DOCUMENTARY HISTORY OF FAITH AND ORDER
1963-1993

DOCUMENTARY HISTORY OF FAITH AND ORDER 1963-1993

Edited by

Günther Gassmann

Faith and Order Paper No. 159

WCC Publications, Geneva

Cover design: Rob Lucas

ISBN 2-8254-1101-9

© 1993 WCC Publications, World Council of Churches,
150 route de Ferney, 1211 Geneva 2, Switzerland

Printed in Switzerland

Contents

IV. SPECIFIC FAITH AND ORDER PROJECTS   *201*

V. ONGOING FAITH AND ORDER TASKS   *323*

Introduction

The Faith and Order Movement and the Commission

Together with the movement for Life and Work and the International Missionary Council, the Faith and Order movement was a major expression of ecumenism during the first half of this century. Following the 1910 world missionary conference in Edinburgh, the convention of the (Anglican) Protestant Episcopal Church in the USA in the same year resolved "that a Joint Commission be appointed to bring about a conference for the consideration of questions touching Faith and Order". Several churches passed similar resolutions and others responded positively to the invitation to join in the preparation for such a world conference. Efforts to win the participation of the Roman Catholic Church met with a negative response.

Thus, the Faith and Order movement was born, and after years of work and a preparatory meeting in Geneva in 1920, the first world conference on faith and order took place in Lausanne in 1927. It provided the first occasion in modern church history for representatives of Orthodox, Anglican, Reformation and Free churches — more than 400 people — to come together to discuss their agreements in faith and the deep differences which had divided them for centuries. The conference met in the context of a new world situation: there was a growing awareness of an interdependent and "smaller" world in which the Christian churches were beginning to discover the need for common mission and service. From these early years onwards Faith and Order has perceived its theological task as one of overcoming church-dividing differences and preparing the way towards visible unity, thereby also supporting this common calling to mission and service.

The second world conference on faith and order in 1937 in Edinburgh was more systematically prepared by a number of commissions. It followed the same comparative methodology of registering agreements and disagreements, but was able to clarify several concepts of church unity with a certain preference for that of organic or corporate union. The conference also agreed, despite some opposing voices, to the proposal to unite the Faith and Order and Life and Work movements "to form a council of churches". This decision was implemented in 1948 at Amsterdam when the World Council of Churches (WCC) was formed.

Within the new structure of the WCC the tasks of the Faith and Order movement were carried on by the Commission on Faith and Order. But the idea of a movement was preserved and expressed in the form of a special constitution (later, by-laws) which provides for membership on the Commission of representatives from churches which do not belong to the WCC, and for the Commission to continue to organize world conferences from time to time. The aim of the Commission, according to the by-laws, is "to proclaim the oneness of the church of Jesus Christ and to call the churches to the goal of visible unity in one faith and one eucharistic fellowship, expressed in worship and in common life in Christ, in order that the world may believe".

In 1952 the Commission organized the third world conference on Faith and Order in Lund, where it moved from the former comparative method to a form of theological dialogue which seeks to bring out agreements and convergences and to struggle with controversial issues by starting from a common biblical and Christological basis. The fourth world conference took place in 1963 in Montreal and the fifth world conference will be held at Santiago de Compostela, Spain, in August 1993.

While the first phase of the Faith and Order movement was marked by the world conferences in 1927 and 1937, since 1948 an increasingly broader programme of studies has developed. This is one of the reasons for the thirty-year interval between the conferences at Montreal and Santiago de Compostela. These studies are planned and discussed at regular Commission meetings (every three or four years), while the Standing Commission (30 members) supervises and implements the study programmes and ongoing work together with the secretariat, which is an integral part of the WCC structure in Geneva.

Also, the composition of the Faith and Order Commission, which now has up to 120 members, has considerably changed during the last decades. The formerly rather small number of Orthodox members has increased to over 20 percent, while representatives of churches from the Southern hemisphere now make up nearly 50 percent. Women theologians, who were earlier virtually absent from the Commission, now represent 34 percent of its membership and include the present moderator, Dr Mary Tanner. Since 1968 the Roman Catholic Church has been officially represented by 12 members and participates in and supports all Faith and Order studies.

There is not the space here to refer to the numerous studies Faith and Order has undertaken during the more than eighty years of its history, but many references and texts can be found in this book (it should be mentioned that although only Faith and Order texts and publications in English are cited, many have been translated and published in other languages as well). There are chapters on Faith and Order in *A History of the Ecumenical Movement 1517-1948*, eds Ruth Rouse and Stephen Charles Neill, London, SPCK, and Philadelphia, Westminster, 1954, 3rd ed. 1986 by the World Council of Churches; and in *The Ecumenical Advance: A History of the Ecumenical Movement, vol. 2, 1948-1968*, ed. Harold E. Fey, London, SPCK, 1970, 2nd ed. 1986 by the World Council of Churches. A more recent and detailed history of Faith and Order has not yet been written. Some other historical surveys are: John E. Skoglund and J. Robert Nelson, *Fifty Years of Faith and Order*, New York, Interseminary Movement, 1963; Reinhard Frieling, *Die Bewegung für Glauben und Kirchenverfassung 1910-1937*, Göttingen, Vandenhoeck & Ruprecht, 1970; Karl-Christoph Epting, *Ein Gespräch beginnt: Die Anfänge der Bewegung für Glauben und Kirchenverfassung 1910-1920*, Zürich, Theologischer Verlag Zürich, 1972. In addition there are a number of studies on specific themes of Faith and Order work. Most of the results of this work can be found in the reports of the world conferences and the Commission meetings and in the two series of Faith and Order Papers 1910-1948 and 1948-. One publication needs special mention because the present book is, in a way, a sequel to it: *A Documentary History of the Faith and Order Movement 1927-1963*, ed. Lukas Vischer, St Louis, MO, Bethany Press, 1963.

There is no doubt that Faith and Order — both the movement and the Commission — has been and is an appropriate and effective instrument of and within the wider ecumenical movement. It has challenged and assisted the churches to overcome their doctrinal differences, to share their diverse spiritual and theological insights and forms of life as a source of mutual enrichment and renewal, and to reappropriate and express together their common heritage in faith, life and witness. All these efforts have as their goal the manifestation of the visible unity of the church of Jesus Christ. This goal is seen in the wider perspective of the calling of the churches, sustained and inspired by the Holy Spirit, to become a credible sign and instrument of God's saving and transforming purpose for all humanity and creation. In this work Faith and Order has on occasion had to struggle to preserve its specific identity and profile as a movement, which is broader than the WCC but at the same time fully committed and accountable to it. The central aim of the ecumenical movement, the concern for the visible unity of the church, requires a particular institutional instrument within, and in co-ordination and collaboration with, all the many other ecumenical efforts. It is on this basis that Faith and Order has been able to make a significant contribution to the radically changed relationships between the churches, their growing communion in faith, life and witness. The fifth world conference will evaluate this contribution, point to its consequences for the churches, and reflect on the future course of Faith and Order's work.

The Purpose of This Book

Many people have found *A Documentary History of the Faith and Order Movement 1927-1963* most helpful. With this in mind, the former moderator of the Faith and Order Commission, Prof. John Deschner, encouraged me some years ago to publish a continuation of that history. Moving towards a world conference in 1993 and looking back over thirty years of Faith and Order work with its broad spectrum of themes, studies and results, convinced me that now was the right time to undertake this task. I have always been conscious of the important heritage of Faith and Order, and impressed by the breadth, richness and diversity of the material from these three decades. Much of it is no longer well known or easy to find. The purpose of this book, therefore, is to make it available for our ecumenical "memory", for students and for all who wish to do further work on ecumenical theological reflection.

Because of the richness of the material I have assembled a series of documents, as in the earlier documentary history, and provided a descriptive and bibliographical framework both for these texts and for those which could not be included because of lack of space. Thus, I hope that all the basic elements for a history of Faith and Order between 1963 and 1993 are present in this volume, and that it will prove to be as useful as the documentary history of my predecessor.

* * *

I am grateful to my Faith and Order colleagues in Geneva for all their assistance, and especially to Béatrice Fleury for typing a manuscript with so many bibliographical details. My thanks also go to WCC Publications for putting all this into printed form.

Geneva, January 1993   GÜNTHER GASSMANN

The style of each document as originally published has been retained.

I
Assemblies of the WCC: Statements on Unity

Results of the work of the Faith and Order Commission have been part of the preparatory material and the deliberations of all WCC assemblies. This is particularly the case with regard to statements on the unity of the church, the fundamental aim both of the WCC and of Faith and Order. The third assembly in New Delhi (1961) was the first time an attempt was made to describe the conditions and expressions of "the unity we seek" in the form of a short, concise statement. Similar statements were adopted by the assemblies at Nairobi (1975) and Canberra (1991). They were all prepared by Faith and Order, but received broader significance by being accepted at assemblies, and they have become basic reference texts for the whole ecumenical movement. A comparison of the three statements indicates both a continuity in identifying the basic conditions of church unity and a development in the historical and theological framework within which these conditions are set.

1. The Third Assembly in New Delhi (1961)

At its meeting in 1960 in St Andrews, Scotland, the Commission on Faith and Order adopted a report to the WCC central committee on "The Future of Faith and Order". One paragraph of this report describes the Commission's understanding of "the unity which is both God's will and His gift to His Church" (*Minutes of the Faith and Order Commission 1960, St Andrews, Scotland*, Faith and Order Paper no. 31, 1960, p.113). With some modification this paragraph became paragraph 2 of the report of section III of the New Delhi assembly. The section report adds a rather extensive commentary on the statement (*The New Delhi Report: The Third Assembly of the World Council of Churches, 1961*, ed. W.A. Visser 't Hooft, London, SCM, 1962, pp.116,117-122; also in Vischer, *op. cit.*, pp.144-145,145-150). • **Document I.1, p.3**

2. The Fourth and Fifth Assemblies in Uppsala (1968) and Nairobi (1975)

The fourth assembly of the WCC in Uppsala (1968) did not formulate a new statement on the unity of the church. However, in its report on section I, "The Holy Spirit and the Catholicity of the Church", Uppsala emphasized the universal dimension of church unity in the sense of "a truly universal, ecumenical, conciliar form of common life and witness". The churches were called to "work for the time when a genuinely universal council may once more speak for all Christians, and lead the way into the future". The report also established a link between the search for the unity of the church and the unity of humankind (*The Uppsala Report 1968: Official Report of the Fourth Assembly of the World Council of Churches*, ed. Norman Goodall, Geneva, WCC, 1968, p.17).

The Uppsala perspective on conciliarity was taken up at a Faith and Order consultation in Salamanca, Spain, in 1973 on "Concepts of Unity and Models of Union". In the report of the consultation on "The Unity of the Church — Next Steps", a new statement on the unity of the church was formulated (*What Kind of Unity?*, Faith and Order Paper no. 69, 1974, p.121). This statement was integrated without modification into the report of section II, "What Unity Requires", of the 1975 Nairobi assembly (*Breaking Barriers: Nairobi 1975. The Official Report of the Fifth Assembly of the World Council of Churches*, ed. David M. Paton, London, SPCK, and Grand Rapids, Eerdmans, 1975, p.60). • **Document I.2, p.3**

3. The Sixth and Seventh Assemblies in Vancouver (1983) and Canberra (1991)

Again, the sixth assembly of the WCC in Vancouver (1983) did not formulate a statement on the unity of the church. In the report of issue group 2, the Nairobi statement was reaffirmed and broadened with the help of a (not yet fully developed) "eucharistic vision". Three "marks" of unity were underlined "which the divided churches do not yet fully share": (1) a common understanding and confession of the apostolic faith; (2) full mutual recognition of baptism, the eucharist and ministry, so that the churches would be able "through their visible communion to let the healing and uniting power of these gifts become more evident amidst the divisions of humankind"; (3) common ways of decision-making and of teaching authoritatively. "Such a unity — overcoming church division, binding us together in the face of racism, sexism, injustice — would be a witnessing unity, a credible sign of the new creation" (*Gathered for Life: Official Report of the Sixth Assembly of the World Council of Churches, Vancouver, 1983*, ed. David Gill, Geneva, WCC, and Grand Rapids, Eerdmans, 1983, pp.44-45).

In 1987 the central committee of the WCC requested Faith and Order to undertake "a fresh consideration of the concepts and forms of the unity we seek" and to prepare a draft statement to be submitted to the 1991 WCC Assembly at Canberra. A Faith and Order consultation in Etchmiadzin, Armenia, in July 1990 and the Faith and Order Standing Commission in Dunblane, Scotland, in August 1990, prepared draft statements (the drafts are printed in *Minutes of the Meeting of the Faith and Order Standing Commission, Rome, Italy, 1991*, Faith and Order Paper no. 157, 1992, pp.82-85). At the Canberra assembly the draft was revised and the statement was adopted (*Signs of the Spirit: Official Report of the Seventh Assembly, Canberra*, ed. Michael Kinnamon, Geneva, WCC, and Grand Rapids, Eerdmans, 1991, pp.172-174). • **Document I.3, p.3**

DOCUMENT I.1

NEW DELHI 1961: SECTION III ON UNITY (§2)

We believe that the unity which is both God's will and his gift to his Church is being made visible as all in each place who are baptized into Jesus Christ and confess him as Lord and Saviour are brought by the Holy Spirit into one fully committed fellowship, holding the one apostolic faith, preaching the one Gospel, breaking the one bread, joining in common prayer, and having a corporate life reaching out in witness and service to all and who at the same time are united with the whole Christian fellowship in all places and all ages in such wise that ministry and members are accepted by all, and that all can act and speak together as occasion requires for the tasks to which God calls his people.

DOCUMENT I.2

NAIROBI 1975: SECTION II ON WHAT UNITY REQUIRES (§3)

The one Church is to be envisioned as a conciliar fellowship of local churches which are themselves truly united. In this conciliar fellowship, each local church possesses, in communion with the others, the fullness of catholicity, witnesses to the same apostolic faith, and therefore recognizes the others as belonging to the same Church of Christ and guided by the same Spirit. As the New Delhi Assembly pointed out, they are bound together because they have received the same baptism and share in the same Eucharist; they recognize each other's members and ministries. They are one in their common commitment to confess the gospel of Christ by proclamation and service to the world. To this end, each church aims at maintaining sustained and sustaining relationships with her sister churches, expressed in conciliar gatherings whenever required for the fulfilment of their common calling.

DOCUMENT I.3

CANBERRA 1991: THE UNITY OF THE CHURCH AS KOINONIA: GIFT AND CALLING

1.1 The purpose of God according to holy scripture is to gather the whole of creation under the Lordship of Christ Jesus in whom, by the power of the Holy Spirit, all are brought into communion with God (Eph. 1). The church is the foretaste of this communion with God and with one another. The grace of our Lord Jesus Christ, the love of God, and the communion of the Holy Spirit enable the one church to live as sign of the reign of God and servant of the reconciliation with God, promised and provided for the whole creation. The purpose of the church is to unite people with Christ in the power of the Spirit, to manifest communion in prayer and action and thus to point to the fullness of communion with God, humanity and the whole creation in the glory of the kingdom.

1.2 The calling of the church is to proclaim reconciliation and provide healing, to overcome divisions based on race, gender, age, culture, colour, and to bring all people into communion with God. Because of sin and the misunderstanding of the diverse gifts of the Spirit, the churches are painfully divided within themselves and among each other. The scandalous divisions damage the credibility of their witness to the world in worship and service. Moreover they contradict not only the church's witness but also its very nature.

1.3 We acknowledge with gratitude to God that in the ecumenical movement the churches walk together in mutual understanding, theological convergence, common suffering and common prayer, shared witness and service as they draw close to one another. This has allowed them to recognize a certain degree of communion already existing between them. This is indeed the fruit of the active presence of the Holy Spirit in the midst of all who believe in Christ Jesus and who struggle for visible unity now. Nevertheless churches have failed to draw the consequences for their life from the degree of communion they have already experienced and the agreements already achieved. They have remained satisfied to co-exist in division.

2.1 The unity of the church to which we are called is a koinonia given and expressed in the common confession of the apostolic faith; a common sacramental life entered by the one baptism and celebrated together in one eucharistic fellowship; a common life in which members and ministries are mutually recognized and reconciled; and a common mission witnessing to the gospel of God's grace to all people and serving the whole of creation. The goal of the search for full communion is realized when all the churches are able to recognize in one another the one, holy, catholic and apostolic church in its fullness. This full communion will be expressed on the local and the universal levels through conciliar forms of life and action. In such communion churches are bound in all aspects of their life together at all levels in confessing the one faith and engaging in worship and witness, deliberation and action.

2.2 Diversities which are rooted in theological traditions, various cultural, ethnic or historical contacts are integral to the nature of communion; yet there are limits to diversity. Diversity is illegitimate when, for instance, it makes impossible the common confession of Jesus Christ as God and Saviour the same yesterday, today and forever (Heb. 13:8); and salvation and the final destiny of humanity as proclaimed in holy scripture and preached by the apostolic community. In communion diversities are brought together in harmony as gifts of the Holy Spirit, contributing to the richness and fullness of the church of God.

3.1 Many things have been done and many remain to be done on the way towards the realization of full communion. Churches have reached agreements in bilateral and multilateral dialogues which are already bearing fruit, renewing their liturgical and spiritual life and their theology. In taking specific steps together the churches express and encourage the enrichment and renewal of Christian life, as they learn from one another, work together for justice and peace, and care together for God's creation.

3.2 The challenge at this moment in the ecumenical movement as a reconciling and renewing movement towards full visible unity is for the seventh assembly of the WCC to call all churches:

— to recognize each other's baptism on the basis of the BEM document;
— to move towards the recognition of the apostolic faith as expressed through the Nicene-Constantinopolitan Creed in the life and witness of one another;
— on the basis of convergence in faith in baptism, eucharist and ministry to consider, wherever appropriate, forms of eucharistic hospitality; we gladly acknowledge that some who do not observe these rites share in the spiritual experience of life in Christ;
— to move towards a mutual recognition of ministries;
— to endeavour in word and deed to give common witness to the gospel as a whole;
— to recommit themselves to work for justice, peace and the integrity of creation, linking more closely the search for the sacramental communion of the church with the struggles for justice and peace;
— to help parishes and communities express in appropriate ways locally the degree of communion that already exists.

4.1 The Holy Spirit as promoter of koinonia (2 Cor. 13:13) gives to those who are still divided the thirst and hunger for full communion. We remain restless until we grow together according to the wish and prayer of Christ that those who believe in him may be one (John 17:21). In the process of praying, working and struggling for unity, the Holy Spirit comforts us in pain, disturbs us when we are satisfied to remain in our division, leads us to repentance, and grants us joy when our communion flourishes.

II
World Conferences
on Faith and Order

1. From Lausanne 1927 to Montreal 1963

The movement on Faith and Order received preliminary structural expression when the general convention of the Protestant Episcopal Church in the USA decided in 1910 to appoint a commission for the preparation of a world conference. All "Christian Communions throughout the world which confess our Lord Jesus Christ as God and Saviour" were to be invited to this conference "for the consideration of questions touching Faith and Order" (cf. Vischer, *op. cit.*, p.199, n.1). Other churches also supported this plan and in 1927 the dream of the pioneers of Faith and Order became real: the *first world conference on faith and order was held in Lausanne, Switzerland*. After centuries of division and enmity, representatives of all the major Christian traditions, with the exception of the Roman Catholic Church, came together. They began to state and compare their differing and often divisive positions in discussions and reports on "The Nature of the Church", "The Church's Common Confession of Faith", "The Ministry of the Church" and "The Sacraments", and discovered their common calling in a divided world. They unanimously adopted "The Call to Unity" and received a report on "The Church's Message to the World — the Gospel" (*Faith and Order: Proceedings of the World Conference, Lausanne 1927*, ed. H.N. Bate, London, SCM, 1927; also in Vischer, *op. cit.*, pp.27-39).

The *second world conference on faith and order in Edinburgh, Scotland* (1937) was more systematically prepared by commissions and larger publications. It received reports on "The Grace of Our Lord Jesus Christ", "The Church of Christ and the Word of God", "The Communion of Saints", "The Church of Christ: Ministry and Sacraments", "The Church's Unity in Life and Worship", highlighting in this last report organic or corporate unity/union as the final goal of the search for church unity (*The Second World Conference on Faith and Order held at Edinburgh, 1937*, ed. Leonard Hodgson, London, SCM, 1938; also in Vischer, *op. cit.*, pp.40-74).

These two world conferences are the most important expressions of the first phase of the Faith and Order movement and are also milestones for the ecumenical movement as a whole.

In 1948 the movements on Faith and Order and Life and Work united to form the World Council of Churches at its first assembly in Amsterdam. By their membership in the Council the churches entered a new and official ecumenical commitment within a more comprehensive ecumenical structure. The special role and continuing significance of the Faith and Order movement was, however, affirmed by establishing a Commission on Faith and Order with its own constitution (later by-laws) which, among other things, allows for the official representation of WCC non-member churches on the Commission and the holding of world conferences from time to time. Thus, four years later in 1952 the *third world conference on faith and order took place in Lund, Sweden*. This conference reflected the growing relationship between the churches by following a new methodology, stating that "we can make no real advance towards unity if we only compare our several conceptions of the nature of the Church... We need, therefore, to penetrate behind our divisions to a deeper and richer understanding of the mystery of the God-given union of Christ with his Church" (Vischer, *op. cit.*, pp.85-86). The resulting strong biblical and Christological emphasis marked the six sections of the conference report: "A Word to the Churches", "Christ and His Church", "Continuity and Unity" (of the church), "Ways of Worship", "Intercommunion" and "Where Do We Stand?" (*The Third World Conference on Faith and Order Held at Lund, 1952*, ed. Oliver S. Tomkins, London, SCM, 1953; also in Vischer, *op. cit.*, pp.85-130). The sections on "Christ and His Church" and "Intercommunion" (with a clarification of terminology and recommendations concerning "Communion Services at Ecumenical Gatherings") received special attention, and one formulation in the first section has entered ecumenical history as the so-called "Lund principle: ...whether they [i.e. the churches] should not act together in all matters except those in which deep differences of conviction compel them to act separately?" (Vischer, *op. cit.*, p.86).

2. The World Conference in Montreal (1963)

Suggestions and emphases of the world conference at Lund led to the establishment of four theological commissions by the Faith and Order Commission and Working Committee in 1953, 1954 and 1955. These commissions dealt with "Institutionalism", "Christ and the Church" (with North American and European sections), "Worship" (with European, East Asian and North American sections) and "Tradition and Traditions" (with North American and European sections). All the commissions published interim reports and/or collected papers: *The Old and the New in the Church*, London, SCM, and Minneapolis, Augsburg, 1961 (containing the reports on "Tradition and Traditions" and "Institutionalism and Church Unity"); *Institutionalism and Church Unity: A Symposium Prepared by the Study Commission on Institutionalism*, eds Nils Ehrenström and Walter G. Muelder, New York, Association Press, 1963; *Schrift und Tradition*, Hrsg. von Kristen E. Skydsgaard and Lukas Vischer, Zurich, EVZ-Verlag, 1963 (papers of the European section); *One Lord, One Baptism*, London, SCM, 1960 (containing the reports "The Divine Trinity and the Unity of the Church" and "The Meaning of Baptism"); *Worship and the Acts of God*, ed. Wiebe Vos, Nieuwendam/Holland, Studia Liturgica Press, 1963 (papers of the European section); East Asian Theological Commission on Worship, *A Report of the Conference on Worship held at Bangalore, March 1955*, published by the Commission.

After the decision had been made to hold the fourth world conference on faith and order in 1963, it was agreed that the final reports of the four theological commissions should serve as the preparatory material (the reports were published individually as Faith and Order Papers nos 37-40 and then together in one volume: *Faith and Order Findings: The Final Report of the Theological Commissions to the Fourth World Conference on Faith and Order, Montreal 1963*, ed. Paul S. Minear, London, SCM, 1963).

The composition of the participants at Montreal reflected new developments in the ecumenical movement. Compared to Lund in 1952 there were many more delegates from the Southern hemisphere, the Orthodox churches were fully represented since several Eastern European Orthodox churches had joined the WCC in 1961, and, for the first time, Roman Catholic representatives participated as speakers and guests — the world conference was held during the time of the Second Vatican Council.

The five sections of the conference and their reports drew on the reports of the four theological commissions and a host of additional material: papers presented to the conference, reports from other sections of the WCC such as, for example, the youth and laity departments, and reports from regional study groups. Section I on "The Church in the Purpose of God" continued the work of Lund on Christ and the church and added a reflection on "The Church and the World Council of Churches" in an attempt to spell out some ecclesiological implications of the existence of a World Council of Churches. Section III on "The Redemptive Work of Christ and the Ministry of His Church" initiated — after a pause since Edinburgh 1937 — a new study on the "special" (i.e. ordained) ministry in the context of the ministries of the people of God. Section IV on "Worship and the Oneness of Christ's Church" included ecumenical perspectives on baptism and the eucharist in its report and developed further the Lund clarifications and recommendations on "Communion Services at Ecumenical Gatherings" (approved by the central committee in Rochester, USA, in August 1963). Section V on "'All in Each Place': The Process of Growing Together" developed the perspective of the New Delhi statement on unity (document I.1) in reflections on the "local church", its relation to the church universal, and its mission and service in a divided world.

However, most attention and continuing study after the world conference was related to the report of section II on "Scripture, Tradition and Traditions" which is reproduced below. The report of the world conference is still available from the WCC (*The Fourth World Conference on Faith and Order, Montreal 1963*, Faith and Order Paper no. 42, eds P.C. Rodger and L. Vischer, London, SCM, 1964). • **Document II.1, p.10**

3. From Montreal 1963 to Santiago de Compostela

Thirty years after Montreal, the *fifth world conference on faith and order will take place in August 1993 in Santiago de Compostela, Spain*. Compared with the time lapse between preceding world conferences this long interval may seem surprising. But in the course of the many studies undertaken by Faith and Order since 1963, it was felt that the time had not yet come for another large conference.

Authorized by the central committee of the WCC as early as 1982 but postponed because of several other major conferences between 1983 and 1991, the fifth world conference comes at an appropriate moment. Results of key Faith and Order studies, such as the broad process of discussion and response initiated by the 1982 *Baptism, Eucharist and Ministry* document and the study documents *Church and World* (1990) and *Confessing the One Faith* (1991) (cf. chapter III), need to be tested and their implications for the churches further discussed. The same applies to the Canberra statement on unity (document I.3) as well as contributions of other studies, bilateral dialogues and united churches to the quest for the visible unity of the church. And there is the more fundamental question of the future direction of the ecumenical movement which needs to be addressed at the end of this "ecumenical century". Thus, with its theme "Towards Koinonia in Faith, Life and Witness" the fifth world conference will endeavour to wrestle with the questions: What has been achieved in our search for visible unity? What are the problems and challenges we still have to face? What are the basic orientations for our ecumenical pilgrimage into the next century?

DOCUMENT II.1

SCRIPTURE, TRADITION AND TRADITIONS (1963)

. . .

Introduction

38. We find ourselves together in Montreal, delegates of churches with many different backgrounds and many different histories. And yet despite these differences we find that we are able to meet one another in faith and hope in the one Father, who by his Son Jesus Christ has sent the Holy Spirit to draw all men into unity with one another and with him. It is on the basis of this faith and hope, and in the context of a common prayer to the one God, Father, Son and Holy Spirit, that we have studied together anew the problem of the one Tradition and the many traditions, and despite the fact of our separations, have found that we can talk with one another and grow in mutual understanding. The Section warmly commends for study by the churches the Report of the Theological Commission on "Tradition and Traditions" (*Faith and Order Findings*, Part IV, pp. 3-63), which was the main documentary foundation of its work.

39. In our report we have distinguished between a number of different meanings of the word *tradition*. We speak of the *Tradition* (with a capital T), *tradition* (with a small t) and *traditions*. By *the Tradition* is meant the Gospel itself, transmitted from generation to generation in and by the Church, Christ himself present in the life of the Church. By *tradition* is meant the traditionary process. The term *traditions* is used in two senses, to indicate both the diversity of forms of expression and also what we call confessional traditions, for instance the Lutheran tradition or the Reformed tradition. In the latter part of our report the word appears in a further sense, when we speak of cultural traditions.

40. Our report contains the substance of the work of three subsections. The first considered the subject of the relation of Tradition to Scripture, regarded as the written prophetic and apostolic testimony to God's act in Christ, whose authority we all accept. The concern of the second was with the problem of the one Tradition and the many traditions of Christendom as they unfold in the course of the Church's history. The third discussed the urgent problems raised both in the life of the younger churches and in the churches of the West, concerning the translation of Christian Tradition into new cultures and languages.

41. Part I received a full discussion and the complete approval of the Section. Owing to the lack of time it was not possible to give the same detailed attention to Parts II and III. The Section in general recommends them for study.

I. Scripture, Tradition and traditions

42. As Christians we all acknowledge with thankfulness that God has revealed himself in the history of the people of God in the Old Testament and in Christ Jesus, his Son, the mediator between God and man. God's mercy and God's glory are the beginning and end of our own history. The testimony of prophets and apostles inaugurated the Tradition of his revelation. The once-for-all disclosure of God in Jesus Christ inspired the apostles and disciples to give witness to the revelation given in the

person and work of Christ. No one could, and no one can, "say that Jesus is Lord, save by the Holy Spirit" (I Cor. 12.3). The oral and written tradition of the prophets and apostles under the guidance of the Holy Spirit led to the formation of Scriptures and to the canonization of the Old and New Testaments as the Bible of the Church. The very fact that Tradition precedes the Scriptures points to the significance of tradition, but also to the Bible as the treasure of the Word of God.

43. The Bible poses the problem of Tradition and Scripture in a more or less implicit manner; the history of Christian theology points to it explicitly. While in the Early Church the relation was not understood as problematical, ever since the Reformation "Scripture and Tradition" has been a matter of controversy in the dialogue between Roman Catholic and Protestant theology. On the Roman Catholic side, tradition has generally been understood as divine truth not expressed in Holy Scripture alone, but orally transmitted. The Protestant position has been an appeal to Holy Scripture alone, as the infallible and sufficient authority in all matters pertaining to salvation, to which all human traditions should be subjected. The voice of the Orthodox Church has hardly been heard in these Western discussions until quite recently.

44. For a variety of reasons, it has now become necessary to reconsider these positions. We are more aware of our living in various confessional traditions, e.g. that stated paradoxically in the saying "It has been the tradition of my church not to attribute any weight to tradition." Historical study and not least the encounter of the churches in the ecumenical movement have led us to realize that the proclamation of the Gospel is always inevitably historically conditioned. We are also aware that in Roman Catholic theology the concept of tradition is undergoing serious reconsideration.

45. In our present situation, we wish to reconsider the problem of Scripture and Tradition, or rather that of Tradition and Scripture. And therefore we wish to propose the following statement as a fruitful way of reformulating the question. Our starting-point is that we are all living in a tradition which goes back to our Lord and has its roots in the Old Testament, and are all indebted to that tradition inasmuch as we have received the revealed truth, the Gospel, through its being transmitted from one generation to another. Thus we can say that we exist as Christians by the Tradition of the Gospel (the *paradosis* of the *kerygma*) testified in Scripture, transmitted in and by the Church through the power of the Holy Spirit. Tradition taken in this sense is actualized in the preaching of the Word, in the administration of the Sacraments and worship, in Christian teaching and theology, and in mission and witness to Christ by the lives of the members of the Church.

46. What is transmitted in the process of tradition is the Christian faith, not only as a sum of tenets, but as a living reality transmitted through the operation of the Holy Spirit. We can speak of the Christian Tradition (with a capital T), whose content is God's revelation and self-giving in Christ, present in the life of the Church.

47. But this Tradition which is the work of the Holy Spirit is embodied in traditions (in the two senses of the word, both as referring to diversity in forms of expression, and in the sense of separate communions). The traditions in Christian history are distinct from, and yet connected with, the Tradition. They are the expressions and manifestations in diverse historical forms of the one truth and reality which is Christ.

48. This evaluation of the traditions poses serious problems. For some, questions such as these are raised. Is it possible to determine more precisely what the content of the one Tradition is, and by what means? Do all traditions which claim to be Christian contain the Tradition? How can we distinguish between traditions embodying the true Tradition and merely human traditions? Where do we find the genuine Tradition, and where impoverished tradition or even distortion of tradition? Tradition can be a faithful transmission of the Gospel, but also a distortion of it. In this ambiguity the seriousness of the problem of tradition is indicated.

49. These questions imply the search for a criterion. This has been a main concern for the Church since its beginning. In the New Testament we find warnings against false teaching and deviations from the truth of the Gospel. For the post-apostolic Church the appeal to the Tradition received from the apostles became the criterion. As this Tradition was embodied in the apostolic writings, it became natural to use those writings as an authority for determining where the true Tradition was to be found. In the midst of all tradition, these early records of divine revelation have a special basic value, because of their apostolic character. But the Gnostic crisis in the second century shows that the mere existence of apostolic writings did not solve the problem. The question of interpretation arose as soon as the appeal to written documents made its appearance. When the canon of the New Testament had been finally defined and recognized by the Church, it was still more natural to use this body of writings as an indispensable criterion.

50. The Tradition in its written form, as Holy Scripture (comprising both the Old and the New Testament), has to be interpreted by the Church in ever new situations. Such interpretation of the Tradition is to be found in the crystallization of tradition in the creeds, the liturgical forms of the sacraments and other forms of worship, and also in the preaching of the Word and in theological expositions of the Church's doctrine. A mere reiteration of the words of Holy Scripture would be a betrayal of the Gospel which has to be made understandable and has to convey a challenge to the world.

51. The necessity of interpretation raises again the question of the criterion for the genuine Tradition. Throughout the history of the Church the criterion has been sought in the Holy Scriptures rightly interpreted. But what is "right interpretation"?

52. The Scriptures as documents can be letter only. It is the Spirit who is the Lord and Giver of life. Accordingly we may say that the right interpretation (taking the words in the widest possible sense) is that interpretation which is guided by the Holy Spirit. But this does not solve the problem of criterion. We arrive at the quest for a hermeneutical principle.

53. This problem has been dealt with in different ways by the various churches. In some confessional traditions the accepted hermeneutical principle has been that any portion of Scripture is to be interpreted in the light of Scripture as a whole. In others the key has been sought in what is considered to be the centre of Holy Scripture, and the emphasis has been primarily on the Incarnation, or on the Atonement and Redemption, or on justification by faith, or again on the message of the nearness of the Kingdom of God, or on the ethical teachings of Jesus. In yet others, all emphasis is laid upon what Scripture says to the individual conscience, under the guidance of the Holy Spirit. In the Orthodox Church the hermeneutical key is found in the mind of the Church, especially as expressed in the Fathers of the Church and in the Ecumenical Councils. In the Roman Catholic Church the key is found in the deposit of faith, of

which the Church's *magisterium* is the guardian. In other traditions again the creeds, complemented by confessional documents or by the definitions of Ecumenical Councils and the witness of the Fathers, are considered to give the right key to the understanding of Scripture. In none of these cases where the principle of interpretation is found elsewhere than in Scripture is the authority thought to be alien to the central concept of Holy Scripture. On the contrary, it is considered as providing just a key to the understanding of what is said in Scripture.

54. Loyalty to our confessional understanding of Holy Scripture produces both convergence and divergence in the interpretation of Scripture. For example, an Anglican and a Baptist will certainly agree on many points when they interpret Holy Scripture (in the wide sense of interpretation), but they will disagree on others. As another example, there may be mentioned the divergent interpretations given to Matt. 16.18 in Roman Catholic theology on the one hand, and in Orthodox or Protestant theology on the other. How can we overcome the situation in which we all read Scripture in the light of our own traditions?

55. Modern biblical scholarship has already done much to bring the different churches together by conducting them towards the Tradition. It is along this line that the necessity for further thinking about the hermeneutical problem arises: i.e. how we can reach an adequate interpretation of the Scriptures, so that the Word of God addresses us and Scripture is safeguarded from subjective or arbitrary exegesis. Should not the very fact that God has blessed the Church with the Scriptures demand that we emphasize more than in the past a common study of Scripture whenever representatives of the various churches meet? Should we not study more the Fathers of all periods of the Church and their interpretations of the Scriptures in the light of our ecumenical task? Does not the ecumenical situation demand that we search for the Tradition by re-examining sincerely our own particular traditions?

II. The unity of Tradition and the diversity of traditions

56. Church and tradition are inseparable. By tradition we do not mean traditionalism. The Tradition of the Church is not an object which we possess, but a reality by which we are possessed. The Church's life has its source in God's act of revelation in Jesus Christ, and in the gift of the Holy Spirit to his people and his work in their history. Through the action of the Holy Spirit, a new community, the Church, is constituted and commissioned, so that the revelation and the life which are in Jesus Christ may be transmitted to the ends of the earth and to the end of time. The Tradition in its content not only looks backward to its origin in the past but also forward to the fulness which shall be revealed. The life of the Church is lived in the continuous recalling, appropriation and transmission of the once-for-all event of Christ's coming in the flesh, and in the eager expectation of his coming in glory. All this finds expression in the Word and in the Sacraments in which "we proclaim the Lord's death till he come" (I Cor. 11.26).

57. There are at least two distinctive types of understanding of the Tradition. Of these, the first is affirmed most clearly by the Orthodox. For them, the Tradition is not only the act of God in Christ, who comes by the work of the Holy Spirit to save all men who believe in him; it is also the Christian faith itself, transmitted in wholeness and purity, and made explicit in unbroken continuity through definite events in the life of the catholic and apostolic Church from generation to generation. For some others, the

Tradition is substantially the same as the revelation in Christ and the preaching of the Word entrusted to the Church which is sustained in being by it, and expressed with different degrees of fidelity in various historically conditioned forms, namely the traditions. There are others whose understanding of the Tradition and the traditions contains elements of both these points of view. Current developments in biblical and historical study, and the experience of ecumenical encounter, are leading many to see new values in positions which they had previously ignored. The subject remains open.

58. In the two distinctive positions mentioned above, the Tradition and the traditions are clearly distinguished. But while in the one case it is held that it is to be found in the organic and concrete unity of the one Church, in the other it is assumed that the one Tradition can express itself in a variety of forms, not necessarily all equally complete. The problem of the many churches and the one Tradition appears very differently from each of those points of view. But though on the one side it is possible to maintain that the Church cannot be, and has not been, divided, and on the other to envisage the existence of many churches sharing in the one Tradition even though not in communion with each other, none would wish to acquiesce in the present state of separation.

59. Many of our misunderstandings and disagreements on this subject arise out of the fact of our long history of estrangement and division. During the centuries the different Christian communions have developed their own traditions of historical study and their own particular ways of viewing the past. The rise of the idea of a strictly scientific study of history, with its spirit of accuracy and objectivity, in some ways ameliorated this situation. But the resultant work so frequently failed to take note of the deeper theological issues involved in church history, that its value was severely limited. More recently, a study of history which is ecumenical in its scope and spirit has appeared.

60. We believe that if such a line of study is pursued, it can be of great relevance to the present life and problems of the Church: "those who fail to comprehend their histories are doomed to re-enact them" (Santayana). We believe, too, that it would have great value in offering possibilities of a new understanding of some of the most contested areas of our common past. We therefore specifically recommend that Faith and Order should seek to promote such studies, ensuring the collaboration of scholars of different confessions, in an attempt to gain a new view of crucial epochs and events in church history, especially those in which discontinuity is evident.

61. But at this point another problem arises. At a moment when mankind is becoming ever more aware of itself as a unity, and we are faced with the development of a global civilization, Christians are called to a new awareness of the universality of the Church, and of its history in relation to the history of mankind. This means that, both at the level of theological study and of pastoral teaching, an attempt has to be made to overcome the parochialism of most studies in church history, and to convey some idea of the history of God's people as a whole. But how is this to be done? Does it not demand the work of historians with more than human capabilities? Is it possible for the scholar, limited as he is by his own cultural, historical and ecclesiastical background, to achieve this vision? Clearly it is not, though we believe that by working in collaboration something could be accomplished. For specialized but limited insights and points of view can be checked and supplemented by those of others; for example, a group may command a larger number of languages and

literatures than is possible for an individual. Questions are being raised in the philosophy and theology of history, pointing both to the danger of mere traditionalism and the permanent value of authentic traditionalism. These demand our constant consideration.

62. Still a third kind of historical concern has been with us. We are aware that during the period of this Conference we have been passing through a new and unprecedented experience in the ecumenical movement. For the first time in the Faith and Order dialogue, the Eastern Orthodox and the other Eastern Churches have been strongly represented in our meetings. A new dimension of Faith and Order has opened up, and we only begin to see its future possibilities. It is clear that many of our problems of communication have arisen from the inadequate understanding of the life and history of the Eastern Churches to be found even among scholars in the West, and *vice versa*. Here again is an area in which we would recommend further study, e.g. of the problem of the *filioque,* its origin and consequences. There are two other studies which we recommend to the Faith and Order Commission. We believe it important to undertake together a study of the Councils of the Early Church, and we recommend an examination of the catechetical material at present in use by the churches, and of the methods whereby it could be revised in the light of the ecumenical movement.

63. In all this we are not blind to the nature of the world in which we live, nor to the cultural and intellectual problems of our day. To many of our contemporaries a concern with the past will immediately appear suspect, as revealing a desire for the mere resuscitation of old customs and ideas, which have no relevance for the urgent questions of our time. We recognize that in many places human traditions — national, social, and indeed religious — are being shaken; and that in this age of scientific and technological achievement many tend to regard the heritage of the past as unimportant. We recognize the positive elements in the present situation. It is for this reason that we have placed the contrast of tradition and traditionalism at the beginning of this part. The past of which we speak is not only a subject which we study from afar. It is a past which has value for us, in so far as we make it our own in an act of personal decision. In the Church it becomes a past by which we live by sharing in the one Tradition, for in it we are united with him who is the Lord of history, who was and is and is to come; and he is God not of the dead but of the living.

III. The Christian Tradition and cultural diversity

64. In what has been written so far, we have been concerned primarily with the understanding of Tradition as it relates to the past, to the once-for-all event of Christ's coming in the flesh, his death and resurrection, and to the continuing work of the Holy Spirit within the Church. But we have recognized throughout, that Tradition looks also to the present and to the future. The Church is sent by Christ to proclaim the Gospel to all men; the Tradition must be handed on in time and also in space. In other words, Tradition has a vital missionary dimension in every land, for the command of the Lord is to go to all nations. Whatever differences of interpretation there may be, all are agreed that there is this dynamic element in the Tradition, which comes from the action of God within the history of his people and its fulfilment in the person and work of Christ, and which looks to the consummation of the victory of the Lord at the end of time.

65. The problems raised by the transmission of the Tradition in different lands and cultures, and by the diversities of traditions in which the one Tradition has been transmitted, are common in varying ways to all Christians. They are to be seen in an acute form in the life of the younger churches of Asia and Africa today, and in a less obvious but no less real form in what was formerly called Western Christendom. To take the problem of the younger churches, in one quite small and typical country there are more than eighty different denominations. How among these traditions are we to find the Tradition? In the building up of new nations there is a particular need for all that will make for unity among men. Are Christians, to whom the ministry of reconciliation has been committed, to be a factor of division at such a time? It is in such testing circumstances as these that the serious problems have to be faced of how the Church may become truly indigenous, bringing into the service of Christ all that is good in the life of every culture and nation, without falling into syncretism.

66. When the Word became flesh, the Gospel came to man through a particular cultural medium, that of the Palestinian world of the time. So when the Church takes the Tradition to new peoples, it is necessary that again the essential content should find expression in terms of new cultures. Thus in the great missionary expansion of the Eastern Church, the Tradition was transmitted through the life of the Church into new languages and cultures, such as those of Russia and the other mission fields. Just as the use of the Slavonic tongue was necessary for the transmission of the Tradition to the Slavs, so today it is necessary to use new languages and new forms of expression which can be understood by those to whom the good news comes. In order that this can be rightly done, it is necessary to draw together knowledge of the culture and language in question, along with a careful study of the languages of the Old and New Testaments, and a thorough knowledge of church history. It is in this context that we begin to understand the meaning of the gift of tongues at Pentecost. By the power of the Holy Spirit the apostles were enabled to preach the mighty works of God to each man in his own tongue, and thus the diversity of nations and cultures was united in the service of God. Through recognizing this, Christians in countries where they are a small minority can avoid the dangers of developing a "ghetto mentality".

67. The content of the Tradition cannot be exactly defined, for the reality it transmits can never be fully contained in propositional forms. In the Orthodox view, Tradition includes an understanding of the events recorded in the New Testament, of the writings of the Fathers, of the ecumenical creeds and Councils, and of the life of the Church throughout the centuries. All member churches of the World Council of Churches are united in confessing the Lord Jesus Christ "as God and Saviour, according to the Scriptures, and in seeking together to fulfil their common calling to the glory of the one God, Father, Son and Holy Spirit". This basis of membership safeguards a position from which we may seek constantly to grow in understanding of the fulness of God's revelation, and to correct partial apprehensions of the truth. In the task of seeking to understand the relation between the Tradition and the traditions, problems are raised as difficult to solve as they are crucial in importance. Such questions often cannot be answered apart from the specific situations which pose them. There are no ready-made solutions. Yet some things may be said.

68. What is basic in the Old and New Testament record and interpretation remains basic for the Church in any situation. Moreover, the Holy Spirit has been given to the Church to guide it into all truth. The decisions which communities of God's believing

people have to take are to be made in reliance on this leading of his Spirit within the Church, and in awareness of God's providential operations in the world. In the process of indigenization (understood in its widest sense), nothing can be admitted which is at variance with the good news of what God has done, is doing and will do, in the redemption of the world through our Lord Jesus Christ, as expressed in terms of the Church's christocentric and trinitarian faith. In each particular situation, the Gospel should be so proclaimed that it will be experienced, not as a burdensome law, but as a "joyful, liberating and reconciling power". The Church must be careful to avoid all unnecessary offence in the proclamation of its message, but the offence of the cross itself, as foolishness to the world, can never be denied. And so the attempt must always be made to transmit the Tradition in its fulness and to remain within the community of the whole of God's people, and the temptation must be avoided of over-emphasizing those elements which are especially congenial to a particular culture. It is in the wholeness of God's truth that the Church will be enabled to fulfil its mission and to bear authentic witness.

69. The traditionary process involves the dialectic, both of relating the Tradition as completely as possible to every separate cultural situation in which men live, and at the same time of demonstrating its transcendence of all that divides men from one another. From this comes the truth that the more the Tradition is expressed in the varying terms of particular cultures, the more will its universal character be fully revealed. It is only "with all the saints" that we come to know the fulness of Christ's love and glory (Eph. 3.18-19).

70. Catholicity, as a gift of God's grace, calls us to a task. It is a concept of immense richness whose definition is not attempted here. It can be sought and received only through consciousness of, and caring for, the wholeness of Christ's body, through witness for Christ's lordship over every area of human life, and through compassionate identification with every man in his own particular need.

71. In the fulfilment of their missionary task most churches claim not merely to be reproducing themselves, but in some sense to be planting the *una sancta ecclesia*. Surely this fact has implications which are scarcely yet realized, let alone worked out, both for the life of the mother-churches, and also for all that is involved in the establishing of any new church in an ecumenical age. It demands that the liberty of newly-founded churches be recognized, so that both mother- and daughter-churches may receive together the one gift of God's grace. This demands faithfulness to the whole *koinonia* of Christ's Church, even when we are engaged with particular problems. In this connection we recognize a vital need for the study of the history of the Church's life and mission, written from an ecumenical perspective. All must labour together in seeking to receive and manifest the fulness of Christ's truth.

72. The problem of communicating this fulness of truth today is felt throughout the whole modern world. This is a result of the emergence in our time of a global civilization, shaped by rapid technological advances, and grounded in a scientific outlook that transforms our concept of the universe. The new cosmology which is taking shape challenges our traditional conceptions of man and of nature, both in themselves and in their inter-relationship with one another. Amid these developments, and to some degree because of them, radical changes in social structure are taking place in every part of the world. The Church is thus faced with a dual responsibility. The Tradition has to be simultaneously transmitted in diverse ways; on the one hand,

in popular everyday language; on the other hand, in terms of the most complex and critical contemporary thought. The seriousness of this revolutionary situation cannot easily be exaggerated. We have seen its inherent dangers, but we must equally seek to realize its enormous potentialities for good.

73. Our thinking about the Christian faith too often lacks a forward-looking vision and orientation. The phrase *"in partibus infidelium"* has already acquired a universal reference. Experiments in pastoral and evangelistic work, such as industrial chaplaincies and "store front parishes", are first attempts at meeting this need. The deepest witness is always borne by the life of the Church itself, through its prayer and sacramental worship, and through the bearing of the cross in silence. As we address ourselves together to our common problems, we may find that God is using the pressures of the world to break the barriers which divide us from one another. We must recognize the opportunity given to us, and with vigour and boldness fulfil the Church's great commission to transmit the Tradition, the word of grace and hope, to men in this new global culture, as in the past it was preached to Jerusalem, to Hellas, Rome and Gaul, and to the uttermost parts of the earth.

III
Main Faith and Order Themes
1963-1993

Concerning the many Faith and Order studies between 1963 and 1993, this and the next chapter follow a thematic order — rather than the chronological order of Faith and Order Commission meetings — which allows for a more coherent presentation of studies in a specific area. The reports and minutes of the Faith and Order Commission and its Working Committee — which in 1977 became the Standing Commission — provide all the information and also much of the relevant material. They are listed here first and are then referred to by place and year and their Faith and Order Paper number (e.g. *Aarhus 1964*, no. 44). All these texts were published by the WCC. (In this and the following chapters, Faith and Order Papers are indicated by their number.)

MINUTES OF THE MEETINGS OF THE FAITH AND ORDER COMMISSION

Montreal, Canada, July 1963; no. 41

Aarhus, Denmark, August 1964; no. 44

Bristol 1967: New Directions in Faith and Order. Reports — Minutes — Documents; no. 50

Uppsala and Sigtuna, Sweden, July 1968; no. 53

Louvain, Belgium, August 1971; no. 60

Louvain 1971: Study Reports and Documents; no. 59

Accra, Ghana, July/August 1974; no. 71

Accra 1974: Uniting in Hope. Reports and Documents from the Meeting of the Faith and Order Commission; no. 72 (1975)

Bangalore, India, August 1978; no. 93

Bangalore 1978: Sharing in One Hope. Reports and Documents from the Meeting of the Faith and Order Commission; no. 92

Lima, Peru, January 1982. *Towards Visible Unity, Vol. I: Minutes and Addresses*, ed. Michael Kinnamon; no. 112

Lima 1982. Towards Visible Unity, Vol. II: Study Papers and Reports, ed. Michael Kinnamon; no. 113

Stavanger, Norway, August 1985. *Faith and Renewal: Reports and Documents*, ed. Thomas F. Best; no. 131

Budapest, Hungary, August 1989. *Faith and Order 1985-1989: The Commission Meeting at Budapest*, ed. Thomas F. Best; no. 148

MINUTES OF THE MEETINGS OF THE FAITH AND ORDER
WORKING COMMITTEE/STANDING COMMISSION

Montreal, Canada, July 1963; no. 41

Aarhus, Denmark, August 1964; no. 44

Bad Saarow, GDR, July 1965; no. 45

Zagorsk, USSR, August/September 1966; no. 48

Bristol, England, July/August 1967; no. 51

Uppsala and Sigtuna, Sweden, July 1968; no. 53

Canterbury, England, July 1969; no. 54

Crêt-Bérard, Switzerland, August 1970; no. 57

Louvain, Belgium, August 1971; no. 60

Utrecht, Netherlands, August 1972; no. 65

Zagorsk, USSR, August 1973; no. 66

Accra, Ghana, July/August 1974; no. 71

Loccum, FRG, July 1977; no. 83

Bangalore, India, August 1978; no. 93

Taizé, France, August 1979; no. 98

Annecy, France, January 1981; no. 106

Lima, Peru, January 1982; no. 112

Crete, Greece, April 1984; no. 121

Potsdam, GDR, July 1986; no. 134

Madrid, Spain, August 1987; no. 141

Boston, USA, September 1988; no. 145

Dunblane, Scotland, August 1990; no. 152

Rome, Italy, June 1991; no. 157

Dublin, Ireland, April 1992; no. 158

Stuttgart, Germany, March/April 1993

Santiago de Compostela, Spain, August 1993

1. The Visible Unity of the Church

Obviously, all studies and documents of Faith and Order are contributions to the implementation of the main mandate of the Faith and Order Commission to serve the churches in their search for the manifestation of the unity of the church of Jesus Christ. But there has also been continuing and specific reflection on the nature of the unity we seek. The most important results of this are the statements of the world conferences of 1927 in Lausanne and 1937 in Edinburgh (cf. Vischer, *op. cit.*, pp.28-29,61-72) and of the WCC assemblies on the unity of the church (cf. chapter I). The Commission proposed at its meeting in 1964 "to study more intensively what is *the nature of unity*, that actual expression of our oneness in the Lord Jesus Christ which He himself wishes to have upon earth" (*Aarhus 1964*, no. 44, p.40).

Nearly ten years later, in September 1973, a Faith and Order consultation on "Concepts of Unity and Models of Union" was held in Salamanca, Spain. The central section of its report was integrated into the report of section II of the Nairobi assembly (cf. chapter I). The Salamanca report was published in *The Ecumenical Review*, vol. XXVI, April 1974, pp.291-303, and in *What Kind of Unity*, no. 69, pp.119-131. • **Document III.1, p.35**

Less than one year after the Salamanca consultation the Faith and Order Commission met in Accra, Ghana. Together with the statements on "One Baptism, One Eucharist and a Mutually Recognized Ministry" and "Towards Unity in Tension" (document III.11), the Commission, following up the work at Salamanca, also adopted a report on "The Unity of the Church: The Goal and the Way" (*Accra 1974: Uniting in Hope*, no. 72, pp.110-123). • **Document III.2, p.50**

In addition to the Salamanca report, several other texts on the unity of the church were submitted to the discussions in section II of the 1975 Nairobi assembly (cf. *What Unity Requires: Papers and Report on the Unity of the Church*, no. 77, 1975). Of continuing significance is the report of a consultation in Geneva in 1975 which reflects not only on the nature of unity and especially on the concept of conciliar fellowship "to be highlighted in the Nairobi report", but also on the role and place of the concern for the unity of the church within the framework of the mandate and programmes of the WCC as a whole (*ibid.*, pp.30-39). • **Document III.3, p.61**

A consultation was organized jointly by Faith and Order and the WCC Sub-unit on Renewal and Congregational Life in Geneva in 1976, in response to the strong emphasis of Nairobi on "congregational life" and the assembly's recommendation that the meaning of the term "local church" as used in the Nairobi statement on unity (cf. document I.2) be further clarified (report and papers: *In Each Place: Towards a Fellowship of Local Churches Truly United*, Geneva, WCC, 1977, report pp.3-12). • **Document III.4, p.69**

In 1978 the Faith and Order Commission met in Bangalore, India, where it concluded its work on the study project "Giving Account of the Hope" (cf. document III.15). At the same time, the Commission continued the process of reflection and clarification on the theme of the visible unity of the church which had received new impetus from the Nairobi statement on unity. The Bangalore meeting agreed that:

> in order to reach visible unity, three fundamental requirements must be met. The churches must reach:
> a) common understanding of the apostolic faith;
> b) full mutual recognition of baptism, the eucharist and the ministry;
> c) agreement on common ways of teaching and decision-making (*Bangalore 1978*, no. 93, p.40).

The Commission divided into five committees, each dealing with one particular aspect of the search for visible unity. Committee I dealt with "Reflections on the Common Goal" and its report is given below (*Bangalore 1978: Sharing in One Hope*, no. 92, pp.237-242). • **Document III.5, p.76**

After Bangalore, the Faith and Order Commission focused its work on "Baptism, Eucharist and Ministry" (Lima 1982) and the broad process of discussion and response that followed, and then, since Lima, on the two study projects "Towards the Common Expression of the Apostolic Faith Today" and "The Unity of the Church and the

Renewal of Human Community". The Commission took up specific reflection on the goal of visible unity again only in 1990 when it prepared the draft of the unity statement of the 1991 Canberra assembly (cf. document I.3). The explication of this statement will be on the agenda of the 1993 world conference.

2. Baptism, Eucharist and Ministry

The discussions on baptism, eucharist and ministry have been at the centre of the Faith and Order movement and Commission from the very beginning. Differences in the understanding and practice of these three foundational expressions of the life of the church have contributed to the divisions between the churches and are still a barrier to eucharistic communion. Consequently, the search for consensus and convergence on these three issues and the common understanding that mutual recognition of baptism, eucharist and ministry is an essential requirement and expression of the visible unity of the church have marked the work of Faith and Order since 1927.

Baptism, the eucharist and the ministry had a prominent place on the agendas of the first two world conferences. There, a first comparison of the teaching and practice of the churches was undertaken and agreements and differences were stated (cf. Vischer, *op. cit.*, pp.34-39,52-61).

a) Eucharist

After the break between 1937 and 1948, the eucharist was the first theme to be taken up in the work of Faith and Order. In the preparatory studies for the third world conference in 1952 in Lund (*Ways of Worship: The Report of a Theological Commission of Faith and Order*, eds P. Edwall, E. Hayman and W. D. Maxwell, London, SCM, 1951; *Intercommunion: The Report of the Theological Commission Appointed by the Continuation Committee of the World Conference on Faith and Order*, eds Donald Baillie and John Marsh, London, SCM, 1952), a number of emerging convergences in the understanding of holy communion were formulated, especially on the relation between word and sacrament and on the sacrificial aspect of the eucharist. These were taken up in the reports of the world conference on "Ways of Worship" and "Intercommunion" (cf. Vischer, *op. cit.*, pp.106-111,115-123). In the report of the fourth world conference in Montreal in 1963 on "Worship and the Oneness of the Church", the convergence is considerably broadened; the anamnetic and epicletic character of the Lord's supper, its universal and eschatological dimensions and the main elements of the eucharistic liturgy — among other aspects — are set forth (cf. *The Fourth World Conference on Faith and Order, op. cit.*, pp.73-75).

The basis for the work leading up to the 1982 Lima document had been laid.

The next step was taken by the Faith and Order Commission in 1964 in Aarhus which, on the basis of the work and a recommendation from Montreal, initiated a study on the eucharist (*Aarhus 1964*, no. 44, pp.54-57). A consultation produced a first draft in 1965, regional groups reacted, and a theological commission finalized the text which was presented to the Commission meeting in Bristol in 1967 (*Bristol 1967: New Directions in Faith and Order*, no. 50, pp.60-68). • **Document III.6, p.81**

The 1968 Uppsala assembly asked the Faith and Order Commission to take up again the question of intercommunion, which had been considered at the world conferences in Lund (Vischer, *op. cit.*, pp.115-125) and Montreal (*The Fourth World Conference on Faith and Order, op. cit.*, pp.74,76-80). This was done — with the participation of Roman Catholic theologians, who were now officially represented on the Commission — at a consultation in Geneva in 1969, whose report was presented to the Commission meeting in 1971 in Louvain (*Louvain 1971: Study Reports and Documents*, no. 59, pp.54-70). • **Document III.7, p.89**

Since Louvain, Faith and Order has not drawn up another comprehensive text on the issue of eucharistic communion, but its entire work remains dedicated to this goal and seeks to contribute to its fulfilment. At Louvain the Commission received a second text on "The Eucharist in Ecumenical Thought" (*ibid.*, pp.71-77) which summarized the basic insights of the Lund and Montreal conferences and especially the Bristol text (cf. document III.6). After further revision it became part of the 1974 Accra document "One Baptism, One Eucharist and a Mutually Recognized Ministry".

b) Baptism

The work on baptism was resumed by the theological commission on "Christ and the Church" (cf. chapter II) which published a first report in 1960 (*One Lord, One Baptism: The Meaning of Baptism*, London, SCM, 1960). A solid foundation for further work was laid by describing the Christological, pneumatological, ecclesiological and eschatological character of baptism and the significance of this sacrament for the whole life of the person baptized. An initial effort was made to reflect on the controversial issues of faith and baptism, infant and adult baptism, baptism and confirmation. In its report on "Worship and the Oneness of the Church of Christ" the Montreal world conference summarized these reflections and added a list of elements which should be part of every service of baptism (cf. *The Fourth World Conference on Faith and Order, op. cit.*, pp.72-73).

On this basis work was continued at two consultations in 1968 (cf. *Study Encounter*, vol. IV, no. 4, 1968, pp.194-198) and 1970, to which regional groups contributed. Their findings were summarized and revised in 1970 by a working group which presented a report to the 1971 Commission meeting in Louvain (*Louvain 1971: Study Reports and Documents*, no. 59, pp.35-49). • **Document III.8, p.104**

The Commission at Louvain added to the above text an appendix, "Ecumenical Agreement on Baptism" (*ibid.*, pp.49-53), in the form of a compilation of quotations from Faith and Order world conferences and WCC assemblies. After revision and considerable expansion, based partly on the above text on "Baptism, Confirmation and Eucharist", it became part of the 1974 Accra document "One Baptism, One Eucharist and a Mutually Recognized Ministry".

c) Ministry

After 1937 the question of the ministry of the church came back on the agenda of Faith and Order only at Montreal 1963. In the report of section III on "The Redemptive Work of Christ and the Ministry of his Church", the "special" or ordained ministry is set in the framework of the general ministry of all believers and developed within a Christological and pneumatological concept of the nature of the church. The character of service of all ministry is underlined, and the need for a renewal of the forms and functions of the ministry within the changing structures of society receives considerable attention. Progress in dealing with controversial issues like ordination, apostolic succession and structures of the ministry was, however, limited (cf. *The Fourth World Conference on Faith and Order, op. cit.*, pp.61-69).

The Commission meetings in Aarhus in 1964 and Bristol in 1967 continued the discussion in the form of short reports on "Christ, the Holy Spirit and the Ministry" (*Aarhus 1964*, no. 44, pp.47-53) and "Ordination" (*Bristol 1967: New Directions in Faith and Order*, no. 50, pp.144-147). A 1968 consultation produced a more extensive working paper, to which 36 regional study groups reacted. This, in turn, led to the text produced by a consultation in 1970 and submitted to the Commission meeting at Louvain (*Louvain 1971: Study Reports and Documents*, no. 59, pp.78-101). • **Document III.9, p.116**

The Louvain text was developed further with the full participation of Roman Catholic theologians, which gave added weight to the issue of the ministry within the search for the visible unity of the church. The text was considerably revised at two consultations, in Marseille in 1972 (cf. *Study Encounter*, vol. VIII, no. 4, 1972) and in Geneva in 1973, and was then presented to the Commission meeting in Accra in 1974. There, after further revision, it became part of the document "One Baptism, One Eucharist and a Mutually Recognized Ministry".

d) Baptism, eucharist and ministry

The three streams of discussion on baptism, the eucharist and the ministry between 1927 and 1964, outlined above, merged at the meeting of the Faith and Order Commission in 1974 in Accra, Ghana. An important stage in the work of Faith and Order had been reached when the Commission decided that the three reports which had been revised at Accra should be sent to the churches and interested groups and individuals for their consideration and comment: *One Baptism, One Eucharist and a Mutually Recognized Ministry*, no. 73, 1975 (the text is too long to be reproduced here).

The Nairobi assembly of the WCC in 1975 authorized the distribution of the Accra statements for study by the churches. They met with much interest and over a hundred comments were received from churches, theological faculties and other sources. At a consultation in 1977 in Crêt-Bérard, Switzerland, these comments were analyzed, agreements and remaining differences noted, and suggestions for further work made (*Towards an Ecumenical Consensus on Baptism, the Eucharist and the Ministry: A Response to the Churches*, no. 84, 1977). As a result, two special consultations were held, one in 1978 in Louisville, USA, focusing on the problem of infant and believer's baptism (*Louisville Consultation on Baptism*, no. 97, special issue of *Review and Expositor* vol. LXXVII, no. 1, Louisville, Southern Baptist Seminary, 1980), and the other, in 1979 in Geneva, on episkopé and the episcopate (*Episcopé and Episcopate in Ecumenical Perspective*, no. 102, 1980). Results of the new bilateral dialogues were of great assistance in the preparation of a new text. An Orthodox consultation in Chambésy/Geneva in 1979 also commented on the new draft text which was prepared by a special steering group. This draft, "Baptism, Eucharist and Ministry", was submitted to the meeting of the Faith and Order Commission in January 1982 in Lima, Peru. After extensive discussion and revision the Commission unanimously agreed to the motion:

> The Commission considers the revised text on Baptism, Eucharist and Ministry to have been brought to such a stage of maturity that it is now ready for transmission to the churches in accordance with the mandate given at the Fifth Assembly of the World Council of Churches, Nairobi 1975, and re-affirmed by the Central Committee, Dresden 1981. (*Lima 1982*, vol. I, no. 112, 1982, p.83)

It was a historical moment when this motion was passed. But probably very few of those present at Lima expected that the "Lima document", soon to be known as BEM, would become the most widely published, translated, discussed and commented text in the history of the ecumenical movement. *Baptism, Eucharist and Ministry* (no. 111, 1982, 26th printing 1992) has been translated into 33 languages, printed in more than 450,000 copies, discussed in thousands of groups, and officially responded to by over 180 churches, including the Roman Catholic Church.

Three interpretative studies were published by Faith and Order: *Ecumenical Perspectives on Baptism, Eucharist and Ministry*, ed. Max Thurian, no. 116, 1983; *Baptism and Eucharist: Ecumenical Convergence in Celebration*, eds Max Thurian and Geoffrey Wainwright, no. 117, 1984; *Orthodox Perspectives on Baptism, Eucharist and Ministry*, eds Gennadios Limouris and Michael Vaporis, no. 128, *The Greek Orthodox Theological Review*, vol. 30, no. 2, 1985. In addition to the study guide published by Faith and Order (*Growing Together in Baptism, Eucharist and Ministry*, ed. William H. Lazareth, no. 114, 1982), many churches developed their own. Hundreds of articles, collections of essays and books on BEM have been published since 1982 (cf. *Bibliography on Baptism, Eucharist and Ministry, 1982-1987*, Leiden-Utrecht, Interuniversitair Instituut voor Missiologie en Oecumenica, 1988). A unique collection representing the ecumenical thinking and the affirmative and critical reactions of the churches to BEM are the six volumes of official responses (*Churches Respond to BEM*, ed. Max Thurian, vols I-VI, 1986-1988).

All this, together with other information and material on the BEM process of discussion and reception, was studied and evaluated by a BEM steering group, a sub-committee of the Faith and Order Standing Commission, which held three consultations (Venice 1986, Annecy 1987 and Turku 1988). A drafting team met three times in 1988, and then together with the steering group in 1989, in order to prepare a report on the BEM process, its impact, and the responses of the churches. This report notes that most churches see in BEM a significant ecumenical breakthrough, but it refers also to their critical comments and responds to them. It concludes by outlining three major issues on which further study is necessary: scripture and Tradition, sacrament and sacramentality, and ecumenical perspectives on ecclesiology (*Baptism, Eucharist and Ministry 1982-1990: Report on the Process and Responses*, no. 149, 1990).

BEM has become an ecumenical reference text for bilateral conversations, agreements between churches, and ongoing ecumenical studies and discussions. The so-called "Lima liturgy", the order of the closing worship at Lima in 1982, has been used on many ecumenical occasions, from Vancouver 1983 to Canberra 1991 (*The Eucharistic Liturgy: Liturgical Expression of Convergence in Faith Achieved in Baptism, Eucharist and Ministry*, 1983, offprint from *Baptism, Eucharist and Ministry: Ecumenical Convergence in Celebration*, op. cit.). But as the Canberra statement on unity underlines (document I.3), the task of the churches is still to receive the achievements of BEM into their thinking and life and to continue in the effort to overcome the remaining divisive differences. The Faith and Order world conference in 1993 will be part of this process.

3. The Unity of the Church and the Renewal of Human Community

The work of Faith and Order for the visible unity of the church was never conceived in a narrow limited manner. The common Christian witness to the gospel and the common Christian service in the wider human family were seen as necessary elements in and fruits of the search for unity.

As a topic for theological reflection, this wider context of world and humanity was prominent on the ecumenical agenda during the 1960s. In Faith and Order this new orientation found expression in the Commission meeting in 1964 in Aarhus, where a study on "Creation, New Creation and the Unity of the Church" was planned, which led to the document "God in Nature and History", adopted by the Commission in Bristol in 1967 (cf. chapter IV). The 1968 Uppsala assembly highlighted the "unity of mankind" in relation to the calling of the church within God's universal history, and formulated the oft-quoted sentence: "The Church is bold in speaking of itself as the sign of the coming unity of mankind" (*The Uppsala Report, op. cit.*, p.17). Uppsala encouraged further work along these lines:

> We are in agreement with the decision of the Faith and Order Commission at its Bristol meeting to pursue its study programme on the unity of the church in the wider context of the study of the unity of mankind and of creation. (*ibid.*, p.223)

a) The unity of the church and the unity of humankind

Thus, the study programme on "The Unity of the Church and the Unity of Mankind" was born. Its stages and main texts (quoted in excerpts) are described and analyzed by Geiko Müller-Fahrenholz in *Unity in Today's World: The Faith and Order Studies on "Unity of the Church — Unity of Humankind"*, no. 88, 1978. In 1969 already, a working paper on the theme was presented to the Faith and Order Working Committee in Canterbury where the whole project was discussed (*Canterbury 1969*, no. 54, pp.6-7). The text reflects on the unity of the human race, theological anthropology, creation and history, and concludes with ecclesiological considerations (*Study Encounter*, vol. V, no. 4, 1969, pp.163-181, also printed in Müller-Fahrenholz, *op. cit.*, pp.29-47). It was discussed and commented in a number of regional study groups (cf. *ibid.*, pp.52-77). The Louvain Commission meeting in 1971 focused on the study project and dealt in five sections with the relationship (or inter-relation) between the unity of the church and (1) the struggle for justice in society, (2) the encounter with living faiths, (3) the struggle against racism, (4) the handicapped in society, (5) the differences in culture (*Louvain 1971: Study Reports and Documents*, no. 59, pp.184-199).

With its broad spectrum of difficult issues, the study project stimulated lively discussion and raised methodological problems and critical questions (e.g. on the title of the study and on the meaning of "unity of mankind", or the relationship between the doxological and missionary/serving function of the unity of the church), but it also led to important new clarifications and perspectives with regard to Faith and Order's traditional area of study: ecclesiology. These new perspectives are formulated in a working document prepared by a small group and discussed by the Faith and Order Working Committee in 1973 in Zagorsk (not published in full, excerpts printed in Müller-Fahrenholz, *op. cit.*, pp.78-88; comments of the Working Committee in *Zagorsk 1973*, no. 66, pp.11-14,43-45). • **Document III.10, p.137**

One year later when the Faith and Order Commission met in Accra, a brief statement on "Towards Unity in Tension" was drawn up which summarized some of the most important insights of the study (*Accra 1974: Uniting in Hope, op. cit.*, pp.90-

94, also in Müller-Fahrenholz, *op. cit.*, pp.89-93). This statement marks the conclusion of the formal study project on "The Unity of the Church and the Unity of Mankind", but it did not signify the end of Faith and Order's efforts to relate its work for the unity of the church to the wider human community and God's purpose for it.
• **Document III.11, p.144**

A year after Accra the Nairobi assembly in 1975 focused again on the relation between the unity of the church and the unity of humankind, but not so much — as at Uppsala — within the framework of a historical-theological vision of God, church and world. The context was more one of a broken world, with a new emphasis: a threatened creation. But the conviction was again expressed strongly that the unity of the church must be envisaged also as a sign and instrument for healing and sustaining both humanity and creation.

b) Racism

Before Faith and Order returned to a specific study of this relationship between the unity of the church and the unity of humankind, it continued work on studies of a more limited nature. One of them was on the issue of racism (cf. *Accra 1974*, no. 71, pp.88,104-106), and a joint consultation with the WCC's Programme to Combat Racism in 1975 produced the report *Racism in Theology — Theology against Racism*, 1975. Following descriptions of the ambiguity of racism, the involvement of church and theology, and the struggle against racism, the report draws some conclusions for the church which are documented here (*ibid.*, pp.13-19). One of the groups at the Commission meeting in Stavanger again discussed this issue (*Faith and Renewal: Stavanger 1985, op. cit.*, pp.93-98). • **Document III.12, p.148**

c) The community of women and men in the church

This area of study was dealt with in a longer and broader process. Its impulse came from the 1974 WCC consultation in Berlin on "Sexism in the 70s", a theme which was taken up by the Faith and Order Commission in Accra the same year (*Accra 1974*, no. 71, pp.88,107-109). It became a joint study between Faith and Order and the Sub-unit on Women in Church and Society, and a special study desk was eventually set up in Faith and Order in 1978. Meanwhile, the programme of the study was further clarified in 1976 by a Faith and Order core group (*For the Years Ahead: Programme of the Commission on Faith and Order*, no. 80, pp.10-13), and the Standing Commission at Loccum in 1977 outlined three areas of particular relevance for Faith and Order:
a) search for signs of unity;
b) exploration of issues of theological language, symbols and images;
c) participation in the "Baptism, Eucharist and Ministry" project, especially on the issue of the ordination of women (*Loccum 1977*, no. 83, pp.28-30).

The third recommendation in this list led to a consultation on "Ordination of Women in Ecumenical Perspective", organized in 1979 in Klingenthal near Strasbourg, France. The results of this consultation, which covered a much wider area than the specific issue of ordination, were summarized in a book which is too extensive to be documented in its entirety, but which is still a basic resource for ecumenical reflection on this topic: *Ordination of Women in Ecumenical Perspective: Workbook for the Church's Future*, ed. Constance F. Parvey, no. 105, 1980. As an example

of the style and way of arguing, chapter VI is reproduced here (*ibid.*, pp.54-59).
• **Document III.13, p.153**

The community study, whose methodology of local discussion groups using an action-reflection process was an important contribution to ecumenical discussion in the 1970s, included two further consultations, both in 1980, which were of significance for Faith and Order: one in Amsterdam on "The Authority of Scripture in Light of the New Experience of Women", and the other in Niederaltaich, Federal Republic of Germany, on "Towards a Theology of Human Wholeness". The reports of these consultations are published in *In God's Image: Reflections on Identity, Human Wholeness and the Authority of Scripture*, eds Janet Crawford and Michael Kinnamon, 1983. The consultation in 1981 in Sheffield marked the formal end of the community study (cf. *The Community of Women and Men in the Church: The Sheffield Report*, ed. Constance F. Parvey, 1983, which includes a description of the whole study process), but the issue of the community of women and men remained on the agenda of the WCC and was taken up again by Faith and Order in the framework of a new study project described below.

d) Other collaborative studies

The initial discussion in Louvain in 1971 on the inter-relation between the unity of the church and the role and place of the handicapped in church and society was taken up again at the Nairobi assembly in 1975. In 1978 a consultation at Bad Saarow, German Democratic Republic, was organized jointly by the WCC Commission on Inter-Church Aid, Refugee and World Service, the Christian Medical Commission and the Commission on Faith and Order, and the resulting publication is of lasting significance (*Partners in Life: The Handicapped and the Church*, ed. Geiko Müller-Fahrenholz, no. 89, 1979). Another effort to further the inclusiveness of the Christian community as part of the search for unity was a consultation in 1980 in Bad Segeberg, Federal Republic of Germany, organized jointly by the WCC Sub-units on Education and Faith and Order, on an issue debated in many churches: the admission of children to holy communion. Again, the report contains ideas and suggestions which can be helpful still today (*...And Do Not Hinder Them: An Ecumenical Plea for the Admission of Children to the Eucharist*, no. 109, 1982).

e) The unity of the church and the renewal of human community

This new study project was accepted by the 1982 Lima Commission meeting as one of the major Faith and Order studies for the coming period (*Lima 1982*, no. 112, vol. I, pp.124,112-124; *Lima 1982*, no. 113, vol. II, pp.123-230). The study was obviously intended as a continuation of the work on the unity of the church and the unity of humankind but was also to serve as a follow-up to the community of women and men study (cf. *op. cit.*, vol. I, pp.126-130; vol. II, pp.153-165). The proposal presented at Lima was prepared by the Standing Commission in 1981 in Annecy (*Annecy 1981*, no. 106, pp.27-37) and a preliminary consultation in Geneva in 1981 which developed the outline for the study (printed in *Lima 1982*, no. 113, vol. II, pp.135-141). • **Document III.14, p.157**

The study came to be seen as a theological investigation into the inter-relation between the concern for the visible unity of the church and the churches' calling to witness and service within the wider human community — areas which have often been regarded as two separate ecumenical agendas. The Vancouver assembly in 1983 welcomed this study and emphasized its ecclesiological focus on the church as "sign" or "prophetic sign" (*Gathered for Life, op. cit.*, p.50). In 1984 the Standing Commission in Crete prepared a programme outline and a proposal for consultations which laid the ecclesiological emphasis on the concept of the church as "mystery" and "prophetic sign". This was to be related to two specific areas of renewal and their ecclesiological implications: the community of women and men in church and society, and the interaction of ideologies, social systems and cultures with issues of justice and peace (*Crete 1984*, no. 121, pp.33-52). Because of the wide range of problems, this second area was limited after 1985 to the concern for justice.

The study process, which sought to combine a "deductive" and a "contextual" methodology and involved local study groups (cf. *Unity and Renewal: A Study Guide for Local Groups*, no. 136, 1987, in several languages), was carried through by a series of consultations, discussions at the Commission meetings in Stavanger (*Stavanger 1985*, no. 131, pp.166-221) and Budapest (*Budapest 1989*, no. 148, pp.134-162), and discussions at the meetings of the Standing Commission between 1984 and 1990. A steering group guided the process and prepared the text for a study document at consultations in 1989 in Leuenberg, Switzerland, and in 1990 in Mandeville, Jamaica. The work on the concept of the church as mystery and prophetic sign was begun at a consultation in 1985 in Chantilly, France (papers and first draft report in *Church-Kingdom-World: The Church as Mystery and Prophetic Sign,* ed. Gennadios Limouris, no. 130, 1986) and the report was revised at Stavanger in 1985 (*op. cit.*, pp.192-207). Three consultations dealt with the community of women and men: in Prague in 1985 (*Beyond Unity-in-Tension: Unity, Renewal and the Community of Women and Men*, ed. Thomas F. Best, no. 138, 1988), Porto Novo, Benin, in 1988, and Cambridge, England, in 1989. Three other consultations were devoted to the ecclesiological significance of the churches' involvement in issues of justice: in Singapore in 1986, Porto Alegre, Brazil, in 1987 (most papers and report in "Justice, Unity and Renewal", a thematic issue of *Mid-Stream*, eds Paul A. Crow, Jr. and Thomas F. Best, vol. XXVIII, no. 1, January 1989; other papers in *The Ecumenical Review*, vol. 39, no. 3, July 1987), and Harlem, USA (with black churches) in 1988 (papers and report in *Mid-Stream*, vol. XXVIII, no. 4, October 1989) (a full list of meetings and publications can be found in the appendices of the study document).

On the basis of these meetings the steering group prepared a draft document which was finalized by the Standing Commission in Dunblane, Scotland, in 1990, and the study document *Church and World: The Unity of the Church and the Renewal of Human Community* was published the same year (no. 151), marking the conclusion of this major Faith and Order study. However, the WCC central committee in 1992 recommended that it should find some continuation after 1993 by dealing with the unity of the church and "emerging new issues such as ethnic tensions and nationalism".

4. Confessing the One Faith

One of the undisputed presuppositions of all ecumenical endeavours towards manifesting the unity of the church was and is that there must be unity in faith. In the statements on the unity of the church adopted by the New Delhi, Nairobi and Canberra assemblies (cf. chapter I), this presupposition is formulated in terms of "holding the one apostolic faith" (New Delhi), "witnesses to the same apostolic faith" (Nairobi), and "common confession of the apostolic faith" (Canberra). According to the revised constitution of the WCC (1975), its first function and purpose is "to call the churches to the goal of visible unity in one faith and in one eucharistic fellowship..." (constitution III.1, in *Breaking Barriers: Nairobi 1975, op. cit.*, p.317). But the content and form of expression of such unity in faith can be interpreted in many different ways. The history of the ecumenical discussion, especially in Faith and Order, has therefore been a continuing search for clarification and explication of the criteria, scope and content of such unity. The whole discussion on scripture and Tradition and on the role of creeds between the world conferences in 1927 in Lausanne and in 1963 in Montreal has been part of this process (cf. chapter II.1), as have been implicitly other Faith and Order studies. As the formulation of the assemblies indicates, there has been an increasing emphasis on the *confession* of the common faith, and that faith has been qualified by the adjective "apostolic" (which requires, of course, further clarification).

a) Work between 1971 and 1982

In a more specific way, the task of the common confession of the apostolic faith was put on the ecumenical agenda by the Nairobi assembly which recommended (*op. cit.*, p.66):

> We ask the churches to undertake a common effort to receive, reappropriate and confess together, as contemporary occasion requires, the Christian truth and faith, delivered through the apostles and handed down through the centuries. Such common action, arising from free and inclusive discussion under the commonly acknowledged authority of God's word, must aim both to clarify and to embody the unity and the diversity which are proper to the church's life and mission (section II, 19).

Already in 1971 at its Commission meeting in Louvain, Faith and Order had decided to approach this task from a particular angle by initiating a study on "Giving Account of the Hope that Is in Us" (cf. 1 Pet. 3:15) (*Louvain 1971: Study Reports and Documents*, no. 59, pp.215-216,239-240). After 40-50 study groups had contributed their experiences and reflections, the Commission meeting in Accra in 1974 prepared a first report which includes witnesses and statements from different regions and situations (*Accra 1974: Uniting in Hope*, no. 72, pp.25-80). Four years later the study came to a conclusion at the Commission meeting in Bangalore. Here, "A Common Account of Hope" was adopted (*Bangalore 1978: Sharing in One Hope*, no. 92, pp.1-11, together with reports, statements, credal formulations, prayers and poems from different regions and areas, pp.51-202; cf. also the statements of discussion groups in the *Bangalore Minutes*, no. 93, pp.45-70). • **Document III.15, p.161**

In Bangalore the Commission took a further step by reflecting on the meaning of the first of the "three requirements for visible unity" highlighted at the meeting (cf. introduction to document III.5): a common understanding of the apostolic faith. As a result and in explicit response to the Nairobi recommendation, a first attempt was made to formulate a common statement of faith (*Bangalore 1978: Sharing in One*

Hope, no. 92, pp.244-246). In its report the group which prepared this statement made an important distinction:

> We are agreed that we must distinguish between faith as commitment and the doctrinal formulation of faith. Faith as the human response to the grace of God, as commitment with love and hope, is essential. The attempt to give it a doctrinal formulation is secondary to it. Therefore, every statement of faith must be recognized as limited in scope, expression and relevance. It cannot itself become the object of our faith. (*ibid.*, p.244)

• Document III.16, p.169

Another contribution to the reflection on the common confession of the apostolic faith came from the Joint Working Group between the Roman Catholic Church and the World Council of Churches. The Group entrusted the organization of a study to the Commission on Faith and Order, on the understanding that its results would be submitted to the Joint Working Group. A colloquium was held in Venice in 1978 and its report was presented the following year to the Joint Working Group. After fifty theologians had sent comments on the draft text, the revised report, qualified as a "working paper", was published in 1980 (*Towards a Confession of the Common Faith*, no. 100, 1980). **• Document III.17, p.171**

Faith and Order took a further initiative in this area by organizing two consultations at Klingenthal near Strasbourg, France, in 1978 and 1979 on the *filioque* clause in the Nicene Creed. This addition to the original text of the Creed has been a major cause of dispute between the Eastern and Western churches. The two consultations formulated a "memorandum" which was transmitted to the churches by the Faith and Order Standing Commission in Taizé in 1979 (papers and memorandum in *Spirit of God, Spirit of Christ: Ecumenical Reflections on the Filioque Controversy*, ed. Lukas Vischer, no. 103. **• Document III.18, p.178**

The preparatory reflections on a study on the common confession or expression of the apostolic faith increasingly referred to the Creed of Nicea-Constantinople of 381 as the only creed shared by churches of the Eastern and Western traditions. The 1600th anniversary of this creed provided an opportunity to consider its significance for the emerging study project. A first consultation was held in July 1981 in Chambésy, near Geneva. Its report, "Towards the Common Expression of the Apostolic Faith Today", was not published (cf. FO/81:9, Faith and Order/apostolic faith archives, WCC), but the text has been integrated with little change into the report of the working group meeting on the apostolic faith study in Lima 1982 (cf. document III.19).

A second consultation, on "The Ecumenical Importance of the Nicene Creed", took place in Odessa in October 1981. Its report was published in *Apostolic Faith Today: A Handbook for Study*, ed. Hans-Georg Link, no. 124, 1985, pp.245-256.

From quite a different angle another contribution was made by an ad hoc working group of American theologians who, at meetings in New York and Princeton in May and September 1981, prepared a substantial report on the contribution of the (nearly finalized) statement on "Baptism, Eucharist and Ministry" to the emerging study project on the apostolic faith (Faith and Order/apostolic faith archives, WCC).

The results of these preparatory consultations were taken up by the Faith and Order Commission at its meeting in 1982 in Lima. There, with the adoption of the report of a working group, the study on "Towards the Common Expression of the Apostolic Faith Today" was officially launched (*Lima 1982*, vol. II, no. 113, pp.28-46). **• Document III.19, p.191**

b) The apostolic faith study 1982-1990
The period between 1982 and 1990 was marked by intensive work on "Towards the Common Expression of the Apostolic Faith Today". The study process, guided by a steering group from the Faith and Order Standing Commission, began with a first consultation in 1983 in Rome on "The Apostolic Faith in the Scriptures and in the Early Church" (papers and report in *The Roots of Our Common Faith: Faith in the Scriptures and in the Early Church*, ed. Hans-Georg Link, no. 119, 1984). A year later, the Standing Commission in Crete decided on a plan for the study (*Crete 1984*, no. 121, pp.11-22). Of the three elements mentioned in the Lima outline (document III.19) — common recognition, explication and confession of the apostolic faith — the second was given priority for the next steps, and in the course of the study it became clear that the work should be limited to the task of jointly explicating the apostolic faith. The other two elements, the mutual recognition of the apostolic faith in each other's faith and life, and the common confession of that faith, would be necessary consequences of a common explication. This common explication would take the Creed of Nicea-Constantinople as a basis and explicate its fundamental affirmations in relation to the biblical witness and to Christian faith and confession today.

Three consultations — in Kottayam, India, in 1984, Chantilly, France, in 1985 and Kinshasa, Zaire, in 1985 — prepared first draft explications of the three articles of the creed, which were revised by the steering group and by the Faith and Order Commission in 1985 in Stavanger (*Faith and Renewal: Stavanger 1985*, no. 131, pp.127-143). Further work on the revised draft was done by the steering group and the Standing Commission in 1986 (an impression of the methodology of such a study process can be seen from the reports of the three consultations and the surveys of the revisions up to 1986, published in *One God, One Lord, One Spirit: On the Explication of the Apostolic Faith Today*, ed. Hans-Georg Link, no. 139, 1988), and in August 1987 the Standing Commission in Madrid approved the study document *Confessing One Faith: Towards an Ecumenical Explication of the Apostolic Faith as Expressed in the Nicene-Constantinopolitan Creed (381)* (no. 140, 1987) in its provisional form. It was sent to the churches and the wider ecumenical public, requesting their study and reactions. During this first phase of the study, in 1985, the handbook *Apostolic Faith Today (op. cit.)* was published which contains a comprehensive documentation of creeds and confessional documents, basic ecumenical texts on the Christian faith and its confession, texts from the preparatory period and first phase of the apostolic faith study, and a historical survey by the editor. At the same time, Faith and Order published four volumes containing contemporary statements of faith (*Confessing Our Faith around the World*, vol. I, ed. C. S. Song, no. 104, 1981; *Confessing Our Faith around the World*, vol. II; vol. III: The Caribbean and Central America; vol. IV: South America; all ed. Hans-Georg Link, nos 120, 123 and 126, 1983, 1984 and 1985).

During the second phase of the study process, 1987-1990, a considerable number of comments and suggestions on the draft "Confessing One Faith" were received from churches, theological faculties, ecumenical commissions and individuals. At three consultations in Porto Alegre, Brazil, in 1987, Rhodes, Greece, in 1988 and Würzburg, Federal Republic of Germany, in 1989, the three parts of "Confessing One Faith" were discussed and related to contemporary issues. Also part of the study were two consultations held jointly with the Sub-unit on Church and Society, in 1986 on "Integrity of Creation" (York, England) and in 1988 on "Creation and the Kingdom of

God" (Dublin, Ireland) (texts in *Creation and the Kingdom of God*, eds D. Gosling and G. Limouris, Church and Society Documents no. 5, 1988). These two consultations, together with that of Porto Alegre in 1987 on the "Doctrine of Creation and its Integrity: A Challenge to the Responsibility of Christianity Today", were also conceived and planned as a contribution to the ecumenical process "Justice, Peace and the Integrity of Creation".

All these reactions and contributions were considered by the Standing Commission in 1988 and the Plenary Commission in Budapest in 1989 (*Budapest 1989: Faith and Order 1985-1989*, no. 148, pp.104-133). On the basis of this material the steering group revised the draft study document and in 1990 the Standing Commission in Dunblane, Scotland, accepted the revised text and authorized its publication: *Confessing the One Faith: An Ecumenical Explication of the Apostolic Faith as It Is Confessed in the Nicene-Constantinopolitan Creed (381). A Faith and Order Study Document*, no. 153, 1991 (the publication includes appendices with a historical overview of the study together with bibliographical references, a glossary and a bibliography). The study document is now being discussed in churches, theological seminaries, ecumenical commissions, etc. It is hoped that it will contribute to a reappropriation of the apostolic faith in the churches so that they may be able to *recognize* in each other's faith and life this same apostolic faith in the unity of its fundamental affirmations and the diversity of its theological expressions, and to *confess* this faith together in our present-day world.

5. Looking towards Santiago de Compostela and beyond

The work on the four main Faith and Order themes between 1963 and 1993 surveyed and documented in this chapter has led to remarkable clarifications, agreements and convergences: (1) on the visible unity of the church up to the 1991 Canberra statement on "The Unity of the Church as Koinonia: Gift and Calling"; (2) on the sacraments and the ministry up to the 1982 Lima document on *Baptism, Eucharist and Ministry* (BEM); (3) on the inter-relation of the efforts for the unity of the church and the renewal of human community up to the study document *Church and World* (1990); and (4) on the common confession of the apostolic faith today up to the study document *Confessing the One Faith* (1991). These results should become part of the ecumenical thinking and life of the churches. One of the major tasks of the *fifth world conference on faith and order* in August 1993 at Santiago de Compostela, Spain, is to identify the remaining differences and problems in these areas and determine ways of dealing with them.

All these four main Faith and Order themes are concerned with fundamental aspects of the nature and mission of the church. This has repeatedly led to the question whether the ecclesiological perspectives implicitly or explicitly operative in the work on these themes are coherent. A first step in response to this question was undertaken by a consultation in 1988 in Pyatigorsk, USSR, on "Ecclesiology — Basic Ecumenical Perspectives" (the report was not published, cf. FO/89:1, Faith and Order/mimeographed texts, archives, WCC). That consultation also considered whether the time had not come for Faith and Order to begin more comprehensive and focused work on the nature and mission of the church. This was further discussed by the Commission at its meeting in Budapest (*Budapest 1989*, no. 148, pp.201-219) and the Commission agreed that Faith and Order should undertake a major study on "Ecumenical Perspectives on Ecclesiology" (*ibid.*, p.219). A consultation in Etchmiadzin, Armenia, USSR, in 1990 prepared a first outline for the study (cf. *Dunblane 1990*, no. 152, pp.32-36) which was revised by the Standing Commission 1990 in Dunblane, Scotland (*ibid.*, pp.68-71). The WCC central committee in 1992 emphasized that this study should be one of the priorities for Faith and Order after the 1993 world conference. Thus, a major study project for the future work has been identified which will be of significance for the WCC and for the ecumenical movement as a whole.

DOCUMENT III.1

THE UNITY OF THE CHURCH — NEXT STEPS (1973)

PART A

I. The context

In the course of the last years much progress has been made in the search for a fuller expression of unity. Most churches have to some degree or other entered the process of exploring and manifesting their unity; in the years since the Fourth Assembly in Uppsala endeavours to overcome the inherited divisions between the separated churches have advanced to such a degree as hardly ever before in such a short space in history. Multilateral theological discussion in the Faith and Order movement has led to agreements which represent a challenge to the churches, especially on the questions of baptism and the eucharist; and issues of controversy are now under discussion which could not have been approached a few years ago. Several interconfessional dialogues, especially between the Roman Catholic Church and other churches, have led to remarkable consensus statements; in some cases, the churches are faced with the question whether they are prepared to draw the logical consequence from the common ground they have discovered and to establish full church fellowship.

The movement for church union has continued to bear fruits. In the past 50 years approximately 60 unions have been consummated; in recent years, united churches in North India, Pakistan and Britain have come into being. In about 30 countries negotiations are being conducted and in several countries plans have been presented to the churches for their decision.

Perhaps even more important is the actual fellowship which in innumerable places has grown among Christians and congregations of different traditions. Coming together in common worship, witness and action, they experience Christian unity to an extent which is not yet possible for their churches as a whole.

At the same time much still needs to be done. The traditional divisions are far from overcome; in some parts of the world their negative force in obscuring common Christian life and witness is still acutely felt. Very often the confessional positions are made even more intransigent by historical, social, political, ethnic and cultural factors. As agreement is being reached on the theological issues which divided the churches in the past, the decisive role of these factors has become even more apparent than before.

But it is not only traditional disagreements that divide us. As the search for unity proceeds, the churches are threatened by new tensions and divisions; many illustrations of these tensions could be given. The search for new expressions of Christian identity, especially in the so-called Third World, and the mutual questioning which results from it, puts strain on the relationship between the churches. Is unity possible between churches in rich and powerful countries and those in poor and oppressed countries? Between churches living in countries with different political systems? Christians facing the issues of the contemporary world often find themselves sharply divided by radically different political and social engagements. They often feel closer to members of other churches sharing the same convictions, experiences and aims than to the members of their own church. The division is often rather between different transconfessional groups and movements than between the churches. How can unity be maintained in these tensions? Can it be maintained at all without betraying the causes recognized by the different groups as imperatives inherent in the Gospel? Is it necessary to give institutional expression to unity? Should there not be, on the contrary, the fullest freedom for new movements to spring up and to grow? Why crush the Spirit by working for the visible manifestation of the communion given by the power of Christ?

Several WCC Assemblies, especially those at New Delhi and Uppsala, have formulated their understanding of the unity to be attained in the ecumenical movement. Their statements are still relevant and need to be reaffirmed. They express the goal of the ecumenical quest for visible unity. But the question arises as to how the search for this goal must be pursued in the present time. Obviously, the vision cannot be realized step by step according to a preconceived plan. The vision granted to the churches may be obscured; they may be tempted to withdraw or they may feel overwhelmed by the magnitude of the issues arising as they seek to witness to the Gospel. Is visible unity a possibility at all in this world? Is the Church not bound to be torn in different directions? Nevertheless, God's promise stands. Christ has prayed for the unity of His disciples and it is on the ground of this prayer that the search for unity can be pursued with the confidence and expectation that the aim will be realized in ever new ways.

II. The unity of the Church in God's purpose for the world

The unity of the Church which we confess in the creed has been given by God in Jesus Christ. It is not the result of human creativity but the living acceptance of God's gift.

God's love has been revealed in and through the life, death and resurrection of Jesus Christ, His son. He has come to reconcile men with God and with one another. He called the disciples. He gave His life for them and His victory over death freed them from the forces of separation. Through the power of the Holy Spirit they were made one in Him. This communion, achieved for the first time in the apostolic community, is at work today as people open their hearts in faith to the Gospel of Jesus Christ.

The unity of the Church stands in relation to God's promise and purpose for the world. Jesus proclaims that the Kingdom of God has drawn near. Sin and its consequences will be overcome. Human self-confidence, rebellion and fear will end. Brokenness and division will be healed and all things will be gathered up under the rule of God. The mystery of the Kingdom was anticipated in Christ's life, death and resurrection, as it is wherever the believing community participates in Him and bears witness to Him.

The one Church today is the continuation of the apostolic community of the first days. If the churches are to overcome their present stage of division, that original communion must be restored among them. But unity does not mean returning to the past. By the power of the Holy Spirit the communion must be realized anew in each period. The Church exists under the call to proclaim God's purpose for the world and to live it out in ever new historical contexts and situations. The mystery of the Kingdom is to be announced today and the unity of the Church will be achieved as Christians are united in the anticipation and expectation of God's future.

God's purpose embraces all people. The Church is called to discern by faith the signs of God's actions in history, in men and women of other faiths and commitments. Their meaning becomes clear only as they are understood in the perspective of Christ's coming. The Church rejoices in these signs and recognizes them as a judgment and bearer of renewal for the Church. In particular, it needs to explore, in its search for unity, both what, out of its own experience, it may contribute to the overcoming of human barriers and divisions and also those insights which others may contribute to the life of the Church itself.

By what terms can the unity of the Church be best described today? Perhaps the terms "sacrament", "sign" and instrument provide the most promising approach.

In the first place, the terms "sacrament" and "sign" refer to the mystery of God's revelation in Jesus Christ — the great mystery that "He was manifested in the flesh, vindicated in Spirit, seen by angels, preached among the nations, believed on in the world, taken up in glory" (I Tim. 3:16 RSV). But in the course of history, the terms have also been used for the community of those who believe in Him. Because this community is an integral part of the mystery of God's action in bringing about His Kingdom, it is, in a derivative sense, "sacrament" and "sign" in history, reflecting God's purpose and promise to all people. As the Church communicates the Gospel, it is "sign" in the sense of instrument. It contributes to the salvation and communion of people with God in Jesus Christ.

When the Church is called "sacrament" and "sign", there cannot be any thought of identifying the Church and the Kingdom of God as if the Church has already arrived at its goal and thus embodied the fulness of God's gift in its historical existence. It is no more than a sign indicating the reality of God's purpose for the world. It might even be said that the sign is often hidden because Christians are disobedient to their call and divided in their response. The Church must confess that it shares in and contributes to the brokenness of the world. The Church is a sign which constantly needs to be made visible. Therefore, the Church must constantly look at the ways in which its sign character has been obscured and needs to be restored.

The terms "sacrament" and "sign" raise many questions which need further attention in the ecumenical movement. How is the sacramentality of the Church to be understood? In what ways does an adequate understanding of this notion challenge the present self-understanding of the churches? What is the relationship between the sacramentality of the Church and the sacraments? A study of these issues may be a priority on the agenda of the Faith and Order Commission.

III. The vision of a united Church as a conciliar fellowship

Jesus Christ founded one Church. Today we live in diverse churches divided from one another. Yet our vision of the future is that we shall once again live as brothers and sisters in one undivided Church. How can this goal be described? We offer the following description to the churches for their consideration: The one Church is to be envisioned as a conciliar fellowship of local churches which are themselves truly united. In this conciliar fellowship each local church possesses, in communion with the others, the fulness of catholicity, witnesses to the same apostolic faith and therefore recognizes the others as belonging to the same Church of Christ and guided by the same spirit. As the New Delhi Assembly pointed out, they are bound together because they have received the same baptism and share in the same eucharist; they recognize each other's members and ministries. They are one in their common commitment to confess the Gospel of Christ by proclamation and service to the world. To this end each church aims at maintaining sustained and sustaining relationships with her sister churches, expressed in conciliar gatherings whenever required for the fulfilment of their common calling.

But how is the relationship between the conciliar fellowship and the local churches to be seen? Further elaboration of each of these two terms is necessary.

Conciliar fellowship

The word *conciliar* refers here to the mutual relationships of local churches within the *one* Church. It is derived from *concilium*. The term does not refer to the councils of divided churches (e.g. the World Council of Churches, National Councils, etc.) which have come into existence in the ecumenical movement as instruments to promote the search for unity and common witness; these, in relation to the goal we seek, are "preconciliar".

Meeting together in representative gatherings is required to proclaim the truth of the Gospel and to carry out the mission of the Church. It is a natural expression of the *communion* among the churches, not simply an organizational pattern. Occasionally when major issues concerning the truth and the unity of the Church need to be faced, the need for universal councils may arise. But maintaining communion calls for a *regular* conciliar practice, in order that legitimate diversity be prevented from deteriorating into division and that conflicts which might lead to trust and growth be "enabled". Meeting in council is a discipline required by communion in Christ; it is verified in the history of the Church. It is an expression of the *relatedness* among all who call on the name of Christ and a means of mutual edification and correction.

This goal may still be in the distant future. But if the churches can accept this description of unity as their goal they must commit themselves to working together towards its achievement. What are the conditions which must first be fulfilled? What are the issues which must receive priority on the ecumenical agenda if we are to advance on the road towards that goal? Already the churches are engaged in multiple dialogues. Already they experience some sort of pre-conciliar fellowship. If all these efforts are directed towards reaching conciliar fellowship certain common priorities can be established. And the conciliar process must be carried on *within* each church as well as among them.

The following considerations regarding conciliar fellowship may be mentioned:

1) Conciliar fellowship can exist only if the churches recognize one another as holding and confessing the same truth. Primary emphasis must, therefore, be placed on the search for a common understanding of the Gospel. This does not necessarily need to be expressed in the same form of words but there needs to be sufficient mutual understanding among the churches to accept one another as living visibly in one and the same truth. Conciliar fellowship requires full reconciliation of the now divided churches. Wherever invalid condemnations have been issued in the past, they must be faced in dialogue and eventually be explicitly shown to have become inapplicable.

2) Conciliar fellowship cannot but be eucharistic fellowship. United by one baptism, members of all local churches should be able to share everywhere in the celebration of the eucharist. No council *(concilium)* can be held without celebrating the eucharist. Many different forms of celebration may be possible as long as the celebration can be recognized by all as the fulfilment of the Lord's commandment,

"Do this in remembrance of me." Priority must be given to reaching such common celebration. Obviously, this means also that different understandings of the ministry need to be clarified.

3) Conciliar fellowship necessitates representative gatherings and this means that thought must be given to the most appropriate ways of representation in the Church. Who speaks for the local church? Who represents the Church at the regional, national or world level? For this reason also the issue of the role of the ministry in the Church must be pursued as a priority. How should the ministry function at various levels of the Church's life and how should these various ministries be related to one another? In particular, the vision of a conciliar fellowship requires a fresh examination of the place of the ordained ministry in the whole people of God. What is the role of the laity — both men and women — in representing the Church in the conciliar process?

4) Conciliar fellowship is concerned with the truth. How can the churches agree on a way of articulating the faith they hold in common? What are the bases of authority; how are they related to each other; who is competent to represent the faithful in synods and councils which decide on both doctrinal and juridical matters affecting the life of the Church? The focus here is twofold: (a) the sacramental and ecclesiological *context* in which authority is exercised, and (b) *how* decisions are made at various levels of the Church's life, in diverse cultures and national settings, as well as at the universal level. Authority is closely and inescapably connected with power. How can the conciliar process contribute to empowering the powerless? While most of us are agreed that the final authority of the Church resides in the whole congregation of the faithful, who through the years either do or do not receive the findings of councils as authoritative, the question of authority in conciliar life is crucial. Councils take decisions which affect the lives of all and require their response. The power inherent in authority must be exercised in overt and transparent ways. How can authority be exercised as a service to the Church, avoiding domination of one part over the other? The statement of the Faith and Order Commission at Louvain puts it pointedly:

> "There must be opportunity within the life of the Church for each community of mankind to develop and express its own authentic selfhood; for the oppressed and exploited to find justice; and for the 'marginal' people in our society — the handicapped in mind and body — to make their own distinctive contribution."[2]

5) The conciliar fellowship is a confessing fellowship. As the churches strive to achieve greater unity, they must begin to engage in common witness and service. But they need constantly to ask "What is the Church for? To what task is God calling each church in its particular time and place?" This implies their facing together the issues arising from their witness in the contemporary world. Many of these issues are new and have not been controversial in the past. But they may be profoundly controversial today, sometimes even dividing the churches in new ways and leading to new transconfessional groupings. But potentially divisive issues should not therefore be avoided. Their preliminary ecumenical fellowship must be used as the place to practise in anticipation that conciliar fellowship the churches are ultimately seeking to build.

As the churches commit themselves to the goals of conciliar fellowship, the following steps may help to initiate and hasten that process.

---

[2] *Faith and Order Louvain 1971*, Geneva: WCC, 1971, pp.226,227. [note 1 omitted here]

(a) The initiative for any advance must primarily come from the churches themselves. Most churches have declared in one way or another that they are committed to the ecumenical movement. But if further progress is to be made, they need to express more clearly how they understand the unity that Christ wills for His Church and above all they need to state how this unity can be reached in a concerted effort with the other churches.

(b) The ecumenical discussion still concentrates too exclusively on the issues which were manifestly controversial in the past. But the agenda of the ecumenical movement is wider. The churches need to face together the issues which arise from their witness in the contemporary world, especially those which may cause new tensions and divisions. What is the role of the Church in the field of political and social responsibility? What is the appropriate relationship between Church and state? Is it essential that each church consider all problems of its life in the light of the ecumenical movement? Common conciliar life can be developed only if common perspectives and mutual understanding emerge at all levels and in connection with all problems. By adopting this ecumenical discipline the churches may gradually become "unitable churches".

(c) The Uppsala statement on "The Holy Spirit and the catholicity of the Church" speaks of the existence of regional councils and the World Council as "a transitional opportunity for eventually actualizing a truly universal, ecumenical, conciliar form of life and witness".[3] There exists a need for relating efforts at all levels — local and universal. Because of this, we recommend that *churches, union negotiating committees, partners in bi- and multi-lateral conversations* use the World Council of Churches and the Faith and Order Commission in coordinating the efforts and collating the results of these diverse efforts towards unity. In this way these efforts could reinforce and aid each other and energy be focused rather than diffused.

Local churches

The second focus of this discussion concerns the local churches. It has been said above that the conciliar fellowship is a fellowship of *local churches,* that is to say, churches which are themselves already one in a locality.

But the term *local* can have different meanings. It can refer to the individual worshipping congregation, to dioceses or other regional groupings as well as to national churches. It means here primarily the eucharistic community in a given place or context. Conciliar fellowship must be realized in the first place among the local eucharistic communities of a given area. It must find expression, however, at all levels of the life of the Church — in regions, nations and eventually at the world level.

But how can the local churches, often divided and in isolation from one another, work towards this unity? In discussing the necessary elements of conciliarity above, some of the ingredients of this search have been described. At this point one expression of local church unity can be mentioned: that *of church union.*

IV. Conciliar fellowship and organic union

The unity described in the preceding section requires union of the churches which are still separated today. There is no contradiction between the vision of a conciliar fellowship of local churches and the goal of organic union. Both terms point to the

[3] *The Uppsala '68 Report*, Geneva: WCC, 1968, p.17.

same calling. The conciliar fellowship requires organic union. The vision of such a conciliar fellowship will, therefore, become a reality only as the churches are prepared to face, at all levels, the implications and challenge of organic union.

In particular, union negotiations at the national level need to be pursued. Since the local churches which form the universal conciliar fellowship must be truly united themselves, division at this level of the Church's life is particularly intolerable. But union negotiations at this level must recognize especially the necessity of finding appropriate ways to provide fully for emerging expressions of human diversities within the united Church, as well as ways of expressing the worldwide dimension of the Christian community.

God's great gift in Jesus Christ is the promise of a new community in which humanity's estrangements are overcome. The churches are called to seek to give visible institutional form to this new community — in a manner which will enable their members in each place to gather around the Word and sacraments and to work out their mission in the world together. Corporate union is such a form.

In many places unions have occurred or are now being considered. Union has repeatedly become the occasion for Christians discovering a deeper identity; it has proved again and again to be a dynamic concept with a capacity to respond to new expressions of human need, making possible the growth of a more inclusive identity and fellowship. Union does this by gathering up into one body the various confessional traditions of the past and thus enriches the life and faith of each member. It thus makes it possible for Christians previously isolated from one another by racial and cultural barriers to learn from one another and in so doing to move towards a fuller involvement in the human community. Church union can also provide a place within the Church for groups now developing that transcend existing confessional and cultural lines.

The relevance and urgency of organic union

The urgency and relevance of organic union has been underlined by several recent developments.

Thus, for example, in union negotiations the churches are rediscovering both what Jesus Christ means for our time and how the community which bears His name witnesses to this faith. Organic union also enables Christians to play a more effective part in the struggle for social justice and peace. It does so by challenging institutional barriers which block effective action, by encouraging and facilitating new strategies for witness and by building patterns of shared life for groups that have been estranged.

God calls the Church into the world to build personal and corporate community, in creating structures of justice and service, in mediating reconciliation. But each of these commissions of Christ is called into question and crippled in implementation by our divisions. By their disunity and competition the churches make fully authentic witness or community impossible and their resources are squandered in an irresponsible fashion. Organic union is an appropriate response to the call for responsible Christian stewardship of personnel and resources.

Finally to be mentioned is the evangelistic commission. Faced by a world that denies the lordship of Christ, the churches need to be united in the task of evangelism, so that their divisions no longer belie the gospel of reconciliation.

A united Church is a necessity. Thus some form of organic union must be the goal of the churches and this goal should be pursued urgently, under divine guidance and compulsion.

Steps on the road to union

As churches grow towards union, they have found a whole number of possible intermediate steps which help to move them towards their goal. Examples of such steps are:
— involvement in joint mission projects;
— shared worship, especially intercommunion, on a regular basis;
— covenanting, by which churches at all levels of their life publicly declare their common intention;
— united theological education, training of the laity, Christian education and literature work, etc.;
— evaluation and re-allocation of funds and programme priorities.

Such typical intermediate steps, however, should not be allowed to become resting places.

It is clear that Councils of Churches can make significant contributions to the union of churches. In some cases Councils have played an initiating role. But even if a Council has not taken an active part, it should be possible that interested member churches in a Council be free to work towards union without breaking the fellowship within that Council. A Council can also help build relationships among churches as a first step in establishing acquaintance and can assist in facilitating greater communication among them even before union is possible.

V. Different levels of unity — Complementarity and interaction

Unity must be established at all levels of the Church's life — congregational, national, regional and worldwide. Basically, unity is the same at all levels. It is lived out as Christians profess the same faith, witnessed to by the one baptism, as they share in one and the same eucharist. But unity requires different expressions at different levels. When efforts towards unity are undertaken, the envisioned goal will inevitably vary according to the level at which they are taking place: e.g. conversations at the world level will not lead to the same type of union as negotiations at the national or local levels. Though the different levels need to be distinguished, they must not be separated from one another. All efforts towards unity depend on one another and must, therefore, be seen in their interaction. There is urgent need for consultation between the different levels as a whole.

Each level has its own proper value and function and none is privileged above another. Initiatives towards fuller unity can and should be proposed from any level. Today we are realizing anew that the local level where Christians come together out of confessional separation to achieve certain common tasks, can often be a vital source of ecumenical initiative. Yet it is in other places the level at which the strongest resistance to moves towards unity is felt.

There is at all levels a serious danger of the further fragmentation of the existing churches. Some are tempted to apply the term "schismatic" to newly constituted transconfessional groups which come together out of a vivid awareness of a common task. Yet there is the real danger that the existing churches may make themselves responsible for schism if they refuse to accept and act upon the true insights expressed in such groups. Situations where the potential for gain or loss exists are found in abundance — mixed marriages, the charismatic renewal, experimental joint congregations, action groups for evangelism or for social action, to name only a few.

In such cases the ordained ministry has an important role to play in maintaining unity and, therefore, particular attention needs to be paid to its exercise. Ordained ministers may often prove to be one of the main links between transconfessional groups and the churches to which their members belong and yet by the same token to be in danger of pulling such groups apart because of inherited separate patterns of training, approach, payment and the like. The ordained ministers should in these cases seek primarily to interpret the insights and experiences of the united groups into other levels of church life so that the church as a whole may learn how to incarnate the truth there perceived. The loosening of traditional disciplines (e.g. of eucharistic fellowship) that some churches now find possible in such circumstances must always be accompanied by a correspondingly eager discipline of interpretation and reception in the wider levels.

Similarly, particular attention needs to be given to the form of the Church's ministry at the world level. Some churches know what they believe to be appropriate here and have patterns of experience (e.g. the communion of the bishops) which witness to that. But many churches have not yet developed clear ideas of what sort of structures are appropriate to the exercise of universal unity. It is at least evident that the present pattern of the World Council of Churches as a world fellowship of churches, while providing useful experience, cannot in itself constitute a satisfactory answer to this ecclesiological question. More thought must be devoted to this problem.

Unity is not something to be created but to be received — yet not passively; rather in an active search. This "reception" of God's gifts demands that we give expression at all levels to these gifts in signs and actions which commit us personally and which can in time commit the churches to which we belong. Ecumenism is essentially a movement in which each step ahead must be translated into visible experience by church members so that it may in turn be lived out by ever wider circles of Christians.

VI. Identity, change and unity

Any advance towards unity calls into question the identity of the now divided churches. But can this identity be abandoned? Is it not the expression of God's faithfulness throughout history? All churches face this dilemma in one way or another. A group of Orthodox theologians has recently described it in the following terms: "The Orthodox emphasize the God-given ontological and indivisible unity of the Body of Christ realized and preserved in history. They believe that this unity has existed continuously and without interruption in the Orthodox Church, its doctrine, its sacraments and its essential order — even if its members either as individuals or corporately fail to realize and manifest the implications of this divine gift. Other churches find it difficult to accept this claim. They share the view that the Church is founded and given in Christ and that it has existed in history without interruption. They cannot share, however, the identification of the one Church with the Orthodox Church. They either identify the one Church with a different historical tradition or believe that the continuity must be affirmed in faith but cannot be identified with one particular historical tradition."[4] Even if the latter view described in this quotation is held, union cannot easily be achieved; the historical identity represents a decisive obstacle.

What can be said about this dilemma? The identity and the unity of the Church have their ultimate and normative reality in Jesus Christ, who comes to us in the power of the Holy Spirit, calling His Church to and empowering it for an ever-renewed testimony to His redeeming and reconciling work. In this living tradition we are one with the Church throughout history and at the same time we are liberated to articulate our witness within the conditions and demands of our present historical moment. Identity and change are not therefore opposed or contradictory. Rather our present identity is to be found as, from within its whole tradition and out of its solidarity with the needs and hopes of the world, the Church undertakes to manifest the Gospel of our Lord Jesus Christ in thought, life and action.

In this effort, the traditional expressions of our identity as confessions and communions are gratefully received as witness of the ever-faithful leading of the Spirit, but they are also time-bound in their terms of reference and relevance. They have helped us to enrich our understanding of the Christian faith and they should also help us in accepting the change that the present moment demands. While we recognize the fundamental unity which Christ gave and wishes for His Church, it is not imperative that we express it today by a return to one of these particular expressions of the living tradition and continuity of the Church, nor by seeking a compromise by combining several historical forms of the past. Rather we are free and compelled to attempt to express in the present, in the variety of our circumstances, the living tradition of the Gospel.

In virtue of this living tradition which expresses the economy of Christ through the Holy Spirit for the salvation of the world, the Church professes the same witness as was professed by the apostolic community, and her ministry continues the apostolic ministry. Her whole life is integrally related to the experience of the whole People of God of all ages, so that the Church is permanently renewed by God in her historical continuity. In this process, historical traditions will at the same time be tested, renewed, transcended and reconstituted in the catholicity and the unity of the Church. Thus we are given, through repentance and conversion, a present identity which we recognize as in some continuity with our common and particular histories but at the same time as a new and original gift of God.

PART B

1. How can consensus (agreed statement on doctrine) contribute to unity among the churches? What use can be made of the consensus on baptism, the eucharist and the ministry?

In the course of the past years, the Faith and Order Commission has spent much time and energy in formulating agreed statements on baptism, the eucharist and the ministry. Draft statements were submitted to the Commission. The texts on baptism

---

[4] See *Minutes of Working Committee,* Faith and Order, Paper No. 66, p.47.

and the eucharist were sent to all member churches of the World Council of Churches with the request that comment be made on them.[5]

One group at the Salamanca consultation was asked to study the significance of such consensus statements. The following observations are the fruits of their discussion.

The consensus as part of a process

It is vital that consensus be understood as part of a process. It is like a single frame taken from a motion picture: the attitudes seen in it indicate the direction of movement but they are fully intelligible only when the whole picture is shown in motion. It is from the life and thought of the People of God that the consensus emerges and it is into that life that it must be fed back. Only in this way is it possible to appreciate the living context which gives meaning to the consensus statements, albeit sometimes divergent meaning in different contexts; and only in this way is it possible to give life to the consensus by hearing the testimonies of those who variously, and sometimes contrastingly, illustrate or challenge the consensus out of their own Christian experience.

The process preceding and following up the establishment of consensus provokes that fermentation of thought and discussion which is essential to the preparation of a future general ecumenical council. A process of true consensus derives from and moves towards Jesus Christ.

The value of consensus

The consensus on baptism and the eucharist creatively emphasizes the fact that baptism and eucharist are essentially concerned with the outpouring of God's love to the world and the consequent responsibility of Christians.

The search for consensus of this kind is an important element in the ecumenical movement. Some see it as the essential method of ecumenical progress, while all the groups would give it an important place along with the complementary exploration of partnership in service and mutual acceptance despite doctrinal diversity.

Churches called to make pastoral decisions, e.g. on confirmation practice in relation to the eucharist, may avoid unhappily divergent decisions if there is widespread achievement of and knowledge of ecumenical consensus.

The consensus, and even more the discipline of arriving at it, can lead participants to a discovery of the riches of Christian insights and experiences other than their own.

A common discovery of revealed truth by opening our hearts and minds to the reception of the Divine Word gradually unites us in the communion of the Holy Spirit and, therefore, in the unity of the one Body of Christ, the Church. Ambiguous diplomatic formulae are to be avoided, but there is a need in many circumstances for a form of words that can register a partial agreement sufficient for the next steps to be taken in cooperation.

The limitations of consensus

This kind of consensus is by its nature verbal and doctrinal. This means that it can be too theoretical, e.g. in defining baptism but failing to indicate which actual rites of Christian initiation fall within the agreed description; it means also that it may bypass

---

[5] Cf. "Ecumenical Agreement on Baptism" and "The Eucharist in Ecumenical Thought", *Faith and Order Louvain 1971*, pp.49-53, 71-77.

the possibilities of mutual acceptance in diversity or mutual challenge by varied witness.

The very desire to encompass the richness of insights mentioned above can make it difficult to express the witness of those Christian bodies whose emphasis is upon the simplicity of the Gospel.

Up to this time the consensus reflects too much the pastoral situation of secularized Europe and North America. The discussion of infant baptism, for instance, shows little awareness of the facts of community solidarity in some parts of the world.

The addressees of the consensus

The consensus is addressed to at least three groups — theologians, church leaders, and the faithful in general. This means that it has a variety of uses but also that it cannot completely satisfy any one group. The theologians demand greater precision, the church leaders more practical application and the faithful in general more clarity and immediate relevance; yet theologians are stimulated to new encounters, church leaders given a basis for decision-making and the faithful in general encouraged to deepen their Christian living together.

The use that can be made of the consensus on baptism and the eucharist

Recognition of the nature and function of consensus as part of the ecumenical process makes possible specific recommendations concerning the use of the consensus on baptism and eucharist. The existing consensus statements are open to many critical comments but they contain such a breadth and richness of material in quite brief compass that they should not be locked away in the files of Faith and Order or at church offices. The consensus will have achieved little unless it be given living expression in the ecumenical movement and in the life of local communities of Christians in many ways, including the following:

1. Worship

The consensus statements on baptism and eucharist should be revised to include ways of understanding and testing the consensus in actual worship; this could be done either by indicating existing liturgies and forms of worship (in which it is believed that the consensus already finds expression) or where necessary by developing new orders of baptism and eucharist.

On particular occasions Christians from a number of local fellowships should gather for the common renewal of their baptismal vows.

Christians of one church should be invited to be present at baptisms in other Christian communities.

The expression of the consensus in relation to eucharistic sharing calls for great pastoral sensitivity both to the existing disciplines of the churches and to the longing of Christians to be at one at the Lord's table.

2. Pastoral relationships

Every effort should be made through teams of clergy and laity (which could be sponsored by local Councils of Churches) to enable Christians to enter into common Christian life experiences. Across a wide spectrum of the ecumenical movement these efforts could be based on the mystical unity of all Christians through their baptism, although for some this would not be the natural starting point.

This general sharing could both be aided by and be of help to the households of mixed marriages among Christians.

3. Study

Consultations concerning the consensus should be encouraged: (a) among the partner churches in bilateral discussions (preferably with consultants from other traditions present); (b) with churches and groups not hitherto involved in the discussions.

There should be common study of those passages of Scripture which are basic to the consensus. Scripture also underlies developed Christian teaching on the meaning of sacraments in general and on this a further consensus still needs to be evolved.

To assist these studies and the wider sharing of the consensus, there will be need for publications at all levels: brief popular pamphlets to state and explain the essential elements of the consensus; catechetical material; study documents suitable for ecumenical use in seminary and university groups.

All these studies need to be kept in relation to the development of other WCC programmes preparing for the next Assembly, in particular the sections on "Confessing Christ Today" and "What Unity Requires".

4. Use in relation to church union negotiations

Church leaders should be encouraged to use the consensus in preparing the way for developments in inter-church relations such as covenanting for union.

The consensus documents should be widely studied in church union negotiations with the recognition that the material will have to be worked through in each particular situation by the negotiators.

II. The role of World Confessional Families in the ecumenical movement

We must emphasize the extreme heterogeneity of the bodies grouped together as World Confessional Families. They have described themselves as follows: "Each World Confessional Family consists of churches belonging to the same tradition and held together by this common heritage; they are conscious of living in the same universal fellowship and give to this consciousness at least some structural expression" (Conference of Secretaries of WCFs, 1967). It is the very disparate nature of this structural expression that makes it very difficult to give precise formulation to the role of the World Confessional Families, and in fact leads to considerable frustration in discussing their role, and in making generalizations about them. We would, however, prefer the term "World Families of Churches" as a more appropriate description to include all those who have become the partners in dialogue referred to below.

Bilateral conversations

Most of these World Families have been in recent years, and still are, engaged in a process of bilateral and multilateral conversations at world and regional levels. An expression of the achievement and range of their conversations can be found in the survey *Confessions in Dialogue* (Geneva: WCC, 1972). The evaluation of this process of interconfessional dialogue raises, among others, the question of the relationship between, and respective functions of, the World Council of Churches and the World Families. It is important that both examine how they can conceive their own role in relation to one another in the pursuit of unity in relation to the ecumenical movement in general.

Concerning the dialogue in which World Families are engaged, we draw attention in particular to the need for adequate coordination between bilateral dialogues, multilateral dialogue and church union negotiations. There is also the need to relate the results of interconfessional dialogues to the decision-making processes of the churches at every level.

We request that at the meeting of General Secretaries of the World Confessional Families in Geneva, 1973, the Roman Catholic Church, the Orthodox Churches and the other World Families should be effectively represented so that plans can be made to constitute an adequate forum for the full exchange of views on bilateral conversations at the world level.

Ecumenical commitment

We appreciate the value of world-wide fellowships which the World Families represent and the way in which, as they engage in interconfessional dialogue, they seek to find a universal expression of the faith. We also appreciate how small and scattered churches are brought into a broader community through the World Families, and how in some cases their member churches are helped to overcome isolation and to enter into real relationship.

On the other hand there are ways in which the World Families may hinder the ecumenical movement, and we suggest that in view of frequently expressed misgivings, World Families should seriously consider whether:

(a) they give sufficient attention to the local situation in the processes of agenda-setting and decision-making;

(b) they engage in sufficient consultation between each other and with the World Council of Churches;

(c) their structures, policies and activities in fact encourage and support their member churches as they move towards union, and do not prevent local ecumenical commitment;

(d) their financial policies, or the policies of the boards or agencies of some of their member churches, lead to domination and a dependence on the part of member churches which restricts ecumenical engagements;

(e) their policies encourage consultation and common planning for mission, service and development at local and national levels.

In the field of theological education World Families cooperate with one another in some places, but we urge that in every local situation there should be consultation between the World Families, the Theological Education Fund and the local churches of whatever denomination with the aim of establishing theological education on an ecumenical basis.

We also request the World Families to ask their member churches to listen to the witness of the unity found in spontaneous groups, and to give a greater hearing to the voices of the Third World, of women and of youth.

In parts of the world member churches of the World Families have crossed their denominational frontiers and joined together in organic union. The very existence of these united churches is a sign of the need to interpret the universal Gospel at the local level. The united churches are a challenge to the World Families, and the problems of those wishing to unite should set the agenda for discussions at the world level. The ecumenical experience of those who have achieved organic union, both in their struggle towards union and in their growing together after union, should be made available to, and made use of by, others as they in their turn move towards union.

In the light of the foregoing we would urge upon the World Families the need to clarify their understanding of the quest for unity by cooperating with the World Council of Churches to develop an agreed discussion paper on the ecumenical roles of the World Families and the World Council of Churches to be used in preparation for their next world assemblies. We request that this concern should become part of the agenda of the meeting of the Conference of General Secretaries of the World Confessional Families in Geneva, November 1973.[6]

---

[6] At their 1973 meeting, the World Families began the planning of a consultation in December 1974 to begin this process.

DOCUMENT III.2

THE UNITY OF THE CHURCH: THE GOAL AND THE WAY (1974)

A. Understanding the Context

Neither the goal of unity nor attempts to come closer to it can be adequately described in abstract and timeless definitions. Any description must be related to the actual historical conditions, the different concerns, emerging in various parts of the world and the struggle to find authentic expressions of Christian faith and life in countries outside the European-North American tradition.

In the years since the Fourth Assembly of the World Council of Churches in Uppsala, endeavours to overcome the traditional confessional divisions between the separated churches have advanced to a remarkable degree. Multilateral theological discussion in the area of Faith and Order has led to agreements which represent a challenge to the churches, especially on the questions of baptism and the eucharist. Other issues of controversy (for example, the ministry) are now under discussion.

Several interconfessional dialogues, especially between the Roman Catholic Church and other churches, have led to important consensus statements. These conversations are an important expression of the ecumenical responsibilities of the World Families of Churches. The churches are faced with the question whether they are prepared to initiate a process of reception with regard to these agreements on all levels of church life with a view to definite steps towards full church fellowship.

This difficult task of overcoming the traditional divisions is still at the centre of ecumenical endeavours in Europe and North America — the continents where these divisions have their historical roots and their formative impact on many aspects of ecclesiastical and secular life. For churches outside these areas, such divisions cannot have the same significance, since they are not really part of their own history. They are, therefore, trying to deal with these divisions on a doctrinal level but incorporating also in their attempts to reach unity other aspects which are of significance for their existence in a different cultural, historical, and socio-economic context.

The movement for church union has continued to bear fruit. In the past fifty years approximately sixty unions have been consummated: in recent years, the united churches in North India, Pakistan, and Britain have come into being. In about thirty countries, negotiations are being conducted, and in several countries plans have been presented to the churches for their decision.

Perhaps even more important is the actual fellowship which in innumerable places has grown among Christians and congregations of different traditions. Coming together in common worship, witness and action, they experience Christian unity to an extent which is not yet possible for their churches as a whole. This experience must be taken up in theological reflection and in decisions of the churches.

In some parts of the world, the traditional confessional positions, whether they are part of the history of a particular country or imposed from outside, are made even more intransigent by historical, social, political, ethnic, and cultural factors (for example, state-church relations in Europe, caste in India, tribalism in Africa, class structures in Latin America, ethnic and social backgrounds in North America, to cite only some indications). Where agreements have been reached on theological issues, the decisive role of these factors has become even more apparent than before.

The struggle for unity among the churches in Asia, Africa and Latin America is also intimately connected with the painful attempts of many of these churches to free themselves from what they regard as the bondage of superimposed Western patterns of theological thinking and method. Accordingly, in Africa, for example, attempts to reach union between separated churches are linked to the struggle to find a truly African identity in Christian and ecclesiastical life by overcoming Western conceptional patterns of thinking, cultural forms and imported divisions. There are analogous tensions between black and white churches in the United States. This painful struggle for authenticity and community requires the freedom to develop its own methods in dealing with the questions of the unity of the Church.

In Asia, the gift and task of unity are more and more seen in the context of finding true expressions of Christian life and witness in the context of a religious and cultural diversity. Here it is strongly felt that the denominational diversity of churches in Europe and North America still has negative consequences for the efforts towards organic union in Asia. The need for a complete independence of the churches in their efforts for unity has to be stressed here as well as in other parts of the world. This challenge from the churches outside the Western hemisphere may also help the churches in Europe and North America to take their obligation to seek organic union or full fellowship among themselves more seriously.

In Latin America, the struggle for social justice is regarded by many as an integral part of attempts to bring the churches closer together. Here, the questions of division, tension, conflict, reconciliation, and fellowship are seen in a socio-political, confessional and spiritual context at the same time. Here, as in other regions of the world, the awareness is growing that the attempts to heal the wounds of the Church have to go hand in hand with efforts to heal the wounds of the body of mankind. One of the longstanding convictions of many, namely that the search for the unity of the people of God is not an end in itself, but is directed to the task and mission of the Church, is finding practical expression in many parts of the world.

The ecumenical situation today is not characterized only by a greater diversity but also by new divisive tensions and polarizations. Conservative evangelical movements, the charismatic movement, and radical socio-political tendencies and groups have emerged within the different churches. These movements exhibit many aspects which allow them to be described as "new confessionalities" — they have their own "creeds" and their own "anathemas". Many of those involved in these movements find in them a warm fellowship which transcends the older divisions. This raises serious questions for the renewal of the traditional churches. They can nevertheless create serious polarizations more acute than the divisions between the traditional churches. All attempts to reach fuller unity have to take these transconfessional, worldwide movements seriously into account.

The aspects of the present situation indicated above make it clear that the search for unity today is becoming a much more complex matter than it has been in previous periods of the ecumenical movement. As a consequence, it is increasingly difficult and inappropriate to apply the same concepts and methods in this search in all places. Therefore, the ecumenical discussion and ecumenical statements on the world level have to allow for a great variety of methods and ways to meet the tasks of different situations. On the other hand, many of the newer tensions and polarizations will always be with us in one form or another. Socio-political conflicts, and the tensions between those who are mainly concerned to guard the heritage and those who are mainly concerned with current challenges, will always be present in the Church. It may be that the distinctive *kairos* which the Holy Spirit is now giving us (as the fruit of the pioneering work of the ecumenical movement) is for the healing of the great confessional divisions of the Church. We must not allow this chance to slip away. In fact the healing of these inherited wounds would enable us to help each other to face together the newer conflicts. Certain basic convictions need to be shared by all who struggle for the fuller manifestation of the unity of Christ's Church in order that the universality of our faith, witness, and fellowship be maintained.

What can we say together, from our many different situations, about the healing of the divisions which keep us apart and stand in the way of common witness?

B. Describing the Goal

When the World Council of Churches was founded, it was made clear that membership in the Council, while committing the churches to the quest for unity, did not commit them to any particular doctrine about the form of that unity. This was spelled out in the Toronto Statement of the Central Committee in 1950. But it was obviously necessary to press on beyond the starting point and to seek to adumbrate — even in the most general terms — a vision of the nature of the unity we seek. This was attempted in the statement of the Third Assembly at New Delhi which spoke of the unity of a fully committed fellowship in each place, linked with the one fellowship everywhere.

In the subsequent discussions, much more attention was paid to the first half of the definition — "in each place" — than to the second. The Fourth Assembly at Uppsala sought to carry the discussion further by invoking the idea of conciliarity as a model for the wider unity of the Church in all places. It spoke of the World Council as a "transitional opportunity for eventually actualizing a truly universal, ecumenical, conciliar form of common life", and suggested that the member churches should "work for the time when a genuinely universal council may once more speak for all Christians and lead the way into the future".

This suggestion was welcomed in many quarters, especially in several of the World Families of Churches, and was taken up at the request of the Central Committee for further clarification at the Faith and Order Commission meeting at Louvain in 1971. The Commission was able to make use of the results of a study on the Council of Chalcedon in undertaking this work. The meeting produced a substantial report which emphasized the value of the conciliar idea as providing a form of unity which could do full justice to the great diversity of human situations.

At the conference called by the Faith and Order Commission at Salamanca in 1973, this concept of conciliarity was further discussed in the context of a study of "Concepts of unity and models of union". In particular, the conference sought to clarify the relation between the two concepts of "conciliarity" and "organic union". It gave the following description of the goal of the ecumenical effort:

> The one Church is to be envisioned as a conciliar fellowship of local churches which are themselves truly united. In this conciliar fellowship, each local church possesses, in communion with others, the fullness of catholicity, witnesses to the same apostolic faith and, therefore, recognizes the others as belonging to the same Church of Christ and guided

by the same spirit. As the New Delhi Assembly pointed out, they are bound together because they have received the same baptism and share in the same eucharist; they recognize each other's members and ministries. They are one in their common commitment to confess the Gospel of Christ by proclamation and service to the world. To this end each church aims at maintaining sustained and sustaining relationships with her sister churches, expressed in conciliar gatherings whenever required for the fulfilment of their common calling.

At our meeting in Accra, we have tried to carry further this discussion. We have found it difficult for several reasons. We have not yet been able to give sufficient theological clarity to the terms "conciliarity" and "organic union" and to the relation between them. Some among us regret the use of the word "conciliarity" as one which limits the range of discussion, describes the nature of the Church in an external way, and suggests something less than full organic union. Others are unwilling to use the phrase "organic union" as the *only* satisfactory definition of the goal. While we have tried to say certain things together, we recognize that there is still much that seems to us obscure and that real differences remain unresolved.

We have devoted most of our discussion to the elucidation of the concept of conciliarity. How far is this concept useful in helping us to envisage — and reach — our goal? Certainly it can be understood in different ways. Councils have performed a variety of different functions. They have been convened to deal with actual or threatened breaches of fellowship, to settle doctrinal disputes, to legislate for the churches, and to provide guidance and renewal. Conciliarism has been a powerful force in the Western Church of the fourteenth and fifteenth centuries and in the Russian Church of the nineteenth — in each case with a somewhat different intention. The local, national and world councils of churches which perform such a vital role in the modern ecumenical movement do not, obviously, conform to the definition of conciliar fellowship given at Salamanca. They are federal in character and do not enjoy either full communion or the capacity to make decisions for all their members. They might properly be described as "pre-conciliar" bodies.

This multiplicity of references makes the word "conciliar" both useful and dangerous. It can evoke a response from many different quarters, but it can also create misunderstanding. Some have taken it to be an easier alternative to the quest for organic union — although the Salamanca Statement has insisted that it in fact requires organic union. To some it may seem a remote idea which has little bearing on present realities. It is welcomed by some as a description of the continued co-existence of separate confessional families in a "reconciled diversity".

In spite of these dangers which must be recognized, it remains true that the concept of conciliarity can play a helpful role at this stage in our pilgrimage towards unity, and this for two reasons:

1. We have noted that the discussion of the New Delhi Statement concentrated mainly on its first part, concerning "all in each place". The concept of conciliarity helps to balance this discussion by providing a possible model for the relation to each other of churches locally united in each place, nation, or region. Most of the plans for organic union in the past fifty years have looked to national united churches as their goal; there has not hitherto been much serious reflection about the form in which the unity of these united churches with one another should be expressed. The concept of conciliarity can provide a model. The recent Conference on Church Union in Africa has advocated the formation of some sort of *concilium* for Africa along these lines.

2. Proposals for organic union among churches frequently meet with the criticism that a church which embraced "all in each place" in one administrative structure could become a denial of legitimate freedom and diversity. To speak of organic union primarily in terms of administrative unification is to misapply the term. It is indeed true that unity can become oppressive and that a powerful church administration can and often does suppress proper diversities.

The concept of conciliarity, as it was developed by the Commission at Louvain in 1971, called for a form of church life in which "there is ample space for diversity and for open mutual confrontation of differing interests and convictions".[1] In this respect, the model of conciliarity is provided by the meeting described in the fifteenth chapter of Acts, where, in the fullest mutual fellowship and trust, it was agreed that different parts of the one Church, remaining in full communion, would pursue the one world mission along different paths and in different styles. But this diversity had at its heart a unity which, as St Paul insisted in his controversy with St Peter at Antioch, must necessarily include fellowship at one table, and, as the same text reminds us, this diversity is held within the fellowship of the one Spirit who guides the whole Council.

In other words, conciliarity can be a way of describing a certain kind of church life — at every level — in which a total mutual acceptance is combined with a deep respect for the "otherness" of those who share the same fellowship but fulfil its obligations in different ways.

The concept of conciliarity is thus not an alternative to that of organic union but rather a way of describing one aspect of a truly organic union at every level from the local to the universal.

Seen in this light, the conciliar idea could be helpful in stimulating fresh thinking about the practical implications of "organic union" at every level. In fact, it is most necessary that fresh and imaginative thought should be given to the forms and structures of a shared church life, so that it may become clear that, in advocating organic union as the goal of our efforts, we are not advocating a form of unity which would deny diversity.

In spite of the differences among us, and the obscurity which still surrounds our use of terms concerning the visible forms of our unity in Christ, we joyfully affirm and confess together the inner reality of that unity which is already given to us in him. That given unity awakens in us all the longing for the one great feast to which the Lord calls his own — the eucharistic feast in which all men and women of every kind are accepted and joyfully accept one another as children of one Father and brothers and sisters of one Lord. In each eucharist — even in our separation — we have both a sign and renewal of the unity for which we long. The vision which draws us is the vision of the one feast — not many and separate feasts — one host and one feast for all the people of God. It is that vision, and the foretaste of it which we have already received, which continually move us to seek together the forms by which the unity of the Church is to be made visible.

---

[1] Minutes of the Meeting of the Commission and Working Committee, Louvain 1971. *Faith and Order Paper*, No. 60, p.227. Geneva: WCC, 1971.

C. Moving into the Fullness of Conciliar Fellowship

If it is accepted that the concept of conciliarity can be helpful in enabling us to describe the goal of our efforts, we must now ask what help it gives us in discerning the way. Some may feel they are already clear about the requirements of the goal, as they understand it; others may feel it to be strange and distant. Some will feel they have already moved from what they were in times past through several stages on the way to it; others may be quite unsure what it might require from them or how they can begin. To all it is clear that the achievement of full conciliar fellowship:
— must involve all who claim Jesus Christ as Lord;
— will inevitably require a long process of striving with one another towards and into that fullness.

Moreover, since what we are concerned with is the integrity of Christ's Church, and since conciliarity, like unity, is not a goal in itself in isolation from other dimensions of the true life of faith, all sorts of other strivings (for example, for justice between rich and poor, for true partnership between men and women, for the proper exercise of human responsibility for the created order, and so on) belong *with* and will play more into the striving for true faith and a common order. What matters is not that all should take up the same causes at the same time, but that each group or church should be moving into the next stage in the way towards wholeness.

It is impossible here and now to lay down any blueprint for the goal towards which we are moving. As we grow into the fullness of conciliar fellowship by living more truly those already conciliar elements in the life of our churches — divided as they are — we shall be given greater clarity and understanding. It is precisely the working things out with one another under the pressure and leading of the Holy Spirit that the whole striving is about. But already now we begin to see some dimension of what will be required of all of us, in one way or another, according to different situations and points at which we must not get stuck.

1. Unity in the *truth of the Gospel*. The churches must be able to recognize one another as holding and confessing the apostolic faith. There must be a common reliance on the Word of God as Scripture. Wherever, for instance, there have been condemnations of one another, the issues involved must be worked at until the condemnations can be seen on all sides to apply no longer. Any new conflicts that arise in the sphere of doctrine and truth (for example, those referred to by "confessing" groups) must be held *within* the fellowship and worked out *together* until they lose their power to divide.

2. Unity around *the table of the Lord*. Baptized into the same Body of the one Lord, the members of local churches must be able to share in the celebration of the eucharist. This in turn deepens our conciliar fellowship at all levels. For this reason, attempts are made to loosen the discipline of churches in order to anticipate greater fullness of fellowship, for example, by permitting some people to share in the eucharist across the barriers. When this is done out of a responsible pastoral judgment, it is to be respected and welcomed. Yet we cannot be satisfied with this as more than a transitional measure. There is thus today in certain situations a greater scandal in the sight of churches permanently offering each other eucharistic hospitality while insisting on retaining their distinct, divided identities than in the longstanding, painful insistence of the other churches that communion must wait on proven willingness to move into the fully committed fellowship of unity.

3. Fellowship in the Church is *for the sake of the quality of human life in the world*. Our current discussions on the relation of church unity to the unity of mankind have clarified many points here. Christians are not to seek fellowship for their own sake but in order that they may together serve and witness in the world and together represent their surrounding world before God. Just as the divisions between the churches have often had tragic results in the wider community (for example, Ireland), so the moving into true unity can be an important witness (for example, South Africa). The wounds to which Christ's healing power is to be brought are first and foremost those of a suffering world; it is that struggle which provides the proper, missionary context for the search for conciliar fellowship.

4. Unity *in each place is basic*. Thus, whatever the forms appropriate to the wider life of the Church, there can be no by-passing the challenge to move into full and effective unity at the local level, as this was memorably spelt out in the New Delhi Statement of 1961. This is often referred to as organic union, i.e. the form of being effectively one that is appropriate to the Body of Christ in each place. More specifically, it is the healing of these wounds that have divided the churches in times past into separate fellowships by the specific repentance, renewal, and restoration of unity that will be appropriate in each case. The approach to this excludes any deliberate proselytism of members of other churches, any mere "peaceful co-existence" in which churches cherish their separate identities without putting to the test their contribution to the whole, and any refusal to enter into a "committed fellowship" in which effective common decisions for the locality can be taken.

The attainment of local unity would mean that the Church would be so plainly united in that place that such questions would not even arise.

5. Conciliar fellowship requires *the mutual acceptance of the appropriate representatives of each expression of the Church*. It is rooted in the very nature of the Church that its members represent Christ to one another and to the world just as they represent the world in intercession before God. This pattern works itself out further in the way the various localities and levels in the Church are represented to each other and receive and transmit the living stream of Tradition. Specifically, the achievement of fuller fellowship cannot by-pass the problem of the nature of the ministries of the Church and of their mutual recognition. In this belong the unresolved questions of the function of a special ordained ministry within the whole and of the appropriate forms of authority at local and world levels of the Church. The fullness of fellowship will for instance lead the Church beyond all forms of "overlapping jurisdictions" where, say, two different bishops or committees both claim a similar authority for the same place or sector of the common life.

6. The fullness of fellowship will thus be *an interlocking scale of corporate relationships,* in which each grouping will have its proper autonomy (in missionary responsibility to the surrounding world) and its proper dependence on the Church as a whole. There will be the conciliar Church in each place meeting from time to time at the Lord's table and under his Word. Each depends entirely on the integrity of the other, and while we are deprived of either the fellowship is enfeebled. Moreover, recent discussions, and, even more, recent explorations in practice have made it clear that between these two levels there is need for a number of other levels of conciliar forms (for example, in a city area, in a province, in a nation, in a continent, and so on), each meeting on occasion at the table. Only those who participate in each can say

what these forms can most usefully be, and they can of course change with circumstances. The important point is that none is privileged above another. Conciliar fellowship means radical interdependence, and is incompatible with any structures of power from on high which inhibit legitimate diversity, or any refusal from below of those relationships by which communion is maintained. While each specific fellowship will have its own burdens, we are all also called to bear each other's burdens in mutual pastoral — not primarily jurisdictional — responsibility.

7. This conciliar fellowship must also lead us into exploration of *the proper forms of fellowship at the universal level*. Some churches know what they believe to be appropriate here (for example, the collegiality of bishops, the ministry of unity of the See of Rome, and so on). Others have few clear ideas on this as yet, and should be invited to give attention to it. Some people talk as if the World Council of Churches, in the 25 years of its existence, had developed some of these appropriate forms. While it may be true that its experience — in practice rather than in ecclesial theory — may provide pointers, these cannot supply a satisfactory answer to the ecclesiological problem. It seems clear, however, that the conciliar fellowship we seek at the universal level must be grounded in that which we know to be appropriate at the local level. A consensus of churches at the national level which fails to make an impact on local practice and fellowship, cannot suffice as a basis for fellowship between them.

8. The counterpart of mutual pastoral responsibility in interdependence is that Councils of the Church at every level are *invested with an appropriate authority*. Who says "authority" says "power", and power in the Church always must be exercised in transparent ways, as a service and not a domination. The characteristic note in the decisions of a Council will be: "It seemed good to the Holy Spirit and us..." A Council is not simply a democratic parliament taking decisions by the desire of the majority. All its members are there to discover the will of the Spirit, so that even when there is a divided opinion, when the minority is outvoted, it must be in such a way that all regard the decision as the way the Spirit is leading. Therefore, an essential part of the authority of any Council is the uncoerced "reception" of decisions (or their rejection) by the churches in whose name they are made. Fellowship must further mean a constant readiness and struggle to know what Christians elsewhere are concerned about and to interpret for all the truth some are given to perceive. This covers equally the need for the churches of the West to hear and respond to what, say, Latin American Christians are saying about the radical injustices of present power structures in the world as for those of, say, Asia to learn from Catholic and Orthodox insistence on the unbroken Tradition of the one Church. Similarly, in terms of time, the Louvain statement said, "Within the living fellowship of the one Church, we are enabled to enter into conversation with the past, to put questions and to receive illumination on our problems... it is an essential part of our growth into full conciliarity that we should be continually engaged in the process of 're-reception' of the Councils of the past, through whose witness — received in living dialogue — the same Holy Spirit who spoke to the Fathers in the past can lead us into his future."

9. Finally, the whole structure of conciliar fellowship depends essentially upon *the active presence of the Holy Spirit* and on the Church's active acknowledgment of his leading. Thus the fundamental question is always: "Are we open to him?" An important test of that is whether any one group is open to another. In that permanent, demanding openness, we shall be given unity and each step into its fullness in God's

good time. Without it — if we are primarily concerned for "our own tradition, heritage, identity, obedience", regarded as ends in themselves or as property to be piously and jealously defended — we need not expect to move very far. Such confidence as we can have in the ecumenical movement is in him — as he speaks to us through each other — and not in ourselves.

D. Taking the Next Steps

When we come to consider the next steps on the way to full *koinonia,* we should thankfully note that we have made considerable progress since the beginning of the ecumenical movement. We can do things together today which would have seemed quite impossible in 1948, or even ten or five years ago. But, of course, we cannot stop here. We are on the way forward, and the frontiers have to be pushed further.

Before speaking of some concrete possibilities, we can make five general remarks:

1. Whatever we may suggest, or may actually do, must be based on a changed attitude. Work for the unity of the Church must have a very high priority. Our Christian identity cannot be in our denomination, but must be in our belonging to Christ and being part of his Body. Therefore, ecumenical commitments must not come at the bottom of our agenda. It must be these, rather than the commitment to building up our own church, which govern our choice of priorities and the use of funds.

2. This particular moment may well offer us specific opportunities which have to be grasped *now*. We must not miss the opportunities given today, for they may never come again, or come only after many years.

3. In extending the area of fellowship already achieved, it may often be necessary to take risks. When we do new things, there is always the possibility that some cannot follow. While we must be as careful as possible not to alienate groups in our churches and thus cause new divisions, we must seek to maintain a mutual respect within which those who are ready to move forward can do so without breaking fellowship with those who cannot.

4. One of the risks to be run is the breaking of church rules and discipline. Some Christians, for the sake of future fellowship, transgress rules which in their eyes have become an obstacle to a shared life in Jesus Christ. No one should take such actions except as a last resort. In fact, it is often the case that the order of churches allows a larger area for experiment than many realize. When individuals or groups, for conscience sake, overstep the borders fixed by their church, they should nevertheless seek in every way to remain within its fellowship. The church for its part should not look at them primarily with distrust, but should face frankly the question which is raised by their action, and which may be a question which the Lord himself is putting to his Church.

5. When two or more churches enter into an agreement, they should take care that they do not unnecessarily alienate other churches. Any agreement should in principle be open-ended so that others may be able to join later.

E. Moving Towards Full Koinonia

We now turn to concrete possibilities for moving ahead on the way to full *koinonia*.

1. Churches considering new steps should not take these without a careful, common analysis of their regional or national situation.[2] Any action, in order not simply to beat the air, should be specifically conceived with regard to what is required and possible in each particular situation and time. Things that might be helpful in one continent or country might prove irrelevant in another. (See the difference between South and North India in the unification of ministries, because of the different traditions of churchmanship with which they had to deal.) That does not, however, preclude learning from attempts to go forward elsewhere.

2. While common worship is in most churches permitted and indeed practised on special occasions, this could become a more regular observance. Some forms of interim eucharistic fellowship can be envisaged, for example where the churches of a country or region openly and publicly declare their common commitment to union (for example, "Covenanting for Union" in Wales). Such a possibility, however, can only be justified if this provisional sharing does not become a resting place, and the search for a fully committed fellowship is not abandoned. It is urgent that the churches be reflecting theologically on what is already happening in this respect and on its implications. In particular, those churches which have for years practised intercommunion without entering into fuller unity should be challenged publicly to state their reasons for not doing so.

3. In order that members of different churches may get to know one another, and to understand each other's traditions, they should be encouraged to participate in the life of each other's churches. Many of the prejudices and caricatures of other churches that we continue to entertain will disappear in the exercise of mutual hospitality (for example, between historic and pentecostal churches).

4. Where the divisions of the churches (as, for example, in Asia) are not rooted in the history of their nation, their calling to give a credible witness among their own people should take priority over their faithfulness to the historical and cultural traditions of the churches from which their missionaries came.

5. Regional and national assemblies too can practise mutual hospitality. At the least, observers from other churches should be invited in order that their very presence can witness to the wider fellowship. The Second Vatican Council has set an admirable example. Churches should further consider whether their policy-making bodies could not now regularly meet together.

6. As a sign of a growing conciliar life, each church should inform all other churches with which it has active contact of major internal decisions it is making, and, even better, ask their counsel before taking any final action. Similarly, all churches taking decisive new steps should realize that their decisions have some bearing on *all* the churches, even on those which are not immediately affected. The World Council of Churches, for example, can play a most useful role in circulating such information and requests for comment.

7. As a consequence of the emerging consensus on baptism, churches should ask themselves whether they are not obliged to recognize each other's baptism and to work out the implications of this recognition. Unless we translate a consensus into the actual

---

[2] See the recent publication *Kenya Churches Handbook: the Development of Kenyan Christianity 1948-1973,* eds. D.B. Barrett, G.K. Mambo, J. McLaughlin and M.J. McVeigh. Kisumu, Kenya: Evangel Publishing House, 1973.

life and relations of our churches, our vision of full unity will be blurred, and our words will sound false. In some churches, it has been possible to publish a common baptism certificate, used and recognized by all.

8. Joint mission projects have become a fairly common feature of our life together, but we could do much more to act together in each place in a common missionary commitment. We should, however, also face together the challenges of the society we live in, and confront together the social and political issues which have to be dealt with in order to heal the brokenness of the wider human community. Responsibility for joint enterprises calls for a procedure whereby the churches together make up a programme of priorities, evaluating their importance and allocating significant amounts of money to a common fund.

9. Our joint education efforts should be expanded to include joint Sunday School classes — not only the material to be used — as well as joint confirmation and church membership classes.

10. Mixed marriages, so often regarded as a "problem", can rather be seen as the connective tissue par excellence between separate Christian communities. Thus the partners deserve to be given all possible pastoral help to share as fully as possible in the life of both communities in which they are involved, and to bring these together.

DOCUMENT III.3

CALLING THE CHURCHES TO THE GOAL OF VISIBLE UNITY
(1975)

In preparation for the Fifth Assembly of the World Council of Churches in Nairobi, a small consultation was called in Geneva, April 6-10, 1975, to consider the question: "How can the World Council of Churches contribute more effectively to the churches' search for visible unity?" The proposed new Constitution of the WCC lists as one of the principal aims of the WCC "to call the churches to the goal of visible unity in one faith and one eucharistic fellowship..." The consultation focused its discussion on exploring the meaning of this phrase. Though theological and ecclesiological questions were discussed, the primary emphasis was rather on the practical implications of the new formulations for the WCC and its member churches. The consultation did not aim at elaborating a detailed description of the "unity we seek". This effort has been made at other conferences (e.g. the meetings at Salamanca, cf. *The Ecumenical Review*, April 1974 and Accra, cf. *Uniting in Hope*, p.110-123). The consultation used the agreement reached at these meetings as its point of departure and sought to answer the question: How can the WCC as a whole and its individual programmes promote the cause of the unity of the Church?

I. Unity is Given in Christ

The unity which is given in Christ is the presupposition of the witness, the mission and the service of the Church. Unity is not the result of human efforts. It is God's gift in Jesus Christ to be received constantly anew by the community of the faithful. Though given, it is not yet fully experienced. The Church *is* one and is constantly on the way of becoming one. The search for unity and the effort to maintain unity must be pursued at all times.

From the beginning of the modern ecumenical movement, the search for unity has been the main focus. The efforts undertaken have been successful in many respects. The isolation between the churches has been broken. They have entered dialogue. Many controversial issues have been clarified. Common prayer, common worship, common witness and service have become possible. The churches are now able to live in fellowship. The progress brings with it the temptation to be satisfied with the degree of unity which has been achieved. The scandal of disunity being removed, the churches can easily settle down and renounce the further efforts towards full unity. Why should further unity be sought? Is it not sufficient to have overcome hostility and to live in dialogue and friendship?

At the same time, the search for full unity is being called into question by new tensions which arise between, and even more within, the churches. Differing political and social commitments, differences of culture, language, race, class, etc. can be the cause of deep conflicts. Sometimes, they lead to new groupings across confessional borderlines. Why then should unity between the confessionally divided churches be pursued?

Facing this present situation, we re-affirm our conviction that the search for visible unity in one faith and one eucharistic fellowship remains one of the primary concerns of the WCC and that it should permeate all its programmes and activities. The concern for unity is not optional; it is based on the Gospel and is inseparably linked with the very essence of faith in Jesus Christ.

Both are required — restoring the unity of the divided churches and maintaining it in the tensions and conflicts of the present time. The churches will be able to face the challenges of our generation only if they stay together in solidarity, mutual openness and correction.[1] Each church must bring its gifts — charismata — and experience into the ecumenical fellowship to enrich others and to be enriched by them. True unity in Christ cannot be separated from the concern for witness, service and justice in the world.

II. Visible Unity in Conciliar Fellowship

At the Faith and Order Conference on "Concepts of Unity and Models of Union", Salamanca, 1973, the vision of the one Church was set forth in the following terms:

> The one Church is to be envisioned as a conciliar fellowship of local churches which are themselves truly united. In this conciliar fellowship each local church possesses, in communion with the others, the fullness of catholicity, witnesses to the same apostolic faith and therefore recognises the others as belonging to the same Church of Christ and guided by the same spirit. They are bound together because they have received the same baptism, and share in the same eucharist; they recognise each other's member and ministries. They are one in their common commitment to confess the Gospel of Christ by proclamation and service to the world. To this end each church aims at maintaining sustained and sustaining relationships with her sister churches, expressed in conciliar gatherings whenever required for the fulfilment of their common calling.[2]

Several implications from this description should be noted:

1. It is essential to note that this conciliar fellowship is rooted in the *common celebration of the eucharist*. In the breaking of the bread, the risen Christ himself constitutes the communion. He precedes all human experience of togetherness and all human efforts of joint action. He recreates the communion where it threatens to fall apart. He enables the members to grow within the one body. Within the present ecumenical fellowship, this eucharistic dimension is only partially experienced; the restoration of full eucharistic fellowship is the goal to which all ecumenical efforts must aspire.

2. The term "conciliar fellowship" indicates that unity is not a situation which can be reached once for all — a static harmony — but is rather a *dynamic movement* to be entered into. The historical differences among the churches must be overcome and union must be achieved. But once the united church has come into existence, the struggle for unity will not cease, because the forces of division will be with her till the end of time. Conciliar fellowship is capable of facing the conflicts which arise as the Church sets out to witness to the Gospel in the tensions of the world.

3. The unity given in Jesus Christ must manifest itself in *community and shared life*. The Church must always point beyond itself, realizing that it cannot work for greater community in society without actualizing community more fully within its own fold. What does that mean? For instance, the Church should be a community which involves the fullest possible participation of all members in its decision-making and

---

[1] Cf. the Statement of the Faith and Order Commission "Towards Unity in Tension", *Uniting in Hope — Accra 1974*, p.90f.

[2] *What Kind of Unity?*, Geneva 1974, p.121.

other activities; the community should be capable of transcending the divisive human barriers like race, class, sex. Thus the life of the Church is characterized by a constant struggle for the fuller manifestation of community. The term "conciliar fellowship" must be understood with this task in mind.

4. The description implies *the need to manifest the unity of the Church at different levels* — local, national, regional and universal. The Church as a whole must be visibly one, but the requirements of unity are different at each level. The primary reality is the common celebration of the eucharist at a given place or in a given context. Jesus Christ is present wherever this celebration takes place, and where he is present the Church is present. Within this eucharistic community, the members receive the gifts of the Spirit which constitute their Christian life.

At the local and national levels, the Christian congregations need to be so united that they are able to share their experiences, to support one another in their witness and to act together. They also need to be able to represent the church of their area to the wider Christian fellowship. The description refers to a "conciliar fellowship of local churches which are themselves truly united". The term "local" here refers to an area (usually a nation) and points to the need for *Christians in that given area to form recognizably one community*. Recognizably united means organically united, i.e. sharing in one eucharistic fellowship, being able to decide together, taking responsibility for missionary tasks in their area, exercising authority on the use of money within the Church and for service in their area, caring for the theological training of their members and ministers, etc. The ecumenical efforts must aim at establishing united churches of this kind in each area.

At the regional and international levels, churches need to meet in representative gatherings, and make possible common witness and action which is required at these levels.

All the levels are interdependent and must not be isolated from one another. Today this interdependence is even more evident than in earlier centuries — because the problems the Church faces at different levels are more intertwined; because there is no real witness and action at the regional or international level without the experience of the local level; because there is no real fulfilment of the calling at the local level without the wider perspective provided by the exchange and common commitment at the regional and international levels. The vision of "conciliar fellowship" places the emphasis on this interdependence.

5. The vision of conciliar fellowship at all levels represents a *challenge to the present situation*. Are the churches free to move towards that goal? Can they form truly united churches in each area? There are many obstacles which need to be overcome. In some countries, through ties with confessional bodies or mission and service agencies, churches have closer links with churches of the same tradition in distant lands than with churches of other traditions in the same area. In some cases, international relations within the same confessional tradition serve to stimulate the churches' local ecumenical involvement; but on the whole, these relations tend to slow down the movement towards local union, and indeed often preserve and strengthen division.

The goal of conciliar fellowship raises the question as to how World Confessional Families contribute to or hinder the growth of unity at the local level. The primary task of confessional organizations should not be seen as the preservation of confessional identity, but rather as the enabling of churches to move towards unity. The call to unity, and the search for authentic selfhood and culturally determined expressions of the Christian faith, challenge the confessional organizations and their member churches to ask anew whether in reality they promote a conciliar fellowship of all churches. They need to examine together what steps could be taken both to remove the obstacles to union and to support those actions which implement the visible unity of the Church today.

6. The description emphasizes the *need for sustained and sustaining relationships* among the various sister churches. Each church needs not only to receive and recognize other churches as belonging to the same Church of Christ, but it is obliged to relate to other churches and to feel accountable to them. The conciliar fellowship is a fellowship of exchange, support and mutual correction. What are the implications of this affirmation? As long as the divisions have not been overcome, communion among churches remains limited. But their communion will grow as they begin to practise conciliar fellowship by anticipation. It is one of the most pressing and immediate ecumenical tasks to begin developing true "sustained and sustaining relationships" among the churches as they look towards the time when they can accept one another as sister churches in full mutual responsibility and solidarity.

What does that mean? Some examples may illustrate it:

a) *Sharing in suffering.* In many countries, the Church is passing through the test of persecution and suffering. In some countries, the Church must pay the price for its witness against a specific political power; in other countries, the Church is under pressure because the Gospel is regarded as incompatible with the ideology underlying the political and social order. The unity of the Church must find an expression in solidarity; for, if one part of the Church is suffering, it must be the concern of the whole church. Ways must be actively sought to participate in the suffering of others. Conciliar fellowship can be promoted by intercession and pastoral visits, by courageous information of public opinion and sometimes by protest.

b) *Common responsibility for mission.* Each church has a certain responsibility for the witness and mission of other churches. There must be a constant exchange between the churches aiming at strengthening the witness to the Gospel. The experience of each church belongs to all churches; the errors and failures affect the whole fellowship. The conciliar fellowship is therefore a fellowship of common responsibility for mission. Obviously, within this fellowship each church has its own specific tasks to fulfil, and the relationships must aim at enabling the church in each area to fulfil these tasks.

c) *Sharing personnel and finance.* For the fulfilment of their common calling, the churches are brought to share their resources in personnel and finance. The need of each church must be met by a concerted effort of the whole fellowship. In developing the fellowship of mutual solidarity, care must be taken that the churches are related to one another in full freedom. Resources in personnel and finance constitute power, and thus their use can easily distort the relations among the churches. Sending personnel and money implies the readiness also to receive — the exchange must be mutual. It is understood that true sharing within a mature partnership means that churches are free to use personnel and financial aid in accordance with their own priorities; they can also decline any support which they feel would not further the cause of the Gospel in their area.

The call for a moratorium, as issued by the All Africa Conference of Churches in Lusaka in 1974, must be understood in this perspective. Its aim is not to end the relations among the churches, but rather to attain a more authentic expression of the universality of the Church. The call implies that only through a temporary suspension of the flow of personnel and finance can the churches truly discover and accept their calling in a given place. The help given by a church must not diminish the freedom of decision and self-reliance of sister churches. In some situations, true partnership can be brought about only by breaking the existing relationship of domination and dependence.

d) *Sharing in the liturgical life of the churches*. Conciliar fellowship requires exchange and mutual visitation. At present many ecumenical visits have an exclusively "technical" character: people are sent to fulfil certain functions in a programme. But, visits as described in the New Testament had a deeper meaning: they were a means of spiritual exchange and mutual strengthening. In order to achieve this today, mutual visitation must involve the participation in the worship life of the churches. Many churches are not yet equipped for this kind of sharing.

e) *Accepting the critical voice of other churches*. At present critical judgment is often viewed as intervention in the internal affairs of another church. Critical questioning, however, should be an integral part of true relations between the churches. Obviously, there must be restraint in addressing questions to another church, but conciliar fellowship can grow only if the churches feel accountable and responsive to one another.

III. The Promotion of Unity through the Programmes and Activities of the World Council of Churches

The task as it is formulated in the proposed Constitution, "to call the churches to the goal of visible unity in one faith and in one eucharistic fellowship" is entrusted to the WCC as a whole. All Units and Sub-Units have a responsible role to play in this overall objective. No doubt the Faith and Order Commission has to maintain a certain specialized role in the promotion of Christian unity. However, this does not mean that this central task of the WCC can be delegated exclusively to one Commission. The overwhelming nature of the concern for the visible unity of the Church and the overriding priority that is accorded to it in the establishment of the WCC require the resources, capabilities and contributions of all Sub-Units.

In how far is the search for the unity of the Church a real concern for the various programmes of the WCC? Of course, one can speak of all programmes in the WCC as interconfessional and, therefore, ecumenical. It can also be said that all programmes in effect bring about a certain measure of understanding and cooperation among the churches. But the question goes beyond this. How far do the Sub-Units, in designing and carrying out their programmes, consciously consider the promotion of Christian unity as one of the criteria?

Some questions may illustrate this:

Of the financial resources which are channelled through the InterChurch Aid programmes and projects, what proportion is aimed at bringing about Church unity? Is the promotion of the unity of the Church an equally valid criterion in InterChurch Aid to the service of human need? Do our studies and programmes in the field of justice give due consideration to the calling of the Church to be "a reconciling community"?

How seriously does our promotion of mission and evangelism take the unity of the Church as a precondition for the credible witness to the Gospel of reconciliation? In the selection of the subjects for study and theological reflection, do we give priority consideration to topics which narrow the existing differences among Christians or which help to develop common understanding on new frontiers?

Finally, should the WCC evolve an overall strategy for the promotion of Christian unity, in which the specific tasks and programmes of the various Units and Sub-Units would be evaluated and assigned?

These questions are raised as indicators for self-examination by each Programme Unit. Their purpose is not to compromise the specific objectives of the various programmes and activities, but to ensure the contribution of all Programme Units to the concern for unity, the central goal of the ecumenical movement.

IV. The Promotion of Unity through National Counterparts

If unity is to be promoted, the WCC needs also to review the relationships to its constituency, specifically to its regional and national counterparts. The way in which these relations are conceived has a deep impact on the search for unity as it emerges at the local, national and regional levels.

1. Most programmes of the WCC relate to different individuals or organizations within the churches in different local situations: study centres, groups involved in the programmes of the Urban Industrial Mission, associations of theological schools, literature commissions, etc. Very often these counterparts have emerged as a local response to an international ecumenical initiative. In the desire to help the renewal and the mission of the local church, the WCC stimulates the creation of those instruments; most of them provide a good service to the churches and to society in the local area. But all of them are under the permanent temptation of becoming isolated either from the main life of the churches or from each other by keeping a direct relationship with the sponsoring body of the WCC, or with funding agencies abroad. In promotion of the unity of the Church at the local level, the WCC needs to challenge itself and these counterparts to work together, be it by cooperation or by confrontation, and to try in every case to relate their being and actions to the life of the local churches. Every attempt by the WCC to relate to the local situation should be made not only with the specific purpose of rendering a particular service, but also with the question of how much this entrance into the local situation helps the renewal of that church community towards the goal of eucharistic fellowship.

2. Among the national counterparts, National Christian Councils hold a special place. Most of them are helpful instruments for cooperation among the churches. But it must be recognized that very often this cooperation becomes a substitute for the genuine searching for visible unity. At this moment, when the WCC in its new Constitution recognizes the particular responsibility of helping the churches to work towards a eucharistic fellowship, is there not need for inviting and urging the councils of churches related to the WCC to participate in this same vocation?

3. While we talk of National Christian Councils in general, it is recognized that they represent very different realities and different possibilities in different countries. In several countries, there are no council structures, but rather there exist ad hoc and sometimes flexible inter-church arrangements for cooperation. All this demands from the WCC a careful analysis of the different situations, and the development of means

of relating to councils that take into consideration their respective possibilities and limitations.

4. The WCC, being a council of *churches*, could and should work for the promotion of church unity at the national level, not only through councils but primarily through its member churches. Such a double, complementary approach would be more fruitful and would help to stimulate the search for a truly conciliar fellowship.

V. Issues and Methods for Continuing Theological Reflection

1. Theological reflection on the basic issues within church life which are important for the unity of the Church has continued over many years within the Faith and Order Commission. After several years of common study, three agreed statements on baptism, the eucharist and the ministry have been sent to the churches for their reaction, evaluation and serious appraisal (*One Baptism, One Eucharist and a Mutually Recognized Ministry*, Geneva 1975). Responses from the churches themselves will point the way ahead in the investigation of these themes. It appears obvious that these topics, specifically the ministry, will need further study in the period ahead. The question is how best this might be done. How are the results so far achieved to be implemented and incorporated into the life of the churches, e.g. catechisms, confirmation classes, interconfessional eucharistic services, etc.? A new level of discussion should be developed to further the progress already achieved.

2. The primary task of the Faith and Order Commission will continue in concentrating its efforts on the central issues which are directly related to the concern for the unity of the Church. This concentration is seen in three areas:

a) Continuing the study on "Giving Account of the Hope that is within us" — which seeks to engage Christians around the world in giving expression to their hope in Jesus Christ within their particular situations and contexts. This study may open a new way to unity as Christians confess together the one faith in Jesus Christ, discovering anew the centrality and power of the Gospel in bringing unity.

b) Continuing to seek to clarify the nature of the unity we seek — keeping prominently before the churches the call to unity by specifying the goal and the implications of that goal for the churches within the fellowship of the WCC. Attempts have been made to give clarity to the goal in setting forth the concept of "conciliar fellowship" (see Part II) above "Visible Unity in Conciliar Fellowship", and the report "The Unity of the Church — the Goal and the Way", *Uniting in Hope-Accra 1974*, p.110).

c) Becoming more reflection-action oriented: maintaining contacts and providing support to specific situations where churches are working for union or are dealing with issues that continue divisions among Christians in their communities. In particular, Faith and Order should assist churches threatened by new divisions. Too often the search for unity is understood as a process of restoration. But in fact the danger of further division is constantly with the churches; if no conscious efforts are made to meet the divisions today, future generations may inherit the unsolved problems of their fathers. The Faith and Order Commission should consider ways and means to meet this problem, e.g. by setting up "ministries of reconciliation" when churches are threatened by conflicts which may further divide their fellowship.

3. There is a widening range of issues emerging within the ecumenical movement which broaden the context of the unity discussion — a new type of ecumenical

collaboration and coordination needs to be developed to meet these issues. This would mean that within the WCC all programmes must continue to do their own theological reflection upon the areas of their activities and concern, but collaboration among the programmes should be developed so that they would constantly keep the horizon and perspective of unity in mind. Such collaboration would enable the WCC to see more clearly the nature of the unity we seek in the wider perspective, based on the active engagement of Christians in the fields of faith and witness, justice and service, and renewal and education.

a) Faith and Order should be a constant reminder of the dimension of unity to other programmes within the WCC; e.g., collaboration already exists with the Programme to Combat Racism as they seek to reflect on their experience and engagement in developing a "Racism in Theology and Theology Against Racism", and there is collaboration with Unit III in the concern to develop a theology of men and women in community. This collaboration should be extended; especially urgent at this time are the areas of power and powerlessness in international relations, finance and Church and State relations.

b) Faith and Order needs to begin to look at all the programmes of the WCC and interpret what their developments mean for the unity of the Church. To accept this mandate would imply some form of regular joint evaluation between Faith and Order and the different programmes within the WCC.

DOCUMENT III.4

A FELLOWSHIP OF LOCAL CHURCHES TRULY UNITED (1976)

The concept of "a fellowship of local churches" presented some difficulties for the WCC's Fifth Assembly. Three reasons for this may be noted:

a) The term "local church" does not have the same meaning in the various confessional traditions. While in some the term refers to the community gathered around word and sacrament in a given place and at a specific moment, in others it is used for larger units, for example, a diocese, a region or even a nation.

b) The translation of the term presents difficulties. The literal equivalents in French or German, for instance, tend to have different connotations. Mutual understanding, therefore, can be reached only by an agreed description of the reality which the term is supposed to designate.

c) The attempt to describe the reality raises other difficulties, however. The first meaning of the term "local" is geographical. Therefore, the term "local church" naturally should be used for the church in a geographically limited place, for example, a village, a neighbourhood, a town. But would such a geographical description do justice to the complicated sociological realities of modern society? More and more the same persons belong to several communities. Their allegiance is divided between the places of residence, work, recreation and so on. What should then be called the local church? Each eucharistic assembly? Or rather the church in the area where a group of Christians moves and meets in varying constellations? If the latter solution is chosen, how should the area be delineated?

The difficulty referred to under c) has already been debated by earlier Assemblies. The Third Assembly in New Delhi made the following comment on the meaning of the term "place":

> This statement used the word "place" both in its primary sense of local neighbourhood and also, under modern conditions, of other areas in which Christians need to express unity in Christ. Thus being one in Christ means that unity among Christians must be found in each school where they study, in each factory or office where they work and in each congregation where they worship, as well as between congregations. "Place" may further imply not only local communities but also wider geographical areas such as states, provinces or nations, and certainly refers to all Christian people in each place regardless of race and class.

By using the term "place" for all levels of the Church's life the Third Assembly avoided a clear definition. The description of the "unity we seek" requires more definite distinctions.

Some comments on the text of Nairobi have understood the term "local church" to mean the Church within a relatively large area, for example, a diocese or a nation. They have interpreted the phrase as having the meaning which is attributed in the Roman Catholic Church to the term "ecclesia particularis". "Fellowship of local churches" would then mean the communion of dioceses or even groups of dioceses. This immediate interpretation must not be too quickly adopted. The meaning can only be determined on the basis of ecclesiological and sociological scrutiny.

In any case, the description offered by the Fifth Assembly presents by its emphasis on the unity of the local church a challenge to the existing reality of the churches.

Disunity is seen as particularly scandalous at the level of the local church. The question arises, therefore, as to how the efforts towards unity can contribute towards restoring the unity of "all in each place". The description implicitly regards the unity at that level as the criterion by which the ecumenical movement must be guided.

I. "Church" and "place": some preliminary theological considerations

Speaking about the Church inevitably implies speaking about people living in specific places, contexts and situations. The Church is not something ready-made which is only secondarily related to places; no, the Church cannot even be conceived apart from the reality of places. It is necessarily and essentially "local".

This observation is, of course, sociologically a truism. But more is involved here than sociological observation. Theologically, the essential relatedness of Church to place is part of the Church's self-understanding as a missionary community. At this level, we have to speak of the necessity for the Church to be conscious of its relatedness to "place" as a relatedness which is missionary in structure and intention. The relation of Church to place receives its final meaning in this perspective, and it must, therefore, permanently be made meaningful in this sense.

Again, to say that the Church has been "placed" in the midst of human communities does not imply that the Church is an accomplished reality in itself prior to or apart from its being "placed". The Church comes into being and it exists as a part of human relations and conditions; yet as such it is part of a missionary movement in history. The Church is part of created humanity and called, as the chosen people, to keep the praise of God going in the world. It bears the marks of sinful humanity and proclaims and represents Christ as the suffering and triumphant servant, thus reminding the world of the renewal and fulfilment which God will grant. All speech about "local church" should be qualified by these considerations.

Now, how should we define "place"? Obviously, a place is not merely a geographical area which can be identified on the map. It has a temporal dimension as well. The people of a specific place have a specific past and future; they have their traditions and expectations. An adequate understanding of "place" is only possible if this temporal dimension is taken into account. This is especially true today, as the pace of history has accelerated: conditions are changing much more rapidly than in earlier centuries. More than ever, therefore, it becomes necessary to emphasize that places are not fixed and static entities.

In the light of the missionary structure and intention of the relation between Church and place, outlined above, this aspect of temporality and change implies the necessity for the Church to be constantly self-critical. Of course, the Church has its share of temporality and change. But the way in which it changes does not automatically imply a continuity in meaningful missionary relatedness. Questions as to the validity of the mode of the Church's presence will have to be asked again and again. The missionary adaptation meant here does not imply that the Church should go along with all fashions and tendencies that manifest themselves in society; its source of self-criticism is ultimately not given with the conditions but with the source of its mission. Only if the Church constantly relates its "place" to that source will it be renewed and transformed, not just by the pressure of time, but by the vision of the coming kingdom.

In that sense the Church's presence and witness will also affect the character of the place and give it a new direction. The Church brings into each place its own past and its own future, Jesus Christ, the source and goal of all things. Though it becomes part of the traditions and expectations of the place to which it is related, its own past and future will qualify those and may even effectively change the character of the place.

The relationship between Church and place always remains provisional. No manifestation of the "local church" can therefore be regarded as definitive or normative. If the Church is to be an effective sign of Christ's presence, the relationship to the place needs to be kept under constant review; and as history moves on, new forms of "local churches" may develop. It belongs to the Church's witness to be constantly on the way and to be open to ever-new ways of relating to the localities in which it is placed. It is by the very acceptance of the conditions of provisionality and change that it will be seen as pointing to the ultimate victory of Christ and the final unambiguous renewal of all things.

II. "Local church" in the confessional traditions

The meaning of the term "local church" is not the same in all confessional traditions. Depending on the understanding of the Church, its life and its structures, the meaning of the term is determined by different factors. For all, the assembly gathered for the celebration of the eucharist is the basic unit in the Church's life. But they differ in the way in which they consider the liturgical assembly to be constituted. Three broad types may be distinguished. They are not entirely coincident with confessional differences.

(1) The "local church" is the Church under the leadership of a bishop. It has its centre in the bishop's see. The bishop, surrounded by his presbyterium, presides over the eucharistic assembly. Ideally, there should be not more than one eucharistic assembly. Practically, there will be several sub-units — parishes which are geographical in nature or communities constituted on a cultural or linguistic basis. Each of these sub-units will be under the care of a presbyter, but they are all understood as extensions of the bishop's eucharistic assembly. This first type is characteristic of the ancient Church.

(2) The "local church" is the Church under the leadership of a presbyter. In this view, a distinction is made between the administrative level of the diocese or region and the liturgical assembly presided over by the presbyter. The term "local church" is reserved for the latter. This second type is characteristic of the Western tradition. It prevailed in the Church of the Middle Ages and is still the common understanding of the Roman Catholic Church (although in response to the Second Vatican Council it is moving today in the direction of the first type). The churches of the Reformation (Lutheran, Reformed and Anglican) have inherited this position and have on the whole maintained it. These churches, especially the Lutheran and Reformed, place less emphasis on the celebration of the eucharist than the Orthodox and Roman Catholic Churches; the centrality of the presbyter is expressed rather through the Ministry of the Word.

(3) The "local church" is the gathered community. In this view, the liturgical assembly constitutes its own centre and periphery. The ordained ministry, where it exists, is seen as rising up from within the community as is expressed in the practice of lay members sharing, together with ordained representatives of the wider Church, in the laying on of hands in the ordination. This third type is characteristic of the Baptist and Congregationalist traditions.

In all traditions the need of a close connection between the "local churches" is felt and recognized. Everywhere, in one form or another, a network of "sustained and sustaining relations" exists. The ground for this network is always the mutual recognition which the "local churches" accord to one another. The ways of mutual recognition vary, however; the variety largely coincides with the three types mentioned above.

(1) In the first type, the communion is established by the mutual recognition of bishops. They, acting not as individuals but as representatives of their church, ensure the unity of the local churches.

(2) In the second type, the communion is usually established by synodical networks. The presbyters and very often members of the laity represent their liturgical assembly in synodical meetings. Methodism represents a variety within this type. The interlocking of society, circuit, district and conference is such that the whole "connexion" is ecclesiologically more basic than any local church. In the Roman Catholic Church the presbyters will meet under the bishop who, in turn, will represent the diocese or other dioceses. Each bishop needs to be in communion with the bishop of Rome.

(3) In the third type, the network of mutual relations is to a large extent determined by a community-to-community recognition. The emphasis is not on a system of representation but rather on the direct fellowship between the communities. Though the "local churches" may consult each other and collaborate in many fields, they will retain, as a rule, a large degree of independence and self-government.

All three views of the local church have their roots in certain historical circumstances and developments. The first type is the result of the expansion of the early Church. The bishop, originally presiding over the one community which existed in a given place, has now the responsibility for several communities; the communities are still regarded as one community. The second type represents a further stage. The role originally played by the bishop has now in part been attributed to the presbyter. The third type is the result of the rediscovery of the charismatic community, often with a strong element of rebellion against hierarchical or political interference and pressure.

Sometimes, structures which had been adopted to meet the needs in particular cultural, social or political circumstances have been perpetuated even after the circumstances have changed. Sometimes, churches maintain in their teaching a certain understanding of the "local church" but allow in reality other approaches to develop. For instance, while the Orthodox Churches officially belong to the first type, in many parts of the world their practice is closer to the second type. Sometimes, in response to changing circumstances the approach has been modified and combined with elements of other approaches. For instance, the Congregationalist approach in the course of the centuries has developed in the direction of the second type.

Obviously, the local church can be described under yet other aspects. There is, for instance, the difference between the approach of the *Volkskirche* and the "voluntarist" approach. The *Volkskirche* claims to include the whole population of a village, region, island, country or nation. The term "local church" in the perspective of the *Volkskirche* has a strong geographical connotation; it refers to the area served by the church. The "voluntarist" approach emphasizes the community which is constituted by the free decision of the people, in response to God's initiative, to covenant together. In this view, the term "local church" refers rather to the gathered community.

Similarly, specific circumstances under which the Church lives have their influence on the way in which the "local church" is conceived, for example, where the Church lives under pressure and persecution or where a hostile state imposes its control on the Church. There is also the difference between the Church in a majority situation and the Church in a minority situation which needs to be taken into account.

III. What is the meaning of the term "local church"?

In the light of these considerations, can the meaning of the term "local church" be determined? The following observations may offer the beginning of an answer.

The term refers to an area where Christians can easily meet and form one committed fellowship in witness and service. Every local church will normally gather in one eucharistic service. The conditions of the area may be such that there is need for several separate services. Even then it must be made evident that these communities understand themselves as one eucharistic fellowship.

The area to be served may vary in size. It may be a village or town; it may be a city or part of a city. It should not be so large that the Christian community loses coherence nor yet so small that its homogeneity favours separatism in the human community. The area should be so chosen that the power of the Gospel to cross human barriers will become manifest.

Modern developments in society lead to a stronger emphasis on larger units in the Church's life. Since people belong to several communities at the same time, there is need for greater transparency and interaction between the communities. Common decisions need to be taken by all and for all communities together. In all confessional traditions, one can observe today a convergent tendency to attach greater importance to the "zone humaine", that is, the area in which a significant grouping of people lives and moves. Local presbyteral parishes, for instance, are being grouped into "deaneries" and larger dioceses are being divided into several "episcopal" areas (sometimes on a geographical basis, as in the Anglican diocese of London; sometimes on a functional basis, as in the Roman Catholic diocese of Liverpool). Whatever name is given to these pastoral units there is need to recognize their increasing role in the life of the Church. Even less than in earlier periods can individual communities fulfil their witness in isolation. They need to be fully part of the whole Christian community in a larger area and to make available their resources for common witness.

This last observation underlines the need for the whole Church, from the local to the regional, national and world levels, to form one living organism. Local churches, in communion with each other, manifest the whole Church, and therefore each local church must participate visibly in the life of the whole Church in as far as it takes place at other than local levels. The term "conciliar fellowship" points to the openness and mutual giving that is required in such participation.

IV. The "local church" in the midst of the human community

A place is not only a geographical but also a human reality. All human beings are shaped by many factors. They are members of a particular race and a particular culture, they formulate their thoughts and purposes in a particular language, they share in the life of agriculture, business, industry or profession and are influenced in their outlook by the activity to which they are committed. These and other similar particularities become part of the life of the Church because of the way in which it is related to the place (see above, Section I).

From very early times, there have been congregations formed by those who shared a common language and this has been widely accepted as legitimate. Can there also be legitimate forms of the Church related to race, culture or daily work? Is it proper to recognize distinct eucharistic assemblies in the same area on the basis of distinct language, race, culture and other factors? The issue is especially acute in areas where, through increased mobility, people of different backgrounds live together.

There is no agreed answer to these questions. Some insist that there can only be one eucharistic assembly in one area and that all must be gathered into it. Others hold that there can and ought to be liberty for separate eucharistic assemblies gathering together those who share the same background.

There is no doubt that according to God's purpose all of every language, race and culture should share in one eucharist. But in the course of its missionary journey into every sector of human society the Church may find it necessary, as a matter of pastoral wisdom, to give provisional recognition to distinct assemblies in one and the same area. For instance, when the Church crosses a barrier and brings the Gospel to a sector of society which lives in a different culture, it cannot be content simply to invite individuals from that culture to join the existing community. Such an invitation would sever the converts from their culture and make them marginal adherents of another culture. Mission would be rendered sterile. Therefore, as a provisional measure, there must be room for the formation of a congregation within that receiving culture, speaking its language and sharing its style of life, through which the full riches of that culture may be brought into the life of the universal Church. The pluriformity that comes into being, and in fact has come into being in the course of the history of the Church, has its obvious assets and liabilities. The strictly provisional character of any separation that is involved will be made manifest if, at the level of the larger pastoral unit, there is a form of church life which enables communities marked by distinct linguistic, racial and cultural styles to share together in full eucharistic fellowship with one another, just as the churches of all regions share in the eucharistic fellowship of a universal council. This is part of what we understand by conciliar fellowship. True conciliar fellowship will provide opportunities for mutual openness and mutual correction so that the provisional separation may not be allowed to harden into permanent separation.

V. The "local church" and the search for the unity of the Church

The local church, in order to be authentically related to the place, needs to be one fully committed fellowship. The existence of several churches in the same place divided along confessional lines is a denial of the nature and the calling of the local church. The present situation must be regarded as an anomaly.

The efforts towards the unity of the Church must aim primarily at enabling "all in each place" to form one "local church". The confessional heritages may have a continuing life in the united Church as long as they nourish the witness of the local church and do not diminish its capacity for responding to the needs of the people whom it is called to serve.

There is need for conversations among the various traditions at all levels. Agreement on the faith and the structure of the Church is essential for the true unity of the Church. Local churches must be able to count on the achievement of such agreement on a wider scale. If the different confessional communities in one place unite without this foundation, they will lack doctrinal profile. Their unity will be based primarily on their common cultural or social outlook. Where only one confessional tradition is represented in one place, the wider agreement will make the local church more fully aware of the extended fellowship. True conciliar relations require a firm common base.

But are there not intermediary stages on the way to the full unity of the Church? Can the unity of the local church not be partially realized? The present situation offers interesting and challenging new developments. In many places, small groups and fellowships have grown around common concerns and interests. They have been formed across the barriers of confessional traditions. There are groups to meet the pastoral needs of people living in mixed marriages, groups offering new insight, spiritual experience or liturgical renewal, new monastic communities, groups responding to particular problems in society, etc. At the moment of their formation, most of these groups do not consider themselves as ecclesial units. But as they begin to share in worship, in the celebration of the sacraments and in mutual pastoral ministry, their fellowship acquires ecclesial quality.

What significance do such groups have for the search for the unity of the Church? No doubt, they are spontaneous responses to the imperative to form a committed fellowship centred in Jesus Christ and inspired by the Holy Spirit. The members of these new fellowships remain within and accept their confessional tradition. But their commitment to the unity of the Church leads them to anticipate the communion of the future. These groups are local. They are responses to needs which present themselves in a particular place. In a certain sense they begin to realize what the local church has been called to be. Therefore their initiative cannot be regarded as entirely local. They reflect the nature of the universal Church in their determination to centre their life on Jesus Christ and to follow the inspiration and guidance of the Holy Spirit. In many cases, ministers of different traditions participate in the life of a group and provide a link with the leadership of the confessional traditions.

Is it not necessary, therefore, to attribute to such groups ecclesial significance? Should they not be regarded as foretaste of the unity to come? In any case, they present a challenge to the churches which continue to live in separation. The spontaneous experience of unity at the local level is another reminder of the urgency of the quest for unity. In response, the churches need to double their efforts to reach the firm agreement which is required for the unity of the Church.

DOCUMENT III.5

REFLECTIONS ON THE COMMON GOAL (1978)

. . .

A re-affirmation of the goal of visible unity

The Faith and Order Commission is committed to keep before the churches this vision and goal. It is its constitutional task to contribute to the creation of conditions which will make it possible for the churches to enter into full communion. They will then recognize each other's ministries; they will share the bread and the cup of their Lord; they will acknowledge each other as belonging to the body of Christ in all places and at all times; they will proclaim together the Gospel to the world; they will serve the needs of humankind in mutual trust and dedication; and for these ends they will plan and take decisions together in assemblies constituted by authorized representatives whenever this is required.

We are fully aware of the sad and scandalous fact that this goal of visible unity is still far away. But we wish to affirm that the vision of unity in such a "conciliar fellowship", sharing the one apostolic faith as well as the gifts of baptism and the eucharist, is alive in us. Although it may seem to be only a distant possibility, the vision provides inspiration and guidance already in the present as we envisage the way ahead. Christ himself summons us to pursue the goal. Since He is the centre of our lives, the realization of the unity for which He prayed is a central task for us. The Gospel to be proclaimed to the world includes as an essential part the communion (koinonia) of the Church with Christ and of Christians with one another. Therefore, division must not be regarded as a secondary issue. Those whom Christ has brought together in his body through his suffering and death on the cross, and through his resurrection, must not be put asunder by anybody. The love which is in Jesus Christ holds us together. Therefore, it is a matter of grateful and obedient discipleship not to acquiesce in the divisions but to engage constantly anew in the struggle to break old and new barriers which separate us from one another.

Why repeat what has been stated many times? Simply because the striving for visible unity is slackening in many quarters. Some who have set out on this road have become victims of frustration. Others declare themselves content with the measure of good will and cooperation which has developed among the churches over the last decades, and cease to reach out to new stages of unity.

This is not to say that no efforts at promoting unity are being undertaken. In fact, the search for unity goes on at all levels of the churches' life. Congregations and groups within congregations are seeking new ways of cooperation. They pray for each other, they seek a deeper mutual understanding. Barriers of distrust are being removed. Joint action expands. Theological commissions are at work, at national, regional and universal levels, to articulate the consensus among the churches. Common understanding is being reached on many issues which, in the past, have caused alienation, division and enmity.

All these efforts are to be welcomed and need to be continued. The search for unity must proceed at many levels and involve more and more Christians. There is no uniform strategy in moving towards unity. According to different situations and conditions, different methods must be employed. The multiplicity of efforts is not without problems, however. We are concerned that instead of being complementary, they might counteract and neutralize each other. There is need to work in concert. The vision of full visible unity in conciliar fellowship provides the frame for working in concert. The agreements which have emerged or are emerging from multilateral and bilateral dialogues must be taken seriously by all churches and, as far as they are acceptable to each church, translated into practical decisions which affect the relations with other churches. The far-reaching results of dialogues present the churches with the challenge to give new expression to the oneness in Christ for the sake of the Gospel and to the glory of God.

a) Visible unity and conciliar fellowship

"... The one Church is to be envisioned as a conciliar fellowship of local churches which are themselves truly united." What does this mean? "Conciliar fellowship" refers to a communion of local churches which is capable of holding assemblies or synods of authorized representatives of the various local churches.

Unity is the presupposition for such assemblies and synods. The primary task of all ecumenical endeavours is therefore the promotion of that unity. Representative conciliar gatherings will be one expression and manifestation of that unity. The World Council of Churches cannot call a universal council. This will be the prerogative of the churches as they unite. But the churches through their common life and work in councils (conseils) at the local, national, regional and universal levels, as well as through other ecumenical efforts, can seek to bring about a situation in which unity can be established and a representative conciliar gathering can be held. To achieve this they need to engage in a movement of ecumenical life based on Christian prayer, repentance, love, dialogue, growth in understanding and actions which open the doors to deeper communion.

The main value of statements such as those of the Assemblies in New Delhi and Nairobi is to provide a framework for the search for unity. It would be simplistic to regard them as solutions of the ecclesiological differences. They rather present a programme for further common studies. They are a challenge to the churches to use the findings of multilateral and bilateral dialogues and whatever other means are available to move forward towards the full rediscovery of the unity in Christ.

They also provide a frame for living, witnessing and serving together. The Church is a sign and instrument of Christ's mission to all humankind. The sign is obscured by the present divisions. Will the churches continue to be a misguiding sign by remaining a divided and fragmented people? Or will they seek to be a reliable, trustworthy sign as a people constantly uniting in mutual forgiveness and reconciliation?

The notion of the Church as sign and instrument has already been discussed by Faith and Order on previous occasions.[2] At Bangalore special mention was made of two aspects. In affirming the sign-character of the Church, two dangers can be avoided. The one would be to imagine that the Church could be called to bring about

---

[2] See: *What Unity Requires*, Faith and Order Paper No. 77, pp.3ff. Geiko Müller-Fahrenholz: *Unity in Today's World*, The Faith and Order Studies on Unity of the Church — Unity of Humankind, WCC, 1978, pp.78ff [note 1 omitted here].

the Kingdom of Christ and to take into its own hands what Christ alone can fulfil. The other would be to be oblivious to the calling visibly and tangibly to manifest our oneness in faith and hope in history. To be a sign and instrument is one way of expressing that Christians are called to be faithful stewards of God's gifts, "in full accord and of one mind" (Phil. 2:2).

The concept of "conciliar fellowship" presents a challenge to all churches. Churches which regard themselves as representing in historical continuity the one, holy, catholic and apostolic Church need to find ways of transcending the canonical boundaries whereby they identify the Church; they must reflect on the possibility of recognizing other churches as holding the same apostolic faith and sharing the same eucharistic fellowship; they need to discover ways of associating with them and moving together with them to full conciliar fellowship. Churches which consider the one, holy, catholic and apostolic Church to be a reality far greater than the historical reality of any church tradition need to reflect on the ways in which the sense of community can be developed which is the presupposition of true conciliar life.

b) ...local churches which are themselves truly united

The report "What Unity Requires" drew attention to the ambiguity of the term "local church". Since the Assembly, the issue has been carefully studied.[3] Clearly, the meaning of the term "local" varies from tradition to tradition.[4] The different uses reflect different ecclesiologies not yet reconciled with one another.

The formula "local churches which are themselves truly united" brings also into the open different approaches to the realization of unity. Many say that true unity requires the gathering of all in each place into one eucharistic community; there would be no room for a continuing life of the confessional traditions. Others say that unity according to Christ's will does not necessarily require the disappearance but rather the transformation of confessional identities to such a degree that unity in full sacramental fellowship, common witness and service, together with some common structural/institutional expression becomes possible. While the first view is rather connected with the concept of "organic unity", the second is held by those proposing the concept "unity in reconciled diversity". The two concepts are not to be seen as alternatives. They may be two different ways of reacting to the ecumenical necessities and possibilities of different situations and of different church traditions.

c) "Council", "councils" and "pre-conciliar"

In English, the term "council" and its derivatives are capable of two different interpretations:
i) The term can refer to a gathering or *assembly of official representatives* of local churches within a fully united sacramental fellowship.
ii) The term can also refer to the *associations of churches* at local, national, regional and universal levels which have come into existence as a fruit of the ecumenical movement. They are not bound together in full sacramental fellowship. They have, however, some features of conciliar life and are instruments for creating closer

---

[3] See *In Each Place,* Towards a Fellowship of Local Churches Truly United, WCC, 1977.
[4] See *In Each Place,* pp.6ff.

relationships between churches separated from one another both confessionally and geographically.

Other languages do not suffer from the same terminological difficulty. They use different terms for the two meanings. The Greek language uses the terms *synodos* and *symboulion;* the Latin *concilium* and *consilium;* the French *concile* and *conseil;* the German *Konzil* and *Rat;* the Russian *sobor* and *sowiet.*

The double meaning in English has sometimes led to misunderstandings. Those who understand the term "conciliar fellowship" in the sense of (ii) are either discontent because it seems to suggest less than the organic unity for which they hope and work, or they rest content because it seems to give support to the view that the associations which exist today are a sufficient expression of the unity we seek.

The report "What Unity Requires" of the Fifth Assembly makes it clear that the term is to be used in the meaning given under (i). Conciliar fellowship means a communion capable of holding representative councils.

How then is the present stage of the ecumenical movement to be described? The report "What Unity Requires" and other documents refer to it as *pre-conciliar*. It is important to agree on the precise meaning of this term. In the Orthodox church the term is used to refer to the period in which a council *(synodos, sobor)* is being directly prepared. The Orthodox churches are today in a pre-conciliar period because they have agreed to prepare for the celebration of a pan-orthodox council. The usage of the term in this particular meaning only makes sense within the context of a fully united sacramental communion. Christians of all traditions, however, are able to use the word "pre-conciliar" in a more general sense in order to refer to the various efforts and developments which prepare for and herald the future conciliar fellowship.

Recommendations

1. The vision of the common goal articulated by the Fifth Assembly needs to be further clarified and explained. This effort should not be seen as a verbal ballet between concepts like "conciliar fellowship", "organic unity" and "unity in reconciled diversity", but rather as a struggle to find a way of presenting the vision that will give real hope to ordinary members of the churches that the vision is, by God's will, both desirable and achievable. It is recommended that the Standing Commission work on a communication to the churches on the common goal.

2. The description of the unity we seek offered by the Fifth Assembly does not overcome the differences in the understanding of the nature of the Church; it provides a common setting and a fresh approach for discussing them. Therefore, it may be advisable to return in future to a study of the fundamental ecclesiological issues which separate the churches. Special attention should be given to a) the Church as effective sign and instrument; b) the ecclesiological implications of the various concepts of unity at present under discussion, for example "organic unity", "unity in reconciled diversity"; c) the ecclesiological implications of the term "local churches which are themselves truly united"; d) ecclesiological aspects of the ecumenical discussion on baptism, the eucharist and the ministry.

3. Fresh attention should be given to intermediary steps between the present stage of the ecumenical movement and the final goal of visible unity.

4. In particular, the Commission should seek to offer guidelines and practical help in finding ways relating the different levels of ecumenical experiences and dialogue to

each other so as to facilitate the process of reception and common growth into unity.

5. The debate on the vision of conciliar fellowship should be continued on as many levels and in as many settings as possible. Special attention should be drawn to two consultations which may be regarded as models: the consultation organized by the Conference of European Churches in Sofia (1977) on "Churches in conciliar fellowship", and the Indian National Consultation on "Conciliar unity" (1978). Churches and families of churches engaged in bilateral conversations should reflect on the concepts of unity underlying their efforts and consider ways in which they can contribute to the clarification of the common goal.

DOCUMENT III.6

THE HOLY EUCHARIST (1967)

I. Introduction

The Commission on Faith and Order at its meeting in Aarhus authorized the Secretariat to get underway a study on the Eucharist. As the unity of the Church receives special expression in the celebration of the Eucharist, it is only natural that this topic holds a dominating position in the Faith and Order movement. The separated churches constantly have to examine anew how they can clear the way to the Lord's Table for their members. The problem cannot, however, be solved if attention is drawn directly and exclusively to intercommunion, and the theological and practical questions immediately related to it. The regulations of the individual churches are deeply grounded and can only be changed when the deeper theological connections are clarified. The Commission therefore recommended that the Secretariat should start an extended study of eucharistic theology, especially in the light of recent developments in ecclesiology. In a short memorandum it summarized the problems to be included in the study.[1]

As a beginning the Secretariat asked Professor J.-J. von Allmen to write a study on the Eucharist especially in relation to the ecumenical movement.[2] It then convened a consultation of about 20 participants (Grandchamp, July 1965) at which this document was discussed in detail. The discussion showed a surprising agreement on a number of problems. In a short report the consultation indicated a few points where a more detailed study might be promising.[3]

The report was sent to a number of regional groups (e.g. in Japan, Cameroon, Brazil, South Africa, Germany, etc.) with the request that they should take the whole problem into consideration and then examine in detail one or more of the questions raised.

Then a theological commission — in accordance with the recommendation of Aarhus — was formed. Its first meeting was held at Crêt-Bérard, Switzerland, April 1967. In the light of the comments sent in it came to the conclusion that an ecumenical discussion could be furthered at the following three points — Anamnesis and Epiclesis, Catholicity of the Eucharist, Eucharist and Agape. The commission therefore submitted a report on these three questions to the Commission on Faith and Order. The appendix on intercommunion shows that the common celebration of the Eucharist has served as a goal in all these reflections.

II. The Anamnetic and Epikletic Character of the Eucharist

The Montreal Report expressed a consensus on the Eucharist in these terms:

...'The Lord's Supper, a gift of God to his Church, is a sacrament of the presence of the crucified and glorified Christ until he comes, and a means whereby the sacrifice

---

[1] *Aarhus Minutes*, pp.54-57.

[2] This study has been published after revision under the title *Essai sur le repas du Seigneur*, Neuchâtel, 1967; the English edition will be published by Lutterworth Press, London; the German edition will be published by Neukirchener Verlag. See also Lukas Vischer, "Questions on the Eucharist, its past and future celebration", *Studia Liturgica*, V, 2, 1966.

[3] *Study Encounter* (former *Bulletin*, Vol X, 2, 1964) and *Studia Liturgica*, V, 2, 1966.

of the cross, which we proclaim, is operative within the Church. In the Lord's Supper the members of the body of Christ are sustained in their unity with their Head and Saviour who offered himself on the cross: by him, with him and in him who is our great High Priest and Intercessor we offer to the Father, in the power of the Holy Spirit, our praise, thanksgiving and intercession. With contrite hearts we offer ourselves as a living and holy sacrifice, a sacrifice which must be expressed in the whole of our daily lives. Thus united to our Lord, and to the Church triumphant, and in fellowship with the whole Church on earth, we are renewed in the covenant sealed by the blood of Christ. In the Supper we also anticipate the marriage-supper of the lamb in the Kingdom of God."[4]

On the basis of this consensus we limit ourselves to a consideration of two aspects which are increasingly recognized as essential to the Eucharist and which have not heretofore been given sufficient attention: the anamnetic and epikletic character of the Eucharist.

1. Christ instituted the Eucharist, sacrament of his body and blood with its focus upon the cross and resurrection, as the anamnesis of the whole of God's reconciling action in him. Christ himself with all he has accomplished for us and for all creation (in his incarnation, servanthood, ministry, teaching, suffering, sacrifice, resurrection, ascension and Pentecost) is present in this anamnesis as is also the foretaste of his Parousia and the fulfilment of the Kingdom. The anamnesis in which Christ acts through the joyful celebration of his Church thus includes this representation and anticipation. It is not only a calling to mind of what is past, or of its significance. It is the Church's effective proclamation of God's mighty acts. By this communion with Christ the Church participates in that reality.

2. Anamnetic representation and anticipation are realized in thanksgiving and intercession. The Church, proclaiming before God the mighty acts of redemption in thanksgiving, beseeches him to give the benefits of these acts to every man. In thanksgiving and intercession, the Church is united with the Son, its great High Priest and Intercessor.

3. The anamnesis of Christ is the basis and source of all Christian prayer. So our prayer relies upon and is united with the continual intercession of the risen Lord. In the Eucharist, Christ empowers us to live with him and to pray with him as justified sinners joyfully and freely fulfilling his will.

4. The anamnesis leads to epiklesis, for Christ in his heavenly intercession prays the Father to send the Spirit upon his children. For this reason, the Church, being under the New Covenant, confidently prays for the Spirit, in order that it may be sanctified and renewed, led into all truth and empowered to fulfil its mission in the world. Anamnesis and epiklesis, being unitive acts, cannot be conceived apart from communion. Moreover it is the Spirit who, in our Eucharist, makes Christ really present and given to us in the bread and wine, according to the words of institution.

5. The liturgy should express adequately both the anamnetic and epikletic character of the Eucharist.

a) Since the anamnesis of Christ is the very essence of the preached Word as it is of the Eucharist, each reinforces the other. Eucharist should not be celebrated without

---

[4] *The Fourth World Conference on Faith and Order: The Report from Montreal*, eds P.C. Rodger and L. Vischer, London, SCM Press, 1964, paragraph 117, p.73f.

the ministry of the Word, and the ministry of the Word points to, and is consummated in the Eucharist.

b) The anamnetic character of the whole Eucharist should be adequately expressed in the prayer of thanksgiving and in a proper "anamnesis".

c) Because of the epikletic character of the whole Eucharist, the epiklesis should be clearly expressed in all liturgies as the invocation of the Spirit upon the people of God and upon the whole eucharistic action, including the elements. The consecration cannot be limited to a particular moment in the liturgy. Nor is the location of the epiklesis in relation to the words of institution of decisive importance. In the early liturgies the whole "prayer action" was thought of as bringing about the reality promised by Christ. A recovery of such an understanding may help to overcome our differences concerning a special moment of consecration.

III. The Catholic Character of the Eucharist

The Christian understanding of the catholicity of the Church and of its local manifestations is rooted in Judaism. The words *qāhāl, ekklesia* (LXX) referred originally to the whole people of God. In post-exilic times, however, the word *ecclesia*, like *synagoge,* came to apply also to local congregations of believers. The New Testament usage continues this double signification. The word *church (ecclesia)* always witnesses to the totality of the people of God. The same is true of other New Testament descriptions of the Church such as "the household of God", "the planting of God", "the bride of Christ", "the body of Christ", etc. This is in line with our understanding of the incarnation: that God sent his only Son, in whom he was pleased to cause his fulness to dwell, into the world as Messiah to reconcile, redeem and glorify it with all its inhabitants. These expressions, therefore, which refer to the Church, even when they refer to local congregations, never lose sight of this totality.

1. Therefore the Eucharist which Jesus Christ, God's Son, instituted, when observed by a local assembly of Christians at any particular time and place, has the fulness of catholicity. The sharing of the common loaf and the common cup in a given place demonstrates the oneness of the sharers with the whole Christ and with their fellow sharers in all times and places. By sharing the common loaf they show their unity with the Church catholic, the mystery of redemption is set forth, and the whole body grows in grace. The Catholic Church, therefore, is more than the summation of the local churches, and is to be fully manifested in each local church.

2. The catholic character of the Eucharist is further seen in that it is in every place both an assurance of redemption and a sign of hope to the whole cosmos. For the world God is reconciling to himself is present at every Eucharist: in the bread and wine, in the persons of the faithful, and in the prayers they offer for themselves and for all men. As the faithful and their prayers are united in the Person of our Lord and to his intercession they are transfigured and accepted. Thus the Eucharist reveals to the world what it must become.

3. When local churches, no matter how humble, share in the Eucharist they experience the wholeness of the Church and reveal it in its fulness: its members, its faith, its history, and its special gifts. Eucharistic celebrations, therefore, are always concerned with the whole Church and the whole Church is concerned with every eucharistic celebration. Since the earliest days Baptism has been understood as the sacrament by which believers are incorporated into the body of Christ and are endowed

by the Holy Spirit. When, therefore, the right of baptized believers and their ministers to participate in and preside over eucharistic celebrations in one church is called in question by those who preside over and are members of other eucharistic congregations, the catholicity of the Eucharist is obscured. On the other hand, insofar as a church claims to be a manifestation of the whole Church, it should recognize that the whole Church is involved in its pastoral and administrative regulations.

4. Because of its catholicity the Eucharist is a radical challenge to the "demonic" tendencies in church life towards estrangement, separation and fragmentation. Lack of local unity in church or society constitutes a challenge to the Christians in that place. A mockery is made of the Eucharist when the walls of separation destroyed by Christ on his cross are allowed to persist: those between races, nationalities, tongues, classes, congregations and confessions, etc.

5. The Church which is Christ's body and is for all men always finds itself in a great variety of cultural and social situations. These inevitably exert their influence upon it. Tensions often arise between local and national churches and between communions and confessions. But the catholic character of the Eucharist requires that the Church be both indigenous and contemporary. Thus the differences between the church of one nation and another nation, between the church of one generation and another, are justified. Its temporal and spatial dimensions make the Church conscious of its catholicity and it rejoices in them. Catholicity welcomes that "particularity" which renounces self-realization at the expense of others and which has allowed itself to be converted by the Gospel, so that it dies to self and lives to Christ.

6. When the church in a certain locality and age, in the midst of a particular cultural situation, asks the church in other places and situations to be allowed to celebrate the Eucharist in its own way, Christian charity will not look upon it as that church's attempt to vindicate itself, nor as an imposition upon catholicity. Rather it will recognize it as an expression of that church's bona fide intention to serve and honour the catholicity of the Church. All churches however, would better evidence the validity of their own eucharistic life in Christ were they to refrain from doing anything which increases misunderstanding, multiplies divisions, or provokes estrangement in the Church. So will they bear a more effective witness before the world to that catholicity all of them claim, and which is embodied in their Eucharists.

IV. Eucharist and Agape

1. Agape in early Christian usage designates a communal meal explicitly observed in the name and presence of Christ. The term reflects God's self-revealed love — between God in Christ and the Church, love between Christians themselves, and love emanating from God and going via his believing people to and for the world in active concern and responsiveness.

2. Although the precise relation of the Agape to the Eucharist in earliest Christian practice is not clear, all communal meals mentioned in the New Testament, if not necessarily eucharistic, were surely intended to be agapeic. The term agapeic here signifies a covenantal relationship in which the members of the community both recognized their common existence in Christ and pledged to live for one another's total welfare according to, and as they were involved in, God's servant-love in Christ.

3. The Eucharist, in the institution at the Last Supper and in subsequent celebrations, involves, as does the Agape, communal eating and drinking. Such action, especially in Hebraic and early Christian thought, implies an agapeic relationship which was meant to find expression in all the affairs of God's people.

4. As the Church's liturgy and structured life developed, these agapeic implications were given specific expression in connection with the Eucharist: for example, in the mutual forgiveness of sins; the kiss of peace; the bringing of gifts for the communal meal and for distribution to the poor brethren; the specific prayer for the needy and suffering; the taking of the Eucharist to the sick and those in prison. In this agapeic realization of eucharistic fulness, the ministry of deacons and deaconesses was especially responsible.[5] The place of such a ministry between the table and the needy properly testifies to the redeeming presence of Christ in the world. All these agapeic features of the Eucharist are directly related to Christ's own testimony as a Servant, in whose servanthood Christians themselves participate by virtue of their union with him. As God in Christ has entered into the human situation, so should eucharistic liturgy be near to the concrete and particular situations of men. This essential agapeic character of the Eucharist needs to be emphasized today.

5. For reasons we cannot fully know, the Agape and the Eucharist became clearly separate observances in the Church. The Agape followed its own ceremonial with emphasis on fraternal responsibility in human affairs. But the danger was always that Agapes would lose their integrity as manifestations of the basic oneness of Christians and the love revealed in Christ. It is significant that they first came under attack for so losing their integrity (I Cor. 11:21-22; Jude 12; cf. II Pet. 2:13). This loss no doubt contributed to the eventual disappearance of the Agape as a regular communal meal in the Church.

6. Today there is a growing interest in the fellowship of Agape-like meals. Various factors may explain this. For example, in a highly technological, specialized society human values are often frustrated and a sense of joyful, responsible community is frequently lacking. Also, in many areas of the world there is a felt need for more meaningful social fellowship within church-life. Although these meals are not eucharistic, the Church cannot ignore contemporary enthusiasm for them. Such meals should be neither condemned nor approved *in themselves*. Historical evidence shows that Agapes are possible in principle, yet are not necessary for all times. Particular observances of the Agape must be assessed in relation to prevailing circumstances. Practical considerations must be weighed to ascertain how far in a particular Agape the Holy Spirit or alien spirits may be at work and whether such a celebration may be approved.

With this in mind the following observations should be considered:

a) The greatest care must be taken to acknowledge and realize the agapeic character of the eucharistic meal, as mentioned above, so that the Lord's Supper may be recognized as the most desirable "Agape". In this regard churches may need to re-examine their understanding and practice of the Eucharist and consider whether new forms for its celebration may be desirable. At this point the renewal of the diaconate office deserves consideration.

---

[5] Cf. Faith and Order studies on the *Ministry of Deacons* and *The Deaconess*, published in World Council Studies No. 2 (1965), No. 4 (1966).

b) In some situations congregational Agapes, when related to eucharistic observances, may serve to enhance the congregation's sense of joyful, responsible
community connoted in the Eucharist itself.

c) Congregational Agapes not related to eucharistic observances may also be of
advantage in special situations: for example, to stimulate both fuller participation
in the whole life of the Church and active concern for the world; to provide
occasions for Christian fellowship whether in urban, industrial, or rural communities; etc. However, there is a danger that such Agapes, if not rightly
understood and observed, can lose their intended purpose, compete with the Lord's
Supper, or even lead to a confusing of the two.

d) Interconfessional Agapes, related to separate confessional observances of the
Eucharist, may foster Christian fellowship and witness. Each confessional family
could celebrate the Eucharist and then join with other Christians in an Agape.

e) This possibility of an Agape should be considered especially with regard to the
Fourth Assembly of WCC at Uppsala. In this connection the guidelines concerning
"Communion Services at Ecumenical Gatherings", adopted by the Central Committee (1963) need to be remembered. They recommend:
   i) that at least two eucharistic services should be held within the programme of
       the meeting, one at which an invitation to "participate and partake is given to
       members of other churches", and another "according to the liturgy of a church
       which cannot conscientiously offer an invitation to members of all other
       churches to partake in the elements", and that all participants in the meeting
       should be invited to be present at both services;
   ii) that provision should be made enabling all participants to communicate
       according to their tradition.[6]

An Agape could be held towards the end of the Assembly after all participants had
the opportunity to communicate and had experienced the problem presented by our
divisions. Such a meal could underline the fellowship which we have in spite of our
divisions. Of course, details would have to be worked out by the appropriate
preparatory committees.

V. Appendix: Intercommunion

The Montreal Report summarized the state of the question about intercommunion
in these terms:

> Some Christians believe that the degree of ecclesial Communion which we have in the
> body of Christ, through baptism and through our fundamental faith, although we are still
> divided on some points, urges us to celebrate Holy Communion together and to promote
> intercommunion between the churches. It is Christ, present in the Eucharist, who invites all
> Christians to his table: this strict invitation of Christ cannot be thwarted by ecclesial
> discipline. In the communion at the same holy table, divided Christians are committed in a
> decisive way to make manifest this total, visible and organic unity.
>
> Some Christians believe that eucharistic communion, being an expression of acceptance
> of the whole Christ, implies full unity in the wholeness of his truth; that there cannot be any

---

[6] *The Fourth World Conference*, *op. cit.*, paragraph 142, p.79.

"intercommunion" between otherwise separated Christians; that communion in the sacraments therefore implies a pattern of doctrine and ministry, which is indivisible; and that "intercommunion" cannot presume upon the union in faith that we still seek.[7]

Since these findings were passed (1963) a number of changes have occurred which affect the discussion of the issue; we point to the following:

a) There has been unprecedented widening of ecumenical contacts. More and more Christians are having the experience of division at the Lord's Table so that whereas the issue could be ignored in the past it leads today to an ever-growing recognition that the problem needs to be faced.

b) An increasing number of churches are involved in liturgical and eucharistic renewal, partly as a result of the Second Vatican Council; questions which seemed closed are now open for discussion. The attempt is being made by many churches to understand afresh the place of the Eucharist in the Church both in theory and in practice.

c) In some places promising decisions have been taken making intercommunion possible between churches, committed to union (e.g. West Africa). In other places the proposal that churches should engage in a covenant for union provides a new setting for the discussion of intercommunion.

d) Sociological pressures continue to exercize their power. Division has always been felt most strongly where people live closest together — in marriage, in education, at work, etc., but as churches come closer to each other this division is felt even more strongly.

There is no fundamental change in the positions as they were formulated at Montreal, and this Theological Commission has not been able to bring them decisively nearer to one another. As they are discussed in this changed situation they appear, however, in a new light. Above all the foregoing considerations make clear the urgent need of a solution.

As our study has shown, the separate churches are becoming increasingly aware that the Eucharist occupies a central place in the life of the Church and that the Eucharist itself must be the basis of their growth into the fulness of communion to which they aspire. Though they cannot participate in the sacrament together they share this conviction. Those who hold the conviction that the Eucharist, "being the expression of acceptance of the whole Christ implies full unity" will consider the Eucharist celebrated by other churches as a witness to their desire to obey the Lord's command and to manifest both his presence and the reconciliation he offers to the world. The separate eucharistic celebrations are all related to the communion we seek to live in, and the hope for breaking the walls rests upon the fact of communion existing within and between separated churches. As the churches in their eucharistic experience move toward the fulness which is in Christ, the problem of intercommunion will move towards its solution.

For the continuing study the following considerations may be of value:

1. If the problems of unity and intercommunion are to be clarified, there is need for a theological and sociological study of disunity.

---

[7] *Op. cit.*, paragraph 138f., p.78.

a) Such a study will ask, as paragraphs 138-139 of Montreal already clearly intimate, for an assessment of the factors of ecclesiality, and of wholeness of tradition, and their importance or irrelevance over against the mere confession of belief in and discipleship of Christ.

b) It will have to consider the importance of mutual canonical (formal) recognition for sacramental intercommunion, and to decide whether such recognition be sufficient in and by itself to secure the theological reality of unity and consequent possibility of sacramental sharing.

c) It will examine the question as to how far divisions are really inside the Church or separate from it. The study will keep in view the terms carefully defined at Lund.

d) This in its turn calls for further study of the limits or boundaries of the Church, and of its membership.

2. The question of intercommunion demands above all an inquiry about the nature, as well as the necessity, of the Ministry in general, and of Episcopacy in particular. The churches should be urged to undertake a positive re-assessment of the Ministry, both as it is manifested in their own Order and in that of other churches. In particular, they should address themselves to the following questions:

a) The "Catholic" churches should ask whether the ministries of non-episcopal churches — quite apart from their possession of apostolic succession or their lack of it — do not in fact contain elements of value (such as charismatic or extraordinary ministries), and if so of what value such elements may be.

b) The "Protestant" churches, on the other hand, should reconsider, in the light of the ecumenical movement, the value of the commonly accepted ministry of the Early Church and of Pre-Reformation times.

c) "Protestant" as well as "Catholic" churches should further ask themselves whether, in spite of the widely divergent appearance of Pre-Reformation and Reformation ministries, a measure of hidden identity may not in fact have been preserved. Does the fact that the Reformers rejected the name or title of a given ecclesiastical order necessarily prove that the reality behind the name was also rejected? Or again, does the fact that a name or title has been preserved, by itself, constitute a proof that the intended reality has been retained? In what cases is the rejection of episcopacy or of priesthood absolute and final? In what cases does the apparent rejection of the old ecclesiastical orders only mean the rejection of certain sociological forms and modalities? How far are they susceptible to the principle of "economy"?

3. We must continue to wrestle with the question, "Why are the churches usually more ready to recognize each other's Baptism than each other's Eucharist?"

DOCUMENT III.7

BEYOND INTERCOMMUNION:
ON THE WAY TO COMMUNION IN THE EUCHARIST (1971)

Preamble

Since its very beginnings the ecumenical movement has been concerned with the question of common eucharistic worship. As Christians from hitherto separated Churches come together in common fellowship they are inevitably confronted with the question whether they can celebrate the Lord's supper together and if so, under what conditions. Precisely because of the fellowship they have begun to experience, the pain of not being able to share in the Lord's table is all the more intense.

Many have worked on the solution of what is usually, if misleadingly, known as the question of intercommunion. Of the ecumenical bodies Faith and Order has known itself commissioned to explore the question's deep roots in the Church's faith and practice. The World Conferences at Edinburgh in 1937[1] and at Lund in 1952[2] went into it at length. The most recent World Conference, at Montreal in 1963,[3] took further the work of a consultation convened jointly with the WCC Youth Department in 1961,[4] on the narrower but crucial question of communion services at ecumenical gatherings. Since then the problem has not been directly discussed by the Faith and Order Commission. The Commission chose rather to deal with the nature and practice of the eucharist in general in the hope that new insights and agreements there would enable advance in turn on this question also.[5]

Meanwhile, however, much has been happening. Experimental and unprecedented ventures of many sorts have been taking place in all parts of Christendom. Previous analyses of the problem are no longer entirely adequate; the terminology suggested for example by the Lund Conference now needs to be revised (cf. Appendix II). The Uppsala Assembly of the World Council of Churches asked the Faith and Order Commission to take up the question again,[6] and this paper is the first-fruits of the new effort. It is the product of a consultation which was held in Geneva (Switzerland) in March 1969.

I. The present stage on the way

Since it has to do with the very centre of Christian faith and of the life of the Church, the eucharist lies inescapably at the heart of the ecumenical movement. All forms of ecumenical activity are constantly throwing up questions about the sacra-

---

[1] Cf. Intercommunion, *The Second World Conference on Faith and Order,* Edinburgh 1937, ed. Leonard Hodgson, pp.251ff.

[2] Cf. Intercommunion, *The Third World Conference on Faith and Order,* Lund 1952, ed. Oliver S. Tomkins, pp.49ff.

[3] Cf. Intercommunion, *The Fourth World Conference on Faith and Order,* Montreal 1963, ed. P.C. Rodger and L. Vischer, pp.72ff.,76ff.

[4] Cf. Report of Consultation on Services of Holy Communion at Ecumenical Gatherings at Bossey (1961), *The Ecumenical Review,* XIII/3, April 1961, pp.353-364.

[5] For the results of this study see *New Directions in Faith and Order,* Bristol 1967, Faith and Order Paper No. 50, pp.60ff.

[6] *Uppsala Report,* see Report of the Assembly Committee on Faith and Order, pp.222ff.

ment, its practice and its discipline. There is a vast mass of evidence of all sorts, which no one can be sure of adequately grasping. This section does no more than point to some of the most salient features. All of them witness to the urgency of the question; many of them deserve a great deal more study.

The discussions of the question of intercommunion run into the existence of two contrasting positions. There are those who, because of their understanding of the nature of the Church and sacraments and because of their concern for the maintenance of the integrity of the Church as essential for the manifestation of its true unity, hold that the eucharist is the sign and reality of the Church's unity. Therefore, the eucharistic observance will gather together those who have found their common life in the *Una Sancta* as both the reality of their oneness in Christ and a witness to it. There are many who, in the present situation, believe that faithful adherence to this position is vital to the ultimate achievement of the true ecumenical goal. There are also those who, believing that the eucharist is not only a sign of unity but also a God-given means by which the grace of unity is imparted, hold that, for those who are committed to the quest of unity in one body, common participation in the eucharist is the proper and grateful use of the means which God has provided. This study starts from the recognition that both of these are largely right, paradoxical as that may sound, and seek to discover how this can be understood and practised.

In recent years the participation in the ecumenical movement has grown. The movement has been enlarged especially by the more general entry of the Roman Catholic Church. While in the past it involved only a certain number of traditions, now the whole spectrum of Christian Churches is represented in the discussion, and this means that the question can at last be seen and tackled in its fulness. This transformation of the ecumenical movement is not merely a quantitative change. It has also opened up new perspectives in theological thinking. The theological discussions between the Churches about ecclesiology have forged ahead and led to new possibilities of discussing points long taken to be immovable stumbling blocks (Appendix III [not reprinted here]). On many sides there is emerging a new awareness of the corporate nature of Christian existence, a sense that communion in the eucharist involves a relationship not only with God but also with fellow Christians. On the basis of these developments some Churches have found it possible to reconsider their policies (cf. the decree *De Oecumenismo* of the Vatican Council, recommendations of the Lambeth Conference, etc.). Especially where Churches are firmly committing themselves to each other on the road to union they find themselves able to adopt new attitudes (the recent recommendations for implementing in Germany the Arnoldshain Theses of 1957, union negotiations in West Africa, etc.). But the growth of the ecumenical movement can be seen especially in the fact that local ecumenical activity and the local ecumenical contacts are increasing, both inside and outside established church structures. Therefore, the question of the common celebration of the eucharist is not confined any more to academic discussions or to the problem of worship at ecumenical gatherings.[7] It is being raised more and more at the local level where many Christians have found that their most significant experiences of fellowship cut across the lines of ecclesiastical separations and are pressing towards the one eucharist as the adequate expression. This inner pressure of the growth of Christians towards one

---

[7] On this see Appendix I for a possible new approach.

another has led to many acts of common eucharistic celebrations not in accordance with the eucharistic discipline of the Churches.

The Week of Prayer for Christian Unity offers an excellent example of this pressure. The Week was started as a vital means of furthering the unity of the Church without suggesting any disloyalty to existing church disciplines. Over the years it has involved more and more Christians from all sorts of churches and has led to marked ecumenical developments in the Roman Catholic Church in particular. The observance of the Week has increasingly taken the form of common corporate worship, in services of the Word and of prayers drawn up for the occasion, and by now many are suggesting that it would be appropriate for it to move one stage further, i.e. into eucharistic worship.

But this is far from the whole story. The pang of separation at the Lord's table is felt no less intensely where Christians are involved in common service and witness in the world. Both the Second Vatican Council and the Uppsala Assembly of the World Council of Churches have forcibly pointed Christians towards a new commitment to corporate action in the world, against hunger, ignorance and oppression and in support of justice, development and peace. Such concerns are today intrinsic, not optional, to Christian obedience. They are crucial in the dynamism of ecumenical advance, nourishing as well as feeding on the new confidence that Christians have in each other, even those separated by centuries of mistrust. Moreover such concerns give new meaning to intentions long expressed in celebrations of the eucharist and are full of eucharistic symbolism and significance.

Many groups of Christians therefore, anticipating the official moves of their Churches along the ecumenical way, have begun to celebrate the sacrament together in ways that transcend existing church disciplines. The bewildering variety of these ventures allows no general judgement. Some represent an implicit protest against forms of authority and established custom felt to be insensitive to the actual contexts in which Christians today live. Others are more clearly fresh restatements of tradition. None however are intended to repudiate the wider fellowship of the Church. On the contrary, at a time when concern for the life of the world is leading many, not least among the responsible and informed, to ignore the Churches or leave them altogether, it is significant that these experimental forms of eucharistic worship make their point by affirming "what the Church is and does".

At the same time the fact must not be overlooked that an increasing number of Christians wrestling with the issues of their contemporary world are no longer content with standard confessional teachings about the meaning and integrity of worship and about the community in which worship takes place. Christ's work of reconciliation in the world requires of his followers not only conciliatory gestures but prophetic words and acts. The complexity and ambiguity of factors involved in a situation may overshadow the central reconciling thrust of the eucharist and make it apparently as much a factor of unrest and division as of peace and unity. Theologians wrestle with the ways in which new understandings of the corporate and missionary character of the sacrament belong with new commitments to effective action in the world, but their findings have not yet been translated into terms that most Christians can grasp and work out in practice.

The fundamental question about the eucharist is thus increasingly seen to be that of the true nature of the human community it both expresses and makes possible.

This *ecclesia* is at the same time a historical, social reality and a participation in the life of God. Where is this reality truly to be found? What are its authentic boundaries? What disciplines are most appropriate to it? These are the questions that challenge the Churches to discern more exactly the nature of the communion we seek.

II. Theology on the way

The Churches engaged in the ecumenical movement do not yet have a common understanding of the nature of the communion they seek. Committed to the search for the unity Christ wills for his Church, they are obliged to question their concepts of unity again and to grow in their obedience to Christ. Many attempts have been made to arrive at an agreed description of the goal of the ecumenical movement. The most notable example is the New Delhi statement on "The Unity We Seek". This section attempts a further contribution to this discussion stating briefly, in terms of the intrinsic character of the eucharist, the goal the Churches are committed to reach (1). It then enumerates, arising out of the increasing consensus between the Churches concerning the eucharist, several theological perspectives which offer hope for advance (2).

1. Communion

Man is created in and for communion with God. In losing this his whole relationship with his fellow-men and with his natural environment is disturbed. In Jesus Christ God renews the communion in both dimensions.

The eucharist is the sacramental event in which this renewed communion is both celebrated and enacted, by the power of the Holy Spirit. Our sharing at the Lord's table thus inseparably involves communion both with God and with our fellow-men, in Jesus Christ. It is the eschatological sign of universal salvation.

The celebration of the Lord's supper will take on its full meaning and truth only if the Church which there receives God's gift is itself a single body. The eucharistic services in which our divisions are made manifest thus raise a question of our faithfulness to God's will. How can our disunity be congruous with a gift given that it might make us all one?

In the past this disunity in the eucharist was an exact and appropriate sign of the Church's decision to excommunicate. Today however the fact that we cannot communicate with one another appears rather as a breach of trust in the gift of communion. Between our Churches we already exchange tokens of reconciliation that are implicitly eucharistic (e.g. the kiss of peace, the saying together of the Lord's prayer). Here we must see a dynamic movement of renewal, the renewed experience of our basic and original unity.

This is why we have today become all the more clearly aware that the Church and the eucharist are signs and tokens of the same mystery of communion (the *koinonia* of the New Testament). Both comprise, in one organic whole, the same essential elements. Today these confront us as questions with which the Spirit is facing the Churches.

Communion is *eschatological;* it is the new day of the Kingdom which already comes amidst our days that are evil (Ephesians 5:16). It inspires *conversion* and conspires to *reconciliation*.

Communion is *kerygmatic;* its first coming was the advent of the Word (John 1:14) which realizes among us our basic communion of *faith,* the first and basic gift of the Kingdom.

Communion, for us who live in these last days, is *sacramental;* Christ gave his Church his communion expressed by the instruments by which the Holy Spirit spreads abroad throughout the world the purposes of God.

Communion is *ministerial;* among these signs are some which give order to the community (baptism-chrismation and ordination). The eucharist implies the sacrament of the royal priesthood as well as that of the apostolic ministry since it is the sacrament both of the whole Christ offered up and of Christ's handing on *(traditio)* communion to his Church. "This is my body *given* for you... this is the new *covenant* in my blood." Yet it is the Holy Spirit who shows forth, makes present and communicates the body and blood of Christ (anaphora of St. Basil). The ministry which witnesses to the incarnation of the Word and makes memorial of Easter is enlivened by the epiclesis, that sacramental Pentecost by which the Holy Spirit nurtures the baptized community — each member according to the gifts bestowed on him for the service of all, and each Church in communion with all others.[8]

Communion is *missionary;* by it is granted to each in his measure and to each Church in her calling the "grace to be a minister of Christ Jesus to the peoples in the priestly service of the gospel of God, so that the offering of the peoples may be acceptable, sanctified by the Holy Spirit" (Romans 15:16).

Communion is *cosmic;* in the body of his Church, Christ the new man acts as priest for all creation, offering up the entire creation as eucharist. The eucharist is thus concerned with the transfiguration and sanctification of all things.

2. Theological issues for further study and exploration

The document "The Eucharist in Ecumenical Thought" (Appendix III [not reprinted here]*) records a degree of agreement in eucharistic doctrine and faith among the Churches' theologians which for many would seem to open the way towards a common celebration of the sacrament.* At least for three long-standing controversies, on the epiclesis, on the real presence of Christ and on eucharistic sacrifice, there are promising signs of progress. This convergence in doctrine is matched by a no less remarkable convergence in the Churches' practices, particularly notable in several recent revisions of eucharistic liturgies, and which is of course rooted in a new appreciation of the Bible. The growing unity at this level strikes many who are quite unaware of theological developments and leads them to question continuing divisions. A major task is therefore already assigned to the Churches to pursue and enact this double convergence, in ever wider circles of their own membership quite as much as in discussions with other Churches.

Those engaged in the teaching processes of the Churches, from Sunday schools to the training of the clergy, will want to look over their materials and ensure that these teach no longer one partial view against another but the fulness of truth that is now available. Traditional practices too will often need revision: How can some continue to accept the fact that most of the faithful present at the eucharist do not receive the bread and wine? How can others continue to celebrate the eucharist infrequently?

---

[8] See *New Directions in Faith and Order*, The Holy Eucharist, pp.61ff.

In many traditions a new awareness of the eschatological nature of the eucharist is suggesting a new openness to each other and a new ordering of priorities. In the eucharist the Church not only remembers Christ's saving death under Pontius Pilate but looks forward to the final fulfilment of the Kingdom, and knows in each new time and place as it did in Jesus' lifetime a foretaste of that reality. The Last Supper is not the only part of the gospels that refers to the later eucharist. The feeding of the five thousand, the parables of the marriage feast and the accounts of Jesus' meals with his disciples in the resurrection are no less suggestive. Here is the source of the joy of the eucharist, that true festival which can be received in time but which time itself cannot give. This foretaste of the Kingdom calls mankind to reconciliation and new life. By its thrust of creative anticipation it overcomes human fears about the future and sets men free to act resolutely within constant change to build a truer human community.

At the same time it recalls that ultimate judgement is in the hands of God and that judgement will call in question all our lesser acts of judgement and division. In this century, as in the early centuries of the Church's history, the reality of martyrdom, of costly witness to Christ, has been given to Christians of many traditions in many places. In the joy of eucharistic anticipation men have found strength to witness to God's kingship despite all appearances and against all expectations. At such moments the barriers fall away.

What does this mean for the balance of our loyalties between that which comes to us from the past and that which we are called to envisage in the future? It is often suggested that the normal situation of Christians is that of their separated fellowships, while only the emergency of the exceptional can justify stepping beyond them. But what is the norm? Persecution, prison and danger of death would seem in New Testament perspective to be promised to the faithful apostle, while divisions such as those in Corinth were exceptional.

In many traditions there is also a renewed sense of the inner dynamism of the eucharist, of the sacrament as means of constituting the fellowship that is the Church. Where we together listen to the proclaimed Word and share the broken bread, there we become one body in Christ. The distinction has often been drawn between those Churches which see the eucharist as the sign of the unity once given and those who see it as a means of restoring that unity. Now it is increasingly known to be both; rather than holding out for their particular and polemic standpoint the faithful Christians are those who try to hold both in balance, taking from each what is true and appropriate for the particular moment on the ecumenical way. As each Church seeks regularly, faithfully and realistically to obey Christ's command in the eucharistic celebration, so the inherent dynamism of the sacrament, the reconciling and healing power of Christ, will be made manifest across our present divisions. Not least does this imply that in our confession of sin before communion we should expressly remember and repent our continued acquiescence in disunity and that in our intercessions we should expressly remember the leaders and members of other Churches than our own.

The prayer of the eucharist always has both a universal and a local character since in the sacrament we participate in the universal acts of Christ made present here and now. The relation between loyalty to the immediate needs of the local community gathered around the table and loyalty to the universal Church with its wider discipline and order has long been one of the most difficult questions of Christian history and needs much further study. But there is hope in recent stress on the biblical teaching that the one, universal eucharist is precisely that which is incarnate in a huge diversity of local celebrations and that each of these is not just a partial and transitory reality but indeed the one and whole Christ praying in his members. This is leading those Churches that have most stressed the visible unity and continuity in time and space to show a new awareness of the proper place of local diversity, and similarly those Churches which have stressed the inner quality of catholicity, the fulness, truth and autonomy of each local community to find a need of structures that assure wider cooperation and unity.

It is easy to say that a proper balance must be achieved. In practice it is extraordinarily difficult. Emphasis on the local, given the bewildering diversity of opinions and situations, can appear dangerously anarchic and liable to lead only to new schism. It may be more positive to study how each local celebration, precisely in and because of its peculiarity, can make a healing contribution to the wholeness of the one Church. On the other hand those who have emphasized a universal discipline are aware how rigid and repressive this can seem. For expressing the unity of the Church a universal discipline of eucharistic practice is neither necessary nor desirable. At a time when most forms of authority are suspect co-responsibility and participation are the order of the day. Such terms usefully suggest the context of diverse commitments within which some form of authority alone appears authentic. How in practice can wider leadership, whether of synods, of bishops or of popes, act less as the final juridical arbiter than as the reconciling enabler of local initiatives?

Divisions in communion have often centred around the question of the ministry. Here, while there is as yet no perfect agreement, there are new and most hopeful approaches towards it. In all Christian traditions the ordained ministry is understood as a service within the body of the faithful. It is a ministry given by God but not over or apart from the people. In the eucharist the whole people together celebrates and offers, in union with the ministry which presides in the action. The thanksgiving is that of a priestly people who participate in the sacrificial offering of Christ. This is the context in which the ministry must be seen as a sign of the action of Christ, the High Priest. The way seems open here to a new agreement on long disputed questions about sacrifice and ministry.

In terms of practice this would suggest that Churches who have insisted on the special status of the ministry should enquire to what extent their lay members are forced to be but passive spectators in a eucharistic action basically conditioned for them by the ministry. How can the ministry truly serve the celebration of the laity? All Churches can usefully ask themselves how much true service of Christ's people they can see in the ministry of other Churches and under what conditions they would be prepared to accept other Churches' ministers as the ministers of their own eucharistic worship.

Similarly in the differences over the Apostolic Succession in the ministry, new light can be found when the ministry is understood as existing in and for the life of the whole body of the faithful, and when the act of ordination is conceived as an act of the Holy Spirit in response to the prayer of the whole congregation. Within this total waiting upon God (epiclesis) there is in all confessions a place for the laying on of hands by those who have already received the ministerial office. Though a sign of continuity with the historical origins of revelation this handing on *(traditio)* of office must never be understood in a mechanical or purely historical sense. The tradition must always be vivified by the ever new action of the Spirit. At this point there is still some difference of understanding and divergence of practice among the Churches. But these differences exist within an area of agreement which should allow Churches which maintain and value historic continuity to recognize in other bodies at least a tradition of ministering and a continuity of invocation, and should allow those who lay less stress on the historic succession to recognize in bodies which preserve it an intention to act as the servants of the Word and the Spirit and thus to reconsider giving expression to the continuity of ministry in their own midst. The very desire to share in sacraments across the barriers which for centuries have kept Christians totally separated from one another witnesses to an implicit acknowledgement of some truth and reality in ministries which have formerly been regarded as null and void.

In terms of practice this would suggest that all Churches do well to examine the relation, in practice and discipline, between the discovery in certain persons of gifts of ministry given by the Spirit and the official recognition and commissioning of persons as life-long ministers of the Church. What openness to ministers outside their own direct fellowship does this suggest?

The eucharist is a celebration of God's reconciling work in the life of the world. While it is an action of the Church it is an action in discipleship to the God who sent his Son because he so loved the world. Moreover the rediscovery of the community-forming power of the eucharist has gone together with a new sense of the necessity of genuine fellowship of life within the local Christian community and of real concern for the life of the world. "The sharing of this bread is the symbol of the sharing of all bread, the unconditional character of this community the pledge of all society restored in Christ."[9] While we do not yet see clearly all the implications of this, practical steps which many are taking in response to this insight are raising new and potentially most important questions, affecting not least the unity and disunity of Christ's people.

For instance: In what ways does our eucharistic worship commit us to certain social (political, economic, etc.) actions, policies and attitudes comparable to the recognition that racial segregation at the Lord's table is a denial of Christ? Conversely, in what ways does the eucharist intrinsically free men from enslaving habits and ideologies?

Or again: In missionary obedience in the world all Christians are prepared to cooperate with Christians from other Churches. Yet how can we restrict the fellowship of worship to a circle narrower than that appropriate for mission? That question frequently arises among Christians, all of whom have been baptized. But at the same time the problem of the Church's borderlines is being raised in an even wider sense. For in missionary obedience Christians will frequently be sharing a common purpose with men of other traditions of religious faith or who believe themselves of none. How can their occasional demand to be admitted to the eucharistic fellowship of the believers be met in a pastoral way so that they are drawn into the fellowship with Christ instead of being estranged from it? Though the eucharist is clearly the worshipping act of the Christian community the questions they may raise about their presence and participation need to be faced.

---

[9] *Intercommunion Today*, London 1968, p.65.

III. Practice on the way

Now that virtually all Churches are at least aware of questions concerning the eucharist, what can be said from one to another about the various practices which are being followed? The first step is clearly to understand what we are talking about. The whole area of question has generally been referred to in the past as the question of "intercommunion", but that one word cannot cover the whole range and has become seriously ambiguous. It will be better to find terms which can exactly describe the different practices and their ecclesiological significance, among which the term "intercommunion" may find its precise and particular place. [10]

The first and most important of the terms proposed is *communion* (cf. previous section). It indicates the goal to be achieved by the ecumenical movement. While this term describes the fellowship willed by Christ the terms which follow refer to the anomalous situations of separation.

1. *Admission*

The term "admission" refers to those cases where a Church in celebrating the eucharist admits to the table members of other Churches. Such admission may be (a) *limited*, (b) *general* or (c) *reciprocal*.

a) Limited admission. This term can mean either (i) exceptional admission for pastoral reasons which is the ground of all exceptional cases in Orthodox and Roman Catholic practice, or (ii) limited admission in a wider sense, based on the awareness that every baptized Christian belongs fundamentally to the one communion of the Church and is directed towards his sanctification in the body of Christ.

The recommendations of the recent Church of England commission provide a clear example of the way in which provisions for limited admission themselves create pressure for a wider admission and at length for fully reciprocal admission. They recommend that individual baptized and communicant members of Churches not in full communion with the Church of England who desire to receive the sacrament and whose informed conscience allows it should be made welcome: *(a)* where particular pastoral conditions warrant it (being cut off from their own Church, when serious considerations of family or other personal relationships are involved, for the sick and in exceptional or emergency situations); *(b)* where the eucharist is regularly celebrated according to the rites of the Church of England in communities where Christians of differing traditions are regularly sharing common life and activity; *(c)* where local congregations or other groups of Christians are meeting together in sustained efforts or on special occasions to promote the unity, ministry or mission of the Church. [11]

Another example is provided by the Lutheran Churches which, though on different grounds than the Anglican Church, started from the practice of limited admission. In many Lutheran Churches this practice has been changed in the course of events. Today it varies from Church to Church. While the attitude of some Churches is still best described as limited admission, others practise general admission, some even reciprocal admission and intercelebration. The change of the earlier practice was usually caused by either special situations (diaspora, etc.) or it was adopted in view of

---

[10] See table of terms printed as Appendix II.
[11] Cf. also The Lambeth Conference, 1968; Resolutions and Reports, London 1968, pp.126ff.

Churches whose doctrine on the eucharist was particularly close to the Lutheran understanding of Christ's real presence in the sacrament. [12]

Questions. All Churches set certain conditions for the admission to communion of their own members. All also set conditions for the admission of others to their communion. What is the relation between these two (groups of) conditions; are they different, and if so, why? This in turn raises the wider question of preparation for communion in general: How seriously do we now take this? What kind of spiritual discipline is appropriate?

Why should admission of members from other Churches ever be limited to exceptional and emergency situations? It is hard enough to define these, but as soon as there are some definitions mutually understood, then decisions about admission can no longer be based on purely individual and fleeting decisions by celebrating ministers and the requesting laity. They will be based on a more or less explicit agreement between the authorities of the Churches — and what does the fact of such agreement suggest for the relations between them?

Some Churches have traditionally laid their chief stress on the fellowship already given and are thus reluctant to welcome others. Yet as this is God's gift and not in man's control, must they not expect in a *de facto* divided Christianity to meet anomalous cases which transcend any regulations? In what sorts of cases have they in fact been prepared to admit outsiders to communion? What are the theological judgements underlying particular pastoral evaluations? If the criterion is purely pastoral, what other situations might be envisaged in which admission might be allowed on the basis of that criterion? If something is possible once, why not always? Can the Church by economy create a sacramental reality *ex nihilo?* If it is not *ex nihilo,* then what is it?

Some Churches have traditionally laid their chief stress on the need for common belief. How can they now maintain and express this at a time when all Churches find among their own members a considerable diversity of views and teaching, a diversity which to many an outsider excluded for lack of the particular belief seems to include views indistinguishable from his own?

Some Churches are prepared to admit others to their communion but much less to permit their own members to share communion with others. This one-sidedness is only comprehensible as a transition stage, marking a step beyond a simple denial of the others' faith but needing to be completed by the further step of full acceptance and communion. If it becomes a permanent policy it is all too liable to be misunderstood — and in some cases misused — as an attempt to absorb the other Church or to win a false prestige over her. How can the provisional character of such a policy be built in to the practice?

Should Churches faced by others with a policy of one-sided admission readily accept to share on those terms? Despite all the psychological barriers they should, since any anticipation of the goal of communion will lead to greater understanding and acceptance.

b) General admission. This is the regular practice of a great number of Protestant Churches. There are, however, different forms. On the one hand, there is the practice

---

[12] Cf. *Church in Fellowship,* Lutheran Inter Church Agreements and Practices, ed. V.Vajta (Minneapolis: Augsburg 1963), p. 259.

of a number of Protestant Churches by which they invite to the Holy Communion baptized and communicant members of other Churches. On the other hand, there is the practice of a number of other Protestant Churches (and of groups within the former) by which the invitation is given to "all who love the Lord Jesus". There are, moreover, times when the growth of ecumenical relationships leads the clergy to remind members of other Churches of the policies of their own communities and thus out of loyalty restrain their general invitation.

Questions. Does a policy of general admission take sufficiently seriously the Christian's decision to belong to one of the separate Churches rather than another? Can it also become a form of confessional triumphalism? If it too is seen as a transition stage on the way to communion, what signs or results of the growing unity it enables should the other Churches expect to be able to see?

Churches practising general admission might well ask: Are there any Christians they would find particularly hard to accept at their table? If so, why particularly they?

Churches practising a general invitation to all who love the Lord Jesus might well ask: What does this mean for the practice of baptism? Does the eucharist itself generate in the non-baptized the appropriate faith and commitment? If so, what signs or results of this are to be expected?

c) Reciprocal admission. This term may be used for two types of situation: (i) the establishment of intercommunion by agreement between two Churches, usually in geographically different regions, and without any question of organic union being raised; (ii) when two Churches are committed to work for organic union, sometimes within a specified period, and enter into this relationship on the ground that the causes of division between them have been, in principle, removed.

An illustration of the former is to be found in the agreement between the Church of Scotland (Presbyterian) and the Church of Sweden (Evangelical-Lutheran) who are prepared to admit each other's members without hesitation and without the question of each other's ministry having been raised. The latter can be seen in the agreement among the Churches negotiating for union in Ceylon that after a service of covenanting for union, by which each Church would commit itself irrevocably to inaugurating the union within a specified period, reciprocal admission would be practised in certain circumstances that bring together members of the different Churches.

Questions. To (i): Is it not an abnormal and anomalous situation that two churches in the same area should practise reciprocal admission without seeking organic unity? What are the questions of Faith and Order that should be settled between two Churches in different areas before entering upon an agreement for reciprocal admission? How can this be justified? To (ii): Where, however, reciprocal admission is seen as a transition stage on the way to communion how can the Churches ensure that it does actively lead along that way and not merely remove the factor of psychological discomfort from separation?

2. *Common celebration*

By this term we designate a form of concelebration by ministers of different confessions on behalf of occasional gatherings of their people, each of the participants being aware of his bringing to the celebration whatever he has received of faith and of ministry, together with his repentance for disunity, his commitment to the overcoming of this and his hope in the unity and fulness that is Christ's will. This kind of celebration is a natural accompaniment of the reciprocal admission just discussed.

One group of Roman Catholics and Protestant theologians has drawn up a set of conditions for it which may be mentioned here:

a) it should involve only groups which are already in existence and which have sought the prior agreement of the Churches.

b) all the participants, clergy and laity, should have had some considerable ecumenical experience and thus be theologically and spiritually prepared.

c) the celebration should not be seen as in any way habitual but take place in the context of a conference or meeting with a precise aim, in study or in action, and including serious doctrinal teaching.

d) there should be no confusion or doubt left about the parts played by the celebrating clergy. Each should perform the actions required for the authenticity of the sacrament in his own Church. There should be no hiding or calling in question the differences in understanding of the ministry that still exist.

e) care should be taken to see that the liturgy used respects the various rules of the Churches, so that all participants may be able to live the sacramental action in full communion with their own Churches and so that they all can receive everything that they receive in their separate communions.

f) the celebration should make vividly clear the penitential character of the action (i.e. its deep relationship with the repentance for which communion in the blood shed for the remission of sins cannot but call) and be performed in close connection with prayer for unity, that prayer not yet fully realized but whose answer is expected with suffering and hope from the grace of the Lord.

Questions. What is the true need and basis for a common celebration as opposed to celebration by a commonly agreed minister? Does it falsely accentuate the part of the clergy vis-à-vis the part of the laity? How can it be prevented from becoming "a cloaking of scruples about the status of the ministries involved"?[13] Is such a form of joint celebration between yet separated Churches at all analogous to the exchange of hospitality practised in the early Church?

3. *Intercelebration*

This term is suggested for those cases where two or more separated Churches are prepared reciprocally to allow their ministers to preside at their eucharistic worship.

Questions. In what respects is this less than a state of communion? How, if it be non-theological factors which hinder unity, can such intercelebration actively contribute to their yielding?

Conclusion

The Uppsala Assembly has suggested that the members of the World Council of Churches should work for the time when a genuinely universal Council may once more speak for all Christians.[14] In our small share in the work of the World Council of Churches we too have been led to see that the natural outcome of the involvement of almost all sectors of Christendom in the modern ecumenical movement, the recent

---

[13] *Intercommunion Today*, para. 200.
[14] *Uppsala Speaks*, p.17. Section I, para. 19.

lifting of certain long-standing anathemata and the growing extent of theological agreement must be the restoration of communion in a single ecclesial fellowship. We cannot be satisfied with less if we are to move along the ecumenical way at the speed Christ demands and are effectively to set ourselves to following up his other and no less urgent work in our contemporary world.

Appendix I: Eucharistic worship in ecumenical contexts

The question which this study paper has considered arises, as has been mentioned, not only within the regular, ordered life of the various Churches in their relationships, but also within the life of the ecumenical movement itself, in a narrow sense, i.e. at times and in communities where Christians of two or more separated Churches come together not in the context of any particular Church but in a specifically ecumenical setting. This poses with particular intensity the question of the appropriate practice and discipline, and for over fifty years ecumenical bodies have been struggling with it.

The present recommendations of the World Council of Churches on this question are those of the Fourth World Conference on Faith and Order, approved by the Central Committee at Rochester in 1963, and those of the first report of the Joint Working Group of the Roman Catholic Church and the World Council of Churches in 1966. These are largely the same. With one or two general provisos about e.g. the possibility for participants to celebrate the sacrament outside conference programmes and the need to consider carefully the building to be used, these rule that no conference can itself take responsibility for this matter, only the Churches, and that there should in general be two services of communion within the programme of the conference, as well as a common service of preparation: one in which a Church or a group of Churches can invite members of other Churches to participate and partake, and one according to the liturgy of a Church which cannot conscientiously offer an invitation to members of all other Churches to partake of the elements.

These recommendations, as drawn up in 1963, referred specifically to meetings of the WCC Assembly, of the Central Committee and other such ecumenical gatherings, i.e. to world conferences to which most of the Churches of Christendom send delegates and which consider publicly a wide range of issues which face the Churches. These recommendations are still an appropriate policy for such meetings. But not all ecumenical meetings are of that type. They occur in every conceivable shape and form. To mention only three other types, they include: (a) smaller occasional conferences, e.g. consultations of a local or national council of Churches, to which representatives are sent by several Churches but which may or may not involve a wide spectrum of Christians, which may meet in private and consider quite limited aspects of Christian obedience; (b) fellowship of Christians, e.g. the YMCA, a Student Christian Movement, the staff of an ecumenical body, who come from different background and traditions but not explicitly as representatives of their Churches, and who pursue together over a longer span of time and with some order in their community a purpose which they hold to be of Christ; (c) gatherings of Christians, e.g. on the march to Selma, who come from different Churches and meet at a particular place and time, often in the context of some worldly situation or activity. They may never meet again in this way and yet find it appropriate to give eucharistic expression to their common worship.

In face of this variety one tendency has been simply to avoid raising the question of the eucharist. Yet in the words of the Joint Working Group "It should not become the rule that the problem of the eucharist is bypassed at ecumenical meetings; and when eucharistic services are held one should not be content with solutions which make visible only one aspect of the problem" *(Ecumenical Review,* 1966, 2, p.254). We suggest therefore that the eucharist ought to be more frequently incorporated, in one way or another, into the life and programme of ecumenical conferences and communities. Yet in face of the variety of situations it would be completely illusory to suggest that there be one common policy and practice followed in them all. Rather we suggest that the attention of those responsible be directed not in the first instance to what is actually done or not done in eucharistic worship but to the way in which this should be approached and prepared.

We are clear that there can be no full and final solution to this question until our Churches are fully united. It is up to the Churches to walk along the way to unity. On that way, it is essential that Christians be able both to hold on to the inevitable tensions and anomalies of the existing situation of division and to take those steps towards unity to which Jesus Christ is calling us and which he makes available.

Therefore we envisage not rules but a pastoral approach, in which the decision reached in any particular situation will be based upon a pastoral assessment, by the planners of the meeting and the appropriate authorities in the Churches, of the readiness and maturity in Christ of the particular people involved in that situation. Whatever the practice adopted it will be seen as belonging to that situation and no other, as a partial and temporary experiment.

The primary consideration in this is that each particular group, within their Christian obedience, be able to worship with integrity. That has immediate connotations:

i)   that the sacrament be not used as an educational device, to instruct some people how others worship. Such a device, if appropriate, belongs at another point in the meeting;

ii) that the worship be deliberately planned in true relationship with the rest of the meeting and not as a pious extra;

iii) that considerable personal, theological and church-diplomatic sensitivity be brought to the planning and preparation of worship in all its aspects;

iv) that the practice contribute to the upbuilding of the total community in Christ and not to its further division, i.e. to the total ecumenical movement of Christ's people;

v)   that this (these) act(s) of worship be deliberately envisaged within the context, not only of the meeting but of the more permanent, "normal" Christian life of those involved;

vi) that this act of worship be deliberately considered in relation to the continuing yet ever new purposes and action of the risen Lord.

Ecumenical committees and other leaders should therefore, we suggest, seek:

a)   with free and sensitive imagination to lay hold of the creative possibilities, in terms of worship as of everything else, in each new meeting (conference, committee, study tour, youth group, etc.). Defensively to do what was done last time or timidly to adopt a practice known to be relatively convenient and undemanding is to fall short of our calling;

b) to be aware that worship is as important a feature as any of the meeting ahead, and therefore to make available as much manpower and money for its preparation as they do for any other;

c) in each case to inform participants in the meeting as fully as is possible about the plans and the reasons for them so that as much confusion and uncertainty as possible is overcome before the act(s) of worship take place. This may include pointing out to participants the implications for their own Churches of the commitment(s) implicit in the worship planned and advising them to consult with the appropriate authorities of their own Churches, both before and after the meeting itself;

d) similarly themselves to consult the Church authorities likely to be most closely involved in the meeting (e.g. of the local Churches in the place of the meeting, the Church(es) from which the celebrating minister(s) comes, the Church(es) who are sponsoring or financing the meeting, etc.).

Appendix II: Terminology: a reference table

Proposed in this Report	Third World Conference on Faith and Order Lund 1952 (pp.51-52)	Lambeth Conference 1968 (Report pp.125-126)
Communion	Full Communion	Full Communion
Limited Admission	Limited Open Communion	Controlled Admission to Communion
General Admission	Open Communion	Open Communion and Free Communion
Reciprocal Admission (= intercommunion)	Mutual Open Communion Intercommunion	Reciprocal Intercommunion
Intercelebration	Intercelebration and Intercommunion	
Common celebration	(Con-celebration)	(Joint celebration)

DOCUMENT III.8
BAPTISM, CONFIRMATION AND EUCHARIST (1971)

Introduction

Baptism and eucharist have always been topics of theological discussion in the ecumenical movement. The present document reports on a study which was initiated in 1967. The Faith and Order Commission had already dealt with the theme of baptism in the period between the Third World Conference on Faith and Order in Lund (1952) and the Fourth in Montreal (1963). The results of that discussion were presented in the report *One Lord, One Baptism*[1] and favourably received by the Fourth World Conference in Montreal.[2] A few years later the Faith and Order Commission decided that the subject should be studied afresh. The report *One Lord, One Baptism* had been concerned primarily with establishing a common understanding of baptism without as yet drawing concrete conclusions for the churches' liturgy and practice. The new study on "Baptism, Confirmation and the Eucharist" was to include these aspects and to explore whether agreement could be reached on them.

Various meetings were held. A first consultation was organized in spring 1968. It produced a brief analysis of the theme[3] which was subsequently discussed and commented on by a large number of regional groups. A second international consultation was held two years later (September 1970 in Revnice, Czechoslovakia) to discuss some problems in more detail. The findings of the whole study were summarized, reconsidered and revised by a working group which met in Geneva in December 1970.

The Churches are agreed that the central meaning of baptism is participation in Christ. Through his baptism in the Jordan Jesus accepted solidarity with sinners; he continued this solidarity as he followed the path of the Suffering Servant through passion, death and resurrection. The Spirit which came upon Jesus when he was baptized comes also on the Church and unites Christ's people with him in death and resurrection, in and through the baptismal action. Baptism is a gift of God's redeeming love to the Church. Those who receive baptism are baptized by the one Spirit into one body; baptism is the sign and seal of their discipleship in obedience to the Lord.[4]

Since there is wide agreement on the meaning of baptism one might expect that the Churches would be able to recognize one another's baptism without restrictions. This is, however, not the case. Baptism has certainly been seen as a unifying bond. But the Churches have not yet succeeded in achieving full mutual recognition. A number of issues have remained unsolved, and as the Churches face the contemporary situation new ones have emerged which require attention. Can the old controversy on believers' and infant baptism be overcome? What is the relation between baptism and chrismation or confirmation? Does one not have to take into account all the stages of Christian initiation if the mutual recognition is to be fully real? Does mutual recognition of

---

[1] *One Lord, One Baptism*, SCM Press, London 1960.

[2] *The Fourth World Conference on Faith and Order*. The Report from Montreal 1963, edited by P.C. Rodger and L. Vischer, Association Press, New York 1964.

[3] See *Study Encounter*, IV/4, 1968, pp.194ff.

[4] All these phrases occur in reports of earlier Faith and Order Conferences. A fuller summary of statements agreed upon at Faith and Order Conferences is attached to this paper (Appendix I [not reprinted here]).

baptism not call for the mutual recognition of the eucharist? Above all, can the Churches maintain their inherited practices without modification? For instance, can they any longer defend, in a secularized society, the practice of indiscriminate baptism?

The present paper makes an attempt to carry the discussion further in the direction of answering these questions. It starts from the assumption that the process of Christian initiation must be looked at as a whole. Baptism, confirmation and the eucharist are inseparable. The paper gives first a brief review of present baptismal practices in the Churches (1). After a few methodological considerations (II) it examines the inter-dependence of ecclesiology and baptismal practice (III) and then lists a number of ethical implications (IV) which are of particular importance for any reform of baptism and confirmation. The following section deals with liturgical aspects (V) and the final chapter deals with the question of mutual recognition of baptism as it presents itself in the life of the Churches today (VI).

I. The Present Practice of the Churches

A brief survey of the practice of the different Churches shows at once the variation in the forms of initiation into the Body of Christ. It is impossible to mention all the differences here; only the most important are given. Clearly too, each tradition leaves certain questions unanswered and must therefore submit to questioning in the light of the practice of the other traditions.

1. In the Eastern tradition baptism and confirmation (chrismation) are administered in immediate succession even when the recipient is an infant. The initiation is then complete. The person baptized is at once admitted to the eucharist without further ceremony. Here the question must be asked whether children are given sufficient opportunity of making for themselves the confession of faith made on their behalf at baptism.

2. In the Western tradition, baptism and the laying on of hands (confirmation) were separated at quite an early date. Whereas baptism could be performed by the priest, the laying on of hands was reserved to the bishop. This meant that usually some time elapsed between baptism and confirmation. Where the person baptized was an infant, the time interval could be of some years. Confirmation thus gradually became independent of baptism although the close connection between the two was never completely forgotten. Confirmation came to mean strengthening by the gift of the Holy Spirit. Admission to eucharistic fellowship could take place either before or after confirmation. All Western Churches face the problem of refusing to admit children to the eucharist even though they have been baptized.

The Western practice of initiation is to be found particularly in the Roman Catholic Church. Recently this Church has been more willing to admit confirmation by a priest in certain special cases, and to emphasize, especially in the case of adults, the unity of the process of initiation.

Western practice prompts the question whether the division of initiation into two related yet distinct sacramental acts does not prejudice the unique once-for-all character of baptism. The Churches of the Reformation sought to reassert the sufficiency of baptism. Since they found no basis in Scripture for confirmation as a sacramental act, it was abandoned. Other reasons, however, led the Churches of the Reformation to adopt an act similar to the sacramental act of confirmation. Baptized children are not admitted to the eucharist until they are able to make for themselves the profession of faith made for them at baptism. Confirmation furnishes the occasion for this act: a service of worship is held in which baptism is recalled and the persons previously baptized make a public profession of faith and are consecrated for their service. From then on they are admitted to the eucharist. This tradition shares the difficulty common to all the Western traditions. But the practice of this kind of confirmation presents a special problem. Confirmation normally takes place when children reach a given age. This frequently makes confirmation into a social formality in practice. Many Protestant Churches have consequently begun to change their practice in this matter, some even going so far as to drop insistence on confirmation as an essential condition for admission to the eucharist.

In Anglicanism the practice of episcopal confirmation was retained. It has always involved both the personal ratification by the candidate of the promises made on his behalf at baptism, and the laying on of hands with prayer for his strengthening by the gift of the Holy Spirit. It is regarded as the way of entrance into communicant status.

The Churches of the Baptist tradition administer baptism only to those who make profession of faith. They have no rite of chrismation or confirmation, but in some Churches there is a laying on of hands upon those who have been baptized. In all cases those who have been baptized are admitted at once to the eucharist. Often the children of baptized parents are dedicated at a special service of worship.

In the 17th century the Society of Friends so stressed the inward life that they were led to reject the outward sacramental signs of both baptism and eucharist. Emphasis on the inward spiritual event has led other Churches to attach no real importance to the external sign of baptism. What really matters is that the Gospel is heard, conversion takes place and a new life begins. Churches born from 18th and 19th century revival movements, therefore, show relatively little interest in the external sign of baptism (e.g. Salvation Army).[5] The question is how rejection of the outward signs can be consistent with the New Testament witness.

3. In almost all Churches baptism is normally performed by the *ordained minister*. On the other hand, almost all the Churches agree that baptism does not have to be administered exclusively by an ordained minister. Thus in certain circumstances it may be performed by lay people.[6] In the episcopal Churches, however, confirmation may only be administered by the bishop or by an ordained minister nominated by him. But since confirmation is usually performed in the presence of the worshipping congregation, even in other Churches it is *de facto* the ordained minister who administers confirmation.

Historical factors have played a large part in determining the role of ordained ministers in baptism and confirmation. For instance, the fact that lay people administer

---

[5] Not all Churches which do not practise water baptism give this as their reason. In certain cases the decision has been determined by historical factors (Kimbanguist Churches, for example).

[6] There are exceptions to this rule. The older Reformed tradition, which is tending to disappear, constitutes one of them. The Reformed attitude has two primary reasons; first that the ministry of the sacraments is closely connected with the ministry of the word in the Reformed tradition; and second that baptism is understood primarily as incorporation into the Body of Christ rather than in terms of individual salvation. Most Churches of the Reformation do not regard water baptism as a condition for salvation, either of infants or adults. Hence the need for lay-administered baptism in cases where death seems imminent is lessened.

baptism is partly explained by the high infant mortality rate of earlier centuries; it was felt essential to administer baptism immediately after birth; at first the lay people involved were usually the midwives.

4. The different practices of the Churches cannot be described without at the same time drawing attention to the fact that many Churches today are seriously concerned about their practice and liturgy of baptism and confirmation. In recent years, a number of Churches including in particular the Roman Catholic Church have introduced far-reaching reforms and revised their liturgical texts. Other Churches are still engaged in such revision and it is probable that this process will continue in the years ahead. Union negotiations provided occasions to review baptismal practices and to relate different approaches to one another. The need for reforms arises, however, also in other contexts. In traditionally Christian countries the question is increasingly being asked: Can the inherited practice continue unchanged? Does the present practice take baptism seriously enough, judged by the light of the New Testament witness? Has not baptism often become more a badge of membership in Christian society than a sign of God's gracious gift in Christ and of the call to serve him? At a time when the Church's relationship to society is clearly undergoing considerable changes, it is not surprising that the question of the nature of baptism should arise simultaneously with fresh urgency in so many Churches. Many Churches have been led to question the indiscriminate baptism of infants and, quite independently of church union negotiations, the view that believers' baptism and infant baptism should be practised side by side in the same Church has been gaining ground.

II. Questions of Approach

How are the Churches to reach agreement in this situation? How are they to advance beyond their differences in doctrine and practice to a common mind? The following methodological reflections may be important for determining the right approach.

1. Clearly the New Testament assumes the practice of baptism though it does not anywhere speak of it systematically nor does it provide us with incontestable historical evidence as to its origin and practice. What is said about baptism occurs in many different contexts and throws light therefore only on certain aspects of baptism in widely varied first century settings. Many questions we should like to have answered today receive no direct answer from the witness of the New Testament. No Church can therefore base its practice on the New Testament evidence alone; tradition and history play a significant role in shaping the Churches' practice and provide the way in which the New Testament is interpreted and understood. The recognition of this fact is important. Churches must exercise caution in their judgements of each other's practice and expose their own practice to the critical questions of others: How far is this practice really governed by the revelation in Christ? The recognition of this fact is also important since it makes it clear that the Church today, like the Church in earlier times, can exercise a certain freedom in determining its practice.

2. The variety of practice in the Ancient Church is also evident. For example, in the Syrian Church chrismation seems to have preceded baptism by water. This variety is significant. Clearly the evidence of the New Testament and of the early centuries does not require a uniform baptismal practice throughout the whole Church. One and the same baptism may be administered in different ways within certain limits in one

and the same Church. This point is important not only for the ecumenical movement but also for new expressions appropriate to baptism in Churches living in other cultural settings (e.g. Africa).

3. Historical events and controversies have greatly influenced the practice of the various Churches. For instance, the christianisation of the Roman Empire and the disappearance of the catechumenate and adult baptism had a profound effect on East and West alike. The Donatist controversy deeply affected the Western tradition. The 16th century controversies between the Reformers and the Anabaptists have influenced and continue to influence the practice of Protestant Churches. The missionary experience outside Europe, which has involved multitudes of adults, has given new insights into the meaning of baptism. It is important to bear such historical factors in mind if we are to arrive at a mature judgement. This is especially important because each Christian has personally undergone one particular form of initiation and instruction and his spiritual life has been influenced by this particular form. He will therefore be inclined to judge all baptismal practices from this standpoint.

4. The history of baptism makes it clear that the rite existed in a developed form from the very earliest times. Particular aspects of baptism had been expressed and stressed by particular actions and gestures. Such adaptations are not merely still possible in principle today, but are actually required. Baptism needs translation and explanation not merely in words but also at the level of signs.

III. Ecclesiology and the Reform of Baptismal and Confirmation Practice

Obviously, there is a close connection between christology, ecclesiology and the understanding and the practice of baptism. Since baptism is the sign of incorporation into the Body of Christ which is the Church, any shift in the understanding of the nature of the Church almost inevitably affects the approach to baptism. In the ecclesiological debate of recent years there is a noticeable convergence on a number of new emphases. It may be useful to list some of them which are particularly relevant for a fresh approach to baptism.

1. *The Church as a Eucharistic Community.* In many Churches there has been a rediscovery of the meaning and the practice of the eucharist. Faith in Christ can be alive only within the fellowship of the Church. Faith requires corporate life. The eucharist is the visible sign giving expression to this communion of Christians with Christ and with one another. This emphasis on the communal aspect of Christian life also has consequences for the understanding of baptism. Baptism is the sign and seal of salvation but it is equally incorporation into the messianic people. It leads into the eucharistic community. This dimension has often been neglected in baptismal and confirmation practice.

2. *The Church as a Genuine Fellowship in the Holy Spirit.* The Church is to be a genuine fellowship in the Spirit. Such fellowship can exist only on the basis of the spontaneous adherence of its members. It cannot be secured by external structures and rules which have to be taken for granted and accepted without too many questions. The Church must be a charismatic fellowship leaving room for new and unexpected charismata. There is an increasing emphasis in contemporary ecclesiological discussions on the work of the Holy Spirit who both gives gifts to each one and at the same time unites all into one, thus reconciling freedom and fellowship. The development of Pentecostal movements reminds the historic Churches how much they have neglected

the life in the Spirit. This has consequences for baptism and confirmation. Baptism is the anointing with the Spirit. Through the Messiah, the Anointed One, the baptized participates in the royal and priestly dignity for which man was created by God. How far does this understanding inform the present practice of baptism and confirmation? How far is it designed to facilitate and promote genuine spontaneous fellowship? Today, baptism and confirmation are felt by many to be no more than external rites which are imposed on people but not really appropriated by them. Should the presence and the demands of Christ not be given fuller expression? Questions like these provide a strong impetus for the reform of both baptism and confirmation.

3. *The Church as a Missionary Fellowship.* The Church is the people which is called to declare the wonderful deeds of Him who called it out of darkness into His marvellous light. It praises its Lord in adoration and gratitude and stands before Him in intercession for the whole world. It can praise Him only if it is a real sign to men of God's presence and love. In each generation this missionary task has to be perceived afresh and it is quite clear today that the Churches are in a new situation. Societies once considered "Christian" can no longer be considered so. Whatever may have been the advantages or disadvantages of the "Christian" society of previous generations, today the Churches have to learn again to be a minority missionary fellowship. More than ever before, such a fellowship calls for Christians who are aware of their fellowship with Christ and recognize the commission this implies. Does this not also mean a shift in the understanding and practice of baptism? Does it not call for a greater emphasis on the note of commission? It is significant that in the Churches which especially associate confirmation with the gift of the Spirit this rite is being given an increasingly missionary perspective.

4. *The Church as a Universal Fellowship.* By its very nature the Church is a fellowship which is intended to include all men. As such it transcends all national, racial, class and other barriers. Almost no ecclesiology has neglected to express this truth, but the course of history has created a new situation. The Church must demonstrate its essential catholicity in a new way. It needs to be freed from the restrictions placed on its catholicity. The principle of catholicity needs to become a reality which is lived and experienced. Baptismal practice must make it clear that Christians, while belonging to a local fellowship, are at the same time members of a fellowship which is universal.

5. *The Church as an Open Fellowship.* For various reasons, ecclesiological discussion today is concerned with the problem of the Church's boundaries. For one thing, the problem arises in connection with the ecumenical movement. Even more urgently it arises in connection with the relationship between Church and world. How can the Church at one and the same time preserve its identity and also be a sign to men of Christ's presence? The Church should not cut itself off from the world. It must identify with the world in ministering to the world's needs but not with the world's estrangement and alienation from God. At present, however, is not its identity too often determined by identification with certain sociological entities, a nation, a particular section of the people, etc.? Are not the present boundaries between Church and world therefore unreal and inadequate? It is not that there will no longer be any boundaries. The problem is rather how to express the real identity of the Church in a convincing way. This raises important questions about baptism and confirmation. The sign of baptism establishes and confirms a boundary. Baptized persons are distin-

guished from non-baptized persons. But is this really the distinguishing line of the Gospel? Many feel that baptism creates an identification with a particular sociological community and for this reason hides rather than expresses its real meaning. How can baptism place the boundary in the right place?

Some even go as far as to ask whether an external sign is not bound to be unreal. A sign which once meant something in a particular situation does not necessarily continue to be meaningful in all situations. It requires at least translation or perhaps transformation. Some even advocate that it should be abandoned altogether. There are not only certain historical groups (e.g. Society of Friends, Salvation Army) which reject the outward sign but there are some in the present generation who, for different reasons, find it difficult to recognize that the sign of baptism is really required. Does it not provide the basis for a dangerous institutionalisation? Are there any decisive reasons why it should be retained under all circumstances? This report assumes that Christ's presence and the promise of freedom and resurrection are expressed and conveyed by the external sign. God became man in Christ. God's revelation took place in history in a particular yet universally relevant event. The outward sign reflects this particularly, and the Church would betray the peculiar character of God's action in Christ if it were to renounce the external sign of baptism. In addition, it is evident that baptism was generally practised from the very beginning. Obviously, the Church regarded itself as bound by the Lord's command to baptize in his name. Christians therefore start simply from baptism as a given sign in the expectation that the promise which goes with it will be fulfilled. The question of the relationship between the external sign and the actual experience, however, remains one which needs to be constantly raised.

IV. Baptismal Life

Baptism has always been understood as the entrance upon a new life. This means that one has died to a previous life and been raised to life with Christ. It means too that he has received the Spirit and been made a sharer in the mystery of Pentecost. This has happened once-and-for-all, but since sin persists, this death and resurrection with Christ is in constant need of renewal. Life under the Lordship of Christ calls us again and again for new acts of repentance and obedience. Life created by baptism can best be described as living in communion with Christ in anticipation of the coming of God's kingdom. The reform of baptism and confirmation requires in the first place a spiritual renewal. It cannot be achieved simply by changing the order or the liturgy. Baptismal life needs to be renewed. In this respect, the following emphases are of particular importance today:

1. When a person is baptized, his whole life is placed under the sign of God's invitation and gift. All that he is now and will be and do in the future is placed at the service of Christ. The future, however, is less predictable today than ever. An awareness that the conditions in which we live are subject to constant change is a feature of our times. Problems need to be faced which could not have been anticipated even a short while before. Ideas, assumptions and aims which even a short while ago seemed assured are being called in question. Faith has to prove itself in constantly changing situations. The commitment which baptism implies cannot, therefore, be defined once and for all by specific ethical claims. The Christian has been given an identity which in communion with Christ he needs to rediscover again and again.

Baptism is to be seen, rather, as the beginning — *initium* — of a new way to be travelled with Christ.

2. When a person is baptized, he becomes a member of the Body of Christ. In other words, he is accepted into a fellowship of baptized persons. Baptism normally takes place in the presence of the local congregation which receives the newly baptized and accepts a certain responsibility for him. Baptism, however, is at the same time incorporation into the universal Church. The baptized person is not only a member of the local congregation which has received him, but at the same time of the universal fellowship which transcends all boundaries and barriers and is characterized by a wide variety. This latter aspect needs to be given particular stress today because it must be realized that the life of the baptized person will be lived in many different contexts and constantly new forms of Christian fellowship. Baptism must direct him towards the whole people of God.

3. When today a person is baptized, he normally becomes a member of a particular Church belonging to a particular confessional tradition. Generally speaking, there is no other way for him to become a member either of a particular fellowship or of the universal fellowship. But the Churches today live in hope of the ending of their divisions. They live today between division and unity. In fact, baptism is one of the grounds for this hope. Baptism may not, therefore, be administered in a way which implies that confessional divisions will continue to the end of time. On the contrary, baptism must be the occasion of giving expression to the hope and the expectation that unity can be achieved.

V. Liturgical Aspects

Baptism should be a congregational act, included in worship, in which God's invitation and gift in Christ are proclaimed and accepted. When the candidate has confessed his faith, he is baptized with water in the name of the Father, the Son and the Holy Spirit.

Adult baptism has to be regarded as the primary form of baptism. The liturgy for infant baptism has therefore been an adaptation of that primary form. It includes the same elements even if in a modified form. The two liturgies should not differ fundamentally. Otherwise they give the impression that adult and infant baptism are two different baptisms.

The liturgy of baptism should provide for the following elements though they need not appear in the order given here:

1. An acknowledgement of God's initiative in salvation, of His continuing faithfulness, and of our total dependence upon His grace.
2. An explanation of the meaning of baptism as it appears from Scripture (reference to participation in the dying and rising of Christ, to the new birth of water and of the Spirit, to the incorporation into his Body, to the forgiveness of sins in and through Christ...).
3. An invocation of the Holy Spirit.
4. A renunciation of evil (possibly accompanied by exorcism).
5. A profession of faith in Christ and the affirmation of allegiance to God: Father, Son and Holy Spirit.
6. A declaration that the person baptized has become a child of God, and witness to the Gospel.

Through baptism the gift of the Spirit is imparted to the baptized. Therefore, it seems appropriate that the baptism in water should be followed by the laying on of hands or a chrismation. For some Churches the strengthening by the gift of the Spirit is the central meaning of confirmation which is conceived of as a separate act, usually not performed at the same time as baptism by water. When confirmation is separated from baptism by an interval of time, should not the imparting of the Spirit be expressed also in the liturgy of baptism itself in order to avoid the impression that the only meaning of baptism is the remission of sins? This is even more important in traditions where confirmation has simply the meaning of recalling baptism and providing the opportunity of making an act of personal commitment. The liturgical action should always enable the candidate and the congregation to participate fully in it. Frequent opportunities should be provided for Christians to recall the meaning of their baptism. It might be helpful to celebrate baptism at Easter or Pentecost, thereby stressing the connection between baptism and Christ's death and resurrection or the outpouring of the Holy Spirit. Other occasions, such as confirmations and eucharists, can be appropriate for administering baptism. In the early centuries baptism was frequently performed by immersion. A recovery of this early form by those who have abandoned it would enhance the symbolism of the liturgy.

Baptismal practice and liturgies should avoid the impression that one can be baptized only as an infant or only as an adult. Older children too may be brought for baptism, in which case the confession of faith should be made both by the parents and the child. [7]

Where baptism is deferred until adulthood, children of Christian parents may be brought for a service of dedication. Of course, this is not a substitute for baptism but an act in preparation of it. It might then be appropriate for the children to be enrolled as catechumens with a view to baptism.

VI. The Unity of Baptismal Initiation

Both the New Testament and the Creeds speak of "one baptism". Baptism is meant to be a sign which in Christ unites people into one fellowship with each other. It is a sign of unity.

Is it really recognized as such? It is often stated that all Churches recognize baptism as God's gift and invitation no matter which Church has administered it. Baptism is therefore regarded by many as the clearest expression of unity which already exists or rather still exists between the Churches. But is this assumption really true? Do all Churches really recognize all other Churches' baptisms?

It can be said that all Churches are convinced that the "one baptism" referred to in the Creeds is a unique and non-repeatable act. [8] If they "repeat" baptism they do so because they believe that the ceremony performed by the other Church has not really been baptism as willed by the Lord. Such difference in interpretation seriously reduces the full mutual recognition of baptism. The difficulty arises particularly between Churches which exclusively practise believers' baptism and those which practise infant baptism as well.

---

[7] The Roman Catholic Church is engaged in preparing such a liturgy.

[8] Some African Independent Churches practise repeated baptism of their own members.

There are, however, other restrictions on the mutual recognition of baptism which need to be taken into account. Recognition of baptism does not usually include recognition of chrismation and confirmation. Many Churches which recognize the baptism administered by other Churches are in the habit of "repeating" confirmation. But baptism and confirmation are inseparably inter-related and baptism is not yet fully recognized if confirmation is not.

This study has been led increasingly to the conviction that this unsatisfactory situation is largely due to the fact that baptismal initiation is not sufficiently recognized as one single coherent process which must always be looked upon as a whole. Baptism is a unique event, and even where the various elements of the rite have been separated in time the basic unity of the baptismal initiation must be retained. Most of the difficulties which today complicate the question of mutual recognition arise from undue separation in this respect. For instance, when the close connection between baptism and confirmation is lost sight of, it is much more difficult to recognize believers' and infant baptism as one and the same baptism. Furthermore, the different concepts of confirmation arising from the separation of the baptismal initiation into two rites constitute a hindrance to full mutual recognition. One may argue that this separation made possible the Western practice of recognizing baptism administered by another Church or outside the Church. Since confirmation was to be performed later by the bishop, baptism could be recognized without compromising the role of the Church and the ministry in administering the sacraments. The fact remains that, in this case, recognition is not complete and that the different concepts of confirmation make it difficult to extend this recognition. Also the uncertainty of the Churches as to the conditions and the time of admission to the eucharist finds its explanation here.

Therefore, the confession of the Church that there is and can be only "one baptism" must be developed afresh in the baptismal practices of the Churches. Their practice must be examined as to whether they obscure this basic affirmation. A new insistence on the unity of the baptismal initiation might open the way to an agreed approach in both the understanding and the practice of baptism. It might also make possible the drastic changes in practice which many call for today.

The General Problem of Mutual Recognition

Conditions for recognizing that baptism administered by another Church has been true baptism are not the same in all Churches. If mutual recognition is to become a full reality it is essential to agree upon certain common criteria.

The following statement is offered here for consideration: Baptism is to be recognized by all Churches when Jesus Christ has been confessed as Lord by the candidate, or, in the case of infant baptism, by the Church on his behalf and when baptism has been performed with water in the name of the Father and the Son and the Holy Spirit.

Of course, this statement is not to be misunderstood as an attempt to reduce the baptismal liturgies to the bare minimum. It simply lists the elements which are of primary importance for the mutual recognition of baptism. The Churches could greatly facilitate mutual recognition if they were to take them into account in their baptismal practice. Generally speaking, the principle of the non-repeatability of baptism needs to be respected even more consistently than it is today if the unique character of baptism is to become manifest among the Churches. Any "repetition" of baptism, even if it is done for valid doctrinal reasons, creates the impression of relativizing the unity of baptismal initiation.

Obviously the above statement leaves many questions open. In particular, it does not yet take the problem of believers' and infant baptism fully into account, nor does it deal with the problem of mutual recognition of confirmation. These questions require special attention (see also note 6).

Believers' and Infant Baptism

Some Churches only baptize adults who are able personally to confess Christ. Other Churches also baptize infants and children. The significance of baptism is often presented so differently in each case that it is difficult to tell whether it is really one and the same baptism. The same often applies to Churches which baptize both adults and infants. The significance given to the act and the liturgies used for it differ so widely that its identity is by no means obvious. In the case of believing adults the baptized person can make his own personal confession of faith and commitment. The baptism of infants looks forward to this personal confession of faith and commitment. Thus the identity of adult believers' baptism and infant baptism can only be evident if the Churches insist on the necessity of the vicarious faith of the congregation as well as of the parents and sponsors. The act of faith also involves the belief that participation in the corporate life of the Body of Christ is an essential element in the salvation of each member and that the baptized infant is initiated into this corporate life. Indiscriminate infant baptism is irresponsible and turns infant baptism into an act which can hardly be understood to be essentially the same as adult believers' baptism.

The problem of the relationship between adult baptism and infant baptism has come into sharper focus through church union negotiations. It is a hopeful sign that in some cases agreement has been possible between Churches which practise only believers' baptism and Churches which have mainly practised infant baptism. United Churches of this kind have been inaugurated in North India and Pakistan. In Ceylon, Ghana, New Zealand and the United States union proposals in which this question figures prominently are before the Churches. In all these schemes it is recognized that in order to hold together the two traditions in one Church there is a need for mutual charity, patience, and respect for differing convictions, but in all cases it is confidently expected that this will be possible. Although in these situations the great majority of Christians concerned come from traditions practising infant baptism, most schemes explicitly recognize that the baptism of adults reveals most clearly the nature of the baptismal act. Great stress is laid on the seriousness of the faith of those bringing children for baptism and on the necessity of ensuring that the child shall grow into the maturity of responsible faith. On the other hand, Churches of the Baptist tradition have found it possible to accept the co-existence of the two practices in view of the fact that the process of Christian initiation — baptism/confirmation/first communion — is understood as one whole.

The importance of the solution favoured in these cases is not confined to the sphere of church union. Even Churches which have not been facing the problem of church union have arrived independently at similar conclusions.

Baptism, Confirmation and Admission to the Eucharist

The different understandings of chrismation and confirmation constitute a particular problem for the mutual recognition of both baptism and confirmation. Here again, much could be gained by stressing the unity of the baptismal initiation. Though initiation may be effected in two stages, the once-for-all character of baptism should not be diminished nor destroyed. Confirmation, whether given sacramental significance or not, tends to give the impression of qualifying the uniqueness of baptism or even of repeating it. But the once-for-all character of baptism must be preserved. Confirmation must not be allowed to take over certain elements which belong properly to baptism alone. For example, though in all traditions in which confirmation (chrismation) is thought of as a sacrament it is associated with the gift of the Spirit, it would be wrong to understand baptism exclusively as the sign of the forgiveness of sins, while the gift of the Spirit is exclusively connected with confirmation. As long as baptism and confirmation are administered simultaneously, there is little danger of such separation. But once baptism and confirmation are separated in time, the once-for-all character of baptism may be lost. Confirmation cannot do more than underline or for some traditions complete what has already been achieved in baptism. If this once-for-all character of baptism is fully recognized the mutual recognition of baptism becomes much more meaningful. The fact that certain Churches confirm baptized persons coming from other Churches is less significant if this confirmation is not to be understood as an essential part of baptism but simply as its recalling or completion.

The baptismal event needs to be recalled, and provision needs to be made so that baptism can be an ever present reality. This is especially important for those who have been baptized as infants. The opportunity must be given for appropriating baptism by personal confession and engagement. In many churches confirmation provides this opportunity. But can this recalling and re-affirmation of baptismal vows take place on one given occasion? Is there not need for several occasions? Does not this "once-for-all" confirmation again rather blur than underline the once-for-all character of baptism? In any case, confirmation should not take place exclusively at a fixed age, but should rather be performed when the candidate is ready for it on his own initiative.

The once-for-all character of baptism calls for immediate admission to the eucharist. If the admission is deferred the impression is created that the incorporation into the Body of Christ has not yet fully taken place. Should baptism not be the gateway to eucharistic fellowship? Several Churches have been led to admit children to the eucharist at a much earlier age than they used to do in the past. They do not regard confirmation or the personal confession as the condition for admission to the eucharist but dissociate admission from confirmation and let it take place at an earlier age. Though this is in the logic of emphasizing the unity of the baptismal initiation, it is recognized that this reform may lead to a greater polarization of the Churches practising infant baptism and those practising believers' baptism. In any case, the insistence on the provision for opportunities of genuine personal commitment (confirmation, confession, etc.) becomes all the more important.

DOCUMENT III.9

THE ORDAINED MINISTRY (1971)

Preface

Many Christians would contend that continued study and discussion regarding Christian ministry in general and ordination in particular is an unfruitful investment of time and effort. They say that the very affirmation of the faith of the Church (which has immediate implications in changing understandings of race, justice and peace, environmental concerns and development) must occupy first place in study today.

But the subject of ordination touches the very heart of the Christian message and action. It is the faith of the Christian that the Church exists to serve the function of reconciliation, which is inseparably bound up with the problems just mentioned. Christ came to serve and not to be served, to heal and unify. As he called and sent apostles to embody his ministry in the world, so he continues to call, and send servants to continue to serve the world. Accordingly whatever keeps the Church from being both an effective sign and instrument of Christ's reconciling presence in the world must be a source of deep and continuing concern to the Christian.

The question of the nature of the ordained ministry is such an element. The table of the Lord is the appointed place for Christians to nourish and express their oneness in Christ Jesus. Yet at just this point of ultimate sharing, many of them are commanded, as part of the sincere belief of their Churches, to part from one another — this because of differing official views on the ordained ministry. Anyone who has experienced the pain of this separation at the celebration of the eucharist will be naturally led to take this problem seriously, because the most basic issues are involved: the nature of the Christian community; the relation of its members to one another and to the world in which the community exists; most fundamentally, the way in which God is at work in the universe and in the hearts of each of his children.

Beside the pressing existential concern there are other reasons for taking up this question again. Perhaps most promising is the fact that the ministry discussion itself is undergoing an evolution in many Churches which makes a more comprehensive and balanced study possible. All Churches are being forced to ask, "How is the whole ministry of Christ being carried out in our tradition, in our ministry to the world?" All are being challenged to look at their total ministry afresh in the light of the Gospel. As a result of such reappraisal the last two decades have witnessed a new sensitivity to the ministry of the whole People of God and the place of the ordained ministry within this People. As the Churches have opened themselves to the questions men are asking, as they are taking more seriously the problem of their task *in* the world, they are beginning to see the place and ministry of the ordained person in a new light also.

These questions are forcing *all* Churches to reconsider the relevance, adequacy, and pragmatic usefulness of their present understanding and employment of ministry, especially in light of the amazing fact that, even though they differ in their understanding of ordination, in considering what forms of ministry best fill the need of the present, they are reaching similar conclusions and initiating similar patterns![1]

---

[1] For particular instances see, for example, S. Mackie, *Patterns of Ministry,* Collins, London 1969.

Also to be mentioned in any list of new factors is the great significance of the Second Vatican Council. Although the full import of this Council will not be known for some time, new doors and avenues were opened there, which will directly stimulate and dramatically broaden the ecumenical conversation about ministry. At several points the Council issued statements concerning ministry. Theological study has devoted close attention to this issue since the Council. This is a new factor in the ecumenical discussion, and is widening it dramatically.

It is in the context of this world and these issues that this study is undertaken. It differs somewhat from such studies in the past, both in the note of urgency imposed upon the Churches and in the realization that the contemporary context is pushing us towards answers that seem to carry the authentic spirit of Jesus Christ within new and sometimes surprising forms. Nevertheless, we take cognizance of the labours of the past and the progress made in earlier studies on the ministry. We make our contribution, as they did, in the context of our times.

Earlier studies on this question laid a necessary foundation for dealing with it today. Discussion on the ministry played an important part in the early Faith and Order Conferences at Lausanne (1927) and Edinburgh (1937). Much time was spent at these meetings in establishing deeper understanding of the varying views held by the Churches on this neuralgic issue. But the end result at that time was an impasse. So deep was the gulf between the Churches on this question that it was simply dropped from the ecumenical agenda.

With the formation of the World Council of Churches in 1948, new possibilities began to present themselves. The impact in Faith and Order studies was felt four years later at the Lund Conference, whence a significant change in methodology emerged. The need was now seen, after an era of "comparative ecclesiology", for the Churches to go together to the sources of their common Christian faith in the future, seeking a consensus on the interpretation of these sources, as well as greater understanding as to how and why the Churches had eventually come to such differing views of their commitment to Christ. Such a change of emphasis was possible because of growing agreement attained by biblical theologians after the Second World War, as exemplified for example by the Wadham College Report, 1951.

Ministry as a formal subject of consideration was to return to the Faith and Order agenda only with the Fourth World Conference in 1963 at Montreal. But disappointingly for many, discussion at Montreal still centred almost completely on the ordained ministry, despite the promise of a larger context held forth by the title of the theme assigned to Section III: "The Redemptive Work of Christ and the Ministry of the Church". Largely because of the dissatisfaction with the Montreal discussion, the Faith and Order staff was mandated to study the topic in the broader context of the general ministry of the Church. This decision was partly motivated by the important work done on the laity *(Laity Bulletin No. 15)* in preparation for Montreal, in which the awareness of the *general* priesthood of the laity as members of the People of God, who through their *baptism* have received their unique ministry in the Church and the world, had been made once again forcefully clear.

The immediate result was the decision by the Faith and Order Commission, at its 1964 meeting in Aarhus, Denmark, to commission a three-year study on "Christ, the Holy Spirit and the Ministry". But the scope of this study proved too broad. Thus at the 1967 meeting of the Commission the theme was delimited to ordination. A 1968 consultation in Geneva produced a working paper which was forwarded by the Geneva Secretariat to study groups around the world for consideration and revision. The present report of the 1970 consultation at Cartigny has benefited from the results of the labours of 36 such study groups, as well as from the work of the study by S. Mackie *(ibid.)* conducted by the Department of Studies in Mission and Evangelism of the World Council of Churches.

At the outset a very brief mention of the order of subjects discussed in this report would be helpful. Thus, the question of the rationale for the continuing of an ordained ministry is raised immediately; the foci of reconciliation, through the kerygmatic word and action, and that of communion are emphasized. Since new dimensions and developments are referred to, a second section looks at the subjects of tradition and change as they relate to ordination. In section III, one example of such a change (the authentication of ministry) is examined.

Inasmuch as the question of the Christian community is continually occupying a more important place in the study of ministry, the relation between and among the community, the ordained person, and new *forms* of community are scrutinized in section IV. Implicit in this discussion is that of the recipient of ordination, which follows directly.

The question of the relation of "professionalism" to the ordained ministry has been given attention in this study; new possibilities offering wider varieties of practice are indicated. And finally, in view of common questions put to the ministries of *all* the Churches, and the results of study and ecumenical discussion in many of them, the report concludes by inquiring how a wider "mutually accepted ministry" might come to be.

I. The Source, Focus and Function of Ordained Ministry

All Churches agree that their ministry has its roots in Christ. He is the true and, strictly speaking, the only minister of his Church. However, Jesus wished his ministry to be continually present and exercised in the world through a community, his Body, which is the Church. It is because the Church is his Body that, right from the Last Supper, it was called to his ministry, and that the apostles, on the day of Pentecost, jointly inaugurated a communal ministry in the power of the Spirit.

The Spirit is always the Enabler, witnessing within the Christian community, within each Christian, to the incarnate and risen Lord. That is, he witnesses always to the ways in which God's redemptive will for the world are to be made effective in terms of flesh and blood, in the form of human (and therefore mortal) institutions, and within the ambiguities of human society. The Spirit distributes particular gifts to particular persons by which the community is built up into the Body of Christ, and made relevant to particular historical situations.

The Priesthood of All

It is essentially through baptism and confirmation that Christians are made members of the Body of Christ and participants in his priesthood. Therefore, any service performed in the Church by a Christian, by virtue of his baptism and confirmation, supposes an offering of his whole person "as a living sacrifice, holy and acceptable to God" (Rom. 12:1) and, consequently, has a priestly character. Thus the royal priesthood of necessity belongs to the People of God, and all forms of ministry within the Church assist, and in a sense must point to that corporate service. The call to be a part of and to serve in Christ's Body is in no way based upon merit, but is simply an undeserved gift of God's grace. *Every* service is by (χάρις), empowered by it, carried out *in* it. And since the Holy Spirit is gracious to every member, there is a *variety* of gifts; each baptized person undertakes an appropriate ministry within the many services.

But it does not appear that all the initiatives, all the charismata, or all the gifts from God should be subsumed under the name of ministry or claim ordination. The reasons for this will appear shortly. It is only necessary that the individual charismata of the non-ordained servants be in no sense regarded as inferior to those of people who are specially commissioned; in the Church there are no second-class citizens. This is simply to say that there is need for *diversified* ministry and service in the Church. For example, it is not necessary that all members of a team ministry be ordained; what is vital is that the whole People of God be built up and equipped for ministry. One of the new incentives of the present time then is brought about by the renewed understanding of this general and essential priesthood of the *whole* People of God.

The Ordained Ministry

But having made this crucial point, it must also be recalled that certain called and set-apart individuals have had a decisive role in the building up of the Church. The New Testament does report a setting apart to special ministry, distinctions of service *were* made. Throughout the Bible the concept of God's selectivity clearly emerges. There *is* a "scandal" of particularity — God called particular people for particular tasks and set them apart to serve the fellowship in distinct ways. Israel's history, its ever-deepening awareness of having been selected by God for particular service, the selection of prophets, priests and kings by God, the Incarnation itself, witness to selectivity and election. God had commonly called and employed individuals and groups to serve him in unique fashion — the selection of apostles continued this tradition, and opened the door to the conception of a called and set-apart ministry. That is to say, the existence of a set-apart ministry is fully consistent with God's *modus operandi* in calling, sending, and empowering individuals for special responsibilities.

Apparently the new relationship with God which Jesus had embodied was most meaningfully communicable and demonstrable by subsequent ministry through *persons*. The apostles were to become visible and personal representatives of Christ, instruments through whom, by life and word, the resurrection would be witnessed, the Church built up, and the ministry of reconciliation continued. Their ministry, though unique and necessarily not repeatable, definitively began and demonstrated the *personal* nature of the Christian gospel and ministry; the good news came to earth in the form of a person, and its communication to others would depend upon the Holy Spirit working through other called persons.

In choosing and sending men to act and speak on his behalf, Christ continued this personal ministry, setting a precedent for the Church. It was the preaching and teaching of the apostles, their understanding of Jesus' life and ministry, which were the basis for kerygma and didache, of the New Testament canon, and the later creeds. The witness and ministry of the apostles, unique as it was, is in a real sense normative in the Church for all time, it is foundational. Thus ministry in the Church in subsequent ages is only truly ministry insofar as it is faithful to and empowered by the apostolic message, insofar as it is congruent with the message and ministry of the apostles. The apostolic ministry continues as a bond of unity for the Church in all times and places.

That is to say, through the commissioning of apostles Jesus bound the Church to the revelation of Himself which occurred during his ministry. It may be said that the Church, in ordaining new persons to ministry in Christ's name, is attempting to follow the mission of the apostles and remain faithful to their teaching; ordination as an act attests the binding of the Church to the historical Jesus and the historical Revelation, at the same time recalling that it is the Risen Lord who is the true Ordainer, who bestows the gift. In ordaining the Church attempts to provide for the faithful proclamation of the Gospel and humble service in Christ's name. The laying on of hands in ordination can be seen as the sign witnessing to the connection of the Church and its ministry with Christ, binding the ministry to a conscious awareness of its anchorage and roots in the revelation accomplished in Him, reminding it to look to Him as the source of its commission.

There has been and still is such a ministry of reconciliation to which certain persons are especially appointed for the service of all; ministers fulfilling such a particular ministry are ambassadors for Christ, God making His appeal through them (II Cor. 5:20). The purpose of this ministry is that the world "may be acceptable, sanctified by the Holy Spirit" (Rom. 15:16). Therefore it would seem that the Churches should be able to agree that this particular ministry constitutes a sacramental reality.

In giving up his own freedom Christ has enabled men to know God in a new way. The living word of reconciliation witnessing to this event makes men capable of true community, and in this community freedom is found. Beside his responsibility in the ministry of reconciliation, the ordained person has a special place in and contribution to make to this community.

Ordination confers an authority (exousia) which is not that of the minister himself, but which demonstrates the authority of God received by the community; it also ratifies and manifests the fact that the minister is called and sent by God. But ordination is not the giving of a "thing" or a "possession" or even an "office" *tout simple;* it arises from and results in a personal, existential relationship with the Holy Spirit, and it inseparably binds the ordained person with the aforementioned community; it is the sign and instrument of Christ in this community.

As an individual assumes his full humanity in relationship with other people, so the gifts given an individual are developed in the Christian community. Ordination is not given or received in a vacuum; it takes place within the Church, the Body of Christ, not in just any gatherings of persons. And by it, the charismata for ministry which the Holy Spirit has given an individual are related to the community in which he has been nurtured, and in which he will exercise his ministry, the community of which Christ is the Head.

Ordination then, in this context, necessarily means commitment to a community — not only to certain ideals or a vague "human unity" but to concrete human beings in whose particular circumstances the ordained person is to be unreservedly involved. Thus the ordinand contributes especially to the communion between Christ and his people, and the relation of these people to one another. The ordinand's role is to minister to this community, to mediate its interior divisions and conflicts through his awareness of, and concern for, the oneness of all. Thus ordination also points to the safeguarding of the unity of the Church which is bound up with the responsibility of the one who presides at the eucharist.

Therefore ordination is at one and the same time:
— an invocation to God that he bestow the power of the Holy Spirit upon the new minister;
— a sign of the granting of this prayer by the Lord who gives the gift of ministry;
— an offering by the Church to God, of the minister consecrated to his service (cf. I Tim. 4:14 and II Tim. 1:6).

The ordained minister fulfils a threefold function:
— gather together, "build up", and oversee the believers, and insure that the community be present in the world; that it be answerable for the yearnings, joys and sufferings of men, and that it may grow in the holiness of the Spirit, in order that it might be the promise of unity for the whole of humanity;
— unceasingly announce and show forth by his life, the good news of the reconciliation — the foundation of man's liberation by God and of the unity of believers in the faith of the apostolic Church;
— preside over baptism and the eucharist — an action of grace on the part of the community and intercession for humanity in its entirety. [2]

II. Tradition and Change

Today all Churches, whatever the inherited pattern of their ministry may be, are having to face the question as to the extent to which the ministry can be changed or adapted. Must it be maintained in its present form? What are the changes or adaptations which are required? There is a growing recognition that changes in both the understanding and practice of the ministry are possible and that they are called for if the needs of the present situation are to be met. The following factors contribute to this recognition:

1. There is today a greater awareness of the historical character of the patterns of ministry within the New Testament. Biblical scholarship has come to the conclusion that it is not possible to ground *one* conception of Church order in the New Testament to the exclusion of others. It appears that in New Testament times differing forms co-existed and differing forms developed simultaneously in various geographical areas. Furthermore, it is increasingly realized that the forms of ministry in the apostolic period were historically, socially, and culturally conditioned and that it is, therefore, justifiable and even necessary in the present time to seek to adapt the patterns of the ministry to the needs of the current situation.

2. Study concerning the various Councils of the Church is leading to a growing recognition of and sophistication about the historical nature of the Councils of the Church. It is recognized that sociological and psychological factors influenced conciliar decisions; there is greater sensitivity to the probability that the intentions of those who framed conciliar statements may have been more modest than subsequent generations believed. For example, development in biblical theology has necessitated a calling into question of Trent's basing its treatment of holy orders on the Epistle to the Hebrews. The historical self-understanding of the Church as a pilgrim people, *in via*, allows the decisions of the Councils to be seen in more dynamic, historical terms.

---

[2] Cf. "The Eucharist in Ecumenical Thought", *Louvain 1971*, above p. 69 *[Louvain 1971]*.

Such sensitivity seems to make possible and necessary the acceptance, by each, of a variety of church orders.

3. In many respects the ministry in its present form does not seem to be fully adequate to its purpose any more. In Western society, traditional and sacred in character, religious ministry conferred its upon holder a central position in the community with almost unequalled status, prestige and power. The minister was in the midst of everything because everyone in the community expected from him either a blessing or moral guidance for human activity.

But modern society tends more to split into innumerable associations and organizations which function according to more rationalistic principles, both scientific and technical. This development has shifted the place of religion to a limited sector of human activity. Thus the professional minister whose duties and activities are dedicated exclusively to this limited religious sector finds himself removed from many functions he was fulfilling in a more "sacred" society. Such deprivation can lead to a serious crisis in the "identity" of the ordained minister.

It should be emphasized that this evolution taking place also has a positive aspect, in that it is freeing and even compelling the Churches to restudy their understanding and deployment of ministry; this study can, in turn, bring about a more biblically faithful and culturally relevant employment of the minister.

4. The experience of different cultural settings and their needs as well as ecumenical contacts have helped relativize claims of permanence which once were attached to certain patterns of ministry. There is also the experience that imaginative changes have contributed to the overcoming of impasse in mission and in the carrying out of pastoral responsibility in the Churches. This experience calls for openness which permits constantly renewed creativity.

Thus all Churches are being confronted with new and, to some extent, similar problems. And it may be said that more and more of them are becoming aware of the need, and the freedom with which they are able to develop their traditional patterns of ministry. But they still differ to a large extent in their ways of realizing adaptations. This is due to their difference in understanding the place of the ministry in the tradition and continuous life of the Church. They are all of the conviction that the Church is apostolic, i.e. that at all times it is and has to be in communion with the apostolic community and ministry. Though it changes in the course of history it must not lose the identity which it has been given by Christ. But in what way does the ministry assure this identity? Is it enough to assure the continuity of content and functions? Or can identity be assured only through certain obligatory patterns?

The Churches also agree that the basic continuity with the apostolic community is provided by the whole People of God. As the Twelve were the image of the new Israel in Christ, so their successors are to be seen in the Church as a whole. The continuity of the ministry is not a continuity independent of, but within, the People of God.

There are, however, different emphases in understanding how the identity given to the Church by Christ is to be faithfully maintained and the relationship of the ministry to this maintenance. To name three:

a) The threefold pattern of ministry, though it developed historically, is to be regarded as divinely given and is, therefore, indispensable for the existence of the Church. It is required for the building up of the communion, or at least as a sign that the People of God are one and the same People in all places and ages. The laying on of hands gives visible expression to this continuity.

b) There are certain functions of ministry which are given and which must be maintained in some way by the Church in every generation; as long as the functions, e.g. *episkope*, faithful preaching, administration of sacraments, and service to humanity are identifiable, the concrete patterns may change.

c) The succession is provided exclusively by the content of the Gospel. The Church is apostolic insofar as it proclaims and serves again and again the same Christ and his liberating and reconciling message. As long as this message is proclaimed and lived ministries and means may change.

These differing views on the place of the ministry in the tradition of the Church influence the attitude of the churches to many of the questions which must be faced today, such as the ordination of women, the possibility of a non-professional ministry, and so forth. But there is evidence now that these three viewpoints are not mutually exclusive. For the third, in practice (for example) has developed a system of comprehensive and orderly oversight and administration of the sacraments intentionally faithful to the apostles (which the first sees as the basis of its position). On the other hand, the first is flexible in the actual practice of its ministries and sees the kerygma involved in the functions it maintains.

There is, then, the continual need of relating the concept of ministry to the experience of it, getting at the mystery of it by employing a multiplicity of images and, eventually, models. The New Testament used many structural images — body, vine, building — but in almost every case growth and flexibility were assumed; *oikodome* was the principle for building up the body. An ever-growing openness to change, and a growing willingness to imitate this New Testament pattern can be discerned; it can be said that the vitality of the Church will be reflected by its openness to experiment with new forms and employ its ordained ministry in ever-new avenues of service.

III. The Authentication of Ministry

The changes affect not only external structures, but the very understanding and exercise of the ministry. Many examples could be given; one will suffice to illustrate the phenomenon — the radically different approaches in past and present to the authentication of the ministry.

An Evolution in Authentication

Generally speaking, in society at large, the criteria enabling a person to acquire and exercise authority (or legitimate power) have changed, and continue to change, considerably. To be sure, there is undoubtedly an unchanging element in the acquisition and use of authority. It can only exist within a relationship of trust built up between a group of people and the holder of a function; it is a result of an acknowledged recognition that one possesses *capabilities* which enable him to fulfil this function, and by definition it excludes authoritarianism. What is subject to variety and change, however, is the kind of capabilities the group considers appropriate and meaningful and the manner in which the authority is exercised. In ever-widening sections of the world, genuine authority is acquired by a leader only within the dynamics of a group in which there is freedom for give and take, exchange and *mutual* reflection and even instruction. And, as mentioned above, such leadership is emerging in the Church and bringing about new experiences of Christian unity.

In traditional society, birth conferred an acknowledged title for ruling a given territory. In the twentieth century however, citizens are more likely to defer to the demonstration of political, economic or social competence on the part of a leader, as over against the fact of his being born into a certain family. A similar change can be seen in the acceptance of almost all social leadership, including business, educational, scientific, and even familial.

Relevant Questions

Such changes in patterns of the authentication of authority would lead a sociologist to raise such questions as the following regarding valid ministry:

1. Acknowledgement of the legitimate authority of ministers was based, in the past, not on the right of birth, but on "anointing". Was not such an anointing usually considered by the faithful as a quasi-physical alteration of the recipient, enabling him to perform certain rituals first legitimately, and later validly, but only in secondary fashion, to rule or guide a community? In such a conception of ordination was not the minister regarded as being related to the individual believer through the administration of the sacraments rather than as being related to the faithful as a *community* in which sacraments and salvation were found in *koinonia*?

2. Was the conception and employment of authority referred to above compatible with the self-authenticating understanding and exercise of authority of Jesus? Does not the emerging understanding seem more in agreement with his practice?

3. This latter view does seem to be gaining wider currency. Does it not imply a modification or supplementation of ordination rites, so that it is made clear that the act of ordination is an expression of the Church's "spiritual" consensus on the aptitudes of a candidate to guide the Church in the name of Christ? Cannot ordination rite(s) and those who participate in it (them) change as long as they express both the relationship to Christ and the proper relationship between the minister, the basic Christian community, and the reachable wider Church?

IV. The Ordained Person and the Community

Every ordination is *within* the Church and *for* the Church, intended to help the Church fulfil its mission in the world. The ordained minister is commissioned to serve some part of the Church, to act in its name, to dramatize and personify its being *sent* and *present*. As is evident in the previous paragraphs, the place and significance of the Christian *community* in regard to ordination are being more clearly recognized. At this point some of the questions raised in this context need to be discussed.

The Ordination Service — in the Community

In order to experience and demonstrate the truth that setting apart is not to some superior level of discipleship, but rather to service *within* the Church, it is important that the entire process of ordination involve the whole body of the people. There needs to be continual emphasis on the fact that ordination is neither "over-against" nor *vis-à-vis* the congregation, but rather, that a person is addressed in the midst of the people. It is also important that the congregation have a part in the calling, choosing, and training of an ordinand, thus preserving the basic significance of the *rite vocatus*. This means more than the inclusion of a sentence or two in the liturgy and ordaining in the *presence* of the laity, important as that may be.

A long and early Christian tradition placed ordination in the context of worship and especially of the eucharist. Such a place for the service of ordination preserves the understanding of ordination as an *act* of the *whole* community, and not of a certain order within it or of the individual ordained. Even if one believes that the act of ordaining belongs to a special order within the Church, it is always important to remember that the entire community is involved in the act. Ordination in association with the eucharist keeps before the Church the truth that it is an act which initiates a person to a *service of the "koinonia"*, a service both to God and to fellow man. It is this *"koinonia"* that the eucharist expresses *par excellence* and by continuing to relate ordination to the eucharist this dimension of ministry is called to mind. Ordination within the service of the eucharist also reminds the Church that the ordained ministry is set apart to point to Christ's own ministry and not to some other. By placing ordination in the context of worship and especially the eucharist, this act is referred to God Himself and the ordained person is dedicated to the service of "His Servant" who offers Himself for the salvation of the world.

Changing Manifestations of Community

But what meaning can be given today to "ordination into a particular community"? There is obviously no place for "detached ministers" (e.g. *episcopi vagantes*). It can no longer be said without qualification, however, that ordination attaches a person to a certain *local* church. For in the twentieth century the meaning of *local* is undergoing extensive modification. Geographical areas no longer delineate certain social entities generally as they once did. Urbanization and the modern organization of society continue to develop; owing to the characteristic mobility, dispersal, and specialization of this society, persons tend to belong to several communities simultaneously, no one of which is primarily geographically defined. This development is tending more to be true of continuing "rural" societies as well.

The neighbourhood community of Christians will continue to be an important and living expression of the Church, and traditional groupings of people and pastor in a relatively homogeneous neighbourhood, where such exist and are meaningful, will continue to be needed and valid. But the new forms of Christian community referred to above are also assuming importance, and are in need of an ordained ministry linked with the wider Church. Is it not necessary for such communities to have the possibility of gathering around the eucharist as well? Are not such communities equally valid congregations of the Church even if they may be of limited duration?

This question is put precisely with the claims of mission in mind, which is the proper orientation of every Christian community and every Christian ministry towards the human community at large. It is not that the minister of the Church should necessarily leave the place where he received the call of God, or the community in which he carries out his service, but he should, as a minister of the Church, take the needs, the worries, and the hopes of his neighbour unto himself, in order that the community may become the place where men can meet God. Such an attitude towards the human community may require the ordained servant to change the locale of his ministry, even though ordained for a particular community.

The emergence of authentic charismatic leadership in new communities needs to be carefully considered. Such leadership is often the channel through which new and deep experiences of Christian unity flow as, for example, when an individual prophetically challenges racism or injustice and a temporary or enduring worshipping community arises out of, and around, this concern. Has not the Holy Spirit brought forth such leaders since biblical times, leaders whose role was not, in the first place, defined by the eucharist? And is it not vital now, as it was then, that such gifted persons be recognized, tested, and authorized by the Church, both for the sake of good order and also that their gifts may be put to the fullest possible use? If such persons are ordained, possibly to new types of ministry, one of the special roles of the bishop could be to keep such a variety of ministries in unity, thus keeping in visible, creative tension the prophetic and priestly ministry of the Church. That is to say, scholars have often theologized from Christ to the ministry, and then to the sacraments and the Church, whereas the more appropriate order might be from Christ to Christian community, and then to ministry and sacraments.

There is, then, a growing need to provide specialized and perhaps limited-term ordained ministers for new forms and types of communities. But a danger at this point must be noted — that emerging communities may themselves tend to become uniform exclusive enclaves. Since the eucharist is the sacrament transcending divisions, the tendency towards homogeneity in this sense must be resisted. It should be borne in mind that unique Christian community cannot be restricted to people of the same sex, occupation, race, age, economic or social level. Thus there is a continuing need for ministers ordained to serve particular communities to provide a bond to the Universal Church.

The Larger Community

Although human degradation is a fact of human history, and people have been, and still are prejudged to have or lack certain qualities, abilities or potentialities on simple grounds of colour, caste, or sex, the Church is that renewed society where there is "neither Jew nor Greek, slave nor free, male nor female, but all are one in Christ Jesus". So long as history lasts, the accomplishment of this vision of full humanity and unity may not be fully realized, but the Church must continually attempt to obediently *live* this new reality, this dimension of the Kingdom of God. The Church is always for the world, and it must obstinately witness to the purposes of God for that world, in the face of all the world's resistance. The Church must always try to claim for God the social environment of which it is a part.

The gift of ministry is therefore essentially related to what God has prepared for His world and which, through the movement of His Spirit, He is realizing in history through the community of His Church; this ministry too does not exist in itself and for itself, but rather *for the world*. There is thus an existential character of the ministry deeply related to the destiny of creation and man's position in this creation. Ordination in this light means an act leading to *existential involvement* in the world and as such, brings the Church into a deep relationship with the world, its needs, its anxieties and possibilities, actually *relating the world to God*. Through ordination the Church is looking out of itself, not by leaving itself behind, but by *involving* itself. This is the *ek-stasis* of communion, which is not only a sending out, but also a being present in the world with its hunger, injustice, pain and sorrow, as well as its joy, thanksgiving and its hope.

V. Who is to be Ordained?

The New Testament suggests two criteria for determining who in particular should be ordained: *a)* an inward and personal call of God to the individual (cf. Gal. 1:15), *b)* a ratification and authentication of that call by the Church, which discerns the individual to have the gifts and potentialities for the ministry in question (cf. I Tim. 3). These two criteria have usually appeared in that order in the tradition of most of our Churches. The reverse order should also be considered; that is *a)* that a person should be sought out, selected and called by the Church to fulfil the ministry in question, and *b)* that he himself should inwardly assent to this call as a call from God.

So in Acts 6: 3 the Church was commanded to find men with gifts appropriate to a particular ministry, upon whom hands could then be laid (and the searching out of such men is one meaning of *episkopein*). The call of God to ordination comes through the Church.

Appointment and Discipline

When a person is to be ordained the determining factor is the discernment by the Church that the person in question has the capacity to fulfil the responsibility which is to be put upon him. What the Church looks for in a person to be ordained is evident spiritual and personal maturity of Christian character, together with a particular aptitude or competence for the performance of the ministry itself, whatever it may be. The Church attempts to identify those to whom the necessary gifts have been given. To those with these gifts, who assent to the call of God through the Church, a further gift is spoken of in I Tim. 4:14 and II Tim. 1: 6, as bestowed through the laying on of hands.

The process of selecting and ordaining particular persons can be seen *both* as the Church's "natural" activity as a social organism, which must supply to itself the leadership and other roles which it needs for its purposes, *and* (more deeply) as the initiative of God at every point for the fulfilment of His plan for the salvation of the world. Seen in this theological perspective, the selecting of the right person for ordination is a matter of grace at every point.

As appointment by the Church, ordination is preceded by preparation, probation and examination. After these responsibilities have been cared for, the Church formally recognizes the gifts and commitments of each ordinand and affirms its belief that he has been chosen and sent by God for ministry in His name and in that of the Church. Because ordination concerns the discernment of spiritual gifts, a risk is involved; thus this discernment must be under constant review. For the ordinand may be mistaken as to his suitability, or on the other hand the Church may not recognize or accept a gift offered to it. This means that ordination is also a testing of the Church, a test of its responsiveness and present openness to new forms of ministry.

Every office of ministry is, therefore, subject to the Church's discipline. The person "in orders" is also "under orders". The Church's responsibility as guardian of the Christian gospel, although vested particularly in those ministerial offices specifically charged with oversight (*episkope*), is in the last analysis a corporate stewardship. By its very act of granting ordination the Church as a body acknowledges the responsibility of the whole company of the faithful for the continuing guardianship of the apostolic testimony.

The Social Milieu

The particular pattern and orientation of ordained ministry, and the particular demands the Church must make upon the ordained ministry, will be prescribed by the needs of the Church in a particular environment and at a particular point of history. The Church never ceases to be part of the world, to be set in this or that socio-cultural matrix, to be in a sense the prisoner of history. Because the Incarnation dictates the radical historicity of the Church, it must always seek to be *contemporary* in its understanding of its task, and therefore of its ministry. When the circumstances of the Church change, its inherited patterns of ministry will need reformulation and reshaping; there is the continual need for the ministry to incarnate itself in the culture in which it finds itself.

Such obedient adaptation is made more difficult when the previous historical experience of the Church is "absolutized" and regarded as normative for all time, or even given an "ontological" rationale. For example, when Christianity was first brought to the Philippine Islands it was not socially possible for Filipinos to be ordained. But there was no justification for perpetuating this tradition for 400 years. Or again, Jesus did not in fact include any women or Gentiles among the Twelve, and there were understandable reasons for this. But it is quite another matter to assert, on this ground, that women, for example, are by nature physically, personally and ontologically incapable of receiving the grace and responsibility given in ordination.

The question of the renewal of each tradition of ministry is seen to be the more urgent when one remembers that it is the Church's task under God, not meekly to accept and follow a society's custom of devaluing certain people by categorizing them and treating them all in a certain manner. Although the Church will inherit the values and attitudes of the society and era of which it is a part, it will nevertheless seek to criticize and transcend these attitudes according to the mind of Christ. It is certain that every culture and every society will have its own difficulties in attaining the full humanization of its inhabitants. Both racism and unjustified prejudice regarding the place and capabilities of women, for example, abound in the Church as well as the world. The Church has to take the limited vision of its people seriously. But it is also bound to bring the judgement of the Gospel to bear upon its cultural predicament. It is also bound to stand as best it can for the principle that it is the gifts and calling of God which should determine the possibility of ordination, not a classification by race, colour, social level, or sex.

The Ordination of Women

Strong emotions are aroused when this subject is discussed. On the one hand, even in societies that no longer generally debar women from any office on grounds of sex alone, there are many men who find it deeply disturbing to be under the authority of a woman. On the other hand, more and more Christian women are expressing frustration in regard to the inability or unwillingness of Churches to consider them as fit candidates for ordination to presbyteral ministry. They feel depersonalized and deprived of the dignity of their adulthood in the Church, and this exclusion is leading in many cases towards feelings of bitterness and militancy.

Since those who advocate the ordination of women do so out of their understanding of the meaning of the Gospel and ordination, and since the experience of the Churches in which women are ordained has been positive and none has found reason to reconsider its decision, the question must be asked as to whether it is not time for all the Churches to confront this matter forthrightly. Churches which ordain women have found that women's gifts and graces are as wide and varied as men's, and that their ministry is fully as blessed by the Holy Spirit as the ministry of men. But even Churches which already ordain women must guard against discriminatory tendencies, since a real ambiguity can be observed in these Churches — the women ordained have usually been given positions of juridical and pastoral inferiority. The force of nineteen centuries of tradition against the ordination of women cannot be lightly ignored. But traditions have been changed in the Church. This question must be faced, and the time to face it is now.

VI. Ordination, Ministry and Profession

Another problem which the Churches confront in their employment of ordained ministers is the increasing uneasiness and uncertainty attached to salaried professionalism.

In a world of rapid change and widely varying conditions, the Church must simultaneously maintain faithfulness through good order and flexibility in the shaping and deploying of its ministry for effectiveness in mission. During recent generations the Churches of the West have developed a presbyteral ministry analogous to the learned professions of law, medicine and teaching; they have set up academic requirements involving extended courses of study in theological (professional) faculties for admission to ordination and they have assumed as normal, or at least as ideal practice, the full-time employment of such ministers in church work. These tendencies have brought important strengths to the ministry "as a profession". In the future many ministers will doubtless require even more extended education than in the past, particularly for various kinds of specialized service. But in some situations it can be said that this kind of professionalizing has led to a kind of clericalism. It must be asked, for example, to what extent the contemporary mood of many theological students to dispense with ordination is due to the association of ordination with a false, but widespread conception of professionalism — i.e. not with the minister as professional in the sense of guaranteeing special training and competence, but as professional in the sense of his being *paid* for his services.

In order that it may more adequately fulfil its pastoral responsibility to Christian people, and its mission of service in the world, the Church needs to avoid a monolithic pattern of professionalism in its ministry. Indeed practice has varied more than many realize, in that large numbers of ministers teach in theological faculties or even in public education, or follow (at least part time) other vocations commonly considered similar or congruous to the ministerial profession. At the same time, in assuming that ministers do not work in factories, for example, or in other positions not characterized by academic attainment, the Churches have lost contact with, and ceased to minister to, important elements of the population.

It is probable that a renewed ordained diaconate offers great hope of meaningfully relating Christian ministry to the service of the world. But in these paragraphs the concern is primarily for ordination as it relates to the presbyter.

A person need not have a degree in theology or a salary from the Church in order to administer the eucharist; what he does need is the request of the Christian community and the Church's recognition of him as a minister. Such a person, who qualifies for ordination, even though a "non-professional", may also prove effective in occasional preaching. If theology is indeed the "attempt to relate the truths of God to the torments of the world", then an attorney, an economist, a youth sensitive to injustice, a housewife, a school teacher, a junior executive, or a scientist, none of whom have ever had formal theological education, may bring the word of God with particular power in certain situations. By a careful drafting of its standards for stated posts or types of appointment, and by more varied and imaginative approaches to education for such persons in the meaning of faith, the Church may use their services without compromising its commitment to learning or to theological responsibility.

Thus at least three sets of educational-economic arrangements respecting ordained ministers can be discerned: *(a)* employment by the Church of some who have formal theological education, *(b)* secular employment for some who have such professional education (i.e. worker-priests or other "tent-making ministers"), *(c)* secular employment for some with other kinds of education or preparation in whom the Church discerns gifts for ordained ministry ("non-professional presbyters").

So long as the Church maintains appropriate discipline or regulations regarding the various forms of ministry, it need not require that all ordained ministers remain dependent upon it financially or give full time to its affairs. Rather, by ordaining to its ministry persons who earn their living in various professions, it may witness more effectively in numerous areas of society and may profit from the insights which these ministers bring to it from their particular disciplines and engagements.

The procedure being discussed seems to hold promise of providing ministry for areas of contemporary life now inadequately served by the Church. As examples, the villages of Asia and Africa, where Western standards for ordination have proved unrealistic, can be cited.

There are also many kinds of "extraordinary situations". In parts of the world the church lives "in diaspora", unable to maintain the institutions of more comfortable times and places and needing all the more a faithful ministry. In some places the Christian community is a tiny minority confronted by a hostile society. Feeling themselves isolated from their neighbours and their fellow believers, the faithful long for a clear witness to the apostolic gospel and regular celebration of the eucharist. Before multiplying the number of denominational ministers in competition with one another, Churches should explore opportunities for ecumenical co-operation and even local union of small congregations. Even so, a part-time or non-professional minister will provide the best answer to many a small community of Christians. Again, certain social classes in many societies have not been reached by "professional" ministers coming from the outside, but have responded to the ministries of persons of their own communities. It would seem to be a mistake to insist that such emergent leaders, accepted by their communities, must be taken out of their socio-cultural *milieu,* to be formally educated at a school of theology outside of that context.

Along this same line, in growing secular cities, groups of younger people often find themselves alienated from the established Church, desiring a ministry which can speak to them in their own idiom in such a way that they can recognize the word of God addressing their own deepest longings. Many naval ships on long tours of lonely and dangerous duty are too small to rate a chaplain. Such worship as is provided must be conducted by lay readers not authorized to minister the eucharist.

Out of such groups as those mentioned here, a person chosen by the community as trust-worthy might well receive ordination from the Church as a non-professional minister, perhaps even for a limited period of time. It is only necessary that such a community hold fast its intention to maintain the unity of the Body of Christ and that the larger Church fulfil its pastoral responsibility in authorizing a minister whom the group recognizes as suited to its particular situation.

Further, the life of many large congregations would conceivably be strengthened by the appointment to their staff of ministers, carefully selected and well qualified persons from various professions to supplement, by their particular gifts and contacts in the world, the skills of the full-time ministers.

A particular problem for any part-time minister will be his sense of identity in society. Will he see himself primarily as a minister or as, for example, a worker in a factory? If he has reasonable "success" in the small community with which he begins his work, he may aspire to "advancement" to ministerial situations for which he lacks adequate education. Such difficulties should not be minimized; nor are there easy answers to all of them. But in its responsibility for exercising *episkope,* the Church must find ways of offering more effective guidance to all its ministers and especially to those who face this kind of problem. At the same time, order and profession (in the sense with which these terms have been employed) are not to be identified.

VII. Mutual Acceptance of Ministry

The New Delhi Assembly of the World Council of Churches, in looking to the future unity of the Church, visualized a concrete vision of Christian unity that would be visible as well as spiritual. It expressed the conviction that the unity which is both God's will and His gift included a ministry accepted by all.[3]

From the perspective of the present study on ordination, it is evident "that the unity which is both God's will and His gift to His Church" will be seriously deficient and even impossible to attain unless all those baptized into Jesus Christ are united with one another in such a way that they are served by a ministry "accepted by all". To come closer to a common understanding of ordained ministry has been a purpose of this study. Therefore in this concluding section it is in order to sketch briefly elements of the convergence of thinking on this subject to illustrate the sources of the growing agreement among many of the Churches. And, since enlarging agreement on the meaning of ordination has implications for and is bound up with the future unity of the Church, a concluding question will be posed: How might this growing agreement on the place and meaning of ordained ministry be influential in the eventual coming into being of a ministry "accepted by all"?

To be sure, there are still differences in understanding ordination among the Churches. The Orthodox Churches stress the threefold pattern of ministry as divinely given. Relation to and ordination by a bishop in the apostolic succession preserves an identity of faith with apostolic teaching within the community; in one form or another it is required for the building up of the communion. It is important that ordination is undertaken within the service of eucharist. Through the community each bishop is

---

[3] *New Delhi Report* (London: SCM Press, 1962), p. 116.

linked to the other bishops, to the apostles and the entire Church. Thus agreement on the meaning of ordination is inseparable from an understanding and agreement regarding the Church.

Further, the Roman Catholic Church teaches that the priesthood of all and the ministerial priesthood are essentially different, although each participates in the priesthood of Christ. But the fullness of priesthood is conferred by episcopal ordination, which confers the *munera* of consecrating the eucharist, teaching, and governing; these *munera* must be exercised in communion with the episcopal college and its head. Those not ordained according to this understanding do not have the power to consecrate the eucharist.

But the Second Vatican Council has made new thinking on the ministry both possible and necessary in the Roman Catholic Church. Today, on the basis of biblical, historical and systematic theological studies, a growing number of Roman Catholic theologians are becoming convinced that there are serious defects in the traditional arguments and approaches used to determine the "validity" of ministry. The following are some of the more important insights leading to this new conviction:

1. There is growing agreement that it is impossible to demonstrate from the New Testament that the only minister of the Lord's Supper was an ordained person. There is no clear biblical evidence that the Twelve were the exclusive ministers of the eucharist in New Testament times or that they appointed the only persons who presided at the eucharist. On the other hand, it may be noted that neither is there evidence that *all* Christians were eligible ministers of the eucharist. While in the local churches, founded by apostles like Paul, there were leaders or persons in authority, very little is said about how such men were appointed and nothing about their presiding at the eucharist.

2. Furthermore, there is ever-greater agreement that the New Testament presents diverse types and even several principles of organization of the Christian communities, according to the difference of authors, places and times. On this basis, there have been developed, in the course of history, multiple forms of church order, each with its own advantages and disadvantages: papal, patriarchal, conciliar, among others. Such diversity suggests the need and freedom to respect and pursue diversity and complementarity in church structures.

3. Growing consensus can likewise be found that, at the beginning of the second century (but perhaps even earlier), as attested by Ignatius of Antioch, the bishop had emerged as the highest authority in the local church and either he or his appointee presided at the eucharist. However, no certainty exists as to how the Ignatian bishop was appointed or whether he stood in a chain of historical succession to the apostles by means of ordination or even that the pattern described by Ignatius was universal in the Church — the fact that he pressed the point so vigorously can well lead to the conclusion that he was attempting to implement greater uniformity on a situation more fluid up till then. Some find in the *Didache*, too, evidence that wandering charismatic prophets could preside at the eucharist.

4. There is further agreement among scholars that although ordination of ministers of the eucharist by bishops was the almost universal practice in the Church very early, it is impossible to show that such a church order existed everywhere in the Church from the earliest times. In fact, there is evidence that even this practice did not become uniform until after several centuries. Further, there have been well-documented cases

later in the Church's history in which priests — not bishops — have ordained other priests to serve at the altar. The Church itself could and did make decisions regarding such cases.

5. Historical investigation has shown that the distinction between "valid" and "licit" ordination as it has been widely used in the past several centuries cannot be found in the primitive Church. There was indeed, in the New Testament itself, as well as in the Early Church Councils, a constant concern for maintaining "order" in the Church. There was also the highest regard for lawful and orderly eucharistic celebration. But it is impossible to find in the ancient Church any universal or authoritative judgement about the sacramental reality of sacraments administered in a "disorderly" or "illicit" manner as, for example, when they were administered by an unauthorized person. There is need for order *(taxis)* in the Church and in the administration of the sacraments of the Church, but such a concern should not militate against Christian Liberty.

6. The concept of "power" that has been attributed to the ordained minister even in the ancient Church was likewise subject to several interpretations. In any case, it is impossible to demonstrate from the Christian literature of the first millennium that the "power" conferred on the ordained minister was absolute in the sense that if no one in a church had received this power, the assembly had to be deprived of the sacrament.

7. A study of church pronouncements during the Middle Ages and at the Council of Trent suggests strongly that even though there is a constant insistence that only ordained priests can consecrate the eucharist, there is no explicit dogma about what happens — or does not happen — when, for evangelical reasons, a baptized but unordained Christian leads the eucharist. Even at Trent the only reservation made about the Protestant ministry was that it was not "legitimate", that is, not established according to canonical norms. At Trent, however, nothing whatever was said about the presence, or absence, of the sacramental body and blood of the Lord in the communion services of the Reformation Churches. Even after Trent Roman Catholics could hold St. Jerome's position that the bishops are superior to priests because of custom rather than because of an ordinance of the Lord. Episcopal church order, therefore, should not be a reason for the division of the Churches.

8. Revealing increased awareness of and sensitivity to such recent historical and theological research into the doctrine of the ministry, the Second Vatican Council held that there is a defect or deficiency in — not a total absence of — ordination in the Protestant Churches. Accordingly, the Council regarded the eucharistic celebrations of Protestant Churches as lacking "the genuine and integral substance of the eucharistic mystery". But it resolutely and explicitly rejected a proposal to the effect that because of the deficiency in Protestant ordinations the Protestant Churches simply have not preserved the eucharist.

Furthermore, the recognition at Vatican II that separated Christian communities have "ecclesial reality" implies, according to many Roman Catholic theologians, that those communities have a competent eucharistic ministry, whatever deficiency that ministry might have from a Roman Catholic perspective. One cannot simply assume, from New Testament evidence at least, that the ultimate ministerial moment is the consecration of the eucharist.

9. Implied in all the above data is the increasing awareness that there is more than one way to validate or legitimatize the ministries of the various Churches. Ordination

by a bishop, which has been called ritual validation, is just one way. Therefore episcopal as over against presbyteral church order cannot be regarded as an adequate justification of division. There can also be what has been termed an ecclesiological validation (which argues from a true manifestation of the Church which Christ founded to true ministry). There is also a charismatic validation, which argues from charismatic church order in Corinth to the possibility of having such a non-episcopal charismatic church order today. Neither of the latter two requires the laying-on of hands by bishops, but both are grounded in the Church's authentic tradition. Thus the question is posed: If the charismatic ministries were laid aside for pastoral and historical reasons, could not these ministries be resumed for similar reasons?

10. The importance of the historic episcopate has not been diminished by the above findings. The only thing that is incompatible with contemporary historical and theological research is the notion that the *episcopal succession* is identical with and embraces the *apostolic succession* of the whole Church. Indeed, more and more Churches are expressing willingness to see episcopacy as a pre-eminent sign of the apostolic succession of the whole Church in faith, life and doctrine, and as such, something that ought to be striven for if absent.

11. Finally, bilateral conversations, Faith and Order studies and statements, and most Plans of Church Union have come close to unanimity in stating that: *(a)* ordination is regarded as divinely instituted, and *(b)* that the prayer of the Church connected with ordination is an efficacious invocation of the Holy Spirit for the strengthening of the one ordained.[4]

Although recognition of ordained ministries is only one element in the bringing about of full communion among Churches, it is clear that mutual acceptance of eucharistic ministries will be a vital step towards all Christians "breaking the one bread" together.

The Way Ahead

From the findings and discussions of two international consultations convened to work with the subject of ordination, plus the reports of thirty-five study groups from around the world, which lie behind this report, certain elements of a possible slowly-emerging conception of ordained ministry can be discerned. Making no attempt to assess priority or give logical order, such elements as these can be included in an enumeration — a ministry called to focus on the apostolic mission of speaking the kerygma, administering the sacraments, building up and overseeing the community, accepted, confirmed, and prayed for by the Church; a ministry related to the world, instituted to serve it in all its joy and torment; a ministry able to change its form according to the mind of Christ as history evolves, in the interest of reconciliation and liberation of men; not necessarily bound to full-time occupation, salary, particular education, or life tenure; a ministry rooted in and related to Christ, but open to the future, free to emerge in different ways in the creation of and nourishment of Christian community in new kinds of situations, and potentially recognizable and confirmed in different ways by the Church in different times and places.

---

[4] See, for example, statements drawn up as a result of Roman Catholic/Reformed and Roman Catholic/Lutheran bilateral conversations.

Before concluding this statement, it would seem valuable to look into the future and envisage possible factors in the bringing about of mutually-accepted ordained ministry. Granting that new insights into Church history exist, and that growing agreement as to the meaning and practice of ordained ministry can be cited (both as sketched above), how can the canonical and juridical structures in which the ordained ministry has been moulded (and by which it has been partly determined) be helped to evolve in consonance with the theological agreement which is emerging?

It must be said at the outset that throughout Church history exceptions and irregularities to perfect order abound, that the Church itself has exercised freedom in recognizing ministries and changing tasks — that exceptional circumstances have called forth fresh approaches and actions on many occasions.

Second, it should be noted that church unions already accomplished reveal that ministries of Churches uniting can be brought together, renewed and enlarged in scope as the Churches themselves come before God in repentance, love and acceptance. Some unions have gained "mutually acceptable ministries" by a mutual laying on of hands of bishops and ministers elected to be bishops, others by mutual acceptance of existing ministry, with all new ordinations to be made by bishops, while others plan a mutual laying on of hands of each, by all. In all union plans, both accomplished and proposed, it is recognized that re-ordination is not being undertaken, but rather, a unique service, attempting to reconcile and unify ministries of previously divided Churches.

Perhaps a mutual recognition of ministries, in the form of an extension of authority or commissioning to a certain work in a united Church, offers a key to further ecumenical discussion and action. Recently such mutual recognition has generally taken place at the time of the union of two or more Churches, when ministries were brought together into the same frame-work to form a new entity.

But this is not to prejudge what form mutual acceptance of ministry might take in the future — it *need* not occur in the context of Churches organically uniting with one another. It could, for example, be declared and implemented when and if two or more world confessional families come into full communion with one another, or when they unite, as the World Alliance of Reformed Churches and the International Congregational Council have recently done; it could take place at the assembly of a genuinely universal Council. In view of the already mentioned ambivalent New Testament witness, the many irregularities of Church history, the intention of faithful ministry in the various traditions, and a desire to be one in the universal Church, could not an initial ministerial unification be accomplished by a *per saltum* acceptance of all existing ministries by the others? Such acceptance could be followed by a sort of re-institution of the process of regularization of those ministries involved. The Church has taken decisions such as this regarding its ministry in the past, albeit on a smaller scale. As some have inquired, might not *Ecclesia supplet* or "economy" be a final hope, even if the principle would have to be extended to situations where it has, as yet, never been applied?

Perhaps until the present, discussions regarding ordination have tended to look too much to the past, that is to concentrate upon bringing together traditional concepts and offices held in the various Churches, not taking seriously enough the challenge of new forms of ministry and the world they reflect. But the fate of Lot's wife should be kept in mind!

Of course it is important that no Christian be required to disavow his own history. Could the introduction of the epiclesis in a eucharistic celebration accompanying some such renewal of ministry be decisive for all? It is the Holy Spirit leading the Churches together; all alike have sin to repent of and treasure to bring. This being the case, the Churches can only be more visibly one through His action, and the introduction of the epiclesis could make this mutual poverty and mutual enrichment unmistakeably clear.

The question of the meaning and use of ordination is Church-wide. And the admission that it *is* a problem is becoming Church-wide. The almost unlimited needs of the world for ministry, and the possibilities of ministry for every Christian are also being recognized. It is also clear that an enlarged, deepened and broadened concept of ordination combining an intentional binding to, and empowerment by, the apostolic ministry with new forms of service in the world, offers itself as an element in the deeper understanding of, and participation in, God's mission in the world.

DOCUMENT III.10

UNITY OF THE CHURCH — UNITY OF MANKIND (1973)

. . .

IV. The Church as "sacrament" and "sign"

How can the Church be described in a way which corresponds to its place in an interdependent world? The New Testament offers many images for the Church. No description of the Church will be adequate which does not take this diversity of New Testament language into account. At different times in its history the Church has chosen particular images to clarify its self-understanding.

Two concepts offer themselves today for describing the Church as confronted with mankind and its growing interdependence. It is hardly by mere coincidence that the II Vatican Council repeatedly speaks of the Church as "sacrament" or "sign". Thus, the constitution on the Church affirms: "By her relationship with Christ, the Church is a kind of sacrament as sign of intimate union with God, and of the unity of all mankind. She is also an instrument for the achievement of such union and unity." (para. 1)

When the Assembly of the World Council at Uppsala (1968) referred to the relationship between Church and mankind, it also, with a certain spontaneity, described the Church as "the sign of the coming unity of mankind" (report of Section I, para. 20). This parallel is significant in itself. It would seem useful to explore the meaning of these concepts.

What is meant by "sacrament" and "sign"?

The two concepts have a long history in the debate on ecclesiology. The New Testament does not directly speak of the Church in these terms. Nonetheless the terminology has many links with New Testament language. It focuses attention in a very pointed way on three aspects: the revelation in Christ, the communion of faith, and the constantly renewed presence of Christ in the worship of the Church. All three aspects are placed under the perspective of the self-communication of God towards men.

This threefold meaning has to be explained further:

1) The concepts are used to grasp the nature of the revelation in Christ. Where the Latin Church spoke of *sacramentum*, the New Testament used the term *mysterion*, mystery. It is an essential characteristic of the revelation in Christ that it both reveals and conceals the truth. "There is no other sign given to you than the sign of Jonah" (Matt.12:39) which is the sign of the crucified Christ calling for repentance. The cross is visible as a sign of God's revelation only to the eyes of faith; it is concealed from unbelief. The sign thus can become transparent, but it also can remain obscure, a sign of folly, of weakness, of rejection, and thus a stumbling-block. Even those who recognize God in Christ are constantly confronted with his hiddenness under the cross.

2) The term *"sacramentum"* has been applied repeatedly in the history of the Church to the community of believers. It points to the presence of Christ *in* the community and stands for the community itself, for Christ is the very centre of the community. Through him and in him the faithful are related to each other. They become a witness for him, a sign or sacrament of his presence in this world.

3) The term finally refers to those signs which in a particular way carry the promise of making Christ effectively present: baptism, and the eucharist. The presence of Christ which constitutes the community of believers is specifically linked to these signs.

The Church as a sign

Where the Church is being referred to as sign of sacrament it is clear that the second among the three meanings serves as the basis. However, the other two aspects are implied as well. What makes the Church a sign is the fact that Christ is truly working in and present among those who follow him in faith. Some observations may render this notion of the Church as sign clearer:

— The Church is sign because it points towards Christ. He is the true sign or sacrament by which God has chosen to communicate himself to men. But he is this sign only in the hiddenness of the cross; the sign is not visible except by the way of repentance. As Christ in his cross and resurrection is the sign of the conflict between the old and the new world, so the Church cannot hope to become an unambiguous sign.

— The Church is sign, because Christ is truly present in the community of believers. He is truly there yet the fullness of what he is and what he has revealed to men will only be grasped imperfectly in any of his present manifestations. Each individual member of the community being in communion with Christ becomes a sign of his presence. "To receive you is to receive me" (Matt. 10:40). Each becomes a "Christ" for the other (M. Luther). But the individual follower of Christ is a sign only in communion with those who believe in Christ. He participates in the sign which the Church is set to be.

— The Church is sign because it points to the future, making present that which is to come. In its witness and in its being, the Church anticipates the end and fulfilment of human history. Through its relationship to Christ, the Church is a sign of that process in which the old is fighting against and is being transformed into the new as the Lordship of Christ over all powers is confronted with the conflicts and demonic aspects of our world. There is but one clear sign of the times, i.e. the sign of Jonah. "Unless you repent, you will all of you come to the same end" (Luke 13:5). Discovering the signs of the time cannot mean to foresee the course of history until the coming of the kingdom. It means to relate the events in human history to the one event of the death and resurrection of Jesus Christ who is the true sign of the fullness of time (Matt. 11:1-6; Luke 4:21).

— The Church is sign, finally, because it lives under the promise that Christ will be present wherever his word is proclaimed and the sacraments, baptism and eucharist, are being celebrated. These sacramental acts constantly remind the Church that it lives not by itself, but is rooted in the life of Jesus Christ. There has been a tendency to restrict the quality of the Church as sign to the performance of these acts. The broader meaning of the notions of sign and sacrament makes clear that the Church is sign only if its whole life and existence, spiritual as well as temporal, liturgical as well as institutional, is expressive of this quality.

Making visible the sign under the conditions of interdependence

The terminology of sacrament and sign has been proposed here because it seems to offer a way to solve the ecclesiological dilemmas arising from the Church's confrontation with growing interdependence. Unless some of the alternatives characterizing ecclesiological debates are overcome, the Church will not find its true place in this situation.

— Is the Church a charismatic community or an institution? Is it a wandering people or a perfect society? Is it ultimately invisible or does its structured visibility belong to its very essence? To speak of the Church as a sign, first of all, underlines the givenness of the Church. It does not owe its existence to human volition and planning. God has set it in Christ to be a sign — and at times a stumbling block — of his salvation and judgment. It is a sign — and nothing but a sign — even against its own desires and expectations. Yet, this sign becomes visible only where it is confronted with the particular conditions of human life in one place. It has to be expressed anew in each new situation and will take on radically different forms and structures. When the Church fails to make the sign visible, it is disobedient to its calling and may turn into an anti-sign.

— How can the Church be open for dialogue and still respond to the obligation of proclaiming the Gospel of Christ to all men? Does God work through his Spirit everywhere in the world or is there no salvation outside the community of the Church? To speak of the Church as a sign emphasizes the aspect of self-realization. Living as a sign means to put no limits to what God may intend to work through the Church and even outside its limits and boundaries. To live as a sign means for the Church to be forgetful of itself and to exist as an invitation to participate in the truth of Christ. As a sign, the Church should respect men's freedom to accept or to reject God's love offered in Christ. Thus, it can be open for dialogue without reservation, concerned only to show forth, as well as it can and to all who may grasp it, the truth which brought it into existence.

— Can the Church identify fully with those who fight for human liberation from all oppression and still be a witness of God's reconciliation? How can the Church at the same time prophetically denounce sin and be a priestly community overcoming the barriers of hatred and violence? To speak of the Church as a sign of God's kingdom emphasizes its identification with the justice of God and the liberating power of his Spirit. Within history the Church is called to live as a sign of that kingdom which transcends and fulfils history. To acknowledge Christ as Lord over the whole universe does not oblige the Church to become the promoter of a universal programme or ideal, nor the catalyst of a new world. It will have to be a prophetic sign calling to repentance over against the temptation both of blind enthusiasm and of paralysing despair. Yet, freed from such temptation, it will be a sign of reconciliation as well as binding together those who are separated by human sin.

— Can the Church ever accept human limitation as final without betraying its hope for ultimate transformation of things? Is it an agent of change or a servant of those left behind by change? To speak of the Church as sign helps to recognize that it can be present in different situations in sometimes contradictory ways without betraying its integrity as a sign. The Church is called to show forth Christ as he becomes alive in a particular situation: as consolation in view of ultimate limits, as liberation and militant courage in view of oppressive powers, as prophetic challenge to any identity based on self-assertion, as acceptance where an identity is in danger of being destroyed. To be a sign means both: to accept the limitations of human existence and to point to him who has broken through all the limits.

V. Unity and diversity

How can the Church visibly manifest its unity in the face of growing cultural diversity. Speaking of the Church as a sign of the coming unity of mankind makes it mandatory that it is a fellowship maintaining a universal oneness without losing its roots in particular settings. As this sign, the Church should set examples or models for holding together unity and diversity. Since this aspect is of special importance for the situation of growing interdependence, the following chapter will explore it further.

A new look at diversity

It is one of the consequences of growing human interdependence that the question of diversity in human life is urgently being raised. Interdependence between the different parts of mankind does not diminish diversity. Rather, by relating the hitherto unrelated, it increases consciousness of the range of human diversity and constitutes a threat to inherited and established identities.

Against this background it is not surprising that the question of diversity should have arisen with pressing urgency within the ecumenical movement as well. This study is in itself an indication of this fact. From the beginning of the modern ecumenical movement, it has been affirmed that Christian unity can only be understood as "unity in diversity". So familiar has this affirmation become that it tends to conceal from the churches the challenge of diversity as it arises in the ecumenical movement today. The pressures of growing interdependence on the one hand and the spread and consequent diversification of the ecumenical movement on the other make it necessary to seek a new appreciation of unity and diversity in the life of the churches and in their relationship with one another.

Diversity can be interpreted from different perspectives. The biblical witness speaks openly about human diversity as a fact given with God's creation. Furthermore, the Christian community is characterized by a diversity of gifts inspired by the Spirit who "apportions to each individually as he wills" (I Cor. 12:4-11). Neither of these two dimensions of diversity necessarily stands in tension with unity. The differences of creation are not exclusive, but complementary and mutually enriching realities manifesting the unity which God intended for his creation. The diversity of gifts is in itself an expression of the unity of all members of the community (I Cor. 14:1-13). The bearers of diverse gifts are all united in the one Spirit who is at work in and through them. The Spirit allows for diversity and through many gifts manifests himself as the centre and source of unity.

Today the question of diversity arises most acutely as Christians and churches try to bear witness to Jesus Christ in specific human situations. In the incarnation, God has revealed himself in the person and life practice of a particular man over against a particular tradition. The truth of Jesus Christ can only be appropriated in as much as it is translated into the corporate life practice of specific human beings in a variety of situations and historical contexts. It invites processes of tradition which lead to diversification. Diversity is not only inevitable, it is the necessary condition for the truth of the incarnation of Jesus Christ to appear in human life.

As long as Christianity shared basic elements of a common cultural and historical tradition, this constitutive diversity could remain relatively unacknowledged even though it has always been present. With the emergence of new Christian traditions, particularly in Asia and Africa, accompanied by the gradual disintegration of the historical Christian cultures, the challenge of this basic diversity takes on new urgency. Diversity is now seen to be rooted in the very understanding and practice of the faith in Jesus Christ. But it is a diversity within the communion which faith creates among men by virtue of the truth revealed in and through Jesus Christ. Through him as the centre, they are related to each other. Any witness of tradition which absolutizes itself and denies its relatedness loses the truth of Christ and turns into untruth.

From this appreciation of diversity emerges an understanding of unity which can be expressed in the phrase "diversity centred on Christ". In him, the tension between unity and diversity is overcome. In witnessing to Jesus Christ the Church is confronted at the same time with the experience of its deepest diversity and with the centre and source of its unity. To speak of unity as "diversity centred on Christ" does not mean a weakening of the obligation to overcome division. However, it underlines the insight that uniformity is not the proper answer to division. In the life of the one Church, there needs to be room for the expression of legitimate diversity. But how do we distinguish between legitimate and sinful diversity, or between *diversity*, i.e. legitimate distinctions, and *division*, i.e. differences which have to be overcome? When does diversity become division? And, when can what appears to be division be properly understood as diversity?

These questions are very timely for the ecumenical movement at the present stage of its development. Many examples could be cited. It may suffice here to refer to two instances. (1) More than fifty years of ecumenical dialogue have led to a new appreciation of the differences in doctrine and order which for long were held to be at the root of the division in the Church. The common effort to reappropriate the "centre of the Gospel", the living truth of Jesus Christ, has forced upon the churches the recognition that many formerly divisive issues had arisen out of the tendency to absolutize particular expressions of the truth of Jesus Christ. Wherever it is possible to reintegrate such controversies into the basic *koinonia* in Christ, they change their quality. What formerly was division can then be understood as a manifestation of legitimate diversity. (2) The ecumenical movement has led to a sharper awareness of the fact that diversities are constantly in danger of being perverted into sinful division which needs to be overcome if the *koinonia* is to be maintained. The most blatant example is offered by racial discrimination in the churches and in society. Racial, as well as cultural and sexual differences are a manifestation of the "created" diversity of mankind. Where such differences are being turned into claims of superiority they divide the fellowship in Christ.

If the unity of the Church is understood as "diversity centred on Christ", the agenda of the ecumenical movement in its search for a fuller manifestation of this unity needs to be reviewed. There is not only division to be overcome and diversity to be respected. There is also false and illegitimate unity to be uncovered and fought against. A unity which is manifested only by a common affirmation of faith without fighting against and overcoming human division and oppression on political, cultural, racial or sexual grounds betrays the unity given in Christ. For, Jesus Christ separates men as he unites; he judges as he reconciles. He stands against "cheap" unity as he opposes "cheap" grace. As the centre, he is the ultimate limit and judge of any manifestation of diversity which regards itself as the last word of truth. But he is also the source of the most radical critique of any unity which is based on the domination and power of man over man. Over against such power is posed the power of the love of

God which expresses itself most fully in the very act when God in his Son renounces all earthly power: *"regnavit a ligno Deus"*.

The catholicity of the Church and the need for indigenization
Understanding the unity of the Church as "diversity centred on Christ" gives new emphasis to the fact that in Christ people of all times, of all races, of all places, of all cultures and conditions are brought into a living fellowship. This is being referred to as the "catholicity of the Church". Catholicity can, in fact, be interpreted as pointing to the basic characteristic of the Church, that it is a fellowship uniting all human diversities around Christ as the centre. "Since Christ lived, died and rose again for all humankind, catholicity is the opposite of all kinds of egoism and particularism. It is the quality by which the Church expresses the fullness, the integrity and totality of its life in Christ" (cf. *The Uppsala Report*, Geneva 1968, Section I, paras. 6 and 7).

Catholicity in its eschatological fulfilment transcends the tension between unity and diversity. The Church is called to anticipate in each historical moment its catholicity in the fullest possible way. This call takes on special significance in a time when churches everywhere are confronted in a new and urgent way with the demand to develop indigenous forms of witness and service. How can the Church maintain its catholicity given in Christ in face of the present struggle about the validity of conflicting forms of indigenization?

Each local congregation, confronted with the differences and tensions between young and old, rich and poor, black and white, sick and healthy, continuously risks losing its catholicity. In baptism the Church recognizes diversities as charismata in the service of a whole community and to that extent affirms them in their own dignity. Thus, the host of diversities which have not found their place in the life of the congregation puts a challenge to the catholicity of the Church. This is particularly true for the powerless and marginalized and continue to have a charismatic task in the congregation.

But the catholicity of the Church is put to a test even more through the needs for "indigenization" in a conflict-torn, interdependent world. This need arises not only when the Gospel confronts traditional cultures. The rapid transformation of all societies calls for ever new forms of Christian presence and proclamation. Congregations and service groups, for example, often take different sides in social and political conflicts. The Church will not preserve its catholicity in such conflicts, when it seeks harmonization at the expense of truth, justice and love.

VI. Conciliarity
What are the forms and structures of fellowship which correspond to the understanding of the Church and its unity as set out before? Where questions of this kind have been asked in recent years, reference has been made at several occasions to the concept of "conciliarity" as it had emerged from studies of the conciliar process of the ancient Church (cf. *Councils and the Ecumenical Movement*, World Council studies no. 5, Geneva 1968). The Uppsala assembly, in speaking about the universality of the Church, called for the realization of a truly conciliar form of life within and among the churches (Section I, para. 19). The Commission on Faith and Order took this debate further by relating it to the concern for the unity of mankind (cf. *Faith and Order, Louvain, 1971*, pp.225ff.). This relationship remained mostly implicit at that time. In

the light of further discussion, the crucial importance of a conciliar form of fellowship for the Church and the ecumenical movement in an interdependent world can be stated more fully.

The quality of ecclesial fellowship

Conciliarity, as the concept is being used in present ecumenical discussions, reflects the conciliar experience of the past and points to the possible event of a future "genuinely universal council". But conciliarity in this sense is not limited to the model of the conciliar processes offered by the ancient Church. This model can be helpful in the attempt to formulate conditions and criteria of conciliarity today; yet the limitation of such historical analogy should constantly be kept in mind. Each generation has to seek forms of conciliarity adequate for its own time.

Conciliarity has a second meaning, influenced partly by the formation of councils of churches at local, national, regional and world levels. Such councils are a distinct feature of the modern ecumenical movement. They reflect, under the conditions of the contemporary world, the need which the Church has faced at all times, namely to find ways of living together in mutual commitment at all levels, which leaves room both for a wide variety of forms of life and of theology, and for differences or even conflicts to be expressed. Conciliarity in this sense goes beyond the pattern of relationships within and between councils of churches and cannot be limited to those aspects of conciliar life already experienced within the structures of councils of churches, including the World Council. While catholicity refers to the nature of the Church and its unity as a "diversity centred on Christ", conciliarity is concerned with the quality of ecclesial fellowship and with the forms of life which correspond to this understanding of the Church.

True conciliarity can only be expressed in a united Church. A united Church necessarily has to be a conciliar Church if it is to hold together the call for catholicity and the need for indigenization, if it is to be a diversity centred on Christ and at the same time a community which in mission reaches out beyond its limits. Surely, the one Church living a truly conciliar life and thus being able to come together in a council remains a vision for the time being, marking the direction into which the ecumenical movement should move. But it seems legitimate to characterize the present ecumenical situation as "pre-conciliar", still lacking some of the essential marks of full conciliarity, yet at the same time presenting to the churches the challenge to anticipate and strive towards "a truly universal, ecumenical, conciliar form of common life and witness".

The characterization of the present ecumenical situation as "pre-conciliar" leads to the questions: (1) How can the quality of fellowship and commitment be deepened so as to help the churches in the ecumenical movement to regain a fuller measure of conciliarity? and (2) What are the minimal conditions to be fulfilled in the life of each individual church and in the relationship of churches with each other in order to enable them one day to unite in a genuinely universal council which may speak for all Christians? The two parts of the question obviously are closely related. For, the minimal conditions of conciliarity represent, in themselves, criteria for the quality of ecclesial fellowship. They can guide churches which are on the way to being reconciled with each other. Only as the churches are ready to mutually recognize and acknowledge each other will they be able to pass beyond the pre-conciliar process into a fully conciliar life.

DOCUMENT III.11

TOWARDS UNITY IN TENSION (1974)

1. Unity in Christ

In pursuing our quest for the visible unity of the Church, we are seeking the fulfilment of God's purpose as it is declared to us in Jesus Christ. This purpose concerns the world, the whole of mankind, and the whole created order. Christ has been lifted up to draw all men to himself, and as all things have been created through him and all men are made in his image, so it is his will that all should be reconciled in him through the "blood of the Cross" (Col. 1:20).

Our concern for the unity of the Church is, therefore, held within a concern for that wider and fuller unity whereof we believe the Church is called to be a sign, first-fruit, and instrument.

Thus it is as part of our faith that we say: "The Church is bold in speaking of itself as the sign of the coming unity of mankind."[1]

2. The Question: Unity in Human Conflict

But in a time when human inter-relatedness has become oppressive for so many, can we speak of "the unity of mankind"? When liberation and struggle have become a vocation for the oppressed, is it enough to speak of "signs" and "church unity"? What does "unity" require of Christians in situations of human conflict?

3. The Unity of Mankind

When we speak of the unity of mankind, we intend to refer to more than the unity of the Church. We speak in the light of the new creation of the human unity in and for which God created mankind, and which he has promised to his children in his Kingdom. It will come in God's own time and power, in judgment and fulfilment, and will be the final definition and realization of mankind's hope for unity.

4. The Just Interdependence of Free People

This unity, whose foretaste we know in the Spirit, demands and enables in history the just interdependence of free people, societies, and nations. It is this just interdependence of which mankind has dreamed, of which its laws and ideologies attempt to speak, and which it continually struggles to attain and protect. Movements of liberation, for instance, derive a large part of their motivation from the sense of solidarity of man with man in the fight for justice and equality. Although this just interdependence is not identical with "the unity of mankind", it is also not separable from it. In this light, humanity's search for a just interdependence is in reality a hunger, implanted by the Creator, a hunger for which Christians share a mutual responsibility with all human beings.

It is part of that travail in which the whole creation groans, longing for liberation (Rom. 8:19-22). It is that longing which Christians share, sustained in it by the work of the Spirit. Therefore, Christians have a mandate for critical, loyal participation in humanity's strivings for a more adequate human community. They are also called to

---

[1] *The Uppsala Report 1968*, p.17. Geneva: WCC, 1968.

recognize, proclaim, and expect God's judgment upon all forms of that community which are unjust and oppressive.

5. Human Inter-relatedness

Mankind's yearning for a just interdependence is magnified today by certain historical factors and forces which are producing an inevitable, fast-developing human inter-relatedness and organization. In speaking of this developing "human inter-relatedness", we intend to refer to a fact of modern life which has both positive and negative aspects.

6. The Possibility in Human Inter-relatedness

On the positive side, a providential increase in the human ability for just interdependence is taking place. World-wide economic structures, mass communication, the development of science and technology, international travel — to name only a few factors — increasingly inter-relate us in one another's economies, societies, politics, cultures, aspirations. They provide a basis for vastly strengthening the just interdependence of free people. We understand this inter-relatedness as extending not only in space but in time. We are increasingly linked with the heritage of past generations and projected into new responsibilities for generations unborn. This makes it all the more urgent and possible to act now to reverse the crisis of our environment and stem the reckless exploitation of this earth's resources.

7. The Threat in Human Inter-relatedness

But the unity of mankind — as the Bible teaches us — bears the mark of Cain. From the beginning, human wickedness has made human history a scene of hostility and alienation. The human quest for a just interdependence is vitiated by sinful self-assertion. In the name of unity and interdependence false structures are created, marked by false dependence and oppression. The powerful exploit the weak in the name of unity. The commercial and financial structures which bind the world together also oppress and enslave. Race oppresses race, and even the Church itself uses its power to subject others to a false unity. Hence it may be more accurate to speak of human brokenness than of mankind's unity.

This universal hostility and alienation has been exposed and condemned in the Cross of Jesus Christ. It is that Cross — the Cross of the one who is risen and who reigns — which marks the birth of a new humanity recreated in him. It gives us our belief in and our hope for the unity of mankind.

8. Liberation and Conflict

We believe that the unity of mankind for which we pray and hope, and the just interdependence of free people inseparable from it, cannot be thought of apart from God's liberating activity and an active human response and participation. Moreover, this liberation is indivisible: it concerns the human soul, mind, and body, and no less mankind in its cultures, societies, and politics. It must confront, struggle against, and overcome whatever alienates human beings from themselves, from each other, and from God. We are aware of limits to liberation which will never be overcome as long as history lasts. The powers of sickness and death will always be present and there will always be suffering people calling for solidarity and love. In recognizing it, our hope in the liberating power of God's Kingdom is reinforced. We are called to that unity where "there shall be an end to death, and to mourning and crying and pain" (Rev. 21:4). And, therefore, we are called to face the problems of suffering and conflict not simply as an unpleasantness to be avoided, or as a disorder to be suppressed, but also as a necessary implication of liberation.

9. Conflict and the Human Sense of Solidarity

We recognize that once men become involved in the struggles for liberation, two factors emerge. A sense of solidarity springs up among those involved together in a common task. But other relationships are strained, even broken, by such engagement. But there is no other way of achieving a just interdependence than by facing the issues, engaging in encounter, and even conflict.

10. Solidarity in Conflict as a Challenge to Church Unity

How does such conflict affect the unity of the Church? What does it mean for the goal of the visible unity of the Church? Christians have a vocation to be the fellowship of reconciliation. But Christians involved in the struggle for liberation in fact often find themselves closer to others who share the struggle with them, Christian or not, than to other Christians who are not committed to it. This problem cannot be avoided. An ecclesiastical unity which would stand in the way of struggles for liberation would be a repressive unity, hindering the just interdependence which Christians are called to serve. We are learning that Church unity can be a "unity in tension".

11. Conflict under the Cross

Christian faith trusts the reality of grace in which it is empowered to bear the tensions of conflicts. Jesus Christ accepted the necessity of conflict, yet transcended it in his death on the Cross. He took upon himself the cost of conflict; forces of divisions are finally overcome in the unity which Christ creates and gives, as he leads all things to unity in himself. The Church has also been given remarkable anticipations of this unity, even in the midst of severe conflict. The Church must, therefore, bear the tension of conflicts within itself, and so fulfil its ministry of reconciliation, in obedience to the Lord who chooses to sacrifice himself rather than to confer on the forces of division any ultimate authority. The Church accordingly is called to work for unity, through suffering, under the sign of the Cross.

12. The Church as "Sign"

The Church is called to be a visible sign of the presence of Christ, who is both hidden and revealed to faith, reconciling and healing human alienation in the worshipping community. The Church's calling to be such a sign includes struggle and conflict for the sake of the just interdependence of mankind.

There is here an enduring tension which will not be resolved until the promise is fulfilled of a new heaven and a new earth. Until that day we have to accept the fact that we do not fully know how to embody in the life of the nations and communities of our time the unity which God wills. There is only one foundation for human unity — the new Man, Jesus Christ. But what we build on that foundation will be tested by fire, and may not pass the test.

We must resolutely refuse any too easy forms of unity, or any misuse of the "sign", that conceal a deeper disunity. At the same time, we may believe in and give witness to our unity in Christ, even with those from whom we may, for his sake, have to part. This means to be prepared to be a "fellowship in darkness" — dependent on the guidance of the Holy Spirit for the form which our fellowship should seek and take; and a "unity in tension" — dependent on the Spirit for the strength to reconcile within the one body of the Church all whom the forces of disunity would otherwise continue to drive apart. For there is no "fellowship in darkness" without some sign of the reconciling judgment and love of Christ.

DOCUMENT III.12

RACISM IN THEOLOGY — THEOLOGY AGAINST RACISM
(1975)

. . .

IV: The Role of the Church: Discipleship and Disciplined Life

We now turn to a few reflections on the role of the Church itself. In the second chapter we tried to describe what the Church ought to be, i.e. a community of disciples which constantly regroups and reconstitutes itself around situations of suffering. What are the consequences of discipleship in terms of "disciplined life"?

1. The Legacy of the Suffering Church in Past and Present

The evil of racism discloses in a new way how often the churches fail to centre around the suffering, dispossessed and degraded members of humanity. The churches are constantly yielding to the temptation to forget those who are forgotten and not heed the voice of the voiceless. They seek to organize and establish themselves along the lines of the main values and dominant forces in their respective societies. In varying degrees the histories of our churches bear witness to their constant drifting away from the poor and powerless to the rich and mighty. The persecutions of defenceless minorities, the ghettoes of Jews in Europe and the recurrent pogroms, the endless stream of refugees, who for the sake of their faith have had to leave their homes and lands — all these have through many centuries left a stain on the history of Christianity. This means that most of our "official" established churches, because of their history and the way their structures have developed, are not equipped to deal with this suffering. There have, of course, been movements within the churches which have had certain insights so radical and onesided that the established, official church at the time has found them threatening. But these movements have often been branded "heretical" or "sectarian". Consequently they have suffered appallingly at the hands of the official Church and of the political authorities in the particular country with which the official Church had aligned itself. Yet it is in many of these expelled groups that the witness of enduring hope in the midst of so much suffering has been kept alive. This presents us with the duty of rescuing this legacy of suffering and resistance, of revolt and silent endurance, hidden in the history of the oppressed. This would give us a truer understanding of what is today being expressed in the theologies of black people, notably in North America and Southern Africa. At the same time, it will help us to a deeper understanding of what it means to die to the might and power of this world and to rise again on the side of suffering. As the churches reflect the ministry of Jesus Christ who "reigns from the Tree", they will regain their authentic ministry. Called constantly to meditate on the cross and resurrection, they will be reminded that their Lord died on the cross because of the combined efforts of an alliance of established religion and power politics. They will need to be constantly on guard against the recurring danger of concluding similar alliances, and become again and again the Church of the suffering servant.

2. Racism — A "Moral Heresy"?

We have tried to reflect on the Church's role with the self-searching that this requires. The sin of racism is so all-pervasive that we are not at liberty to judge or condemn others. Nevertheless, we have to face up to the issue of "moral heresy" to which much attention has been given in recent years, particularly in connection with the Programme to Combat Racism. In our view, the concept of "heresy" is not in practice a very helpful standpoint from which to consider racism. Certainly we recognize that some of the theories and beliefs advanced to justify racism may be heretical, but the discussion of racism must not be side-tracked into an academic discussion of what is or is not formal heresy. On the other hand, we recognize that orthodoxy and orthopraxy are intimately related. As we have already noted, Christian doctrine cannot be divorced from its practical implications. All heretical teaching is likely to produce moral distortions of one sort or another.

Equally, behind every discriminative action, if accepted and justified as a Christian mode of behaviour, there lies some hidden heresy. But our main concern should not be to denounce groups or churches as morally heretical. Rather, we should be consistently attentive to possibly negative effects of certain beliefs and practices, and to help each other to discover and overcome them.

The concept of moral heresy, it seems to us, was originally intended to make a preacher's point. The legitimacy of this is hardly open to dispute. But endless complications and difficulties arise when it is transplanted into formal theological discourse, particularly in the context of the ecumenical movement, which has no constitutional claims on its member churches.

3. Church Discipline

From our understanding of discipleship we would be inclined rather to focus our attention on the discipline of the church. If "being the Church" means "re-establishing community in situations of suffering", it means leading a disciplined life according to this criterion. "Disciplined life" means that all decisions and actions at all levels of church life are related to this central notion of discipleship. As such it does not imply rigidity and isolation but rather consistent flexibility and openness: not an openness towards all kinds of things, but towards people and communities of people (including other churches) in whose life suffering for the sake of freedom and reconciliation has somehow become constitutive. Only in the context of this disciplined life does the concept of *unity* take on meaning and substance. Only in the context of this disciplined life can the unity of the Church be called a sign of the unity of mankind.

We are very much aware of the fact that in the course of church history church discipline has been organized according to certain patterns and that in some churches it has become an important part of their life and structure. We would invite all churches, however, to consider whether some of these patterns of church discipline have not in fact moved away from the notion of discipleship that we are trying to spell out here. At this point, we would like to suggest two points:

a) In the first place we submit that the notion of church discipline has become too individualistic in many churches. It is the individual church member who is "disciplined". The process of repentance that we have been trying to describe, however, makes it difficult to maintain this emphasis. In sins like racism men and women are involved collectively and it is the same in the Church. We cannot assume a clean Church over against a possibly unclean individual. Discipline in this sense must mean helping one another relentlessly to become aware of the dimensions of evil and of our involvement in it. Discipline in this sense can only be judging if it is simultaneously self-judging and if it leads to common efforts at repentance-action. Of course these things have always been important in the understanding of church discipline. But it seems to us that they take on new meaning in the light of the discoveries we have made.

Yet this is not the most radical reason why an individualistic conception of church discipline seems to be inadequate. In the light of our understanding of discipleship as constant re-grouping around real suffering, discipline means a consistent effort to help each other to share constructively and hopefully in the suffering that is the result of sin.

b) In the second place we submit that in most churches the notion of church discipline has become too exclusive in the sense that it is automatically associated with excommunication. We are not prepared to eliminate this notion of excommunication entirely; we feel that it has its legitimate place in a Church that seeks to lead a disciplined life. But neither are we prepared to use the notion of excommunication directly, for instance by saying that the Church should excommunicate all racists. Our understanding of the sin of racism, as we have sought to describe it, and of the nature of discipleship in view of racism, clearly prohibits this.

Most important, however, is that our churches still lack the fruit of credibility that would grow out of a disciplined life around situations of real suffering; and we feel that responsible discussion of excommunication can only take place on the basis of such fruit. Until we have made some real progress on this road, we are not free on the ground of racism either to excommunicate certain churches from the fellowship of churches.

On the whole, it is much more important to work for authenticity at the centre than for a rigid definition of boundaries. Authenticity at the centre implies solidarity in being the body of Christ in the world. That is not an uncritical solidarity that knows no limits; it is a solidarity that keeps defining and redefining itself from the centre. In that process the so-called boundaries of the Church might become visible to people simply by what the Church is and does, rather than by what it says and defines.

4. Forms of Disciplined Life

Only in the context of this positive understanding of discipline can we say that the Church should examine its own life relentlessly in order to ascertain and eliminate institutional racism in itself. Only in the context of this positive understanding of discipline can we try to avoid both the arrogant aloofness of those who feel that they are too important to get their hands soiled in the mundane struggle against racism as well as the self-righteous, sectarian attitude of those who believe that they alone are the Lord's true disciples because they march against racism in advance of the Church. And only in the context of this positive understanding of discipline will submerged people and groups within the Church be enabled to rise and take in hand their own responsibilities as members of the body of Christ.

What does this mean for the life of the Church?

We have given our attention to the following concerns:

4.1. Discipline in Worship and Sacraments

Firstly it appears that the Church needs to be based more decisively on "disciplined worship". This would imply that we seek a new discipline in the sacraments of Baptism and the Eucharist. Through Baptism every person is made part of the Christian Community, and this inclusiveness of our corporate identity in Christ must be taken literally. In the same way the Eucharist is the celebration of oneness in Christ and it is rendered incredible where it is not lived out in a consistent and committed practice of solidarity between black and white, between races and sexes.

The disciplined life in the sacraments and the worship of God provokes rigorous prophetic preaching. Unrepentant racists need to be exhorted that for the health of their souls they are not welcome at the Lord's table until they truly repent. The leadership of the Church needs to be vigorous enough to eradicate preaching and teaching which conforms to personal and institutional racism, and to support preachers and teachers who work against racism. For indifference to racism in the Church is indifference to the worship and service of God.

At the same time our discipline of worship will have to be much more pastoral insofar as it seeks to draw into communion with Christ those who truly repent and are burdened with unacquitted guilt, hidden fears and loneliness. A disciplined worship will be worship which is unqualifiedly hospitable to all who seek Christ. Of course, each congregation has a definite character. But truly united worship will always include those who do not fit in. They are an indispensable sign of how radical the communication of God is. We ought to work hard to prevent totally homogeneous congregations, to secure worship which is truly hospitable to the wide diversity of Christian identity. So, as a consequence of disciplined worship, the Church discovers how deeply its prophetic and pastoral tasks are intertwined and how they flow together in the building up of the healing community in this world. The inclusiveness of the Church will reveal itself in the integrity and comprehensiveness with which it denounces sin, gives new heart to the broken and disheartened, heals the depressed, and sets free the oppressed.

4.2. Disciplined Life in Education

The disciplined life in the Church not only expresses itself in the central activity of worship, in preaching and administration of the sacraments. The discovery of the pervasive and contaminating character of racism must lead us also to reflect on other dimensions of the churches' life. We would in particular like to mention some aspects in the areas of education and renewal.

The brief reference to church history forces us to conclude that the task of teaching in the Church will have to include the critical reassessment of the extent to which our perception of our history still reflects and perpetuates discrimination against minority groups. There is need to reevaluate the important contributions and insights for which many marginalized and rejected groups have struggled and suffered. In addition to this there is need to correct the often false ways in which history books and other theological textbooks present the stories of these groups and movements. To relive the past by rediscovering the role of the Church of Christ from the viewpoint of the suffering Church will help us greatly to see ourselves today in that self-scrutinizing and repentant manner of which we have tried to speak. This will help us both as teachers and as students of theology today to become aware of the on-going cultural, ethnocentric and linguistic presumptions which, in different ways, still reinforce racist features in our theology. Such a self-scrutinizing style of doing theology will lead us to seek ways of inter-cultural, inter-racial and thereby truly ecumenical confrontation and correction. It will also make it mandatory to seek a deeper understanding of the sociological, psychological, economic and other elements which need to be taken into account in order not only to assess fully the churches' involvement in racism and the mechanisms which enforce it but also to provoke changes with sufficient care and vigour.

Again, only on the basis of such a self-critical approach would we be entitled to attack prophetically the unjust features, economic, political and otherwise, of entrenched racism.

An obvious consequence of all this is the need to revise the curricula of education in schools and other institutions of learning. This not only relates to history books, but also to the literature we use in our worship services. Hymnbooks and liturgies need to be checked and new formulae suggested which take into account the experiences of churches and movements that are constantly being overlooked, distrusted or rejected. Disciplined life should be marked by the imagination and joy of discovering the experiences with Christ which such groups represent.

Another vital aspect of renewing educational efforts needs to be a new emphasis on enabling the marginalized to make full use of their potential. Provisions must be made to help these groups to defend and express themselves not in the spirit of benevolent remedial activity but in an attempt to share resources, insights and gifts which exist in the one body of Christ and which must not be left to suffer lest the whole body suffer.

4.3. Disciplined Life in Renewal

The collective and pervasive sin of racism has led us to understand more fully that the discipline of renewal must constantly seek to meet the requirements of inclusiveness, mutual accountability and comprehensiveness. Honest attempts at active repentance will lead to a close combination of work and reflection, of witness and commitment. It will also penetrate the on-going evangelistic task of the churches. This is a formidable task because in many churches, the emphasis on evangelism tends to be separated from the insistence on social action and the radical transformation of society. But we affirm that conversion to God calls for a second conversion to the world, especially to those who are in suffering and pain.

The enormity of the problem of racism has perplexed and frustrated many and the struggle against it in its many different forms has exhausted many groups. Others have sunk back into resignation and apathy.

The quality of the discipline of the healing sacramental community of Christians will therefore be determined, particularly at the local level, by the sharing love, pastoral concern and prophetic solidarity in suffering which refuse to leave brothers and sisters to stand alone. The Church must enfold them in its protective arms, encourage, correct and sustain them to return to and persist in the battle against racism.

DOCUMENT III.13

ORDINATION OF WOMEN IN ECUMENICAL PERSPECTIVE
(1979)

The following propositions do not attempt to be a comprehensive statement on the ministry of the Church, either in the New Testament or in its historical development. Rather, they attempt to raise certain points that are often neglected in ecumenical discussions, which put the question of women's ordination in a new perspective. These six points, stated in the form of questions, may be useful in raising new aspects of the women's ordination issue in view of growing ecumenical consensus on baptism, eucharist and ministry.

1. The new community of the Church

On the question of women's ordination, the nature of the Church is an essential starting point. How does the way in which a church tradition describes the nature of the Church affect its views of the possibility of women's ordination?

All ministry is to be understood in the light of him who came "not to be served, but to serve" (Mark 10:45). In describing the nature of the Church, we should not bypass the witness of the historical community around Jesus. Contemporary Christians have recognized anew the radical nature of the fellowship drawn to Jesus. This fellowship broke through traditional social barriers. It included women as well as men in unconventional ways. It included those who were socially despised. It is even said "that prostitutes and tax collectors will go into the Kingdom of God ahead of the conventional religious leaders, scribes and pharisees" (Matt. 21:31).

This sense of a new community is empowered by the resurrection and Pentecost. Paul speaks of those who are in Christ as being "neither Jew nor Greek, not bond nor free, not male nor female; for all are one in Christ Jesus" (Gal. 3:28). This text is generally understood to have reflected a baptismal creed of the Church. It reflects the sense of oneness in Christ in a new creation, which is anticipated in the Church.

All Christians belong to the Royal Priesthood (I Pet. 2:9). The Christian is one who has been redeemed from earlier states of dependency and enslavement. We are the offspring of the free woman, not the slave woman (Gal. 4:31). We have been freed from the childhood state to become responsible adults (Gal. 3:23-26).

This sense of the Church as a community of equals is not simply a matter of early lack of organization. It contains an enduring insight into the nature of the redeemed humanity in Christ that is a constant source for the renewal of the Church. What is specific to some views of ordained ministry that excludes some baptized Christians, i.e. women, from this ministry? How can this be compatible with the nature of the Church as reflective of oneness in Christ wherein previously justified inequalities are nullified?

2. The Church in ministries

What is the significance of the variety of ministries in the New Testament, shown by current New Testament research, for the understanding of ministry and for the debate on the ordination of women to the ministry?

In the earliest Church there were different gifts and ministries which may serve as paradigms for ministry today, for example, that of prophet or teacher in the local church, or of apostle in the mission of the Church. The paradigms for ministry were linked to various charismata. Women also received the charismata and acted as prophets (Acts 21:9), teachers (Acts 18:26) and missionaries (I Cor. 16:13; Rom. 16:1ff). (Further research is also needed on the issue of "Junias" Rom. 6:7, and on the distinction between prophesying (propheteuein) and speaking (lalein) in the New Testament: I Cor. 11:15, I Cor. 14:31-35, Gal. 1:6-8).

There are differences in the use of "apostolos" in the epistles of St. Paul and in Acts, where the title "apostolos" is reserved for the Twelve. Some interpret the role of the Twelve as specific and symbolic: they represented the 12 tribes of Israel who were to be gathered in with the coming of the Messiah; they are to sit on the 12 thrones of Israel, judging the tribes of Israel (Matt. 19:28). They had of necessity to be men — no woman could be a patriarch of Israel — as by the same token they had to be Jews. Is it important to distinguish between the unique function of the Twelve and the broader idea of apostleship which existed in the Church from the beginning?

In the early Church a new priesthood developed which was meant to be neither Jewish nor Hellenistic. Some traditions today affirm that development as legitimate; others do not, holding that Christ completed and abolished the priesthood, according to the letter to the Hebrews. Is the development of priesthood in some churches an impediment to the ordination of women to the full sacramental ministry in these churches?[1]

The emphasis on the paradigm of teacher likewise contributed to the exclusion of women, not only for sociological reasons but also out of a hesitancy to hand over the Holy Scriptures to women. The Jewish custom of male teachers may have influenced this development. Given the new conditions for women today, must not the churches reconsider the teaching ministries of women?

In the New Testament times the "prophet" was an important paradigm for ministry. The early Christians preached the Christ as the fulfilment of the hope of Israel, interpreting the Scriptures and the signs of the time. They saw themselves as authorized to do this by the Spirit, quoting for example from Joel (Acts 2). These prophets were both men and women. What relevance has the demise of the role of the prophet for the ministry and for the exclusion of women from the ministry? Some churches have revitalized the prophetic ministry; what impact might this development have on ministry and on participation by women today?

The various churches have given greater emphasis to one or the other of the various paradigms of ministry. Is it possible to achieve a new sense of the wholeness of ministry by reconsidering those paradigms which have fallen into disuse?

3. Apostolic succession and Tradition

What is the relation of the understanding of apostolic succession and Tradition to the understanding of ministry and to the question of the ordination of women?

The continuity which is designated "apostolic succession" was in the early Church primarily understood to be the handing on of the deposit of faith, though this was tied

---

[1] Refers to "The Preacher and the Priest: Two Typologies of Ministry and the Ordination of Women", by Rosemary Ruether, a paper prepared for the Klingenthal meeting and included as the appendix [not reprinted here].

to ministry insofar as the bishop was seen as the guardian of faith. Apostolic succession can be seen as much broader than simply ministerial succession.

"The fullness of the apostolic succession of the whole Church involves continuity in the permanent characteristics of the Church of the apostles: witness to the apostolic faith, proclamation and fresh interpretation of the apostolic gospel, transmission of ministerial responsibility, sacramental life, community in love, service for the needy, unity among local churches and sharing the gifts which the Lord has given to each."[2]

If apostolic succession is understood in this wider sense, does this influence our thinking as to whether women can be ordained?

The use of Tradition and of Scripture in the Church urgently calls for further study. Scripture and Tradition both belong to a continuing, living transmission process guided by the Spirit in which the Gospel is being brought to fulfilment.[3] How are we then, while not losing continuity with the past, to move into the future?

It must also be said that certain arguments put forward in the past against ordaining women must be called into question. What does our present knowledge of human reproduction and evolution, as well as different anthropologies and sociology, have to say to the question of the ordination of women?

4. Incarnation and priesthood

Is the maleness of the historical Jesus essential to the meaning of the incarnation? Does Christ have to be represented by a male priesthood?

Some argue that the incarnation of God in the male Jesus requires the representation of Christ to be through a male priesthood.

One Orthodox position would speak of priesthood in the following, somewhat different manner. There is only one Priest, Jesus Christ, in the full sense of the word, who (according to the Liturgy of St John Chrysostom) at the same time offers and is offered. In him the Old Testament priesthood finds its fulfilment. The Church is the place where the Holy Spirit works. By the gift of the Holy Spirit the Church participates in the unique priesthood of the Son of God Incarnate. Such is the meaning of the royal priesthood of all believers. But the Church charges certain of its members in whom it discerns such a charisma to actualize in one place here and now the unique priesthood of the God/Man, the very priesthood in which it participates. Such is the meaning of priestly ordination and of the special grace which it confers. The universal priesthood of all believers and the sacramental priesthood *both* derive from the unique priesthood. The bishop and the priest only actualize, by the grace of the Holy Spirit in time and space, the unique and eternal priesthood of the High Priest.

This argument would continue that, on the basis of biblical anthropology, men and women are different and at the same time one both in accordance with the order of creation and the order of redemption. This unity/diversity can be signified in the reconciled new creation which is beginning in the Church here and now, through the

---

[2] "One Baptism, One Eucharist and a Mutually Recognized Ministry: Three Agreed Statements", *Faith and Order Paper* No. 73, 1978, p.36.

[3] See *The Fourth World Conference on Faith and Order*, eds P.C. Rodger and L. Vischer, London, SCM Press, 1964, p.50ff., and also "Episkopé and Episcopate in Ecumenical Perspective", *Faith and Order Paper* No. 102, 1980.

presence at the altar of a man and a woman, both ordained to ministries of equal dignity, though of different symbolic significance. Others would ask yet further, is not this truth of creation and redemption best exemplified when both women and men stand at the altar as priests?

5. The "particular role" of women in the Church

Do women have particular contributions to offer to the life of the Church that are different from or complementary to the contributions of men?

Does the answer to this question, whether yes or no, have any implications for the ordination of women?

In "One Baptism, One Eucharist and a Mutually Recognized Ministry", p.45, it is said: "Both men and women need to discover the full meaning of their specific contribution to the ministry of Christ. The Church is entitled to the style of ministry which can be provided by women as well as that which can be provided by men."

Many agree with the above statement. Others hesitate to use this language of "specific contributions" because they believe it creates certain expectations of women and of men which limit the fulfilment of their potential as persons.

Many say that the Church especially needs the caring, nourishing and nurturing that women have traditionally provided. Some emphasize that these qualities in women will bring a style of leadership to the Church that encourages partnership rather than domination/submission. Others believe that emphasizing these qualities in women leads to assigning them to specialized and/or secondary roles. Another way of addressing this problem may be: Can there be wholeness in the life of the Church and its ministry before both men and women fully contribute and participate in it?

6. Personal vocation and true ministry of the Church

What is the relation between personal vocation and the criteria for ministry applied by the Church?

There is a strong stream in Christianity which bases authority of ministry on the call of God. It is this call, tested as to its authenticity in various ways by the Church, which undergirds the authorization to minister.

Many in this stream of Christianity believe that insofar as the call of God is the foundation of ministry, and God calls whom God chooses, and since we cannot limit the outpouring of God's gift, basic questions are raised about the obedience of the Church to God if the Church refuses to test the vocations of some who believe themselves to be called to the ordained ministry.

Comment

These six propositions, coming out of an ecumenical dialogue, both narrow and intensify the discussion. They are posed, not with the hope of agreement, but with the aim of discerning which issues are central and which are marginal to the work of achieving mutual understanding.

DOCUMENT III.14

BASES AND OUTLINE OF A STUDY ON THE UNITY OF THE CHURCH AND THE RENEWAL OF HUMAN COMMUNITY (1981)

What is the aim of the study?

In the report from the group on "The Unity of the Church and the Renewal of Human Community" at the Faith and Order Standing Commission meeting in January 1981, there are these words:

> The aim of the proposed study is to place it [the Faith and Order concern on the unity of the Church] in a broadened horizon and to develop its implications for Christian service and mission in the contemporary world.

This aim, if carried out faithfully and boldly, must affect the self-understanding of the Church, reinforce the prophetic imperative of the unity it seeks, and strengthen its mission of reconciliation in human community. The unity of the divided Church and the renewal of the broken human community are closely inter-related.

What is the theological method of the study?

We are discovering today new insights about the formation of scripture and traditions which can serve as a paradigm for us as we engage in theological reflection. We are beginning to understand this formation as an ongoing process in which we share, even today, as we reflect on our inherited faith and realities of our life and world.

In the Bible, the Israel of the Old Testament and the community of the New Testament express ever-new insights into the being and action of God, of God's demands upon, and desires for, them and through them for all creation. These insights came as they reflected upon their inherited traditions in the light of their present experience and on their present experience in the light of those inherited traditions. In the Old Testament, the inherited traditions centre around the action of God in calling and covenanting with the people. In the New Testament, the new, decisive and determinative event which judges and affirms all else is the life, death and resurrection of Christ. In both instances there is a *double dynamic* at work in which light is shed on present experience as well as on inherited traditions. The biblical writers testify that such reflection was at the direction of, and under the power they identified as, the hand, the word, the spirit of God.

If we are to be faithful to this biblical paradigm of doing theology, we must engage in the same double dynamic. We must seek to wrestle with our Christian inheritance in the light of our lived experience so that our inheritance speaks to and judges our experience, but also to reflect upon our inheritance in the light of our experience so that in its turn it speaks to and brings alive what we have received. Such reflection must be undertaken under the power and guidance of the Spirit. There must be no theological enterprise which does not attempt to take seriously both what we inherit and also our lived experience.

In our search for the unity of the Church and the renewal of human community, the demands upon us are immense. We have to take account of the multiplicity of secular and ecumenical contexts, with their conflicts and brokenness as well as their joys and signs of renewal. But the multiplicity and diversity of contexts open up new possibilities for enquiry and exchange and hold promise of deeper and richer understandings of God and God's intention for creation, for we believe that God is already there in the midst ahead of us. A global context provides the opportunity to examine our Christian inheritance in the light of our own experience but also the opportunity to listen to and enter upon the lived experience and insights of others. It is a gift we offer one another in the ecumenical movement of opening ourselves to others, of receiving them back, and of becoming identified with one another in sufferings and joys. In such reciprocal involvement we are recreated by our common tradition under the power of the Spirit and together discover new insights in our shared inheritance. Such mutual understanding and identification involves accepting vulnerability, but through it we believe we discover truths about the nature and work of God the creator, redeemer and sustainer and about God's demands upon us. So we become more truly united with each other in the body of Christ and dedicate ourselves to the renewal of human community. There can be no convergence towards the unity of the Church which does not speak to the renewal of human community, and no renewal of human community that does not carry implications for the unity of the Church in its confession of faith, in its sacramental life, in its pastoral care and its mission in the contemporary world. The unity in Christ, and its eschatological vision of the one kingdom, is at the same time the fulfilment of our hopes for unity *and* the judgment on false dreams and realities of human unity.

Already the studies on the issues of racism and on the Community of Women and Men in the Church have sought to use this method of shared reflection and action which we may describe as the *inter-relational method*. Both studies point to the possibilities of enlarging and enriching our understanding of the unity of the Church and the renewal of human community and to the very real connections between and interdependence of the two.

What is the theological focus of the study?

The aim of placing the Faith and Order concern for the unity of the Church in a broadened horizon and of developing its implications for Christian service and mission demands a clear theological focus. It would be wrong, however, to seek this focus by dealing with the relation between "Church" and "human community" in general, abstract concepts. This is not to say that such reflection is unnecessary or undesirable — far from it. The study, however, should suspend such reflection because our subject directs us, first of all, not to theological problems but to situations where Church and human community are part of actual human problems. These situations, therefore, will constitute the primary contexts of our study.

Suspension of a general conceptual reflection is stressed here because such reflection can result, and often has resulted, in either overlooking or escaping the problems posed by the situations in which the urgent need for renewal of the human community presents challenges to the faith and unity of Christians. General theological reflection tends to shy away from rigorous verification in those situations and to become a closed circuit. The very aim of our study requires of us an effort to avoid such a tendency.

The focus on situations mentioned above is determined by the faith that the triune God is involved in human history and that the brokenness of human community is God's concern. Thus, when we look at the Church in situations where it itself is deeply affected by that brokenness, we are confronted not only with deplorable failures on the part of the Church, but with the frontiers of faith and unity that call for new ways of giving witness to God's involvement. Standing at those frontiers of conflicts and tensions often implies judgment and conversion. At the same time, it is through those frontiers that a fresh understanding of God's acts and the mission of the Church may develop. In this sense, the unity of the Church and its witness to the renewal of human community are inseparable. The experience of humanity as being *en route* to the kingdom is inherent to the experience of unity and disunity in the Church.

This amounts to saying that in order to be able to *speak* about the Church we must *see* the ways in which the Church is involved in human history. We cannot talk about the body of Christ except in the face of the brokenness of the human community. In other words, the theological focus of the study is the point at which faith in God's involvement in human history expresses itself as an effort to speak about that involvement on the basis of actual experiences of brokenness and renewal. In this way we, like Israel and the New Testament community, learn again and again what God's creating and renewing action means. This is what has been described as inter-relational method in the previous section.

The history of the Church and manifestations of its unity and division are inseparably related to the situations in which the confession of faith in Christ and the development of Christian community are actually affected by the ruptures and conflicts that beset human community. Realization of this fact keeps challenging Christians to understand the role they play in the existence and perpetuation of brokenness in human community, and to become engaged in costly acts of repentance and renewal. The Church cannot serve the renewal of human community without itself becoming part of that renewal movement out of a deep sense of repentance.

When Christians take up this challenge, their understanding of faith and inherited traditions can be deepened. Experience of suffering, for example, can throw new light on the meaning of redemption; experience of renewal in human community can help grasp the meaning of resurrection, and so on. All theological thinking has its roots in life situations such as these. In order for theology to maintain its integrity, it has to strike root again and again in new life situations. Only then will it become and remain truly incarnational.

There is always a danger of losing sight of this basic inter-relatedness of Church and human community that constitutes our theological focus. The study is an effort to face that inter-relatedness and to stress the incarnational nature of theology and ecclesiology. It may prove to be an exciting exploration. Since the global contexts of pluralism, conflicts and interdependence are "the great fact of our time" constituting an inescapable challenge for Christian faith and theology, our exploration is both timely and necessary.

What is the process of the study?

On the basis of the considerations above, we envision a study process which will occupy Faith and Order for the coming several years. The basic study resources will have to come from a number of groups to be formed in different world contexts. These groups would consist of persons conscious of living in situations of conflict and renewal in which both Church and human community are involved. Their concerns may be related to issues of historical conflict (e.g. racism, the rich-poor struggle, the armament question), alienation (e.g. sexism, generation conflict), cultural diversity, or relation to nature (e.g. ecological problems). The groups will be asked to consider how their intuitive approach to, as well as their conscious reflection on, faith and community are affected by these issues. In many cases the groups may find it necessary to reinterpret certain aspects of the theological thinking they have inherited and to seek new engagement in their situations, a process similar to that which has led some women's groups to reconsider traditional views on creation and anthropology. All these findings will have to be described in the reports submitted by the groups.

It is important to emphasize that the study process should remain focused on local situations. This means, among other things, that reports from the groups must not be regarded as illustrations or derivatives of some general conception of faith and unity. But this does not suggest that the study intends to consider experiences and reflections of the groups as normative for theological thinking on faith and unity. What is important is that the reflections of the groups are respected in their situational integrity as they arise out of the frontiers of Church and human community. They are brought into common discussion neither as normative reflections nor as examples of or, perhaps, deviations from "given" norms. Rather, they are challenges by which all partners in the worldwide Christian community are stimulated to reconsider their own positions and conceptions. This can be foreseen as an ongoing process since there is almost no limit to the variety of situations and to the challenges these situations pose to Christians. Thus, doing theology within the ecumenical movement must face the fact that no Christians, either as individuals or as community, can ultimately ignore the need to relate their own "double dynamic" to that of others.

Towards the final stage of the study, an effort should be made, of course, to draw conclusions, on the basis of reports from the groups, about the ways in which ecumenical theological reflections can profit from taking seriously unity, conflict and renewal experienced in local situations. It is hoped that these conclusions will highlight new insights about the Church and its mission which are developing in a variety of situations and places. Further, they may point to the ways in which Christians may engage themselves in the practice of and reflection on their faith at the frontiers where Church and human community meet.

In this process of study, how does the unity of the Church remain the central concern? The answer is twofold. In the first place, involvement at the "frontiers" will undoubtedly lead to discovery of new aspects of the problems of unity and division and of new insights into the meaning and shape of communion in Christ. Secondly, when the problem of unity is dealt with in a *global* context, the unity of the Church may be perceived not only as reconciliation of traditions of faith, but also as closely related to diverse and varied ways in which renewal of human community is conceived, expressed and attempted.

In this way, the study on "The Unity of the Church and the Renewal of Human Community" has its own special focus and method but also remains closely related to other Faith and Order concerns such as the apostolic faith, agreed statements on baptism, eucharist and ministry, the community of women and men in the Church, and so on. The present study is to be understood as one contribution to the Faith and Order concern for unity with a specific assignment: to explore the implications of Christian unity in relation to some of the most crucial challenges confronting us in this broken community of our world.

DOCUMENT III.15

A COMMON ACCOUNT OF HOPE (1978)

I. Thanksgiving

Blessed be God! The Father and the Son and the Holy Spirit. Christ is our hope: the power of love stronger than the world. He lived on the earth: God's Yes for the world's salvation. He was crucified and is risen: the first fruit of the new humanity.

He is present in his Church; He is present in those who suffer;
— He is with us.
He will appear again in glory: our judgment and our hope,
— Unveiling this Yes of salvation.
We have this gift from the living God.
— His Spirit poured into our hearts.
Let us give thanks with rejoicing!

II. Voices of hope

In many places all over the world people are participating in this "yes". Even among the cries of despair we hear voices of hope.

A Latin American song:

Since He came into the world and into history;
 broke down silence and suffering;
 filled the world with his glory;
 was the light in the coldness of our night;
 was born in a dark manger;
 in His life sowed love and light;
 broke hardened hearts
 but lifted up dejected souls;
So today we have hope;
 today we persevere in our struggle;
 today we face our future with confidence,
in this land which is ours.

Everywhere songs of hope and longing are being sung. We have been able to listen to many of them in the accounts of hope which we have studied. There is a bewildering variety: from those who hunger for bread, justice and peace; those who long for freedom from religious or political persecution; those who hope for deliverance from infirmities of body and mind; those seeking a new community of women and men; those who search for cultural authenticity; those who hope for a responsible use of science and technology; those who evangelize and work for the spread of the Gospel; those who labour for the visible unity of the churches. We have even become aware of intimations of hope from those who are silenced. In their silence itself is a word for those who can hear it.

III. Hopes encounter hopes

We have been listening to these voices because we ourselves are called to give an account of our hope (I Peter 3:15). We are a group of 160 Christians gathered in India from many churches in every continent as the Faith and Order Commission of the World Council of Churches. Our mandate from the churches is to further the cause of visible Church unity. Central to that task is the growth of an ability among the churches to bear common witness to their faith.

As a preliminary step, the Commission has been working since 1971 to formulate a common account of hope. Today, we want to speak of our common future to church members everywhere and to any others who may be willing to listen. The problems have been formidable: confessional and cultural diversity, sharply divided political and social situations, the threat to relevance in a rapidly changing world, the need to draw upon new voices which have been marginal to the discussion of theology thus far. Yet, the common attempt itself has become a source of hope. We have discovered afresh the force of the Gospel to inspire common witness. We have been drawn together and new ways of communication have been established among those who hope.

The common account is based on the encounter among various accounts of hope. This encounter has proved significant. It has helped us distinguish between one level where specific things are hoped for, for example, to have enough to eat, and another level where the question emerges: "Why do you hope at all for what you cannot see?" (cf. Rom. 8:25).

The encounter has been *humbling* because of the provocation to become more self-critical. It is necessary to distinguish hopes from desires or wishes. Some of our expectations are little more than unexamined desires and wishes, or expressions of fears and anxieties. And these often contradict one another. A desire for an expanding economy in one country can cause poverty in another. A necessary struggle for power in one country may appear to contradict the responsible use of power in another. Some even say: "One's hopes become another's despair."

But we refuse to believe that the hopes of humankind are ultimately contradictory: God-given hopes are many-faceted and complementary. But human hearts are sinful, and their desires can be false. They need to be judged and purified. Christ is the judge of human hopes. He weighs our desires.

The encounter of human hopes is also *encouraging* to us, for in it we become aware of the power and direction of the Holy Spirit. Through that Spirit the hopes of others speak to us, often unintentionally, sometimes unexpectedly. The encounter of hopes points to a wider communion of hope with each other and with God's Spirit. Beyond that it can point to a wider communion between those who believe in Christ and those who do not. "One's hope becomes another's hope!"

IV. Our hope in God

The Church is a fellowship of those who hope in God, and therefore a real encounter among our hopes is possible.

We are not the first to express such faith and hope. Many have gone before us. A cloud of witness surrounds us who gave their testimony even at the cost of their lives. The faithful witness of the human hope in God is Jesus Christ. And every time we celebrate the remembrance of him, we receive grace and power to give our testimony.

Jesus Christ is our hope. In his life He was completely obedient to God the Father. He identified himself with those who were despised by society. He preached a message of God's coming kingdom which sustains us with its vision of a tomorrow that cannot be denied. He was arrested, tortured and killed. In his cross and resurrection God dethroned the forces of sin, guilt, death and evil. God reconciled the world to himself. God defended his image in all — children, women and men — and opened to them a new dignity as the children of God. That is why we hope that everything which threatens human dignity, including death itself, will ultimately be destroyed: ultimately, for in this world those threatening forces, though overcome, are not yet destroyed; our present hope is anchored in God's actions in history and in the eternal life of the age to come. But we know that we are accepted by God as forgiven sinners, and therefore we are certain that we can here and now be co-workers with God in pointing to his rule. In Christ as in a mirror we see the will of God. Christ will come as the revelation of truth and righteousness. The ultimate judgment of the world is his, our assurance that the murderer will never ultimately triumph over the victim. This ultimate hope in the lordship of Christ and the coming kingdom of God cannot be divorced from, or identified with, our historical hopes for freedom, justice, equality and peace. Our struggles for human well-being are judged and transfigured in a life with God marked by the free gifts of forgiveness, new life and salvation. In anticipation we dare to hope that human longings and struggles are justified and that their ultimate outcome is in God's hands.

In giving his Son not to condemn the world but that the world might be saved through him (John 3:17), *God the Father* affirmed the world as his creation and manifested his faithfulness to it. We too will be faithful to the world. He loved the work of his hands and called it good. Therefore we hope for a society which does not violate the goodness of nature. In trust that He has willed the creative powers of the human creature as well, we have hope that human reason can be used responsibly in shaping the future. The Creator is righteous; his law and his justice will restore the right of those who are oppressed. Therefore we have hope in our striving for justice and human rights. This world is full of suffering and injustice, but as God's world it is the place of our obedience in the confidence that He will not let it fall out of his hand. When, following Christ, we fight against evil, we do so not only in the hope for more human happiness; we do it also in the hope that oppressors will repent and be oppressors no longer, and that all will turn to God in faith and together receive the blessing that He wills for them.

The living God becomes accessible to us by the *Holy Spirit* who confirms God's presence in our lives and makes us members of Christ's Body, the Church. By the Holy Spirit, we have hope that already our lives can show signs of the new creation. By the Spirit, God gives us his power and guidance. The Spirit sets us free from the powers of darkness, stirs up our spirits, rekindles our energies, gives us visions and dreams, presses us to work for real communion, overcoming the barriers which sin has erected. Through the Holy Spirit, God's love is poured into our hearts. There can be no real hope without love. Acting in hope is possible for all: for those who can work openly and visibly, and also for those whose love and action are expressed in suffering and prayer. Since God's promises concern the whole of humanity, we hope and pray that the Spirit will empower us to proclaim the good news of salvation and to strive for its realization in life. That is the one mission of the individual and of the Church as such.

V. The Church: a communion of hope

"The Lord is risen!" He is present and powerful in the midst of his people, making them members of one another and of his Body, the Church. He is the Master; they are the disciples. He is the vine; they are the branches. To those who put their faith in him, He gives a communion of hope, and He sends them as a sign of hope for all humanity.

They share his own divine life, the communion of the Father, Son and Holy Spirit, one God whose own being is mirrored in all creaturely love. In the Christian community of faith, sharing in the confession of the apostles, gathered around God's Word and partaking of the sacraments, we are given the power to share with each other. We can rejoice with those who rejoice and weep with those who weep. We can bear one another's burdens. It is in this communion that we also learn to share one another's hopes. This encounter of hope in itself has been made by God to be a sign in every situation and place: Christ our hope, the power of love!

Because this is the spiritual reality of the Church, we are ashamed of how we in our churches actually look. The communion of hope is so obscured that it is almost unrecognizable. The common witness is wounded by divisions. Too often and too transparently, our churches reflect the sins of society, and are found on the side of the privileged and the powerful. Women are often denied their rightful places of leadership in church life. Members and ministers do not fully recognize each other. More scandalous still, our churches do not yet worship God together around the common table. Many of our contemporaries think it a travesty to call this people a sign of hope. Hope for the renewal and unity of our churches is often our most difficult spiritual task.

Nevertheless, we do hope for the Church of Christ to become more manifest in our churches. We hope for the recovery and fruitfulness of their mission. The communion, though obscured, is not lost; it is grounded not in its members, but in God. The Word has been given to it and the Word endures. The Spirit which has been at work throughout the ages is present in our times to re-establish a credible communion. Built on such foundations, this community will become a community of repentance!

Of this power among the churches we are witnesses. We do have hope for this communion. And we believe that this communion, incomplete as it is, can become a sign of hope for others. Communion in Christ provides the possibility of encounter across the human barriers. It re-establishes relations in mutual respect without sacrificing convictions. It can be a testing ground for the witness which each church bears. Without being pressed into conformity, churches can become accountable to each other. It is also a source of hope because as they live by God's forgiveness, they can extend forgiveness to other churches as well, and find in the witness and commitment of others an enrichment of their own. Finally, communion in Christ is a source of hope when it anticipates the reign of God and does not acquiesce in things as they are.

So the Church thanks God for a foretaste, here and now, of what it hopes for. Long since, it has anticipated its hope in its prayer: "Your kingdom come. Your will be done, on earth as in heaven. Give us our daily bread. Forgive us our sins. Deliver us from evil."

VI. Shared hopes in the face of the common future

"Christ is risen!" What does it mean to have common hope in a world where we face common threats? There are common Christian commitments; concerted action is possible, although the emphases are different in different parts of the world.

Our common hope is threatened by *increasing and already excessive concentrations of power with their threats of exploitation and poverty*. They are responsible for the ever-widening gap between rich and poor, not only between nations but within individual nations. Political exploitation and dependency, hunger and malnutrition are the price paid by the poor for the superabundance of goods and power enjoyed by the rich. Concentration of power also leads to the preservation of the existing and the formation of new class distinctions.

Nevertheless, we share a common hope; for we believe that God has taken sides in this struggle (Ps. 103:6).

Our common future is dominated by our *increasing capacity to shape the physical world*. Science and technology have bettered the human lot. Wisely used, they can help to feed the hungry, heal the sick, develop communication, strengthen community. The refusal to use these powers responsibly on the part of all people everywhere, and especially the ability of the affluent to appropriate these benefits for themselves, threatens us with environmental collapse, biological catastrophes and nuclear destruction. Nevertheless, we hope in the continual action of the Creator Spirit who will not abandon his creatures and who can prompt us to act responsibly as stewards of creation.

The most alarming concentration of power in our time is the *seemingly uncontrollable growth of armaments*. The present arsenal of nuclear warheads held by the superpowers numbers well above 10,000 — more than a million times the annihilating power which devastated Hiroshima. Even the so-called Third World has increased its commitment to armament from eight billion dollars in 1957 to forty billion in 1977. It is important not to overstate our hopes, but God's Spirit opens doors beyond human expectations. Evil is not necessary. The Spirit can plant the leaven of peace in unexpected surroundings, and create hope that it is possible to establish justice without resorting to war.

There are pressures and forces everywhere which threaten to disintegrate the human community. Races, classes, sexes, even religions are set against each other. In all places inherited patterns of society are dissolving and weakening the sense of belonging which community provides. At the same time new forms of community are emerging which in their newness can also create anxieties. Nevertheless, the Spirit works with a surprising freedom, preserving that which sustains life and bringing to birth something genuinely new. Therefore, we can have courage to experiment with new forms of association, new structures and institutions, new forms of human relationships.

Our common hope is threatened by *assaults on human dignity*. Statistics for programmes, stereotypes for discrimination, slaves, victims, or simply the forgotten. Human persons and human possibilities are everywhere threatened today. Individual human rights are violated by arbitrary arrest and "disappearances". We are appalled at the growing numbers of "prisoners of conscience" and at the increasingly systematic use of torture as an ordinary method of exercising power. But social human rights are likewise violated by denial of food, housing, jobs, education and health care, compounded by racism and sexism. There is no part of the world where some of these violations are not present. Those who dehumanize others thereby dehumanize themselves. Nevertheless, we have hope because God affirms the dignity of "the very last".

Commitment to the common future and life itself are eroded by *meaninglessness and absurdity*. In situations of affluence, this may result from "playing by the rules of the game" in a success-oriented culture. In situations of rapid cultural or social change, it may arise in the confusion of being called to fill previously undefined roles. In situations of exploitation, dependency and "marginalization" it may be imposed by the sense of impotence and frustration which comes from the inability to act for oneself or one's class. Nevertheless, we share a common hope, for the Son of God himself withstood the threat of meaninglessness and absurdity. God's healing word will come with different accents: to the affluent it is the challenge to renounce false gods; to the confused it offers the light of Jesus' life to clarify perplexity; to the dispossessed it comes as a challenge and empowerment to take up the struggle. To all it promises that life makes sense.

The problems seem overwhelming. The cry for realism is deep in each one of us, and it expresses a kind of ultimate question about Christian hope. But we believe that each rightful action counts because God blesses it. With the five loaves and two fishes which the young man brought to him, Jesus fed the multitude. Hope lives with special power in small actions.

Above all, we dare to hope in the face of *death*, the ultimate threat to our aspirations and actions. As sinners under the judgment of God we are bound to die. Therefore death is the "last enemy" of our hopes. It penetrates life with paralyzing power, especially where it takes away people before they have had a chance to live. Yet hope in Christ focuses precisely on this enemy. The triumph of God's grace is the resurrection — Christ's victory over death and sin with all their allies. The Apostle says: "If in this life only we have hope in Christ, we are of all men most miserable" (I Cor. 15:19). We rejoice that his crucial *if* is answered unequivocally: *not only* in this life. It is this "not only" that gives life its hopeful horizon. Fate is broken. There is a tomorrow for us today — and in the day of our death.

The Christian hope is a resistance movement against fatalism.

VII. Hope as the invitation to risk

"Christ is risen!" But the risen one is the crucified. This means that our life in hope is not a guarantee of safety, but an invitation to risk. To live in hope is never to have reached our goal, but always to be on a risk-laden journey.

To live in hope is to risk *struggle*. We are denied the privilege of being "neither hot nor cold", of adopting a pseudo-neutrality that covertly supports those in power. To struggle is to take sides openly, saying "yes" to some at the cost of saying "no" to others. If patient endurance is all that is possible, that too can be a form of protest. We can afford to fail, since God can use our failures in the fulfilment of his purposes. Hope embraces the risk of struggle.

To live in hope is to risk *the use of power*. Some have too much power to be trusted; most have too little to be effective. It is not right that a few should impose their decisions on the many. We must seek identification with the powerless and help them escape a life of dependency on others. But we must also minister to those in power, asking them to listen to "the wretched of the earth", to use power justly and share it with those who stand outside. Hope embraces the risk of the responsible use of power.

To live in hope is to risk *affirming the new and re-affirming the old*. To affirm the new is to acknowledge that Christ goes before us; to reaffirm the old is to acknowledge that He did not come to destroy, but to fulfil, for He is the same yesterday, today and forever. Hope sends us on untried ways and calls us to discover the new whether it is represented by the challenge of new cultural contexts, the call for new life-styles or previously unheeded cries for liberation. When we lock ourselves to the past we may become deaf to the groanings and pleadings of the Spirit. Yet, the Spirit will always reaffirm the truth of Christ. Therefore, hope embraces the risk both of new departures and of faithfulness to the past against the temptation of passing fashions.

To live in hope is to risk *self-criticism as the channel of renewal*. Within culture and within the Church, renewal comes through challenge to what is established, so that it can be revitalized or cast aside. But renewal in the true sense of the word is not within our power. It arises as we are judged by God and driven to repent and bear fruits worthy of repentance. This can also include, however, a certain light-heartedness, a willingness not to take ourselves too seriously. Only those who can smile at themselves can be ultimately serious about other selves. Hope embraces the risk of self-criticism as the way to renewal.

To live in hope is to risk *dialogue*. Genuine encounter with others can challenge us to vacate positions of special privilege and render ourselves vulnerable. To enter dialogue with people of other faiths and ideologies is to risk having one's own faith shaken and to discover that there are other ways to state the truth than we have yet learned ourselves. The dialogue with Jews holds special promise and difficulties; promise of enrichment, because with no other people are our common roots so deep; difficulties, because the theological and political questions which arise threaten to divide us from one another as well as from them. Because in dialogue we can receive a fuller understanding of our own faith and a deeper understanding of our neighbour, hope is not afraid of dialogue.

To live in hope is to risk *cooperation with those from whom we differ*. When we join with others in immediate human tasks we risk being used and absorbed. But when we find those who, not acknowledging the name of Christ, are serving humanity, we can side with them, both for the sake of all God's children and, if occasion permits, to give account of our own hope. Hope is willing to risk cooperation with those who are different.

To live in hope is to risk *new forms of community between women and men*. This calls for a grace and understanding that can take past structures, stereotypes and resentments and transmute them into new forms of living together, both inside and outside the Church. We are challenged to discover on the basis of scripture and tradition contemporary ways to express mutuality and equality, and especially to understand anew what it means to be created in the image of God.

To live in hope is to risk *scorn*. To most of our contemporaries our hope appears vain; it is at best irrelevant, at worst malevolent. To live in hope is nevertheless to continue to witness to the saving power of Jesus Christ, whether we are ignored or attacked. Because to spread the Gospel is not only our mission but also our privilege and joy, we can run the risk of ridicule.

To live in hope is to risk *death for the sake of that hope*. No Christian may decide that someone else should be a martyr. But each of us confronts the likelihood that faithful witness can be costly witness. The Christian hope is not that death can be avoided, but that death can be overcome. Those who truly live in hope have come to terms with death and can risk dying with Christ. For some that is rhetoric; for others it is the bedrock assurance from which they face each new day. To live in hope is to embrace the risk of death for the sake of that hope.

> The saying is sure
>> if we have died with him, we shall also live with him;
>> if we suffer, we shall also reign with him;
>> if we deny him, he also will deny us;
>> if we are faithless, he remains faithful;
> for he cannot deny himself. (II Tim. 2:11-13)

DOCUMENT III.16

A COMMON STATEMENT OF OUR FAITH (1978)

Preamble

As we seek to give a common statement of our faith, we are mindful of the existing fellowship of churches which is marked by a common confession of "the Lord Jesus Christ as God and Saviour according to the Scriptures". Already we have joined hands seeking to fulfil together our "common calling to the glory of the one God, Father, Son and Holy Spirit".

Because we have travelled together on the road of faith, experiencing, in spite of our historical divisions, the unifying power of Jesus Christ and his salvation and growing together in his service, we desire to express more fully our common faith in the triune God who has called us to himself and wants us to share in his mission for the salvation of all humankind.

As we seek to confess our faith together, we want to be faithful to the apostolic faith according to the Scriptures, handed down to us through the centuries. At the same time we want to face the new situation and the challenge for mission today. Furthermore, we are aware that a common confession of faith should be the sign of our reconciliation.

Part I

As Christians we confess Jesus Christ, the only source of salvation for humankind and for each individual human person. He is the one Lord of his Church, the cornerstone of its unity. The Church is based on his ministry, remembers in her worship his incarnation, his suffering, crucifixion and death, proclaims with joy his resurrection and eagerly awaits his second coming. As our Saviour he is truly God and truly man. He has authority to grant us communion with God in the presence of his reign, which overcomes the power of death and sin and every misery, division and separation among us; but he also shares in our sufferings and temptations so that in spite of them we may have confidence in him and in the promise of his kingdom. He is the new Adam, in whom we recognize the destiny of human beings and into whose image our lives shall be transformed.

In Jesus' ministry we encounter the one God and creator of all things, whose eternal love is concerned for every single human person and thus constitutes the dignity of each human being. God, the Holy Spirit, is the eternal link of love, between God the Father, and God the Son, and spreads abroad God's love to all his creatures to overcome their miseries and separations. In the ministry of the Spirit we receive life and are transfigured, inspired and liberated by the divine presence among his creatures and are sealed in hope. God, the Father, Son and Holy Spirit extends love and judgment to all creation to overcome its separations and calls the Church into the unity of one body, in order to be more fully the sign of a new humanity.

The one faith is confessed and lived in the community of the faithful who have been called through the preaching of the Gospel and gather around the Lord in the Spirit. We enter into this community through baptism which is our participation in the death and resurrection of Jesus Christ. We are incorporated into the eucharistic community in which the Word is proclaimed and the sacrament duly celebrated.

The one faith is the full responsibility of each member of the community, not, however, separately one from the other, but in communion. The presence of the Lord in the midst of his people expresses itself in a variety of charisms and services, which equip them for their mission among men. Such charisms and services are the instruments of the Holy Spirit in the building up of the Church, enabling its community to persevere in the apostolic teaching, in fraternal communion, in the breaking of bread, and in prayer (cf. Acts 2:42). The one(s) who presides over the community has the particular responsibility of being, in the Holy Spirit, the servant of the unity of the Church by the proclamation of the Word in the eucharistic community. His (their) service aims at reinforcing the communication in the community, with a vision of fuller communion.

The confession of the one faith is not a question of majority, but rather, it is a confession in one Spirit. Such a confession naturally implies a total commitment of life on the part of all members of the community.

The community experiences a communion in one Spirit which is not limited to one period in time or to one given place *(hic et nunc);* it is the communion with all witnesses to the apostolic faith in all places and at all times. It is a confession in the communion of saints.

Part II

Growing together in one faith, the divided Christian communities are prepared to share already now a doxology, taken from our common heritage, the Scriptures. One passage which condenses many aspects of our common confession is to be found in Ephesians 1:3-15.

Together with this doxology:

We confess God's involvement in the history of humankind, revealed through Israel, fulfilled in Jesus Christ, communicated to us by the Holy Spirit, into which fulfilment all humanity is called;

we confess the destiny and dignity of all *human beings,* rooted in God's initiative and design;

we confess our dependence upon *God's redeeming and liberating grace,* because we are caught up in the ambiguities of our history and because we live in sin;

we confess the reality of the *Event of Jesus Christ* — his life, his death, his resurrection — and the reality of our answer of faith, given to that Event, that brings us, through the Spirit, to the incorporation into Christ, which means our salvation;

we confess the reality of *the Church,* being the Body of Christ, called to be the nucleus and servant of the unity of humankind and of the universe. We confess our responsibility as Christians to have the mind of Christ and to live and act accordingly in the community of humankind; faith without work is dead;

we confess the presence and the working of *the Spirit,* the pledge and seal of the kingdom, into which we are confirmed.

DOCUMENT III.17

TOWARDS A CONFESSION OF THE COMMON FAITH (1980)

1. Unity in the Faith

The last decade could be judged a stage of capital importance in the common search for the unity willed by Christ. Important strides have been made in essential areas: growth in mutual understanding, respect for different traditions, common commitment to the service of the world in the name of the Gospel, concerted efforts with a view to evangelization. More important still, despite still unresolved difficulties, consensus documents regarding essential points are being worked out not only as the outcome of bilateral dialogues but even at the level of the Christian churches and communions as a whole. A case in point is the agreement prepared by the Faith and Order Commission on baptism, eucharist and ministry, of which a revised text is being prepared.

This gives ground for hope. In our present divided state, in fact, visible unity cannot be restored unless, turning towards Christ, each Church takes the decision to repent in so far as it is a community of sinful Christians. Its repentance will be genuine only to the extent to which it implies a resolve to what the complete re-establishment of communion demands of it: conversion through a constant return to the source which is Christ, a persevering effort of purification, a desire for authentic change. Such repentance will be truly constructive of unity only if it leads it to offer to others its own characteristic goods and to receive from others what it lacks itself.

Now, at the heart of such repentance is the need to reach agreement on a common profession of faith which, after centuries of mutual exclusion, will permit the churches to recognize each other as true brothers, to live in communion, and to commit themselves together to mission without any reservations. For faith is expressed in different ways: the principal ones are liturgical life, catechetical instruction, explicit proclamation of the Word, witness before the world. For to believe really implies a life lived in fidelity to Christ, the submission to his authority of one's whole existence and one's every action. This is why it is that wherever Christians, in the name of the faith, take certain attitudes or stand together for values commended by the Gospel, such common action itself represents a confession in practice of their faith. But they must also know who it is they believe in, who is the God to whom He bears witness, what is the content of the salvation He brings. The different practical expressions of faith in Christ are all linked to and in a way governed by doctrinal expressions that translate the essential of the Christian mystery and constitute, beyond words, what is called the *regula fidei*. This represents, as it were, the understanding of the Gospel by the Church. Full ecclesial communion, then, requires that one comes to confess the faith in common in prayer, action and witness, but also in doctrinal formulas. It is with these above all that we are concerned here. Nevertheless, we shall try not to isolate them from the whole dynamic of the common search for unity. Just as a theology "in act" normally precedes the enunciation of doctrines, so communion in common commitment in the name of the faith leads to the profession of common faith. It is in doing the truth that we come to the light.

2. The Apostolic Faith

The essential elements of the Christian mystery are known to us through the witness of the apostolic community, transmitted in the Scriptures. These are the fruit of the Gospel and of the action of the Spirit in the primitive Church. On the one hand, they bear witness of the apostolic Church's understanding of the mystery of Christ. On the other hand, however, the truth they transmit could be fully grasped only in the context of the life of that early community faithful to the teaching of the apostles, to the fellowship of the brethren, to the breaking of bread and to prayer (cf. Acts 2:42). And so we can say that we exist as Christians through the apostolic tradition (the *paradosis* of the *kerygma*), attested in Scripture and transmitted in and through the Church by the power of the Holy Spirit. Tradition thus understood is made a present reality in the preaching of the Word, the administration of the sacraments, worship, Christian instruction, theology, mission, the witness given to Christ by the life of Christians (cf. Montreal 1963, Section II, 45-46).

After the, normative, apostolic period the Church, bearer of the Spirit but engaged in history, saw itself led to make more explicit the faith it had received from the apostles. What it lived in its liturgy and bore witness to, sometimes to the point of martyrdom, it had to express in terms which would allow it to safeguard its unity and give an account of its hope. At that time it was immersed in a particular culture, permeated with the concepts of a Greek philosophy, and subject to various political situations. However, this effort to find in this new cultural and historical context an adequate expression of its faith was an essential contribution to the course of its history. In formulating the faith it enriched the Christian heritage. In fact the Spirit then led the Church to make explicit the elements necessary for its communion with the apostolic faith.

This building-period is that of the Fathers, of the creeds, of the birth of the great liturgies, of the great Councils. The conciliar definitions about God-in-Trinity and the person of Christ Jesus, particularly, gave the Church a steady vision of the points that are at the very heart of its understanding of the Christian mystery. Certainly, in every age the Church lives and grows in the Holy Spirit and thus builds itself up in charity and faith. Moreover, since their divisions the churches have each given for themselves either conciliar decrees or confessions to which they attach a real authority. But this authority remains always subject not only to the authority of Scripture but also to that of those universally received documents which concern the centre of faith and which the Church holds from this period which was qualified to be its building-period.

3. The Content of the Apostolic Faith

The New Testament itself bears witness to the way in which, in different contexts and situations, the apostolic Church understood the essentials of the faith necessary for salvation. Some very short affirmations — such as "Jesus is Lord" — were made more explicit in fuller professions of faith. Thus two verses of the Epistle to the Romans put the emphasis on the event of the death and resurrection as the heart of the faith: "If you confess with your lips that Jesus is Lord and believe in your heart that God raised him from the dead, you will be saved" (10:8-9). A text like John 3:16 insists above all on the source and purpose of the mystery of faith, that is, the love of the Father and eternal life: "God so loved the world that he gave his only Son, that whoever believes in him should not perish but should have eternal life." In another context, probably liturgical (Eph. 1:3-23), expression of the faith takes on such breadth as to include a synthetic reminder of the history of salvation, contain the roots of a trinitarian confession, and conclude in a vision of the Church, the Body of Christ, looking forward to its fullness.

In that apostolic period and in the subsequent building-period, cultural contexts and historical situations explain the diversity of ways in which the mystery is grasped and of the forms then taken by profession of the one faith. The profession of ecclesial faith is made in reliance on Jesus' own promise to save those who will acknowledge him before the world (Luke 12:8-9). Its purpose is always to make entry into salvation possible for every Christian. But to this is added the need for a liturgical proclamation of the faith by the community gathered for worship. From this will derive the baptismal professions which will be, so to speak, the liturgical seal on the process of catechesis, summarizing its essential axial points. Very soon the denial of central points of faith within the community provokes, as early as the New Testament period, declarations like that in I John 4:2-3 in face of gnostic infiltrations: "Every spirit which confesses that Jesus Christ has come in the flesh is of God, and every spirit which does not confess Jesus is not of God." Peter's preaching on the day of Pentecost is itself conditioned by the Jewish context. The classical creeds, in their turn, differ according to the circumstances in which they appeared: the apostles' creed comes from the baptismal liturgy, while that of Nicaea (Constantinople) was composed to act as a barrier against deviations from the traditional faith. But all insist on the person and the work of Jesus. Salvation — through the remission of sins and the coming of the new world which the resurrection inaugurates — is, they say, the purpose of God's coming in flesh. Inserted into the baptismal and then into the eucharistic liturgy, these creeds will be important for the course of tradition. They will, in fact, become the sign and the test of fidelity to the content of the apostolic faith.

The rise of heresies and the need to express the Gospel in relation to new cultures will soon oblige the churches to expound the meaning of the profession of faith in Jesus as Lord and Saviour. He will be affirmed to be true God and true man, two natures united in one person. This will be the work of the great Councils. They will say of the God of faith that He is one God in three persons. The Church will further assert that from Pentecost to the parousia it has the mission of being the Spirit's instrument to liberate humanity through the forgiveness of sins and the inauguration of the new life, above all through the preaching of the Word and the celebration of the sacraments of the Lord.

Yet the faith thus translated in the creeds and conciliar definitions is also that which is expressed, nourished and deepened in the life of the community. Formulas of faith find their meaning only as closely linked to the whole of the Christian experience. This is, moreover, why, in what we have called the building-period, there was unanimous recognition that the fidelity which seals adherence to dogmatic affirmations is professed par excellence in the eucharistic memorial, the sacrament of communion in the Body of Christ. As custodian of the good deposit of faith, the apostolic ministry has the function of guaranteeing the bond between the eucharistic celebration of each community — and so also of its faith — and that of other communities, and also the bond between all and the apostolic community.

Ceaselessly threatened by schism, the Christian community has known tension and even divisions from its very beginning. Later on, several of these even led to fundamental divergences on how the Church sees itself as Church and how it understands its own nature. The churches continue not to agree on what constitutes the full manifestation of God's plan through them. Some, in fact, attribute essential importance to visible elements, in particular to the sacraments, while others hold that the invisible reality of grace is the sole essential even in the time between Easter and the definitive coming of the reign of God. These divergences are, moreover, closely tied to different views of justification. Even so it must be recognized that this has not prevented the churches calling themselves bearers of the Spirit, commissioned to bring salvation to the world. Despite divisions, Christ has not withdrawn his grace, and baptism celebrated in fidelity to the apostolic tradition inserts all believers into his ecclesial Body. But the fact remains that the scandal of our division is a grave wound to God's will for his people and is one of the chief obstacles to the credibility of our witness.

4. The Form of a Profession of Faith Today

The ancient professions of faith and the great conciliar definitions were very often in response either to the challenges posed by tensions between the adequate expression of the faith and the new cultures, or to the internal problems of the Christian community. It was necessary to remain faithful both to the catholicity of an evangelical message destined to humanity as a whole at all times and in all environments, and to its authentic content, above all in what concerns the person of Jesus, revelation of God's saving grace. Thus the formulas of faith shed light on Christian existence by recalling to it its deepest source and meaning. At the same time they permitted each community to remain united in itself and in communion with the whole sum of Christian communities, despite temptations to division, even to schism.

Today the Church finds itself faced with analogous difficulties. They come both from the churches' new realization of a close relationship with the cultures in which they have taken root, and also from the situation of division which is ours today. So the Church needs to discover how to live the faith in such a way that it will meet the aspirations on which peoples and persons set their hopes today, and how to proclaim this faith unanimously by overcoming its divisions. In fact, these two tasks are complementary. The Church is required to proclaim the traditional faith in new ways, in response to the new conditions of humanity; but it cannot do this in a credible way unless it relies on the witness of its unity in confessing Christ. Moreover, to get out of the impasse into which confessional divisions have led it, it has need of an expression of its faith, which, at this fundamental level, will re-establish mutual confidence between the churches and clear away suspicions or reservations. For the state of disunity, reinforced by a long history of polemics, means that we are not always sure of being unanimous even on essential points, fearing lest a difference in interpretation may conceal a more profound disagreement that touches on the faith itself.

In our world the apostolic faith is challenged from all sides. This questioning touches first of all on belief in a Creator God who is leading the world to its fulfilment. Without the sense of a divine mystery, transcendant and yet present at the heart of the world with the power to reconcile it and renew it while bringing it to perfection, the Christian faith would lose its foundation. For it is this mystery of the transcendant God that makes itself present to the world through Jesus Christ in his Church. Now this truth is contested today — as much as and more than by theoretical atheism — by the very widespread practical attitude which sees the visible and finite world as the only sure reality with which humanity has to reckon. The churches therefore have to speak once again the word of faith, handed down ever since the apostolic community, which will bring light in this situation. But they must express it in a new way which will save our contemporaries from the illusion that they are emancipated from all dependence (even on God) and from the dream of attaining fulfilment through human powers alone. For the faith, which knows that a person is perfectly free only within his relationship to God, that illusion leads to the loss of true liberty. And because the Church knows that human beings are fully human only under the grace of God, it also holds that humanity's community vocation is not fully satisfied in the social and political community (with the necessary transformations) but in the Kingdom of God. Awaited in relationship to the resurrection of the dead, this is already mysteriously present under the signs of the sacramental life. Occasionally, moreover, elements from the Christian tradition, even the faith itself, are appropriated by political powers or movements of the left or of the right for goals which are radically incompatible with the spirit of the Gospel. So it is important to draw out all there is in the faith that is opposed to such cases. But simple protests or vague accusations are not enough in such cases. There is need for firm and precise expression of evangelical conviction and of what it rests on.

Other needs of the contemporary world could lead the churches to give new emphasis to aspects of the apostolic texts which in the past were not included in the explicit object of professions of faith. Confessing Christ implies today a special insistence on the connection between Christian salvation and the realization in our world of a state of justice and peace, abolishing discriminations, and thus announcing the reign of God inaugurated in Jesus. This can become a priority when there is question of defending the dignity of the person in regions or circumstances where it is threatened. It is clear, however, that this verbal profession will be authentic only if what it expresses in words finds its practical expression in the activity of ecclesial communities to second the efforts being made everywhere in the world for the establishment of this justice and of respect for these human rights. For this is a matter of confessing the same apostolic faith, but now in its "existential" aspect without which the profession of the creeds of the past would be seriously weakened. The confession of Christ through action is, in fact, the logical outcome of adherence to the fundamental articles of faith in God the Creator and in the Incarnation "for us men and for our salvation".

It is, then, for each church not, of course, to rewrite the traditional creed, but to translate the confession of apostolic faith with a view to its own cultural context or its own historical situation. Clearly it must be careful not to push into the background that personal communion with God to which faith opens the way by reason of the mystery of Christ. For the act of faith does not stop at formulas giving intelligible expression to the mystery of God or laying down an evangelical mode of behaviour. Its goal is the very person of God, beyond any image or idea which, through revelation, we form for ourselves but always in a limited way. The apostolic texts present the faith to us as a vital dynamism by which the whole person (spirit, heart, will), recognizing in Jesus Christ his God and his Saviour, welcomes him through the Holy Spirit and in doing so yields himself to him in all that his mystery admits of and promises. For in giving himself to us He enables us, always in the Holy Spirit, to give ourselves to him also.

Conversion and docility to the Spirit find their source here. And this explains the coming together of the churches in efforts to enable the new creation of which the Risen Christ is the Lord to shine forth even now.

5. Unity of Faith and Communion of Churches

Since the Nairobi Assembly Faith and Order has been concentrating mainly on the "conciliar community" as final result of the ecumenical quest, since this would bind the churches in an authentic communion. To bring this about there has even been talk of all the churches committing themselves in advance to preparation for a council. However, if the aim is that this should really have the ecumenical character of the first Council it is necessary that the churches taking part should first mutually recognize each other in the same faith, the same baptism and the same eucharist while admitting the equivalence of their respective ministries. For this purpose an assembly of reconciliation could be envisaged as the conclusion of the preparation on which we are already implicitly engaged. The consensus on baptism, eucharist and ministry, once it has been completed and accepted by all the churches, would be a promising step along this path.

But such a reconciliation also requires that the churches should have successfully completed their search for an authentic consensus concerning the faith with a view to the time when they will come to the point of proclaiming that faith "with one heart and one voice to the glory of God, the Father of the Lord Jesus Christ" (Rom. 15:6). In our present context, to have some impact and to serve as a firm basis for witness, the profession of faith must, in fact, be ecumenical. Certainly, to the extent to which it does not stop short at propositions to which the believing intelligence assents but attains to the transcendant reality which the words seek to express, the act of faith transcends divisions or confessional quarrels. But this does not suppress their object, nor their importance, nor the need to try to overcome them if the churches mean to respond fully to God's plan as Jesus proclaimed it: "That all may be one so that the world may believe that thou hast sent me."

At the basis of this search should be the will to understand other churches and no longer to anathematize them, without, however, giving up the task of discovering the objective reasons that show that this or that position held on principle by a church is opposed to the truth of the faith. The translation of the apostolic faith by a church in view of its particular situation should not, certainly not, lead to destruction of the profession of ecclesial faith. Where this translation maintains what the Church in its building-period saw as essential to its faith, the churches of other regions — especially those which have contributed to the appearance of new Christianities elsewhere than in the western world — should be ready to accept it. This recognition of the true faith under forms which are, perhaps, no longer those bequeathed to them, forms part of their conversion to the practical requirements of unity in the circumstances which will be ours henceforth. Such recognition also represents a communion in the mystery of the One who "was rich and became poor" so that the Father's plan might be fulfilled.

There must also be readiness not to demand more than is required for a true communion that bears on what may be called the essential core of the Christian faith. By this is meant one which contains, at least implicitly, all that without which the mystery of Jesus Christ would be irremediably falsified or so impoverished that the master-conviction of the apostolic community would lose its meaning. Churches for which the content of the faith is expressed in a fuller form must not *a priori* consider other churches, whose doctrinal traditions are less explicit, as willingly or through ill-will betraying the wholeness of the Christian heritage. They must put trust in what is implicit and in the way of life it permits. In their turn, clearly, churches which are more restrained in their doctrinal affirmations and in their sacramental life must be on their guard against considering *a priori* that other churches, with richer formulas of faith and rites, are polluting the purity of faith with adventitious or parasitical additions. They should not deny, but should leave the question open. The churches have then to state precisely what in their corpus of doctrine they judge to be either a point on which they must require an explicit affirmation from other churches so that the unity God himself wishes to give to his Church may become a reality at the level of faith, or, on the contrary, to be an aspect which can remain implicit without thereby radically compromising unity of faith. Once reconciled, they will grow together towards the fullness of truth.

Diversity of doctrinal expressions is not necessarily a sign of rupture of faith. Only what is contradictory to or denies the apostolic faith should be seen as an obstacle to ecclesial communion. Moreover, unity of faith is not merely not opposed to allowing a diversity of traditions, doctrinal emphases and theological syntheses; very often it requires them. In this way are shown both the transcendance and the inexhaustible richness of the object of faith.

Conclusion

This paper has stressed the importance of the common commitment of Christians to the evangelization of the world and to efforts to make it "the world which God wants". Here they are often already living the mystery of a communion of faith which they have not yet come to express adequately in wholly satisfactory doctrinal agreements. Already engaged as they are in a movement towards the "conciliar community", the churches can already join in a doxological proclamation of their faith, that which we find in the hymn which opens the Epistle to the Ephesians (Eph. 1:3-23) even while they continue their search for doctrinal agreement. If faith is directed towards God, doxological language expresses it just as much as do the words of dogmatic creeds. This inspired text, which belongs to our common heritage and takes up the truth of faith while being free of doctrinal controversies, could become the opening blessing of our ecumenical meetings and the common profession of that faith whose demands we are trying to discern more clearly.

THE FILIOQUE CLAUSE IN ECUMENICAL PERSPECTIVE (1979)

Preliminary note

The following memorandum has been drawn up by a group of theologians from eastern and different western traditions who met at Schloss Klingenthal near Strasbourg, France, 26-29 October 1978 and 23-27 May 1979. An initial draft was composed after the first meeting and circulated for comment to a number of other specialists. At the second meeting, the document was revised and expanded in the light of their reactions. A large number of specially prepared papers was presented at these meetings.

I. Introduction

The Niceno-Constantinopolitan Creed, often called simply "the Nicene Creed", which dates from the fourth century, has for over 1500 years been regarded as a primary formulation of the common faith of the Christian people. It has been used in many ways in the worship and teaching of different churches throughout the world, and holds a unique place as the Creed which is most widely received and recognized throughout the various Christian traditions.

There have, however, been significant differences between churches in the use that they have made of this Creed and in the authority they have ascribed to it. In the Eastern Orthodox churches it displaced all other credal formulations and came to be seen as the authoritative expression of the faith. In the western Church it only more gradually came into regular use alongside other, distinctively western formulae: the so-called Apostles' and Athanasian Creeds. It became and has remained the Creed regularly used in the Roman Catholic mass. At the Reformation, many of the Protestant churches (including the Anglican) continued to use it, or made reference to it in their own confessions of faith, though some have in effect ceased to make any use of it at all.

Alongside these variations in attitude and practice, there is a further contrast between the broad eastern and western traditions. In the West the wording of the third article was expanded by the addition of the "*filioque* clause". This supplemented the description of the Holy Spirit as "proceeding from the Father" with the Latin *filioque*, "and (from) the Son". In the background to this lay certain differences between the eastern and western approaches to understanding and expressing the mystery of the Trinity. The clause itself was one of several principal factors in the schism between East and West in the Middle Ages, and has continued to the present day to be a matter of controversy and a cause of offence to the Orthodox churches. So the Nicene Creed itself has come to be a focus of division rather than of unity in common faith.

Three distinct issues may be recognized in this situation. First, there is the divergence of approach to the Trinity. Second, we are presented with the particular problem of the wording of the Creed and the *filioque*. Third, the question needs to be faced of the standing and potential ecumenical significance of the Nicene Creed itself. All of these matters have taken on a new urgency and relevance in our present time. There is a widespread feeling that, especially in the West, the trinitarian nature of God needs again to be brought into the centre of Christian theological concern. The new ecumenical climate of recent years poses afresh the question of a reconciliation between East and West — a question which inevitably involves that of *the filioque*. This in turn gives a new sharpness to the question whether the Nicene Creed itself can again be received and appropriated afresh as a shared statement of the Christian faith. These questions are a challenge to all the churches; they are placed on the agenda by our present theological and ecumenical setting; and they deserve to be widely and seriously considered.

II. The Nicene Creed and the filioque clause

A. THE HISTORY AND RECEPTION OF THE NICENE CREED

In spite of its name, this Creed is not in fact that of the Council of Nicea (A.D. 325). In the form in which it has been handed down, it dates from the Council of Constantinople in A.D. 381, though it does include the main emphases of the original formulation of Nicea, if not always in exactly the same words. The full text of the Creed was reproduced by the Council of Chalcedon in A.D. 451, and since then it has been seen as the classical and definitive expression of the orthodox Christian faith as developed and articulated in the controversies of the fourth and fifth centuries.

In the Eastern Orthodox churches, this same Creed was also seen as the heir and beneficiary of the instruction made by the Council of Ephesus (A.D. 431) that no other Creed than that of Nicea should be used. The force of this regulation was primarily directed against any attempt to return behind the affirmations of the Council of Nicea concerning the full divinity of Jesus Christ; but it came in the East to have a further significance as ratifying the sanctity of the Creed framed at Constantinople, which was seen as possessing the same authority and, with it, the same exclusive status.

In the West, by contrast, the process of "reception" of this Creed was a slower one in the sense that while its canonical authority was not questioned, its actual use in the life and teaching of the Church was for many centuries distinctly limited. The western Church already possessed and continued to use the various local forms of the Old Roman Creed, from which in the eighth century the "Apostles' Creed" finally evolved; and also the "Athanasian Creed", which is not in any way connected with Athanasius, but dates from sixth century Gaul. The use of the Nicene Creed spread gradually through the western Church, and it was only as late as ca. 1014 that its singing was introduced into the liturgy of the mass in Rome itself. It was at the same time that the addition of the *filioque* was sanctioned by the Pope.

B. THE ADDITION OF THE FILIOQUE

Although the *filioque* was officially added to the Creed throughout the western Church only in the eleventh century, its history runs back very much further. As early as the fourth century, some Latin writers spoke of the Holy Spirit as "proceeding from the Father and the Son", or "from both", or in other similar ways directly linked the person of the Son with the procession of the Spirit. This understanding was developed further by Augustine in the early fifth century, and between his day and the eighth century it spread throughout the West. What may be called "*filioque* theology" thus came to be deeply anchored in the minds and hearts of western Christians. This represents the first stage of the development and the necessary background to what followed.

The next stage was the appearance of the *filioque* in official statements — e.g. the Canons of the Council of Toledo in A.D. 589 — and in the Athanasian Creed. At that time there was no apparent intention thereby to oppose the teaching of the Church in the East. (Many scholars have thought that the main concern was to counter western forms of Arianism by using the *filioque* as an affirmation of the divine status of the Son.)

By the end of the eighth century the *filioque* had come in many places in the West to be added to the Nicene Creed itself — one of these places being the court of the Emperor Charlemagne at Aachen. Charlemagne and his theologians attempted to persuade Pope Leo III (795-816) to ratify the alteration; but Leo, though seeming to agree with the theology of the *filioque*, refused to sanction an addition to the wording of the Creed which had been drawn up by an Ecumenical Council and reaffirmed by others. The expanded form of the Creed continued, however, to be widely used in the West; and two centuries later Pope Benedict VIII (1012-1024) finally authorized and approved it. Since then the western form of the Creed has included the *filioque*.

Attempts were made at the Councils of Lyons (1274) and Florence (1439) to impose the *filioque* on the East. These attempts were unsuccessful, however, and their effect in the long run was to intensify the bitterness felt in the eastern Church at the unilateral action of the West — not least because of the *anathema* which Lyons laid on those who rejected the clause. Eastern and western theologies of the Trinity and of the procession of the Holy Spirit came very much to stand over against each other, and the differences in approach which the *filioque* problem highlighted hardened into what were felt to be mutually exclusive positions.

While the Reformers were very critical of many of the developments in medieval theology, the question of the *filioque* was not seriously raised in the sixteenth century. Most Protestant churches accepted the clause and its underlying theology and continued to subscribe to both. It has only been much more recently that a new perspective has opened up. The last hundred years have brought many fresh contacts between East and West and enabled a new dialogue between them — a dialogue that is still growing today. The question of the *filioque* is now being discussed in a climate very different from that of the medieval Councils.

In this new climate, the possibility of returning to the original wording of the Creed has suggested itself to more than one western Church. The Old Catholic churches already began to make this change in the nineteenth century; the Lambeth Conference of 1978 has asked the churches of the Anglican Communion to consider doing the same; other churches too are exploring the question. It is our hope that yet more will give it serious consideration. Even those which make relatively little (or even no) use of the Nicene Creed have an interest in the matter in so far as they too are heirs of the western theological tradition and concerned both with the issues involved in the *filioque* and the progress of the ecumenical movement.

III. The Trinity and the procession of the Holy Spirit

The *filioque* question demands some consideration of the relation between the doctrines of the Trinity, of the "eternal procession" and of the "temporal mission" of the Holy Spirit. This is offered in the following four sub-sections which deal in turn with the Church's faith in and experience of the triune God (A), with biblical reflections upon the Spirit and the mystery of Christ (B), with the implications of the

Spirit's temporal mission for relations between the persons of the Trinity (C), and with the way in which the Church always has to do with the Father, Son and Holy Spirit (D).

A. From its beginnings in the second and third centuries, the doctrine of the Trinity was intended to be a help for Christian believers, not an obstacle or an abstract intellectual superimposition upon the "simple faith". For it was in simple faith that the early Christians experienced the presence of the triune God; and it was in that presence that were gathered and held together the remembrance of the God of Israel, the presence within the congregation of the crucified and risen Christ and, from Pentecost, the power to hope in God's coming Kingdom which is the future of humankind.

This perception, celebrated in worship, strengthened and renewed by word and sacrament, and expressed in the individual and corporate lives and actions of believers, was not "dogmatic" or "conceptual" in the sense of enabling them to distinguish between "the advent of the risen Christ", "the presence of the Spirit" and "the presence of the Father". Their experience was — as it still is today — of the unity of the triune God. Both their prayerful acceptance and their rational under- standing of this gift of God's presence, however, were articulated in terms of his triune life and being. This enabled the early Church — as it enables the Church today — to see itself as belonging within the story which God began with Abraham and Sara, which culminated in the coming, teaching, suffering, death, resurrection and ascension of Jesus Christ, and which marks out the way of the Church ever since Pentecost.

It was for this reason that the early Fathers gave witness to God's activity in Israel, his speaking through the prophets, in Jesus of Nazareth, and in the apostolic Church, as the activity of the triune God. They did not deduce their theological conclusions from a preconceived trinitarian concept. So, too, today in any reconsideration of trinitarian concepts as they have come to be developed, it is desirable that we should retrace and follow through the cognitive process of the early Church. The communion of the Church as articulated in ecclesiology seems to be the appropriate theological starting point for re-examining the function of trinitarian thought in the Church's faith, life and work. God is received, thought of and praised in the Church as God in his triune life: as Creator and God of Israel, as God the Logos and Son, as God the Spirit. It is this insight which preserves the biblical and historical roots of Christian faith in the living God.

B. The most personal Christian experience grafts us into the very heart of the mystery of Christ: sharing in the work of salvation, we are introduced into the divine life, into the heart of the deepest trinitarian intimacy. It is thus that, through the whole experience of the Church, the mystery of Christ is realized in a trinitarian perspective of salvation. New life in Christ is inseparable from the work of the Spirit. In its depths, the Church is nothing other than the manifestation of the risen Lord, whom the Holy Spirit renders present in the eucharistic community of the Church. There is a profound correspondence between the mystery of the Church and of Christian life on the one side, and the earthly life and work of Jesus himself on the other. It is thus not possible to speak of the mystery of Christ, of his person and work, without at once speaking not only of his relation to the Father, but also of the Holy Spirit.

In the earthly life of Jesus, the Spirit seems to be focused in him. The Spirit brings about his conception and birth (Matt. 1:18, Luke 1:35), manifests him at his baptism in the Jordan (Mark 1:9-11 and par.), drives him into the desert to be tested (Mark 1:12-13 and par.), empowers him in his return to Galilee (Luke 4:14) and rests in fullness upon him (Luke 4:18). It is thus in the permanent presence of the Spirit that Jesus himself lives, prays, acts, speaks and heals. It is in the Spirit and through the Spirit that Jesus is turned totally towards the Father, and also totally towards humankind, giving his life for the life of the world. Through his passion, his sacrifice on the cross "through the eternal Spirit" (Heb. 9:14), and his resurrection by the power of the Spirit (Rom. 8:11, etc.), it is in the Spirit that henceforth Jesus comes to us in his risen body, penetrated and suffused by the energies of the Spirit, and communicating to us in our turn power from on high. The humanity of Christ, full of the Holy Spirit, is real and authentic humanity; and it is by the Holy Spirit that we, too, become a new creation (John 3:5), sharing in the humanity of Christ (Eph. 2:15). We are "christified", "made christs", in the Church by the indwelling in us of the Holy Spirit who communicates the very life of Christ to us, who in Christ makes us the brothers and sisters of Christ, and strengthens us in our new condition as the adopted children of the heavenly Father.

The Spirit thus appears in the New Testament at once as he who rests upon Jesus and fills him in his humanity, and as he whom Jesus promises to send us from the Father, the Spirit of Truth who proceeds from the Father (John 15:26). The Spirit therefore does not have an action separate from that of Christ himself. He acts in us so that Christ may be our life (Col. 3:4), so that Christ may dwell in our hearts by faith (Eph. 3:12). The Spirit, who proceeds from the Father, is also therefore the Spirit of Jesus Christ himself (Rom. 8:9, Phil. 1:19) who rests in him (Luke 3:22, John 1:32-33), in whom alone we can confess Jesus as Lord (I Cor. 12:3), the Spirit of the Son (Gal. 4:6). These and many other New Testament passages reflect the Church's deep experience of the Spirit-filled and Spirit-giving being of Jesus himself. Here can be seen a full and constant reciprocity of the incarnate Word and the Holy Spirit, a reciprocity whose depths are further revealed in the fact that the sending of the Spirit had as its result the formation of the mystical body of Christ, the Church. This reciprocity must be emphasized as a fundamental principle of Christian theology. It is from this interaction, at once christological and trinitarian, that the divine plan for the salvation of the world is to be viewed in its continuity and coherence from the beginning of creation and the call of Israel to the coming of Christ. Further, all the life of the Church, indeed all Christian life, carries the imprint of this reciprocity from the time of Pentecost till the final coming of Christ. If it loses that vision, it can only suffer grievously from its lack.

C. The points of the Holy Spirit's contact with God's people are manifold. While one might be inclined to connect the coming of the Spirit exclusively with Pentecost, it must be remembered that any such limitation tends towards Marcionism in its patent neglect of the Old Testament witness to the presence and activity of the Spirit in Israel. Moreover, the Spirit is confessed to have been instrumental in the coming of Christ ("conceived by the Holy Spirit"), and to have been the life-giving power of God in his resurrection. Jesus during his ministry promised the sending of the Spirit, and the earliest Christians understood the pouring out of the Spirit at Pentecost to be the fulfilment of that promise. Thus the Spirit *precedes* the coming of Jesus, is active *throughout* his life, death and resurrection, and is *also sent* as the Paraclete by Jesus to the believers, who by this sending and receiving are constituted the Church. This chain of observations suggests that it would be insufficient and indeed illegitimate to "read back" into the Trinity only those New Testament passages which refer to the sending of the Spirit by Jesus Christ.

In the New Testament, the relation between the Spirit and Jesus Christ is not described solely in a linear or one-directional fashion. On the contrary, it is clear that there is a mutuality and reciprocity which must be taken into account in theological reflection upon the Trinity itself. The "eternal procession" of the Spirit of which trinitarian theology speaks as the ground which underlies and is opened up to us in his "temporal mission" cannot be properly characterized if only one aspect of the latter is taken into account. This raises certain questions about the *filioque*. Does it involve an unbiblical subordination of the Spirit to the Son? Does it do justice to the necessary reciprocity between the Son and the Spirit? If its intention is to safeguard the insight that the Holy Spirit is truly the Spirit of the Father *in Jesus Christ,* could other arguments and formulations defend that insight as well or even better? Is it possible that the *filioque,* or certain understandings of it, may have been understandable and indeed helpful in their essential intention in the context of particular theological debates, but yet inadequate as articulations of a full or balanced doctrine of the Trinity?

In approaching these questions it is imperative to remember that any reference to the Trinity is originally *doxological* in nature. This is all the more important in our own time, when talk of God is so severely challenged and trinitarian thinking so obviously neglected. Doxology is not merely the language of direct prayer and praise, but all forms of thought, feeling, action and hope directed and offered by believers to the living God. Doxological affirmations are therefore not primarily definitions or descriptions. They are performative and ascriptive, lines of thought, speech and action which, as they are offered, open up into the living reality of God himself. Trinitarian thought in the early Church originated within that doxological context, and only within it are we able to speak of the "inner life" of the triune God. Further, as fathers like Athanasius and Basil made clear, all such doxological references to that inner life must be checked by reference back to the biblical message concerning God's activity and presence with his people.

D. Conceptual distinctions between the "economic" and "immanent" Trinity, or between "temporal mission" and "eternal procession" should not be taken as separating off from each other two quite different realities which must then be somehow reconnected. Rather, they serve the witness to the triune God as the living God. In calling upon God, we turn and open ourselves to the God who is none other than he has revealed himself in his Word. This calling upon his name is the essential expression of doxology, that is, of trust, praise and thanks that the living God from eternity to eternity was, is and will be none other ("immanent Trinity") than he has shown himself to be in history ("economic Trinity").

In our calling upon him, the mystery of the Trinity itself is actualized. So we pray with Christ and in the power of the Spirit when we call on God his Father as *our* Father. So too we have a share in the joy of God when we allow ourselves to be told again that "for us a child is born". So too we pray in the Holy Spirit and he intercedes in us when we call on the Father in the name of the Son. In the calling upon the Father, the Spirit who proceeds from the Father, and we who worship in the Spirit, witness to Jesus Christ (John 15:26-7). The Spirit who proceeds from the Father of the Son is he whom the risen and ascended Christ sends, and by whose reception we are made the children of God.

IV. Theological aspects of the filioque

A. THE APPROACHES OF EASTERN AND WESTERN TRINITARIAN THEOLOGY

In its origins the Latin tradition of the *filioque* served as an affirmation of the consubstantiality of the Father, Son and Holy Spirit, and also gave expression to the deeply-rooted concern in western piety to declare that the Spirit is the Spirit of the Son. The theology of Augustine marked a definite stage in the development of this tradition by articulating with particular clarity its fundamental concern for the oneness of the divine being, and by setting out on that basis to conceive of the Trinity in terms of a dialectic of oneness-in-threeness and threeness-in-oneness. In subsequent interpretation and application, this approach crystallized into a formal system which became the standard western teaching, and to which all the authority of the name of Augustine himself was attached. The introduction in the West of the logical procedures of medieval scholastic theology brought this form of trinitarian thinking to a new level of definition. One result of this development was to make dialogue with the East increasingly more difficult: hence arose the polemical frustrations of medieval controversy.

The eastern tradition of teaching about the Holy Trinity had from the beginnings somewhat different emphases. A central concern from the time of the Cappadocians in the late fourth century has been to affirm the irreducible distinctiveness of each of the divine hypostases (or, in the term more familiar in the West, "persons") of the Father, Son and Holy Spirit and at the same time, the uniqueness of the Father as the sole principle (ἀρχή), "source" (πηγή) and "cause" (αἰτία) of divinity. Thus, while Greek theologians could and did use such expressions as "from the Father through the Son", they could not accept the western "from the Father and the Son" as a suitable formulation for describing the procession of the Holy Spirit. This difference in emphasis, combined with the virtual absence in the East of the scholastic methods developed in the medieval West, made it difficult for the eastern Church to appreciate the western attitude. The controversies of the ninth century between Constantinople and the West — controversies, it must be said, which were as much political as theological — were the occasion of a further definition of the eastern position in the teaching of Patriarch Photius and his famous formula, "the Spirit proceeds from the Father *alone*". This tradition was continued and further developed by the work of Gregory the Cypriot and Gregory Palamas. Both these writers sought to respond to the controversy with the West by distinguishing between the *procession* of the Spirit from the Father and an "eternal *manifestation* of the Spirit through the Son".

What is striking is that, despite the evident differences between East and West before the eleventh century, communion was maintained between them. The two traditions of trinitarian theological teaching, though divergent and at times in friction with each other, were not considered to be mutually exclusive. In the seventh century indeed, a notable attempt to explain and reconcile them was made in the work of

Maximus the Confessor, a Greek Father who spent a large part of his life in the West. Only after the eleventh century did the two traditions come to be felt to be altogether irreconcilable.

B. TWO CENTRAL ISSUES

In the debate between East and West about the *filioque,* two sets of questions can be seen as central. The first has to do with the traditional eastern insistence that the Spirit proceeds from the Father "alone"; the second with the western concern to discern a connexion between the Son and the procession of the Spirit.

1. Procession from the Father "alone"

According to the eastern tradition, the Holy Spirit proceeds from the Father *alone* for the following reasons:

a) The Father is the principle and cause of the Son and the Holy Spirit because it is an "hypostatic" (or "personal") property *of the Father* (and *not* of the shared divine nature) to "bring forth" the other two persons. The Son and the Holy Spirit do not derive their existence from the common essence, but from the hypostasis of the Father, from which the divine essence is conferred.

b) On the ground of the distinction between *ousia* ("being" or "essence") and hypostasis — which corresponds to the difference between what is "common" or "shared" and what is "particular" — the common properties of the divine nature do not apply to the hypostasis, and the distinctive properties of each of the three hypostases do not belong either to the common nature or to the other two hypostases. On account of his own hypostatic property, the Father derives his being from himself, and brings forth the Son and the Holy Spirit. The Son comes forth by γέννησις ("generation" or "begetting"), and his hypostatic property is to be begotten. The Holy Spirit comes forth by ἐκπόρευσις ("procession"), and that is his own distinctive hypostatic property. Because these hypostatic properties are not interchangeable or confused, the Father is the only cause of the being of the Son and of the Holy Spirit, and they are themselves caused by him.

c) In no way does the Father communicate or convey his own particular hypostatic property to either of the other two persons. Any idea that the Son together with the Father is the cause of the Holy Spirit's "mode of existence" (τρόπος τῆς ὑπάρξεως) was felt in the East to introduce two causes, two sources, two principles into the Holy Trinity. It is of course impossible to reconcile any such teaching with the divine μοναρχία ("monarchy") of the Father, that is, with his being the sole "principle" (ἀρχή).

d) In asserting in its theology, though not in the wording of the Creed, that the Spirit proceeds from the Father alone, the eastern Church does not believe that it is adding to the meaning of the original statement of the Creed. It holds, rather, that it is merely clarifying what was implicit in that original wording but had come to be denied by the West.

From a western point of view, which at the same time appreciates the concerns of the eastern tradition, it may be said that neither the early Latin Fathers, such as Ambrose and Augustine, nor the subsequent medieval tradition ever believed that they were damaging the principle of the Father's "monarchy" by affirming the *filioque.* The West declared itself to be as much attached to this principle as were the eastern

Fathers. But by describing the Son as the "secondary cause" of the procession of the Holy Spirit, the doctrine of the *filioque* gave the impression of introducing "two principles" into the Holy Trinity; and by treating the Son in his consubstantiality and unity with the Father as the origin of the person of the Holy Spirit, it seemed to obscure the difference between the persons of the Father and the Son.

Nonetheless, an important fact remains. Quite apart from the — more or less happy or unhappy — formulations of the *filioque* advanced in western theology (which one must be careful not to treat as dogmas), and even if western Christians are prepared simply to confess in the original terms of the Creed that the Holy Spirit "proceeds from the Father" (without mentioning any secondary causality on the part of the Son), many would still maintain that the Holy Spirit *only proceeds from the Father as the Father is also Father of the Son*. Without necessarily wishing to insist on their own traditional understanding of a logical priority of the generation of the Son over the procession of the Spirit, they believe nonetheless that the trinitarian order (or, in Greek, τάξις) of Father-Son-Holy Spirit is a *datum* of revelation confessed by the Creed itself when it declares that the Spirit is to be "worshipped and glorified together with the Father and the Son". Thus they might indeed be ready to confess that the Holy Spirit proceeds "from the Father alone"; but by this they would not mean, "from the Father in isolation from the Son" (as if the Son were a stranger to the procession of the Holy Spirit), but rather, "from the Father alone, who is the only Father of his Only-begotten Son". The Spirit, who is not a "second Son", proceeds in his own unique and absolutely originated way from the Father who, as Father, is in relation to the Son.

2. The place of the Son in relation to the procession of the Holy Spirit

The Creed in its original form does not mention any participation of the Son in the procession of the Spirit from the Father, nor does it indicate the relationship between the Son and the Spirit. This may be because of the conflict with various current heresies which subordinated the Spirit to the Son, and reduced him to the level of a mere creature. However this may be, the absence of any clear statement on the relation between the Son and the Holy Spirit faces dogmatic theology with a problem which the West in the past attempted to solve by means of the *filioque*. In the Creed's lack of clarity on the point lies at least one of the roots of the divergence between later eastern and western theology of the Trinity. This means that even if agreement were reached on returning to the original wording of the Creed, that by itself would not be enough. In the longer term an answer must be given to the question of the relation between the Son and the Holy Spirit.

The observations which follow are advanced as a suggestion on the way in which western theology might move forward towards a closer understanding with the East, while still maintaining its concern to link the persons of the Son and the Spirit:

a) The Son's participation in the procession of the Spirit from the Father cannot be understood merely in terms of the *temporal mission* of the Spirit, as has sometimes been suggested. In other words, it cannot be restricted to the "economy" of the history of salvation as if it had no reference to, no bearing upon and no connexion with the "immanent" Trinity and the relation within the divine life itself between the three consubstantial persons. The freedom of God in his own being and as he acts in history must always be respected; but it is impossible to accept that what is valid for his revelation of his own being in history is not in some sense also valid for his eternal being and essence.

b) There is a sense in which it is correct to say that the Holy Spirit proceeds from the Father *alone* (ἐκ μόνου τοῦ Πατρός). This "alone" refers to the unique procession of the Spirit from the Father, and to his particular personal being (ὑπόστασις or *hyparxis*) which he receives from the Father. But it does not exclude a relationship with the Son as well as with the Father. On the one hand, the procession (ἐκπόρευσις) of the Spirit must be distinguished from the begetting (γέννησις) of the Son; but on the other hand this procession must be related to the begetting of the Son by the Father alone. While the Holy Spirit proceeds from the Father alone, his procession is nevertheless connected with the relationship within the Trinity between the Father and the Son, in virtue of which the Father acts *as Father*. The begetting of the Son from the Father thus qualifies the procession of the Spirit as *a procession from the Father of the Son*.

c) From this fundamental thesis, two things follow. *First, it should not be said* that the Spirit proceeds "from the Father and the Son", for this would efface the difference in his relationship to the Father and to the Son. *Second, it should be said* that the procession of the Spirit from the Father presupposes the relationship existing within the Trinity between the Father and the Son, for the Son is eternally in and with the Father, and the Father is never without the Son. Eastern theology has traditionally emphasized the first of these two conclusions. The Latin Fathers were already exploring the implications of the second long before the *filioque* had finally been clarified and introduced into the Creed.

d) Along these lines, western trinitarian theology could come to understand the procession of the Holy Spirit in the way suggested by such patristic formulations as "the Spirit proceeds from the Father and receives from the Son". This underlines the fact that the Son is indeed not alien to the procession of the Spirit, nor the Spirit to the begetting of the Son — something which has also been indicated in eastern theology when it has spoken of the Spirit as "resting upon" or "shining out through" the Son, and insisted that the generation of the Son and procession of the Spirit must be *distinguished* but not *separated*. Differences certainly remain still in this area, for eastern theology is not easily able to agree that there is any *priority* of the generation of the Son over the procession of the Spirit, and desires rather to emphasize the "simultaneity" of the two, and to see the one as "accompanying" the other. Nonetheless, there does open up here a field for further exploration. So far as western theology is concerned, the Spirit could then be seen as receiving his complete existence (hypostasis) from the Father, but as existing in relation to both the Father and the Son. This would follow the principle that because the Father is the source of divinity, the Spirit does proceed from him "alone". At the same time, however, it would express what that principle alone and by itself cannot: the relation of the Spirit as a person within the Trinity to the Son as well as to the Father. The *filioque,* on this suggestion, would have valid meaning with reference to the relationship of the three hypostases within the divine triunity, but not with regard to the procession of the complete and perfect hypostasis of the Spirit from the Father.

e) These suggestions raise the further question of whether new or at least alternative formulations might be found which could express what the *filioque* validly

sought to convey. Several old-established expressions have been mentioned in this section of the memorandum, viz:
— the Spirit proceeds from the Father of the Son;
— the Spirit proceeds from the Father through the Son;
— the Spirit proceeds from the Father and receives from the Son;
— the Spirit proceeds from the Father and rests on the Son;
— the Spirit proceeds from the Father and shines out through the Son.
These and possibly other formulations as well deserve to be given attention and consideration in future discussion.

V. The relevance of the question

These ancient controversies about what at first sight seems to be a strictly limited point of doctrine have, we believe, an unexpectedly urgent relevance. The study of the *filioque* question can be the point of entry into a wider exploration of the person and work of the Holy Spirit, of the relation of the Spirit to Jesus Christ, and indeed of the whole of trinitarian theology. The feeling that in all the western traditions something has been lacking in our experience and understanding of the Holy Spirit has grown rapidly in recent years. This tendency has carried with it a sense that the doctrine of the Trinity as such has come to appear remote and abstract to many, indeed very many Christian people. As Lesslie Newbigin writes: "It has been said that the question of the Trinity is the one theological question that has been really settled. It would, I think, be nearer the truth to say that the Nicene formula has been so devoutly hallowed that it is effectively put out of circulation."[1] In the western Christian world, while the churches continue to repeat the trinitarian formula, the trinitarian experience seems distant from many ordinary Christians. To them the word "God" is more likely to evoke thoughts of a supreme Monad than of the triune being of the Father, the Son and the Holy Spirit.

In the course of our discussions, we have realized that the question of the Trinity is one which is very far from being "settled". We have found in this fact not only a source of difficulties which have still to be tackled and overcome, but also at the same time a source of hope. In many different quarters it seems as if these basic articles of the Christian faith were coming to be the centre of new enquiry and fresh reflection. While we have not been able to agree as to how far the addition of the *filioque* clause was the cause of the differences between East and West on this whole subject, we have come to see that at least it has become a sign or indication of an underlying difference in theological approach. For the first ten centuries of the Christian era this difference was contained within a unity of faith and sacramental communion; since then it has been one of the primary causes of the continuing division between Orthodoxy on the one side and the Roman Catholic, Anglican and Protestant churches on the other. Within the last century, however, this situation has begun to change. First among the Old Catholics, then amongst Anglicans and others, the position of the *filioque* clause in the Creed has come under question. The whole matter of trinitarian theology has begun to be approached afresh. It has seemed to many that the balance and fullness of trinitarian doctrine, the reciprocity of the action of the Son and the Spirit, have been to some extent obscured in the West. It is not at all easy to trace the links of cause and effect in such areas. We do not say that the doctrine of the *filioque* was the cause of

---

[1] *The Open Secret,* Grand Rapids, Mich., Eerdmans, 1978, p.30.

these developments. It may be that they have other origins. But certainly there is an interaction between one point of doctrine and others, between teaching and faith, between doctrinal formulations and the growth of Christian life.

In our discussion two points in particular have been suggested as opening up the wider bearing of the *filioque* debate. Both have figured especially in modern discussion of the issue. As they arise out of the concern to see the doctrine of the Trinity in connexion with the experience and practice of the Church, we must take them seriously into account.

A. On the one hand, it can be argued that the *filioque* underlines the fact that the Holy Spirit is none other than the Spirit of Jesus Christ; that this understanding of the Spirit is fundamental to the New Testament witness; and that the *filioque* is a necessary bulwark against the dangers of christologically uncontrolled "charismatic enthusiasm", dangers against which the churches today need to be on guard.

In no way would we wish to underplay the significance of this concern. At the same time, the Spirit too must not be "quenched" (I Thess. 5:19). Justice can be done to both sides of the matter only if in our speaking of the relation between the Spirit and the Son we do not give the impression of a one-sided dependence of the Spirit upon Christ, but express the reciprocity between them mentioned above in Section III B.

B. On the other hand, it can be maintained that the filioque subordinates the Holy Spirit to Christ; that it tends to "depersonalize" him as if he were a mere "instrument" or "power"; and that this tendency can also encourage a subordination of the Spirit to the Church in which the Church itself becomes hardened in authoritarian institutionalism.

This warning, too, must be taken seriously. It is admittedly an open question whether and how far connexions of this kind can be historically demonstrated in the development of the western Church. Nevertheless, this danger too can only be met and countered on solid theological ground by the recognition of the reciprocity and mutual interaction of the Son and Holy Spirit.

VI. Recommendations

We therefore recommend:

A. That the new possibilities of discussion about the meaning of our faith in God, Father, Son and Holy Spirit, which are now opening up, and which we have begun to explore in this memorandum, should be pursued by all the churches; and that there should be a deeper effort to see how this faith is to be expressed in the forms of Christian worship, in the structures of the Church, and in the patterns of Christian life, so that the Holy Trinity may be seen as the foundation of Christian life and experience. This will require in particular a new sensitivity to the person and work of the Holy Spirit as the one who in his fullness both rests upon Jesus Christ and is the gift of Christ to the Church, the Lord and Giver of life to humankind and all creation.

B. That the original form of the third article of the Creed, without the *filioque*, should everywhere be recognized as the normative one and restored, so that the whole Christian people may be able, in this formula, to confess their common faith in the Holy Spirit:

And we believe in the Holy Spirit,
    the Lord and Giver of life,
    who proceeds from the Father,
    who with the Father and the Son together is
        worshipped and glorified,
    who spoke by the prophets.

C. That the different churches should respond to these suggestions in ways appropriate to their own historical and theological situations. For some, this will involve a more living appreciation of formulae whose authority has never been questioned. For others, it will mean a wholly new appreciation of the value and significance of this ancient ecumenical confession of faith. For some in which the Creed is constantly used in public worship, it will imply liturgical changes which will need to be introduced step by step. In all these various ways a renewed reception of the Nicene Creed can play a vital role in the growing together of the separated Christian traditions into the unity of faith.

DOCUMENT III.19

TOWARDS THE COMMON EXPRESSION OF THE APOSTOLIC FAITH TODAY (1982)

Introduction: the importance of this study as an ecumenical project

1. In our present divided state, visible unity cannot be restored unless each church becomes aware of the painful situation of our divisions and takes decisions to overcome our disobedience to the will of Christ as expressed in his prayer for unity (John 17:1-26). These decisions will be genuine only to the extent to which they imply a resolve to do what the re-establishment of communion demands: conversion through a constant return to the source which is God as revealed in Jesus Christ through the Holy Spirit. Such a conversion requires an effort to express the content of the faith in such a way that the life of the community is consonant with the word of God.

2. At its Fifth Assembly in Nairobi in December 1975, the World Council of Churches, after its discussion of "conciliar fellowship", adopted the following recommendation:

> We ask the churches to undertake a common effort to receive, reappropriate and confess together, as contemporary occasion requires, the Christian truth and faith, delivered through the apostles and handed down through the centuries. Such common action, arising from free and inclusive discussion under the commonly acknowledged authority of God's word, must aim both to clarify and to embody the unity and the diversity which are proper to the church's life and mission (Section II, 19).

The same assembly, in revising "The Constitution of the World Council of Churches", adopted the following statement as the first of the purposes of the Council:

> (i) To call the churches to the goal of visible unity in one faith and in one eucharistic fellowship expressed in worship and in common life in Christ, and to advance towards that unity in order that the world may believe (Art. III, 1).

The intention of the Faith and Order Commission in formulating the following project is to help the World Council to fulfil its recommendation, and so to advance towards the realization of its first purpose.

3. A primary assumption of this project is the recognition of the special rank and function of the Nicene Creed.[1] For, together with a growing convergence in our understanding of baptism, eucharist and ministry, the appeal for a common expression of the apostolic faith belongs to the movement towards the unity of the Church. In the attempt to work out such a common expression, it is impossible to disregard the special place of the Nicene Creed. It is the one common creed which is most universally accepted as formulation of the apostolic faith by churches in all parts of the world, where it primarily serves as the confession of faith in the eucharistic liturgy.[2]

---

[1] Throughout this paper the reference is always to the Creed commonly believed to be of the Second Ecumenical Council at Constantinople in 381 AD, although various customary terms are used, such as "the Nicean Creed", "the Nicene Creed", "the Creed commonly called Nicene", "the Nicene Symbol", "the Ecumenical Creed", etc.

[2] Thus, the Faith and Order Conference in Lausanne in 1927 referred to its members as "united in a common Christian faith which is proclaimed in the holy scriptures and is witnessed to and safeguarded in the Ecumenical Creed, commonly called Nicene, and in the Apostles' Creed" (Sect. IV).

4. The *koinonia* of the eucharistic community, which is united to Christ by baptism, is grounded on the apostolic proclamation of the crucified and risen Christ which is documented in the scriptures, summarized in the creed of the church and is served by the minister who presides over the eucharistic celebration. The common understanding of the apostolic faith was expressed by the ancient Church in the Ecumenical Creed of Nicea (325), complemented at Constantinople (381) and solemnly received at Chalcedon (451) as the authentic symbol of the Christian faith, witnessing to the fullness of the Christian faith and life and authoritative for the entire Church.

5. The eucharist builds up the Church and visibly manifests its unity. The apostolic faith, fruit of the Holy Spirit, is the ground of that unity. The outward expression of this intimate relationship of faith and eucharistic celebration is therefore essential to the visible unity of the Church, so much so that without common recognition of the Nicene Creed as the ecumenical symbol of the apostolic faith, it is difficult if not impossible to understand how we are to advance "to the goal of visible unity in one faith and in one eucharistic fellowship expressed in worship and in common life in Christ... in order that the world may believe" (WCC Constitution III, 1). Thus, together with a growing convergence in our understanding of baptism, eucharist and ministry, the appeal for common expression of the apostolic faith of the one, holy, catholic and apostolic Church as expressed in its Ecumenical Symbol of faith belongs to movement towards the unity of the Church.

6. It should be remembered how well this Creed has served millions of Christians, with whom we are also bound together in the unity of the Church, in the past. Its brief statement of the essential faith has provided at least formally a thread of unity down through the centuries. In one form or another, this Creed has been used by the Orthodox churches, by the Roman Catholic and Anglican churches, and by most of the churches of the Protestant Reformation, and in all parts of the world. It has helped the churches to affirm their fundamental belief in God, in the Lord Jesus Christ and his saving action, in the Holy Spirit and the Church, and in the life of the kingdom to come. Some have used it as a baptismal confession, others as a central standard of doctrine. It has been read and sung at the eucharist and other liturgical services and has been used as a statement of belief at the ordination of church ministers. As the product of a council received by the churches in a time of great confusion and strife, it has stood as a model of ecumenical confession, both in the method of its formulation and in the content of its definition. As such, it has inspired theologians, hymn writers, preachers and artists in all ages. It seems appropriate, therefore, to ask the churches, when they try to express their common understanding of the apostolic faith today, to recognize this Creed from the time of the early Church as the ecumenical expression of the apostolic faith which unites Christians of all ages in all places.

7. Such recognition would call each church to examine its beliefs and actions today in relation to that Ecumenical Creed and so to express and interpret its meaning today theologically, ethically, liturgically, socially in terms understandable in that church's everyday life and in society.

8. We are convinced that any real progress among the divided churches towards the common expression of the apostolic faith today will require a twofold movement, towards unity in faith with the early Church, and towards unity in mission with the Church of the future. The word "towards" is important: both movements are actually,

from our present divided situation, movements towards the future. Our hope then is that we can initiate a threefold study project, aiming:
a) to ask the churches to make a common recognition of the apostolic faith as expressed in the Ecumenical Symbol of that faith: the Nicene Creed (Chapter I);
b) to ask the churches how they understand its content today in their own particular situations of worship, fellowship and witness (Chapter II); and
c) to ask the churches "to undertake a common effort to confess together, as contemporary occasion requires, the Christian truth and faith, delivered through the Apostles and handed down through the centuries" (Chapter III).

9. We believe that this project will guide the churches to confess Christ in their life, and lead them towards the common celebration of the eucharist where "we proclaim the Lord's death until he comes" (1 Cor. 11:26).

I. Towards the common recognition of the apostolic faith as expressed in the Ecumenical Symbol of that faith: the Nicene Creed

10. Our hope is that all the churches will recognize the Symbol of Nicea-Constantinople as the common expression of the faith of the Church because:
a) The Nicene Creed over the centuries has been, and is now very widely acknowledged as, the Ecumenical Symbol of the apostolic faith, a fact of fundamental significance for an ecumenism which seeks the unity of the Church "in all places and all ages" (New Delhi statement). We therefore plead with those churches that do not acknowledge it, or, while acknowledging it in reality disregard it, that they ask themselves whether for the sake of unity they might agree to reconsider their attitude.
b) While the act of confessing the contemporary meaning of the apostolic faith has to be done again and again in different situations and in different forms, and this life of contemporary confessing and witness must never be interrupted, nevertheless we consider that designing a new creed, intended to replace the Nicene Creed as the Ecumenical Symbol of the apostolic faith, is not appropriate.
c) The World Council of Churches is not authorized to propose a new creed.
d) Proposing an ecumenical symbol of the apostolic faith clearly presupposes the authority of an ecumenical council. Such a council would have as an essential purpose the confession of the apostolic faith on behalf of the whole Church in the situation of its own present day. Among the important preparatory steps for just such an event would be what this project calls for: a wider recognition among the churches of the Ecumenical Symbol of Nicea.

11. The plurality and variety of documents which occur in the act of confessing in particular situations do not imply that each new creed or symbol binds the whole catholic Church. It is true that Christian witness should always aim to express the whole faith of the one Church; but the whole Church is not thereby bound to each particular act of confessing. These various acts and documents of confession rather apply the one apostolic faith to particular situations, and are to be judged, therefore, by the criterion of their consonance with that apostolic faith as confessed in the Ecumenical Creed of the Church.

12. How shall we understand the relation of scripture and the Creed? This, of course, is a principal question to be studied ecumenically in the project we are proposing. Here we can only indicate some points to be considered in that study.

a) Christian identity is rooted in the acceptance of God's revelation of himself through Jesus Christ and the Holy Spirit. Initiated in creation, witnessed to in the Old Testament, this revelation of God's identity was fully manifested in the mystery of Jesus Christ. Transmitted in the power of the Holy Spirit by the preaching of the apostles, it is the great gift of God to humanity. And the Christian community has the mission to keep it and transmit it to all humankind.

b) It is this revelation, already understood and lived out in various ways by the first Christian communities, that the scriptures record. It is significant, however, that already in the documents of the New Testament we can see the need for some brief statements in which at least the main elements of the revelation are brought together in such a way that they help the Christian communities to test the consonance of their beliefs with what God did and said in the Holy Spirit by Jesus Christ.

c) The creeds of the first centuries, in a more elaborated form, tried to continue this service. Their language was, indeed, dependent on the culture, the needs, the situations of their time. But they were intended to convey a summary of the central teaching of the scriptures. Their authority, however, comes from the consonance of their content with the revelation itself. They are instruments for its acceptance by faith, and its proclamation in the life of the Christian community.

13. It is sometimes asked whether the Nicene Creed can be considered "sufficient" to express the Christian faith for contemporary Christians. It is pointed out that some biblical themes and concepts, indispensable for Christian life and thought, are not explicitly treated in the Creed. Again it is noticed that there are many contemporary questions and issues which are urgent for Christian obedience today, but which were simply not actual when the Creed was written.

a) It is, of course, true that not everything is said explicitly in the Creed, and that certain affirmations came into focus for historical reasons. The Creed is also historically conditioned in its language, its concepts, its thought forms. Moreover, the Creed aims to fulfil particular functions, and its language is sometimes doxological, sometimes dogmatic.

b) The question of the Creed's "sufficiency", however, leads to the authority of the Creed, and it must be clearly said that the Creed's authority for contemporary Christian life and thought does not lie in the extensiveness with which it treats either the biblical witness or contemporary questions, but in its consonance — claimed and recognized in the Church — with the testimony of the apostles to God's revelation in Jesus Christ. The urgent question for Christian witness is, "Who is Jesus Christ for us today?" This question has been faced and answered in all ages, and the adequacy of any answer, however relevant to its age it may appear to be, ultimately is grounded in its participation in the authority with which the apostles and the early Church bear witness to the revelation of God in Jesus Christ.

c) But the element of mystery must be noted, both in the Creed and in any attempt to verbalize the Christian faith. When the word was made flesh, the inexpressible became expressed. Words can express the mystery, yet it remains a mystery, and the words used to express it must respect the fullness of it. Every creed and all our attempts to formulate or explicate our faith have their limits before the mystery of what they try to express. In that perspective, it is wrong to expect either too much or too little, also from the Creed.

14. In order to rediscover the unity of faith, therefore, it would be an important step if the churches would remind themselves again of the significance of the Nicene Creed as Ecumenical Symbol of the one, apostolic faith, implying as it does temporal as well as geographical universality. As such it is not merely to be considered as a first stage in the development of definitions of the faith, but also as intimately connected with the unity of the one, holy, catholic and apostolic Church.

15. Therefore, the World Council of Churches might ask the churches to recognize anew that integral unity of the Christian faith expressed in the Symbol of Nicea-Constantinople, to reconsider the status of their own teaching in its light, to affirm its content as the basis of more comprehensive church unity, and to strengthen its place in the liturgical life of the churches wherever necessary and possible under circumstances of pastoral responsibility.

16. In view of research and recent proposals concerning the *filioque* clause in the Faith and Order Commission, we propose for purposes of this study to use the original Greek text of the Nicene Creed, without thereby prejudging in any way the theological views of the churches on this issue,[3] as follows:

> And we believe in the Holy Spirit,
> the Lord and Giver of life,
> who proceeds from the Father,
> who with the Father and the Son together is
> worshipped and glorified,
> who spoke by the prophets.

II. Towards the common explication of this apostolic faith in the contemporary situations of the churches

17. The content of this apostolic faith, although it is the ground in itself for Church unity and contemporary witness, finds its context in the divided state of the Church and the alienation of humankind. This ground can only become effectual as, given time and opportunity, we appropriate it for ourselves in our times, seek to grasp and understand its meaning in our own language and attempt to share and bear its witness in ways which others in turn can understand. Authoritative in itself, it manifests its authority in the midst of that divided state of the Church and that alienation of humankind, as it asks for and empowers contemporary interpretation of its meaning in the countless particular languages, cultures and crises of today.

18. This was already the case, for example, when the Council of Chalcedon (451 AD) reaffirmed the Creed of Nicea, even as it proceeded to formulate its own definition, more than a century afterwards, of the doctrine of Christ. The procedure was repeated as the Reformers reaffirmed the Apostles' Creed and the Creed of Nicea, and in so doing confessed their recognition of the relation between apostolic faith and their context of sixteenth century questions about justification and sanctification. And it appears likely that ecumenical renewal today will once again open our eyes to the authority of the Creed and our communion with those who assembled at Nicea. At the same time, it can open our eyes to our vocation to explicate the power and meaning of that faith in the many diverse fields of contemporary Church life and witness.

---

[3] See *Spirit of God-Spirit of Christ: Ecumenical Reflections on the Filioque Controversy*, ed. Lukas Vischer, Faith and Order Paper No. 103, London, SPCK, and Geneva, WCC, 1981.

19. The place of the Creed itself in making such a contemporary interpretation will be matter for study and debate, owing to the differing status it is accorded in different churches. In some traditions, the expression of the faith today is quite inconceivable without giving a central and decisive role to the Creed itself, not only in its substantial contents but even in its wording. Others would see themselves as more or less urgently bound by the substance of the Creed but would be more willing to attempt modern statements of the heart of the faith. Still others might value the Creed above all as a procedural model for a task which needs to be accomplished ever anew, namely the confession of the faith in particular circumstances and with the conceptual and linguistic tools available at the time. Even those churches which do not use the Nicene Creed, or indeed any other creed, are usually ready to acknowledge that the Creed deals with matters that are vital for Christian confession.

20. A common expression of the apostolic faith today will necessarily involve some attempt to relate Creed to contemporary situation and contemporary situation to Creed in such a way that each throws its distinct light on the other. "The unity of the Church is a sign of the coming unity of humankind" (Uppsala, I), and it is the apostolic faith which unites us for the renewal of human community.

21. What kind of questions would such a contemporary explication of the Nicene faith need to address? In the following we offer some tentative examples of such questions. Other clearer formulations of such questions would need to be developed in the study itself. These examples pose questions not only of a social and personal character in the context of our alienation and divisions as women and men but also pose questions of an ecclesial nature in the divided state of the Church.

a) The Ecumenical Creed confesses faith in one God. How do we explicate that over against tendencies to absolutize today's finite realities, aspirations, historical situations? What does faith in one God mean for human community torn by poverty, militarism, racism?

b) The Ecumenical Creed confesses faith in the triune God, Father, Son and Holy Spirit. How do we explicate that to those of other faiths or of no faith who charge us with having surrendered the unity of God?

c) The Ecumenical Creed confesses that this one God created all things. How do we explicate that to persons who consider God to be a human creation, a projection of human wishes and realities?

d) The Ecumenical Creed confesses faith in one Lord, Jesus Christ. How do we explicate that to contemporaries in a myriad of cultural and religious situations who, venerating Jesus, understand him to be a mere human being? Or who refuse to see his lordship in social, economic, political life?

e) The Ecumenical Creed confesses Jesus Christ, God's only begotten Son, to be "of one essence" with the Father. How do we explicate today this claim that human salvation and liberation cannot be real without our participation in what is divine and eternal? How are we to understand such a term as "essence" today as a way of speaking about God.

f) The Ecumenical Creed confesses that God's own Son has become human. How do we explicate to present-day men and women in the many relationships of their lives that it is this incarnation that provides meaning for human life? How does this faith in the incarnate God illumine our understanding of human creation as well as human redemption? Of human community and the cosmos as well as the human self?

g) The Ecumenical Creed confesses that Jesus Christ was crucified for us under Pontius Pilate. How do we make clear to our contemporaries that salvation has historical character, that it is no mere cosmological speculation, but a matter of divine election and mission to all humanity? How do we proclaim God's coming into human suffering in the cross, strengthening and empowering as well as consoling those who are oppressed by sin and evil?

h) The Ecumenical Creed confesses that on the third day Jesus Christ arose according to the scriptures. How do we make clear in our twentieth century world that this cross and this resurrection lie at the roots of a new life, liberate and reconcile us, and stand at the centre of all we can say about God's love and justice for God's creatures.

i) The Ecumenical Creed confesses faith in the Holy Spirit. How can we explain the many ways in which we discern the life, the truth, the communion, the morale in which the Spirit creates the life of God in us in the everydayness of our locations and predicaments? At the same time, how does that same Spirit come to us with prophetic authority? By what means do we recognize that it is the same Spirit who is speaking today who spoke through the prophets? What does the discernment of the Spirit mean for the common recognition of the teaching function of the Church, not only in the church authorities but in the inter-relatedness of the contemporary theological enterprise?

j) The Ecumenical Creed confesses one, holy, catholic and apostolic Church. How can we bear witness individually, corporately and representatively to the reality of this community of faith as a liberating and reconciling people of God, confessing one faith and one baptism, sharing one table, and hospitable to all, especially to each other's members and ministers?

k) The Ecumenical Creed confesses one baptism for the forgiveness of sins. How can we strive towards the recognition of that one baptism in each other's churches today? How can we more closely relate baptism and the experience of our forgiveness before God and neighbour? How can we today share in a reconciliation and redemption among women and men, among persons of all races and classes, which is appropriate to the costliness of God's forgiveness of us all in Christ?

l) The Ecumenical Creed confesses the life of the age to come. How can we explain to twentieth century neighbours an understanding of life which transcends death, yet can be lived now? How can we explicate a Christian hope, rooted and grounded in eternal life with God, which addresses urgent human problems, which illumines human suffering and persecution, which clarifies and judges human utopias in the light of God's coming kingdom? How can we attest the unity in this hope and eternal life which we share with the saints, the ancestors, the church of other ages?

22. It is obvious that such contemporary explication will generate much diversity in confessing the faith. Is that consonant with the common confession of which the WCC recommendation speaks?

23. We believe that it is. We believe that diversity is a necessary feature of any serious attempt to recognize and explicate the one apostolic faith today. The one faith is for all. It is universally relevant. But that means it is for each one, each relationship, each family, each group, each class, each culture, each nation. The Christian gospel entered Greco-Roman culture, and the Church accepted the pluralism which that meant for Christian *koinonia* and witness.

24. Nevertheless, although the Creed of Nicea is widely used by churches all over the world, many Christians are asking legitimately whether confessing the faith of the Creed of Nicea means being bound to ancient Greco-Roman forms of thought and speech. Recognizing this, we nevertheless believe that participation in this project could help all churches to receive their common tradition, and link them with other Christians in other parts of the world and in all time.

25. To speak about "the common expression of the apostolic faith", then, does not necessarily mean a single verbal formulation. Faith may be common even where wordings differ. The immediate task is to move towards mutually recognizable expressions of faith. This does not exclude the possibility that a growing mutual understanding could eventually lead to the widespread acceptance of one expression of faith, without abandoning other congruous forms that exist already or could later be formulated. None of this entails the replacement of the Nicene Creed as the Ecumenical Symbol of the apostolic faith.

III. Towards a common confession of the apostolic faith today

26. *The need for and meaning of "common confession":*

a) Interpreting the Creed of the church is not the same thing as actually confessing the faith expressed in the Creed. The act of confession is always personal, even if it is done in community. It is personal also in the sense that it finally relates to the person of Jesus Christ and to the personal reality of the triune God. It means taking sides with Jesus (Luke 12:9) for the truth and love he proclaimed. This also involves assertions concerning who Jesus is, but those assertions are subservient to the intention of acclaiming Jesus as Lord and of joining in his mission to humanity and in his proclamation of the kingdom to come.

b) Confessing Jesus Christ is a communal event, because after Easter it is the apostolic Church in which Jesus is present and which proclaims who Jesus is. To confess Jesus Christ now means to share in the Church's acclamation of Jesus as Lord (Rom. 10:9) through the Holy Spirit (1 Cor. 12:3), and in the profession of the apostolic faith (1 John 4:2-3). Therefore the personal confession of individual Christians is embedded in the community of the Church, even when it occurs in particular situations and is expressed in specific ways. In his or her personal confession, the individual Christian is supported and encouraged by the confessing community. The common confession of the Church does not preclude individual modifications according to specific situations, provided that it is the same faith that comes to expression. Unity is not uniformity. In fact, uniform repetition of the Creed of the Church can become a device in evading a personal confession to Jesus Christ in an actual situation.

c) The normal place for confessing the Creed in the life of the Church is its liturgy. Here all Christians are united in praise and glorification of their Lord. Thus they devote themselves to the Lord so that they may share communion with him in the eucharistic meal.

d) This common confession in the liturgy is expressed in a language of glorification of Jesus Christ and of the triune God and of hope for participation in that glory. It also includes narrative elements that serve to identify the Jesus of history and his relation to the Father and to the Spirit. It is based on repentance, because a conversion to God is required, turning to God from bondage to a world that separated itself from God. Only by way of such conversion can Christians share in God's salvation.

e) If confession means participation in the unity of the body of Christ by joining the acclamation of Jesus as Lord, it must overcome the inherited divisions among the faithful. Therefore the element of repentance and conversion in the act of confession also applies to the separation and division of the churches. Our separations are against the will of the Lord. It is important for the apostolic faith to be confessed by the churches as one and the same faith, so that when the individual shares in the liturgical confession of the Church, he or she will be assured of turning to the one Jesus Christ. The very fact that the act of confession is communal, therefore, obliges the churches to overcome their divisions and to seek a common confession of the apostolic faith that would enable them to enter again into conciliar fellowship.

f) A common confession of faith is also required in view of the challenges arising from contemporary experience which extend to all Christian churches alike, although their focus may be different in different situations. As every form of confession to Jesus Christ involves repentance, conversion and renewal on the part of the confessing person, so also a common confession of the churches responding to the challenges of the time must involve conversion and renewal in the human community. This applies in the first place to community within the Church and among churches, a community of women and men across all barriers of races, classes and cultures. But it also extends to the human community at large, to its economic and political conflicts in the national as well as international context, because the Church witnesses to the kingdom of God, the goal of all human community. The Church is called to be a symbol of that eschatological community of justice and peace. But it lives up to this function only to the degree that the community of the Church itself is truly united through the love of Christ.

27. *The Creed as criterion for a common confession of the apostolic faith:*

a) The challenges of the present world, as well as a widespread feeling that these challenges are not answered in the wording of the traditional creeds and other confessional documents of the churches, have given rise to a wide range of contemporary statements of the Christian faith. They come from entire churches as well as from individuals and groups. Besides, there are confessional documents of the past that are cherished by particular churches as expressing the faith of their fathers. How is this variety of confessional documents and traditions related to the unity of the Christian faith and to the task of a common confession of that faith? The unity of the apostolic faith is expressed in the Ecumenical Creed, proclaimed on behalf of the entire Church as a summary of the central teaching of the scripture and therefore serving as a criterion for the unity of other statements of faith with the teaching of the Church. In relation to the Ecumenical Creed later confessing documents, including those from the present age, will be evaluated as to their witness to the same Lord, expressing the same Spirit that unites the Church in the same faith. But the Creed will also be read with different eyes in new situations so that its assertions may reveal new insights.

b) When on the basis of the Ecumenical Creed later confessional documents are evaluated, the churches may also rediscover in that Creed the basic unity of the faith which they have in common in spite of their separation. The more they come to evaluate their particular confessional traditions in the light of the Creed, the more they may learn to understand other traditions as expressing the same faith under different circumstances and in different situations. While each church should be ready to interpret its own confessional heritage in the light of the apostolic faith as summarized in the Ecumenical Creed, it might also be able to accept other churches and their confessional heritage on the same basis.

c) In such a process of interpreting the confessional positions of one's own church on this basis, it might become possible to overcome condemnations (anathemas) that have been formulated and understood in the past to exclude the teaching of other churches. Without necessarily dissociating themselves from these judgments as such, the churches might discover that they do not apply to those other churches as they are at present. Perhaps particular condemnations never applied to the basic intentions of those positions that occasioned them. This is not to say that the Church can always avoid condemning false teaching and disciplining its adherents. This expresses an element which is essential to the act of confession as taking sides with Jesus in situations where his claim is disputed. But whether this condemnation actually applies to a particular opponent remains open to reconsideration.

28. *On the way to a common confession:*

a) A specific challenge that requires the confession of the Church to Jesus Christ and to the triune God emerges in the encounter with other faiths and ideologies, especially as they influence the mind of the Christian people. But other faiths and ideologies are not simply opposed to Jesus Christ. They can contain many elements of truth which the Christian Church should acknowledge and even appropriate to its own life and understanding. Even explicit rejection of the Christian proclamation may often be conditioned by partial misrepresentations of the truth of the gospel by the churches themselves.

b) Elements of a common confession to Jesus Christ and the triune God are implicit in many documents of ecumenical dialogue, especially in "Baptism, Eucharist and Ministry", but also in many bilateral agreements between particular churches. They should be taken into consideration when the churches move towards confessing together the apostolic faith in the context of the challenges of the contemporary world and on the basis of their common heritage.

c) A common confession of the apostolic faith today will exhibit the potential of the Creed as a summary of the apostolic teaching to illumine the experience of Christians and of their churches in a secularized world and in the particular context of their different cultures. It will help to transform those experiences through the power of the life-giving Spirit by responding to the challenges of the time and thus reassuring the Christian conscience of the truth of the apostolic faith.

IV
Specific Faith and Order Projects

This chapter surveys those studies of the Commission on Faith and Order between 1963 and 1993 which were not pursued continuously throughout this period, but were on the agenda for a limited space of time only. Like the main studies described in the preceding chapter, these more limited studies were in several cases related to each other and also to the main studies. They are an indication of the wide range of themes which were addressed by Faith and Order in the fulfilment of its ecumenical theological task.

1. The Authority and Interpretation of Holy Scripture

In the history of Faith and Order, as in that of the ecumenical movement in general, the fundamental significance of holy scripture for Christian faith and for the search for the visible unity of the church has been an unquestioned presupposition. A problem which was raised already at the world conference of 1927 in Lausanne, however, was the relationship between *scripture and Tradition*. Both in Lausanne and in 1937 in Edinburgh this issue was primarily discussed in relation to the role and significance of the early creeds and later confessions. In Edinburgh new perspectives emerged which went beyond an affirmation of the authority of the Bible in a formal sense by emphasizing its authority in terms of its content, its authoritative witness. Similarly, already at Edinburgh a more dynamic and comprehensive understanding of "Tradition" began to develop (cf. Vischer, *op. cit.*, Lausanne: pp.33-34; Edinburgh: pp.44-45,64-65).

These two developments were taken up within the new theological and ecumenical context after the founding of the WCC in 1948, when European and North American sections of the theological commission on "Tradition and Traditions" prepared reports which served as a basis for the work of the 1963 world conference on faith and order in Montreal. The report of section II of that conference, "Scripture, Tradition and Traditions" (cf. document II.1 and chapter II.2), differentiates between (1) Tradition as the gospel or God's revelation in Christ together with its transmission through history in and by the church, and (2) traditions as the churches' diverse expressions of the one Tradition. The Bible is shown as being both part of Tradition and the criterion for the genuine Tradition. Montreal thus opened up a new understanding of the relationship between scripture and Tradition which is of lasting importance for ecumenical dialogue and still needs to be more fully received by the churches (cf. the re-emergence of the scripture-Tradition issue in the responses of the churches to BEM as described in *Baptism, Eucharist and Ministry 1982-1990: Report on the Process and Responses, op. cit.*, pp.131-142).

But it also became clear at Montreal that the statement that the criterion for the genuine Tradition is to be found in holy scripture "rightly interpreted" immediately raises the problem of the diverse (confessional and other) interpretations of scripture. Consequently, Montreal recommended a study on *biblical interpretation*. A first preparatory consultation took place at Bad Schauenburg near Basel, Switzerland, in 1964. Its results were presented to the Faith and Order Commission in the same year at Aarhus in the form of an outline for a study programme (*Aarhus 1964*, no. 44, pp.61-69), and studies on "the problem of biblical hermeneutics and its significance for the ecumenical movement" were authorized (*ibid.*, pp.41-42). Five regional study groups were formed and in 1967 their results were summarized at a meeting in Heidelberg, Federal Republic of Germany, and published in a report, "The Significance of the Hermeneutical Problem for the Ecumenical Movement". This report was presented to the Commission meeting in Bristol the same year and was printed in *Bristol 1967: New Directions in Faith and Order*, no. 50, pp.32-41.

The Commission recommended that following the study of the hermeneutical problem, a study on "The Authority of the Bible" be undertaken (*ibid.*, pp.59,156). It was initiated by a consultation at Boldern near Zürich, Switzerland, in 1968. With the help of a study outline summarized by James Barr in the paper "The Authority of the Bible: A Study Outline" (*The Ecumenical Review*, vol. XXI, 1969, pp.135-150), a number of groups in different countries discussed the issue. Their comments were summarized, and at Cartigny near Geneva in 1971 representatives of these groups prepared a final report on "The Authority of the Bible". The report was accepted by the Faith and Order Commission in 1971 in Louvain (*Louvain 1971: Study Reports and Documents*, no. 59, pp.9-23).

A further step was taken in Louvain with the recommendation that "the relationship of Old and New Testaments and particularly the contemporary significance of the Old Testament should be given careful study" (*ibid.*, p.214). A study group in the Netherlands was asked to prepare a first report, which was discussed by the Faith and Order Working Committee in 1973 in Zagorsk and by the Commission in Accra in 1974. The Commission recommended requesting reactions to the report from individuals and groups. These provided the basis for further discussion and revision of the first report by a small group from the Faith and Order Standing Commission in 1977 in Loccum. Its report, "The Significance of the Old Testament in Relation to the New", was accepted by the Standing Commission at Bangalore and the proposal was endorsed to publish together the three reports of the whole study process (*Bangalore 1978*, no. 93, p.5). Accordingly, the reports "The Significance of the Hermeneutical Problem for the Ecumenical Movement" (1967), "The Authority of the Bible" (1971), and "The Significance of the Old Testament in its Relation to the New" (1978) were published again in *The Bible: Its Authority and Interpretation in the Ecumenical Movement*, ed. Ellen Flesseman-van Leer, no. 99, 1980 (2nd ed. 1983). This volume also includes an earlier ecumenical text, "Guiding Principles for the Interpretation of the Bible" (1949), and the section II report of Montreal on "Scripture, Tradition and Traditions", together with an introduction by Dr Flesseman-van Leer, bibliographical references to each document and a bibliography. This documentation is still available and is therefore not reproduced here.

Questions of biblical authority and hermeneutics obviously continue to be part of the ecumenical discussion. They have been taken up again in several bilateral dialogues. New questions have arisen with the development of biblical studies and the emphasis on the hermeneutical significance of different contexts for the interpretation and authority of the Bible. They need to be addressed, bearing in mind the results achieved in the earlier studies.

2. Councils and Conciliarity

The New Delhi assembly of the WCC in 1961 recommended a study of "the conciliar process in the Church of the early centuries" (*The New Delhi Report, op. cit.*, p.131). Behind this recommendation lies the question whether there exists a relationship between the conciliar process of the first centuries and the modern ecumenical movement, and whether therefore a study of the councils could be of help in deepening the understanding of the ecumenical movement and its goal of visible unity. The New Delhi recommendation was confirmed at the 1963 Montreal world conference on faith and order and in 1964 the Commission approved a study outline (*Aarhus 1964*, no. 44, pp.70-71,41). The outline also refers to the convocation of the Second Vatican Council which gave added urgency to the study (*ibid.*, p.70). The study should "throw valuable light both on the nature of the Church's unity and continuity and also on the modern problems of the ecumenical movement. Further, this study should be a fruitful area of dialogue between the Orthodox and other churches" (*ibid.*, p.41). A study commission met in Oxford, England, in 1965 and Bad Gastein, Austria, in 1966. Its report was submitted to and welcomed by the Commission in Bristol in 1967 (*Bristol 1967: New Directions in Faith and Order*, no. 50, pp.49-58; it is also printed, together with papers, in *Councils and the Ecumenical Movement*, World Council Studies no. 5, 1968). • **Document IV.1, p.209**

The new interest in conciliarity and the attention it created for the possibility of conciliar life in the future was taken up by the 1968 Uppsala assembly with its affirmation of "a genuinely universal council" as the common ecumenical goal (*The Uppsala Report 1968, op. cit.*, p.17).

Connected in several ways with the work on councils and the conciliar process was a study on patristics, welcomed by the Faith and Order Working Committee in 1962 in Paris (*Paris 1962*, no. 36, p.8). The Commission at Aarhus recommended the continuation of this study which was to consider the importance of the whole area of patristics for the churches and the ecumenical movement today (*Aarhus 1964*, no. 44, p.42). The study group met in 1964 in Aarhus, Denmark, in 1965 in Hamburg, Federal Republic of Germany, and in 1966 in Saloniki, Greece. It presented its report to the Commission in 1967 in Bristol where it was approved (*Bristol 1967: New Directions in Faith and Order*, no. 50, pp.41-49). • **Document IV.2, p.218**

Bristol recommended that a study project on "the Significance of the Council of Chalcedon and its Reception by the Churches" be undertaken, thus continuing the studies on patristics and the councils (*ibid.*, p.156). This was done at a consultation in Geneva in 1969 which prepared a report for the Commission meeting in Louvain (*Louvain 1971: Study Reports and Documents*, no. 59, pp.23-34,224). • **Document IV.3, p.226**

At Louvain itself, one of the committees made an attempt, from the work so far done, to draw some conclusions in relation to the concepts of conciliarity, councils of the church, contemporary ecumenical councils of churches and the World Council of Churches (*ibid.*, pp.225-229). • **Document IV.4, p.236**

In 1974 the West German Ecumenical Study Committee presented a résumé of the ecumenical discussion on conciliarity and developed it further by means of an analysis of conciliar history, the ecclesiological significance of conciliarity, conciliarity and the search for truth, and conciliarity and the struggle for unity (*Councils, Conciliarity and a Genuinely Universal Council*, no. 70, 1974, reprinted from *Study Encounter*, vol. X, no. 2, 1974).

With the help of these studies the concept of conciliarity had become part of the ecumenical reflection on the church and church unity, and it was introduced into the description of church unity at the Faith and Order consultation in Salamanca in 1973 and then at the assembly in Nairobi in 1975, where the goal of the search for the visible unity of the church was described as a "conciliar fellowship of churches" (cf. document I.2), a phrase which has become celebrated.

3. Teaching Authority in the Church

While considering these three study processes on biblical interpretation, patristics and conciliarity, the Faith and Order Commission in Bristol in 1967 realized that they all "pose in common the problem of authority" (*Bristol 1967: New Directions in Faith and Order*, no. 50, p.154). Ongoing studies on "The Authority of the Bible", "The Significance of the Council of Chalcedon", "Spirit, Order and Organization" (cf. document IV.7), "Authority and Freedom in the Church" and "Ordination" should all "be gathered around the focal question of authority in the church, both in faith and in order" (*ibid.*, p.156). But the study on "Giving Account of the Hope" also led the Faith and Order Working Committee in Zagorsk in 1973 to the conclusion that the Commission should "look afresh at certain traditional theological problems... for instance, the teaching authority of the Church and the magisterium in the different traditions" (*Zagorsk 1973*, no. 66, p.39).

A year later the Commission in Accra decided to initiate a study on the teaching authority of the church (*Accra 1974*, no. 71, pp.91-95). This decision was welcomed by the 1975 Nairobi assembly and in 1976 a small consultation in Geneva prepared a working paper for the study, "How Does the Church Teach Authoritatively Today?" A study document was prepared by Faith and Order (in *One in Christ*, 1976, nos 3 and 4, offprint). Four study groups dealt with the issue and their reports were presented to a consultation in 1977 in Odessa which formulated its findings in a report (*How Does the Church Teach Authoritatively Today?*, no. 91, reprinted from *The Ecumenical Review*, vol. 31, January 1979). • **Document IV.5, p.240**

In 1978 the Commission in Bangalore reaffirmed the importance of this study by emphasizing "Common Ways of Teaching and Decision-Making" as one of three requirements for visible unity (together with unity in one faith and mutual recognition of baptism, eucharist and ministry). It again referred to the studies on the authority of the Bible, councils and conciliarity, patristics and, especially, the 1977 Odessa report. For the next Commission meeting it requested a comprehensive report on the basis of these studies, a study of New Testament concepts of doctrine and authority, and special attention to teaching authority in the ongoing work on episkopé and episcopacy (*Bangalore 1978*, no. 93, p.41). The work was not continued in its specific Bangalore formulation, however, even though the new study "Towards the Common Expression of the Apostolic Faith Today" is not without relevance for the issue of common teaching and decision-making. The 1983 Vancouver assembly reminded Faith and

Order of its unfinished task. It referred to the forthcoming responses of the churches to the BEM document as providing

> an ecumenical context within which the churches can learn to understand and encounter each other's ways of making decisions about church teaching. The significance of this opportunity needs to be emphasized, for common agreement about ways of teaching and decision-making is one of the fundamental marks of Church unity. Earlier ecumenical studies of how the Church teaches authoritatively today need to be taken up again in this new context (*Gathered for Life, op. cit.*, p.50).

It is foreseen that the fifth world conference on faith and order in 1993 will take up the question of teaching authority and decision-making and will, hopefully, provide directions for dealing with this issue in the context of a future major study on "Ecumenical Perspectives on Ecclesiology".

4. The Ecumenical Significance of Worship

Common prayer and worship has been and is the most profound resource for the ecumenical movement. The Faith and Order movement began to support efforts for common Christian prayer for unity at an early stage, and in 1926 published "Suggestions for an Octave of Prayer for Christian Unity". The Edinburgh world conference in 1937 requested the "study of liturgical questions" with a view to promoting growth in mutual understanding. Accordingly, in 1939 a theological commission was appointed which, after the second world war, prepared a report and a comprehensive volume for the world conference in Lund in 1952 (*Ways of Worship*, eds P. Edwall, E. Hayman and W. D. Maxwell, London, SCM, 1951). At Lund a whole section was devoted to the subject (cf. Vischer, *op. cit.*, pp.106-115). In continuation of this work three regional groups of the theological commission on worship prepared reports for the 1963 world conference in Montreal (cf. chapter II.2) where one of the sections dealt with "Worship and the Oneness of Christ's Church" (*The Fourth World Conference on Faith and Order, op. cit.*, pp.69-80).

In 1967 the Faith and Order Commission in Bristol recommended the continuation of the study on worship (*Bristol 1967: New Directions in Faith and Order*, no. 50, p.156), while at the same time issues of worship were also included in the work on baptism and eucharist (cf. chapter III.2). A new impulse came from the 1968 Uppsala assembly, whose section V on "Worship" asked the Faith and Order Commission to pursue further work on issues of worship in an ecumenical and contemporary context. In response, a consultation on "Worship in a Secular Age" was held in Geneva in 1969 and its report was submitted to the Louvain Commission meeting (*Louvain 1971: Study Reports and Document*, no. 59, pp.102-116,217-219; the papers of the consultation are published in *Studia Liturgica*, vol. 7, 1970, nos 2/3, ed. Wiebe Voss).
• **Document IV.6, p.256**

The Commission at Louvain in 1971, in receiving this report, recommended that "in all Faith and Order studies the importance of considering the subject in close relation to its expression in worship should continually be remembered". It also recommended that the social significance of the eucharist be taken into account, that contemporary worship material should be collected and that in the preparatory work for the Week of Prayer for Christian Unity the diversity of local situations should be borne in mind (*ibid.*, pp.218-219).

Faith and Order has not continued a specific study on worship but it has in different ways been involved with issues of worship, e.g. in the work on BEM including the much-used Lima liturgy (*The Eucharistic Liturgy: Liturgical Expression of Convergence in Faith Achieved in Baptism, Eucharist and Ministry*, 1983) which was published, with an introduction by Max Thurian, in the comprehensive collection of liturgies of baptism and of the eucharist (*Baptism and Eucharist: Ecumenical Convergence in Celebration*, eds Max Thurian and Geoffrey Wainwright, *op. cit.*). Faith and Order was very much involved in the preparation of *Cantate Domino: An Ecumenical Hymn Book* (Kassel-Basel-London, Bärenreiter, 1974) and carried special responsibility, together with the WCC Sub-unit on Renewal and Congregational Life, for the preparation of *For All God's People: Ecumenical Prayer Cycle* (Geneva, WCC, 1978) and *With All God's People: The New Ecumenical Prayer Cycle* (compiled by John Carden, Geneva, WCC, 1989). As a contribution to ecumenical spirituality a volume of essays on icons was published in 1990 (*Icons: Windows on Eternity. Theology and Spirituality in Colour*, compiled by Gennadios Limouris, no. 147, 1990). And there is the continuing task of preparing the material for the Week of Prayer for Christian Unity (cf. chapter V).

Especially since the 1983 Vancouver assembly, ecumenical worship and spirituality has become a major expression of the communion already achieved and a painful reminder of the still-existing barriers to full eucharistic communion. To overcome these barriers remains the final goal of Faith and Order work.

5. Institution, Law and State

The divisions between the churches and the search for their unity are not conditioned solely by differences and agreements in the area of doctrine but also by social, political, cultural and other factors. This was understood rather early in the Faith and Order movement and presented in a preparatory document for the 1937 Edinburgh world conference, "The Non-Theological Factors in the Making and Unmaking of Church Union" (old series no. 84, London/New York, Harper, 1937). Thus the term "non-theological factors" entered ecumenical language, though its appropriateness was later questioned and alternative terms, such as for example "non-doctrinal", were proposed. For the world conferences in Lund and Montreal in 1952 and 1963 studies on "Social and Cultural Factors in Church Divisions" and "Institutionalism" were prepared (cf. the survey and bibliographical references in part I of document IV.7 below, to which should be added *The Report of the Study Commission on Institutionalism*, no. 37, 1963).

The Commission meeting in Aarhus in 1964 took up the proposal of Montreal to undertake a study of the relation between the work of the Holy Spirit and the nature of the church as an institution, and the outline for a study on "Spirit, Order and Institution" was accepted (*Aarhus 1964*, no. 44, pp.41, 58-60). Two consultations of a special study group in Geneva, in 1965 and 1966, dealt with the methodological and theological aspects of the theme. The 1967 Bristol Commission meeting commented on the study process and a concluding report was presented to the Commission meeting in Louvain (*Louvain 1971: Study Reports and Documents*, no. 59 pp.116-132). • **Document IV.7, p.269**

This study was not pursued further, mainly because of lack of funds. A new, more limited attempt to continue work on "non-theological factors" was made at the Accra

Commission meeting in 1974, where it was decided to consider the role of constitutional matters (church law) in efforts towards the visible unity of the church. An outline for this study was accepted (*Accra 1974*, no. 71, pp.85-86 and esp. 96-103).
• **Document IV.8, p.283**

At Bangalore in 1978 the director of Faith and Order reported to the Commission that, concerning the study on church law, "not much progress has been made on this proposal and, given the limited resources available to the Commission, the study will probably never get very far" (*Bangalore 1978: Sharing in One Hope*, no. 92, p.35). However, one aspect of this issue was taken up at a joint consultation of Faith and Order and the Bossey Ecumenical Institute which produced a report on *Church and State: Opening a New Ecumenical Discussion*, no. 85, 1978.

Limited financial and personnel resources and, consequently, the need to concentrate on a few major studies have prevented Faith and Order from implementing these initiatives in the areas of institution, church law, and church and state. But questions and conflicts in these areas have accompanied the ecumenical movement ever since, which confirms the foresight of those earlier initiatives and the need to take them up once again.

6. God in Nature and History

The Faith and Order Commission meeting in Aarhus in 1965 made an effort to go beyond the obvious controversial issues which have divided the churches by taking up some of the fundamental themes of the Christian faith, which are basic for the doctrine and life of the church. Thus, following a proposal of the 1963 Montreal world conference (*The Fourth World Conference on Faith and Order, op. cit.*, pp.42ff.), the Commission discussed the doctrines of creation and redemption and, as a result, arrived at an outline for a study on "Creation, New Creation and the Unity of the Church" (*Aarhus 1965*, no. 44, pp.43-46). This study was linked with one of the WCC Division of Studies on "The Finality of Christ in an Age of Universal History". A joint meeting in 1965 considered the orientation of the study under its new title "God in Nature and History" and a first draft by Prof. Hendrikus Berkhof was published in 1965 (*Study Encounter*, vol. I, no. 3). This draft was discussed by regional study groups and individuals, and on the basis of their comments a group of theologians, natural scientists and historians prepared a report which was presented to the Commission in Bristol (*Bristol 1967: New Directions in Faith and Order*, no. 50, pp.7-30, comments of the Commission pp.30-31,88-92,130-133). • **Document IV.9, p.289**

One year after Bristol the 1968 Uppsala assembly recommended studies which pursued several elements of the reflection on "God in Nature and History": the WCC-wide "Humanum" study (*The Humanum Studies: A Collection of Documents*, 1975) and the Faith and Order study on the unity of the church and the unity of humankind (cf. chapter III.3).

7. The Church and the Jewish People

Dialogue with people of other faiths has not been a task of Faith and Order. In the ecumenical "division of labour" this increasingly important area of ecumenical reflection and work had become very much part of the programme of the International Missionary Council which was integrated with the WCC in 1961, and in recent decades of specialized committees, commissions and a sub-unit within the WCC. However, in the Faith and Order programme of the 1960s and 1970s, which had widened to include efforts to reflect on the unity of the church in the context of history and humanity, considerable attention was given to the task and understanding of dialogue. In the framework of the concerns of Faith and Order, the relation between the church and the Jewish people was of particular relevance. The 1963 Montreal world conference recommended a study on the place of the people of Israel in relation to God's purpose in the old and new covenant (*The Fourth World Conference, op. cit.*, p.44). One year later the Commission accepted this recommendation (*Aarhus 1964*, no. 44, p.42) and a joint study with the WCC's Committee on the Church and the Jewish People was undertaken. A report was drafted at a consultation in 1964 and then revised following reactions and comments from many groups and individuals. In Bristol the Commission accepted the report "The Church and the Jewish People" with the comment that a more thorough study was required on such issues as (1) the concepts of salvation and election, and (2) the nature of God in relation to the concepts of the people of God and the body of Christ (*Bristol 1967: New Directions in Faith and Order*, no. 50, pp.69-80). • **Document IV.10, p.312**

A number of issues raised in this report were taken up again in the study and report on "The Significance of the Old Testament in its Relation to the New" (cf. here part IV.1, printed in *The Bible: Its Authority and Interpretation in the Ecumenical Movement, op. cit.*, pp.59-76).

Also the broader issue of dialogue with people of other faiths was from time to time included in Faith and Order reflections and there were regular contacts with the WCC Sub-unit on Dialogue. In the context of the study on the unity of the church and the unity of humankind, one section of the Louvain Commission meeting dealt with "The Unity of the Church and the Encounter with Living Faiths" (*Louvain 1971: Study Reports and Documents*, no. 59, pp.191-192). The Commission meetings in Accra (*Accra 1974: Minutes*, no. 71, p.88) and Bangalore (*Bangalore 1978: Minutes*, no. 93, pp.25-26,43) considered the Faith and Order focus on the unity of the church also in relation to dialogue. But no specific studies were undertaken. Since 1992 Faith and Order has been co-operating with the new WCC Office on Inter-religious Relations with the specific mandate of theological reflection on Christian-Jewish dialogue.

DOCUMENT IV.1

THE IMPORTANCE OF THE CONCILIAR PROCESS IN THE ANCIENT CHURCH FOR THE ECUMENICAL MOVEMENT (1967)

The following report is the result of a study which had been recommended by the Third Assembly of the World Council of Churches.[1] *It was hoped that "a fresh general study of the conciliar process in the Church of the early centuries" could help the World Council of Churches towards a better self-understanding. At the Fourth World Conference on Faith and Order it was decided that the Commission should take up this topic, and at Aarhus in 1964 the Commission approved a study outline.*[2] *Because of the particular importance of the councils for the Orthodox churches the choice of participants in this group (similarly in the Patristic Study Group) was so made that the Eastern and Western member churches of the World Council of Churches had equal representation. Two meetings have taken place: the first in Oxford, England (1965), and the second at Bad Gastein, Austria (1966).*

Introduction

In recent decades the churches of divided Christendom have entered a new stage of relations, a state of permanent conversation. They sit down frequently to talk together and so seek to deepen their unity. They have also begun to do things together. How is the fellowship which has developed through this to be understood? What direction should its future development take?

When we raise these questions, we look quite naturally for guidance to the first centuries of the Church. Can we understand the ecumenical movement as a parallel to the synods and councils of the ancient Church? Or can we say that in some way the ecumenical movement continues the conciliar process of the first centuries? In other words, can study of the first centuries teach us something for the future of the ecumenical movement?

In raising these questions we must be aware that the time of the ancient Church cannot be compared *simpliciter* with our own age. If our considerations are to have any validity at all, we must take into account the different presuppositions then and now. The councils of the ancient Church belong to a particular epoch. They were deter-mined by the thought and problems of their time. At that time the Church had not experienced division in the way we have. This difference is reflected in the variant usage of the word "ecumenical". Then it designated the Church spread throughout the entire empire; today it can be used for everything that has to do with the re-creation of the Church's unity.

Nevertheless, the comparison is of great importance. If it is affirmed that some connection exists, it may be that the clarification of this connection can advance the churches on their way towards unity. Examination of the Early Church councils may therefore contribute to the ecumenical movement by bringing more concrete results into reach.

---

[1] *The New Delhi Report*, edited by W. A. Visser' t Hooft, London 1962, page 131, para. 47.

[2] *Aarhus Minutes*, Faith and Order Paper No. 44, pp.70f.

I. Council and Church

1. Conciliarity and Councils

If we are rightly to understand the importance of synods and councils for the life of the Church, it is wise to begin with the general notion of "conciliarity". By conciliarity we mean the fact that the Church in all times needs assemblies to represent it and has in fact felt this need. These assemblies may differ greatly from one another; however, conciliarity, the necessity *that* they take place, is a constant structure of the Church, a dimension which belongs to its nature. As the Church itself is an "assembly" and appears as assembly both in worship and many other expressions of its life, so it needs both at the local and on all other possible levels representative assemblies in order to answer the questions which it faces.

Synods and councils are the historical expression of this basic necessity. They are to be found in one form or another in all churches. Everywhere and at all times there are assemblies which not only serve for joint counsel, but also confront the local church, larger groups of congregations, or even the totality of the churches with an authoritative claim.

Since the Church is not an abstract, but rather an historical entity, one cannot speak of the conciliarity of the Church *in abstracto*. In the course of the centuries it has had a multiplex development. Although the structure of counsel and decision in representative assemblies is to be found everywhere, we find a great variety of forms. They are distinguished in importance, form, and authority both from century to century and from one tradition to another. Often great differences are to be found even within the same tradition.

This history cannot be related in detail here. Only the most important stages will be mentioned: the time up to the Constantinian establishment, the period of the ecumenical imperial councils from 523 to 787, the synodal life of the Eastern churches, the sequence of Western papal councils up to the reform and union councils of the late Middle Ages and the post-Reformation Roman Catholic councils, the new synodal patterns of the Reformation and their subsequent developments, and finally the period of new forms of church assemblies in the context of the ecumenical movement.

Even this most simple over-view allows us to see that the variety of conciliar forms is founded both on the changes in historical relationships and conditions and on variations in theological, especially ecclesiological, assumptions. The history of the Church has led to different types of assemblies, and these types in turn have had further historical consequences. The various types correspond generally to successive or partially concurrent stages. At the risk of over-simplification, we may identify the following nine types:

a) the earliest synods which were of local churches
b) the synods of bishops of a smaller or larger region, as well as the less formal episcopal assemblies and conferences for particular purposes
c) the ecumenical synods in the period of the Christian Roman Empire
d) the *synodon endemousa* and its secondary form in the "Holy Synod" of the Eastern churches
e) the papal council which developed out of the Roman episcopal synod under the influence of the increasing dominance of the idea of primacy
f) the reform and union councils of the late Middle Ages

g) the synod as *ecclesia repraesentativa* on the basis of the Reformation understanding of Scripture and community

h) the synod of delegates oriented on modern parliamentary democracy

i) the new form of responsible counsel and decision in the ecumenical assemblies of
the most recent period.

In order really to understand the variety of conciliar forms, we must also keep in
mind the general distinction between synods which occur at regular intervals and those
which take place because of a particular necessity or for a particular task without
having a permanent place in the institutional structure. The former have more of an
institutional character, the latter more the character of a new event. While the synods
of the third century belong more to the first group, the classical Ecumenical Councils
of the following centuries should be counted more to the second. Although they had
certain institutional characteristics, they were never institutions. The councils with the
character of events were of much greater importance for the history of the Church and
theology than those councils of the first group which tended to be jurisdictional and
administrative.

2. Conciliarity and the Unity of the Church

Conciliarity is indissolubly bound to the unity of the Church. Representative
assemblies are necessary, among other reasons, for the sake of unity. Almost all of the
councils of the ancient Church were called because unity was threatened by heresy or
was broken by schism; all had directly or indirectly the task of protecting or re-
establishing unity. In that the councils of the Church called into remembrance the truth
as it is witnessed to in the Scriptures and passed on by the Church, they sought to
maintain unity on the basis of this truth. The full community in the body of Christ
should be preserved.

This close relationship between the councils and the unity of the Church has its
roots in the Church's liturgical life. This becomes particularly clear when we think
first of all of the representative assemblies which developed in the local church. They
were in the closest relationship to the eucharistic life of the congregation and had,
among others, the task to guard the true unity of the congregation in the Eucharist. The
bishop who presided at the eucharistic celebrations was at the same time the sign of
their unity.

The close relationship is no less valid for later forms of conciliar life. This can be
seen in that the councils may not be understood as organizational super-structures, but
always are connected to the nature of the Church as the eucharistic assembly. In any
case, the principle intention of all of the councils was to preserve the fellowship of the
Church in the Eucharist. They met in the eucharistic fellowship and sought to
strengthen this bond. On the other hand, conciliar decisions often led to excommunication and the destruction of the eucharistic fellowship. This result also shows, however,
the rooting of the councils in the eucharistic fellowship of the Church.

Councils were not only concerned with guarding unity. Often they attempted to
restore the broken fellowship or to heal an existing schism. This attempt often found
expression exclusively in the demand for penitence and return to the fellowship.
Sometimes it was also expressed in theological discussions, in the attempt to clarify
terms and through discussion to overcome misunderstandings between the divided
parties. In these attempts to bring about reconciliation, reference was made from time

to time to baptism as the sacramental bond which still joined the divided groups. Conciliarity is also bound to the unity of the Church to the extent that councils can open the way to restoration of full unity in the faith and in the sacramental life.

II. The Pattern of Councils

Here we cannot deal in detail with all the various forms of conciliarity. We will limit ourselves to the following comments, primarily to the type of the Ecumenical Councils of the Christian Roman Empire. They deserve particular attention insofar as they have taken a very determinative position in the history of the church. When the question is asked what form a general council should have today, it can be answered only in critical confrontation with this type.

1. The Calling of the Ecumenical Councils

The classical Ecumenical Councils met in the period of the Roman Empire. The Christian emperor called them together, often led their deliberations, approved their results, and gave them juridical status. This can be explained from the historical situation. The fourth century considered it self-evident that the emperor, who had become a Christian, should assume responsibility for the Church. This does not imply that an Ecumenical Council must necessarily be called by an emperor. The problem inherent in the organic union of state and Church has become evident in the course of history. It was already evident when churches which lay outside the boundaries of the empire or which were in opposition within the Empire rejected the imperial councils for political, as well as theological and religious, reasons. Subsequent history has brought the problem much more clearly into the foreground in a way that could not have been seen at the beginning of the Christian Empire. After this has been recognized, we can no longer simply return to the example of the first Ecumenical Councils. The question of the calling of the council must be answered differently today. The initiative can come from one or several churches. What is important is that the council met on the basis of a consensus of all the churches involved.

2. Membership

A mark of the councils of the ancient Church was that they were composed of bishops. Eusebius reports meetings to combat the Montanists which may have included bishops and laymen. The later synods and councils were assemblies of bishops, however. This is closely related to the understanding of the bishop's office as it had developed at that time. Bishops received the charisma and the task of protecting the truth in the Church entrusted to them. Therefore it is natural that they were the ones who met in synods and councils. They represented their church at the synod and stood not only for themselves but also for the whole Church. Of course, theologians who were priests, deacons or laymen also took part in several councils, but only in an advisory capacity.

The presence and active role of the emperor raises particular questions about membership. To be sure, he was not a bishop; he cannot simply be called a layman, however.

We are not in agreement whether exclusively episcopal composition is essential or not for a council. We are all of the opinion that a council is a matter for the whole Church and that, therefore, the churches must be represented to the greatest extent possible. Some say that this happens through the bishops who have received the charisma of their office; others are of the opinion that other forms of representation can be found today. They think especially of a mixed assembly (clergy and laity).

3. Geographic Representation

The ancient Church did not have firm rules as to the way in which the individual parts of the Church should be represented in an Ecumenical Council. Therefore it is not clear to what extent the authority of a council was dependent on representation from the entire Church. The emperor issued the invitations, presumably after previous discussion with ecclesiastical advisers. His selection could vary. He could have begun with the idea that the provinces, rather than the individual dioceses, should be represented, for example. In any case, from the composition of the Ecumenical Councils it cannot be decided that an Ecumenical Council *must* be composed of representatives of all dioceses if possible.

None of the great councils was completely representative geographically. Parts of the Church were either not invited or did not participate for particular reasons.

Their absence sometimes produced inadequate representation of certain theological positions or ecclesiastical interests. We are agreed that the largest possible number of individual countries should be represented. Precisely when we understand the word "ecumenical" in its original sense, this necessity becomes self-evident. The ecumenicity of a council does not finally depend on representation of the "whole world", however; rather it is an inner quality which must show itself in the reception (see Chapter III).

4. Norms of the Councils

1) The councils of the Early Church issued doctrinal decrees and determined Canon Law. As a rule, they came together to protect the truth against error or internal danger. They fulfilled a task in a particular historical moment. They taught a *necessarium,* but did not present a compendium of theological truths. They emphasized fundamental truths, given in the tradition of the Church.

It is an important observation that the first councils met after the canon was closed. It was the council's task to protect the apostolic tradition witnessed in the canon. They are subject to the Scriptures as their norm.

The councils appealed to the tradition within which and from which the Church lives.

2) The truth which is hers to preserve and to which she bears witness. Proof must therefore always be offered that what a council teaches is in continuity with the truth to which she has borne witness before.

3) In the sphere of Canon Law the councils had more scope for their own decision. But this freedom left no room for arbitrary decisions. The life and order of the Church are here at stake, as determined by truth handed down from the past.

5. Methods of Discussion

The Ecumenical Councils of the ancient Church met to witness to the truth. In the first instance they wanted to be a common act of witness. Councils are not conferences. They do not exist primarily as a confrontation of as many opinions as possible. Rather they issue a call to truth.

It is in part for this reason that discussion in most of the Ecumenical Councils was not broad enough for modern feelings. The results were often determined in advance and were not worked out gradually in fraternal consultation. The councils saw their task in confessing the truth which had already been given.

This characteristic of the ancient councils has a lasting significance. An Ecumenical Council comes together to express the truth of the Gospel in a binding way. A council would not have fulfilled its function if it only resulted in the opposition of theological opinions. At the same time it must be said that the procedure of the ancient councils has only limited validity as a model for today. With time the importance of discussion as a means for the clarification of truth has become more clearly recognized. The rule that each must have the right of expression has shown itself to be a requirement which results from the spirit of the Gospel. Therefore, discussion must play a greater role, either during a council or before its meeting, than was the case in the first centuries.

III. Authority and Impact of the Councils

1. The Claim of the Councils

Since their inception synods have met to protect the ancient faith of the Church against error or to establish church law. For both tasks the councils understood themselves to be both dependent on the Holy Spirit and authorized by Him to make decisions which demanded obedience. This was true for all synods, whether they were more institutional or eventful in character. Basically even a small, merely locally limited synod is thus accorded the highest authority. This principle was limited, however, in that since the fourth century appeal can be made from a local to a general synod; and canons, in distinction to dogmas, do not have unchangeable validity.

Regardless of whether a synod as a constitutional organ of the Church received a clearly defined and thereby limited legal authority or whether it could appeal to other external signs of authority, its claim finally remains spiritually founded. This is especially true of the dogmas proclaimed by the Ecumenical Councils.

At first the Church had not developed a theory about the theological basis of the councils' authority. But from the beginning it was true that councils had their place within the Church and confronted it with authority. They understood themselves increasingly as an instrument of the Holy Spirit, as a voice which therefore must be heard. This relationship is comparable to that of the preacher to his congregation. He belongs to it as a member, but nevertheless confronts it with authority. The fact that councils have their place in the Church makes it clear that their claim does not exclude reception, but rather has it as a goal.

2. Reception

a) By "reception" we designate the process by which the local churches accept the decision of a council and thereby recognize its authority. Such reception refers only to the conciliar decisions and does not necessarily include a position towards the proceedings during the council by which they came into being. Naturally, however, a refusal of reception can be based on the judgment that the council was illegal or, especially, that it did not hold to the norms of preserving apostolic tradition.

Reception is not something added to the inner authority of a council, but confirms it. Nevertheless, it is not without significance, not only for the historical effect but also for the theological evaluation of a council, whether it is recognized only in a small area or by the whole Church. From the perspective of reception, an Ecumenical Council is a council which has been recognized by the Church scattered throughout the world.

b) Reception is a multiplex process and has not always occurred in the same way. In the pre-Nicean Church it was a manifestation of fraternal fellowship. The council informed the important congregations which were not represented about its decisions, and the local churches or synods could accept them if they felt affected by the question dealt with. Churches outside the empire later received decisions of the Ecumenical Councils in basically the same way.

In the church of the Christian Roman Empire itself, reception seems to have been much more an act of constitutional obedience. Synods became constitutional organs; the emperor not only called special imperial synods together, but also demanded that their decisions be accepted. History shows, however, that this description does not suffice; even synods which were legally called and confirmed by the emperor were disputed, and some of them never finally found recognition. The reception of the dogmatic decisions of extraordinary imperial synods almost always took place in a process of critical appropriation which could last for centuries. The formal conclusion of this process and thus the canonical reception of a council's doctrinal formula was usually a new council which confirmed the validity of the earlier decisions.

c) The criteria for the reception of a council, especially of its dogmatic decisions, was whether it was legally held or especially whether it conformed to the norm, to which it knew itself to be subject, namely to hold fast the ancient apostolic tradition against new heresies. Although non-theological factors were no less at work in reception than in the conciliar process, reception is to be understood at its core as a spiritual process, even where it seems to be an act of constitutional obedience. Proof is precisely the long process of critical appropriation which both preceded the formal reception and followed it. Reception as a spiritual event corresponds to the council's claim to be the voice of the Holy Spirit. This presupposes that the same spirit of God who leads to all truth by witnessing to Jesus, the incarnate Word of God, is at work both in the council and the Church as a whole.

Councils can lead to deep disagreements in the Church, even to divisions. The decision for or against a council can divide churches from one another. The legally binding reception of conciliar dogmatic decisions determines the confession of a local or particular church, and reception can thus lead to cementing disagreements. But we must also remember that the reception of a council never took place in all particular churches at the same time. Some churches are convinced that a council has opened up the truth of God for them; other particular or confessional churches have not received or have not wanted to receive this council. Because of their conviction, the former will always want to offer this truth to those churches which are separated from them. In contrast, the churches which have not received a council continually pose the question whether it has been received properly and with justification. From this point of view the reception of the ancient Church councils is a still open process. This is even more true of the dogmatic, in most cases also conciliar, decisions of later centuries, especially the sixteenth century, which have fundamental significance for many churches. We can therefore say that in the ecumenical movement we find ourselves in a process of continuing or renewed reception.

d) During the period of critical appropriation of a conciliar decision before the concluding legal reception, the understanding of such a decision is often deepened. For example, only in this new, better, and modified understanding were the decisions of Nicea in 381 and those of Chalcedon in 553 adopted in Constantinople. This situation points to a further dimension of the process of reception. Reception refers to decisions made at particular councils. In most cases the legally binding reception occurred centuries ago. The claim of the councils is also valid today, however. They are a reality for all churches, especially for those which are expressly bound by their decisions. They must be constantly newly appropriated, and this new appropriation presupposes a constant new interpretation. Reception is from this point of view as well an open process. This lasting openness is a task and a promise for the individual churches as well as for their fellowship in the ecumenical movement. Only as this process is kept alive can the critical mutual reception of old and newer councils take place, and thereby the overcoming of confessional divisions as well.

IV. Conciliarity and the Church Today

Following these observations we return to the question which we posed at the beginning: what importance does the conciliar process in the ancient Church have for the Church today? To what extent can the modern Ecumenical Movement, especially, be understood as the expression of the conciliarity of the Church?

We must emphasize here again that in many respects we are in a quite different situation today and that, therefore, direct comparison is not possible. The conciliar process in the ancient Church took place in a still unbroken fellowship, generally speaking. Certainly unity was threatened by disagreements over the truth. Although the councils sought to bring about unity in truth, they were not finally able to succeed in maintaining the community of all Christians of that period. The conciliar process in the ancient Church took place, nevertheless, on the basis of the existing fellowship. Today, however, the point of departure is one of plural ecclesiastical communities in confrontation with one another. They differ in their confession of the truth. They are determined by a particular historical inheritance, and are not all in a position to recognize each other fully as churches. The restoration of fellowship is the task with which they see themselves faced in the ecumenical movement.

We have seen that conciliarity necessarily belongs to the life of the Church. The conciliar process continues, therefore, in the separated churches. The conciliarity of the Church creates expression for itself in some form or other everywhere. The individual forms are determined by the particular historical and ecclesiological presuppositions and might present a distortion of true conciliarity in the judgment of other churches. The fact must be underscored that the individual churches, as well, have always seen it necessary to solve the problems placed before them through synods or councils.

Division has made impossible councils which deserve the name "ecumenical". Such a council would have to be in the position to speak for the whole of Christianity and to meet in the hope of being received by all or at least most churches. What individual churches formulate in particular situations of the past may basically be directed to the whole of Christianity. The existing disagreements were, however, so deep that it could not be heard and understood, much less received. The churches must begin to listen to one another in such a way that the disagreements do not remain a dead opposition, but rather that they come into a living relationship. In order that this can happen, it is necessary that the individual churches recognize and develop conciliarity as a necessary element in the life of the Church.

The presupposition for holding an Ecumenical Council is the unity of the Church. An assembly which is sent by separated churches which do not live in eucharistic fellowship can decisively advance unity, but it cannot be designated as a council. Eucharistic fellowship must be the beginning point. That does not mean that the division and differences must be fully overcome. Councils were often held precisely when the eucharistic fellowship was most seriously endangered and the signs of rupture were clearly visible. Precisely through posing a burning question, a council can lead churches together. This can only take place when it speaks and acts out of an at least potentially present eucharistic fellowship, however.

The form of future Ecumenical Councils is not definite. We have already seen that the Ecumenical Councils of the ancient Church are primarily to be understood as an event, and that the historical forms of conciliarity changed in the course of the centuries. A council is not ecumenical just because it meets particular conditions determined by the historical prototype of the ancient Church. Councils are ecumenical primarily through their content, the truth of the Gospel, and their reception by the Church. The external conditions are variable within certain limits (see Chapter II).

In the light of these statements, how is the ecumenical movement and especially the World Council of Churches to be understood? It can be seen as a tool for the preparation of a true Ecumenical Council. It works in this direction in a dual way:

a) On the one hand, it forces the churches to re-examine past decisions which divided them. It contributes to the maintenance of the lively process of progressive and renewed reception and is as the fellowship of various churches at the same time the place in which this can take place in the most fruitful way.

b) On the other hand, it also makes it possible for the churches to formulate a consensus on questions which have not touched the Church before or which have not become an object of division. All the churches today face similar problems. They must confess the Gospel in new situations in terms of new questions. This task is so huge that many traditional divisions seem to have lost their significance. Facing the new tasks together, the churches will led to deeper fellowship.

In working towards the time when the churches, in spite of their existing differences, could accept each other in the eucharistic fellowship, the ecumenical movement also works towards the time when a true Ecumenical Council can become an event.

DOCUMENT IV.2

PATRISTICS STUDIES FROM AN ECUMENICAL VIEWPOINT
(1967)

Preface

What significance do studies on patristics have for the ecumenical movement? All churches share the common foundation of the Fathers, but they are not accorded the same authority by all the churches, and patristics study is carried on by various methods and with unequal intensity. Therefore it is of great importance for the further development of the ecumenical movement that we come to a common understanding of the Fathers.

This problem appeared early in the ecumenical movement. Its urgency has become especially clear, however, since the family of Orthodox churches began to participate fully in the World Council of Churches. For this reason the Faith and Order Commission gave the secretariat the assignment of calling together a group of theologians to study this question. In view of the special significance of the problem for the relationships between Orthodox and western member churches, the group was to be composed of an equal number of participants from East and West. Following a first preparatory meeting in Paris (1962), the study group met for three extended sessions in Aarhus (1964), Hamburg (1965), and Saloniki (1966).

The Patristic Study Group did not begin its work with a general discussion of the patristic period. Rather it came to the conclusion that common results could only be realized by beginning with a particular dogmatically important text from the first centuries. Therefore, the text of Basil of Caesarea ("the Great") on the Holy Spirit (375) was selected as the object of joint study. This document was supplemented by the four letters from Athanasius of Alexandria to Serapion of Thmuis on the divinity of the Spirit (ca. 359), among others. The choice of text was determined by the special significance of pneumatology in the contemporary discussion on the unity of the Church.

The study group agreed that historical-critical analysis of the text is the presupposition for understanding it properly. The study should not be limited to this, however. The text should also be evaluated theologically. It is clear that the real difficulties begin only at this level. Although broad methodological agreement may be found in historical-critical analysis, the attempt at theological interpretation brings to light both agreement and differences.

We now present the results of our endeavours. The first section contains what we were able to formulate jointly about the significance of the patristic study for the ecumenical movement. In the second section follows a series of methodological considerations which have arisen during the study of the text chosen; we think that they have general relevance for the study of patristic texts. With the question of the theological evaluation of a patristic text, we encounter the hermeneutical problem of the translation of the Fathers' message into our idiom and the dogmatic re-actualization *(Nachvollzug)* of their decision. The third section summarizes some results of the discussion. A fourth section presents some recommendations to the Commission on Faith and Order.

I. The Significance of Patristic Study for Ecumenical Discussion

1. *The study of the Fathers of the Early Church is motivated by the recognition that the separated churches confront one another not only as geographical neighbours (ecumenism in space), but also as communities which have a history (ecumenism in time).*

The separated Christian traditions have their common ground and origin in the revelation of God in Jesus Christ, as it is witnessed to in Holy Scripture. The Word of God is heard and proclaimed in a particular time and situation; thereby it has also an historical continuity in which it unremittingly works anew and unfolds itself in its fullness.

In all understanding and proclamation of the Word today, we come from and are dependent on the tradition of the Fathers as those who have spoken the Word to us (Heb. 13:7), whether we know it or not.

2. *Because God has not only chosen the path of historical revelation, but also the path of historical mediation, historical continuity belongs to the nature of the proclamation of Christ. Within this historical mediation, the patristic period has a fundamental significance.*

The Fathers of the Early Church belong to the common basis of all subsequent, divided traditions. They lived in a time in which the Church saw itself for the first time placed before fundamental tasks: the missionary penetration of other cultures, the confrontation between faith and reason, the clarification of the relationship between Church and society in a time in which Christianity was gradually attaining universal recognition, etc.

The Fathers of the Early Church formulated fundamental decisions for the doctrine of the Trinity and Christology. The churches in the World Council together affirm those decisions today in the *Basis*.

The first centuries were certainly not a golden age, and the Early Church Fathers had no different task from what we have today, namely, the transmission of the apostolic message. Nevertheless they embody the "primitive" tradition of the Church from which we all come.

The study of the Fathers is not therefore just a specialists' hobby. Rather it is a fundamental task of theology to penetrate with understanding the historical continuity. The patristic period has both constitutive and paradigmatic significance for the Church today.

3. *The particular significance of the patristic period does not exclude critical examination and confrontation. Rather it demands it since we must hear the Fathers against the background of the apostolic work which they wanted to transmit in their own time.*

In order to do justice to this task, it is first necessary to take into account the formulation and content of the patristic texts and to examine how the proclamation of Christ occurred there. A simply historical analysis is not sufficient. Rather one must recognize and show how the Fathers in their time, in their office, and in their work built on the base of the apostles and prophets of which Jesus is the corner stone (Eph. 2:20).

Study of the patristic texts in the framework of ecumenical discussion is based on the great interest in patristics which has been awakened in both East and West in the last decades. We must especially mention the work of the International Patristics Conference in Oxford (since 1951) where specialists of the most varied churches and confessions work together. The numerous new critical editions of texts and patristic *lexica* which form a common basis for patristic research in all churches and confessions should also be mentioned here. Joint theological evaluation has only just begun, however.

II. De Spiritu Sancto in its Historical Framework

In the hope that the experience, limited as it is, of our work together on the text *De Spiritu Sancto* of Basil of Caesarea could be applied to other texts as well, we present here the following points of reference.

The historical framework which is determinative for a more exact understanding of the text *De Spiritu Sancto* can be outlined under three points: 1. the historical and biographical situation of its composition; 2. the form and structure of the text itself; 3. the main themes of the text.

1. *The historical context of the text* De Spiritu Sancto. *Each text has an historical framework which conditions it, on the one hand, and offers a key to a more exact understanding of it, on the other. It must not be removed from this framework; otherwise there is the danger that irrelevant presuppositions will be brought into the interpretation and that the original content will be lost. For the historical and biographical situation of the composition of* De Spiritu Sancto *(375), the following factors would receive special consideration:*

a) The historical situation. Christianity was on its way to becoming the state religion. It was gradually becoming a matter of course. This is one motive for the search for a new way of holiness, a consciously Christian existence. Thus the monastic movement spread into Cappadocia where it had been previously unknown. Out of the same motivation grew the conviction that the centre of theology is mystery. On the other hand, the Arians took the opposite course, a philosophical and scientific penetration of the Christian proclamation.

b) The ecclesiastical and theological situation. Theological controversies were not only symptomatic for the disintegration of church unity. Rather the struggle over truth is always a struggle for unity. This is to be seen in an especially impressive way in Basil in the co-existence of dogmatic controversy and efforts toward unity. In the failure, the tragedy of the unavoidable and the unwanted is always to be felt.

De Spiritu Sancto was written in the post-Nicaean period, particularly, in the time of conflict with the various groups of "Pneumatomachoi". Of special importance in this regard is the conflict with Eustathius of Sebaste, Basil's former teacher and friend,[1] who was the leader of the Homoiousians, as well as the primary founder of the monastic movement in Asia Minor.

Also significant are Basil's connections with Athanasius of Alexandria and, after his death, with Damasus of Rome. With them Basil raised primarily the question of church unity in the oriental churches, as well as the recognition of Meletius of Antioch by Alexandria and Rome. In the failure of these negotiations the difference between oriental and occidental ecclesiology can already be seen.[2]

---

[1] Cf. the studies of H. Dörries, J. Gribomont, and the critique of their conclusions by B. Pruche, *Autour du traité sur le Saint-Esprit de Saint Basile de Césarée*, in RSR 52 (1964), pp.233-247.

[2] Cf. Emmanuel Amand de Medieta, "Basile de Césarée et Damase de Rome: Les causes de l'échec de leurs négociations", *Biblical and Patristic Studies in Memory of Robert Pierce Casey*, ed. J. Neville Birdsall and Robert W. Thomson, 1965, pp.122-166.

c) The cultural and intellectual situation. Precise analysis must clarify in detail, against the background of the education of his time, Basil's intellectual environment and theological thought forms.

Particularly relevant in this connection are the influences of Hellenistic philosophy, and especially of Neoplatonism (Plotinus), on Basil's thought and terminology.[3] One can clearly see that Basil makes critical use of Neoplatonic ideas. In comparison with his earlier works (such as *Contra Eunomium* or *De Spiritu*, for example), the Neoplatonic influence in *De Spiritu Sancto* is much less marked. His polemic against Eunomius, a strongly Neoplatonic theologian, demonstrates how even in the earlier period, Basil pressed forward to a theological modification of the presupposed concepts: the relationship between the individual soul and the world soul becomes for Basil the relationship between the Holy Spirit and the human spirit.

d) The biographical situation of the author and his work. *De Spiritu Sancto* is a late work of Basil, written while he was Bishop of Caesarea. From the same period comes Ep. 128. In contrast, the three authentic books of *Contra Eunomium* date from the earlier period when he was still a monk. Between these two texts there can be ascertained a noticeable development and deepening in Basil's pneumatology.

2. *Form and structure of the text.*

After the historical situation is taken into account, the substantial content of the text is further illuminated by consideration of its specific form and original intention.

a) In literary form *De Spiritu Sancto* is not a systematic treatise, but an occasional writing (H. Dörries) of an apologetic-polemic character. Basil had to defend himself against the charge that in addition to the traditional trinitarian doxology "*through* (dia) the Son *in* (en) the Holy Spirit", he had used in the liturgy another formula "*with* (meta) the Son *together with* (syn) the Holy Spirit".

b) The following factors determine the formal character of the text: the objection raised against the trinitarian doxology which Basil used, an objection which covered the continuation of an earlier conflict with the Pneumatomachoi over the divinity of the Spirit; the response to a question addressed to Basil in this context by his friend Amphilochius of Iconium; apology; polemic; doctrine, and dogmatic reflections.

c) The statements on pneumatology in *De Spiritu Sancto* are not developed, therefore, in theoretical reflection, but rather in response to a concrete challenge in a particular situation and direction. As a bishop with the responsibility for the purity of doctrine and the unity of the Church, Basil had to answer the *homoiousian* tendencies of the Pneumatomachoi. This is to be seen especially in the remarkable tension between a central decision, on the one hand, and the concern for mediation, on the other; between the public address or confessional stand (kerygma) and the core (dogma) of the Christian faith; between necessary speech and appropriate silence for the sake of the cause (oikonomia).

3. *The main themes in the text.*

The main themes in De Spiritu Sancto *can be comprehended from two sides: in the question first about the presuppositions and second about the content of the theological assertions.*

---

[3] Cf. H. Dehnhard, *Das Problem der Abhängigkeit des Basilius von Plotin*, 1964.

a) The methodological presuppositions which distinguish Basil from his opponents are expressed in that he forcefully emphasizes both in theology and in ecclesiastical (liturgical) practice and piety the apostolic doctrinal tradition, of which Scripture is the centre, over a primacy of philosophical conceptions. Logical argument has a subsidiary, not a constitutive function for him.

b) In subject and structure, his theological argument has a trinitarian orientation, especially because it begins with the commission to baptize and returns to it again and again. One can understand the unique character of the trinitarian theology only against the background of the question about the proper praise of God (doxology) in the Church. It is definitely not a purely speculative problem. Basil's key concept, the *homotimia* of the Spirit, is characteristic. In the history of dogma this forms, admittedly, only a preliminary step toward the doctrine of the *homoousion* of the Spirit. Nevertheless, it clearly shows the original roots of dogmatic reflection in the Church's liturgical practice, in its doxology.

c) In this sense, Basil's theology cannot be understood exclusively as a reflected translation of the revelation into the concepts and thought patterns of a particular time. This process stands much more within the more inclusive framework of the Church's total life, of piety, of liturgy, of doctrine, and finally also of systematic reflection.

III. The Significance and Message of Patristic Texts for Today
The patristic period is a living tradition for the churches, not a fossilized deposit. As a living tradition it must be repeatedly rediscovered and made fruitful.

1. *The significance of the text according to its content.*

a) In its content, *De Spiritu Sancto* makes a decisive contribution to the dogmatic understanding of the divinity of the Spirit in a concrete, historical situation, as well as in the individual theological development of Basil. Although this problem was in no way settled by Basil, he reached the decisive clarification that the Holy Spirit is not a creature and that he is to be honoured equally with God the Father and the Son.

b) Therefore today the accent falls on the significance of this text, not as a final definition, but on the dogmatic decision it reveals, a decision with guiding and exemplary character. It is one voice in a choir of voices.

c) The special weight of this text is also to be seen in the history of its influence both in the West and the East.

2. *The re-actualization of Basil's decision.*

a) Although Basil's dogmatic decision has permanent significance, this does not imply that the cognitive presuppositions which led to it can also claim permanent and binding validity. The thought forms and idiom of that time raise particular difficulties for interpretation.

b) With the re-actualization of the decision, one must ask whether the translation of the philosophical conceptions and terms of that time into the more or less corresponding contemporary conceptions is really possible and necessary.

c) Clarity on the problem of re-actualization can only be achieved when the problem of the development or evolution of dogma is thoroughly discussed.

3. *The contemporary significance of the dogmatic decision can only be developed in critically re-tracing its course.*

a) A schematizing distinction between a permanent content and a changing form is an extremely problematic undertaking, theologically and historically, in which the historicity of the Church and its proclamation are not taken into account.

b) It is much more important to understand the appropriateness of the theological statements in their historical conditionedness. If the appropriateness of the statements about the divinity of the Holy Spirit is so recognized, the dogmatic considerations which Basil formed in his concrete situation can acquire new significance, basically as well as exemplarily, for the doxology, the proclamation of the trinitarian God, and the theological reflection of the present time.

c) In this sense, the contemporary significance of this patristic text resides in its hermeneutical function for the understanding of Scripture with reference to interpretation and proclamation.

4. *The permanent significance and the message for the present day appear in the uniqueness and identity of the divine revelation, in the witness of Scripture, and in the historical continuity in which God through the Holy Spirit fulfills the promise given to his Church, in which men are called and commissioned to preach and teach.*

a) To listen today to the message of the Fathers is basically only possible within the context of listening to the Word of God, preached by the Church and active in it. The message of the Fathers is the expression of the living reality of the Holy Spirit in the Church through all time.

b) To listen today to the message of the Fathers is at the same time to join in the praise of the trinitarian God and thus to found a community in time between the right praise of God in the past and in the present.

c) Finally to listen today to the message of the Fathers also provides an occasion for renewed reflection on the truth and purity of Christian preaching in the past as in the present.

5. *A problem of particular importance, especially in the ecumenical study of the Fathers, is the question about the significance of a particular Church Father, and of the consensus patrum, and about the definition and special position of the patristic period. This can be summarized in the question about the Fathers' authority in principle.*

a) In a definition of the authority of a Church Father there are various factors, e.g. his conformity to Scripture and the purity of his doctrine, his ecclesiastical position as shepherd or teacher, his spiritual authority, his personal life, the judgment of the Church, or the special recognition and honour accorded him within a particular church. These factors are not necessarily mutually exclusive; neither do they necessarily belong together.

b) The facts of church history show that the recognition of the authority of a Father was always also determined by a critical view of his person and his work. (Cf. here, for example, the millenarianism of Ireneus; the controversial doctrine of the *apokatastasis* in Gregory of Nyssa; the problem of Dionysius, the Pseudo-Areopagite; the shifting recognition of Theodoret; the *Retractationes* of Augustine, etc.) Without doubt, the patristic epoch cannot be seen only from the aspect of an unbroken tradition in which error was excluded. It was rather, even among the Fathers of orthodoxy (in the dogmatic sense), a critical process in which the question of truth was raised ever anew.

c) The concept of the authority of the Fathers within the Church in her earthly pilgrimage, fraught with conflict, is always characterized by the provisional nature of all Christian activity in the aeon before the last judgment. It is relative, not only in its historical conditionedness, but also in its eschatological aspect. This provisional character must not be artificially harmonized or eliminated.

IV. Recommendations

Our work so far and our conclusions represent no more than an initial effort. All participants were nevertheless convinced, on the basis of these results, that patristic studies are a necessary part of ecumenical concerns and must be expanded. From our experience we formulate here several concrete suggestions and recommendations.

1. *The study of the Fathers must play a greater role in ecumenical discussion.*

a) In dealing with theological questions more attention must be paid to the witness of the patristic period. We should find here the real roots of a number of ecumenical problems. Ecumenical groups should also increasingly study patristic texts and documents of the Early Councils.

b) In the establishment of such study groups it is important to show that our concern with patristics is not determined by particular confessional or technical interests. We believe, rather, that this work can also be an enrichment for those church fellowships which do not have a dogmatically developed principle of tradition or which in their historical form and self-understanding no longer have a direct connection with the patristic period.

c) Further it seems to us helpful and necessary that exegetes and dogmaticians should participate along with patristic scholars in this work. In this way the questions of New Testament exegesis as well as problems of contemporary doctrine and preaching could be given more comprehensive treatment to their mutual enrichment.

2. *For a continuation of the work we can point to particular problems which can be dealt with and clarified only in a broader context.*

a) Special consideration should be given to the process of selection in which particular traditions have been received and others excluded or simply ignored by the individual churches in the course of historical development.

b) At this point it is necessary to see even in the patristic period the co-existence of various traditions and to ask to what extent they are differentiated by factors of dogmatic principle, church politics or by non-theological considerations.

c) Further one should ask *how*, within the individual traditions and in the co-existence of various traditions, the process of doctrinal development and the history of proclamation has occurred within Christianity.

3. *Patristic studies from an ecumenical viewpoint raise problems and point to relationships which have only been touched on or have even been completely ignored by historians of dogma in the past. At the same time, these studies permit us to see that the patristic period has not just historical significance as the beginning for the*

historical development of the Church and the churches, but is also important for the development of the Church in its present form and reality.

a) The translation of the Christian proclamation into various cultural contexts, a process which we can see happening in the first centuries of the Christian era, constitutes a problem which retains a permanent, basic, and exemplary significance for the subsequent history of the Church up to the present day.

b) The development of independent ecclesiastical traditions is such a problem, e.g. the division between Chalcedonian and pre-Chalcedonian churches which was completed in the patristic period and the division between the churches of East and West which was only begun.

c) Patristic studies also have basic and exemplary significance for the churches which grew out of the modern missionary movement and which must struggle for their independence and the purity of their proclamation in a non-Christian cultural milieu. The participation in this study of representatives of these churches would greatly enrich the understanding of the process of tradition and also be of value to these churches themselves.

DOCUMENT IV.3

THE COUNCIL OF CHALCEDON AND ITS
SIGNIFICANCE FOR THE ECUMENICAL MOVEMENT (1971)

Introduction

The work done in the past by the two study groups, one of which worked on St. Basil's *De Spiritu Sancto* and another on the Councils of the Early Church,[1] has shown that such a common study of the patristic period could now be continued in a form that would combine the work of these two groups. This combination could be achieved by concentrating on the study of one particular Council of the Early Church and on its implications and significance for the present day ecumenical situation.

The Commission on Faith and Order at its meeting in Bristol decided that the Council of Chalcedon should be the subject of such a combined study. Such a study is not of mere historical interest. The importance of Chalcedon for the ecumenical movement is manifold and has to do with many issues which occupy us today. The following are some points which may serve as an illustration of this.

1. Chalcedon represents a crucial point in Church History. Whether one accepts this Council or not, one is compelled to place oneself in relation to it in one way or another.

2. Chalcedon has entered deeply into the tradition of various Churches which claim to have received it. At the same time this Council gave rise to strong objections by other Churches and therefore to divisions which have survived up to now. Its study becomes inevitable for an understanding among these two groups of Churches.

3. The doctrine of Chalcedon raises a number of issues on which the East and the West are not in full agreement. These issues need further clarification through ecumenical conversations. They come up as soon as each tradition examines its reception of this doctrine in the course of history. For example, the Reformation Churches found themselves in a tradition which had accepted Chalcedon and did not formally repudiate it, but this acceptance may have been essentially affected through the adoption of certain creeds, etc.

4. Dealing with the Council of Chalcedon raises the general question of the Churches' attitude towards the authority of the Councils in general. Chalcedon, being itself a controversial Council, puts to us the question of what it means to accept or reject a particular Council or Councils in general.

5. The reception of the Council of Chalcedon appears to be particularly difficult today. It is of special importance for the Churches today to examine in what way the doctrine of Chalcedon can be integrated into the modern discussions on the "humanum" and the "secular", etc.

For the purpose of studying the Council of Chalcedon in its bearing upon the ecumenical movement a consultation was convened in Geneva by the Faith and Order Secretariat from August 31 to September 6, 1969.[2] During the consultation a number of papers were read, covering the historical ground of the proceedings of the Council itself, the reception of the Council by the various traditions and the bearing of the

---

[1] Cf. the reports in *New Directions in Faith and Order,* Bristol 1967. WCC, Geneva 1968; pp.41ff, 49ff.
[2] For a list of participants s. Appendix [not reprinted here].

doctrine of Chalcedon upon the anthropological discussions of our time.[3] The discussions which took place on the basis of these papers proved to be very useful for understanding the importance of Chalcedon for the ecumenical movement. In the following lines an attempt will be made to summarize and present the main issues which have emerged from these discussions for the ecumenical movement.

I. Problems arising from the historical evidence available concerning Chalcedon and their bearing on ecumenical discussions

In dealing with historical material concerning the Council of Chalcedon one is confronted with many differences of view which are due to our various presuppositions. We immediately find ourselves inclined towards certain choices of interpretation stemming from our particular background. It is, therefore, always necessary not only with regard to theology, but also with regard to history, that the various traditions examine themselves in the light of common ecumenical discussion. In connection with our study of Chalcedon the following points have come up more clearly:

1. There is a considerable limitation in the historical evidence at our disposal. It is, of course, true that in comparison with other ecumenical Councils Chalcedon offers us a great amount of source material. Yet this material is not enough to adequately and fully understand all the historical aspects of an event in which a complex of factors have been interwoven, especially concerning discussions in smaller groups or behind the scenes.

This remark refers to the fact that the interpretation of the existing source material is of great importance for a common understanding of Chalcedon by the Churches today. This is illustrated, for example, by the questions raised immediately below concerning the influence of the Emperor on Chalcedon, the role played by the various ecclesiastical sees at that time, etc.

2. The role of the Emperor or his commissioners in the proceedings of Chalcedon present us with the following questions

a) To what extent did this role influence the content of the decision of the Council? Was this role restricted to a simple direction of the agenda (e.g. pressure towards the production of a doctrinal definition) or did it reach the substance of the definition itself? To what extent was the concern for the unity of the Empire determinative for the Council? Was it important only for the formulation of certain canons or was it also a motivation in formulating the doctrine itself?

This question is very much behind the discussions between Chalcedonians and Non-Chalcedonians today. These discussions have shown that to many non-Chalcedonian scholars the essence of Chalcedonian faith appears acceptable. Although this ought to be accepted with the caution that scholars might be ahead of the bulk of membership, it points to the fact that it is essential to establish a distinction between the proceedings of the Council of Chalcedon and the faith which it proclaimed. Thus, although either side in these discussions today may make different use of the views of the historians on the role of the Emperor in the Council, the question remains whether or not these sides agree on the significance of the content of the Chalcedon definition.

---

[3] The papers are published in *The Ecumenical Review*, XXII/4 (1970), pp.30ff.

b) What was the primary imperial concern (motive) in this Council? Was it only or mainly the concern for maintaining one faith in one Empire? Or should we see other political aims behind it?

The reason for raising this question lies again in the fact that in ecumenical discussions the accent is often one-sidedly placed on either the political motivation of the Byzantine Emperors in their concern for the convocation of a Council or on their strictly religious concern for maintaining the orthodox faith in their Empire. It is probably true that in order to find the right motive historically one must take into account the role orthodox faith played for the unity of the Empire in the minds of the people of that time. In any case, the way this question is answered depends to a great extent, and for many Christians today, on the authority a conciliar decision bears.

c) Was Chalcedon influenced by imperial intervention more than previous Councils?

In the conversations between Chalcedonians and Non-Chalcedonians the latter insist on the authority of Nicaea (325) which they consider as final in its proclamation of faith. Constantinople I and Ephesus are accepted by them as commentators on I Nicaea and not as a "new faith" which for them Chalcedon appears to be. In denying the authority of Chalcedon, Non-Chalcedonians point out what they see as imperial intervention and influence on this Council. This raises the question for historical research whether this imperial influence applies more to Chalcedon than to the previous ecumenical Councils.

d) What was the importance of the fact that the faith of Chalcedon had, as in other cases, to be promulgated by special imperial decrees?

This question is connected again with the entire issue of imperial influence on the Council of Chalcedon and the degree to which this issue affects the authority which Chalcedon bears in our ecumenical discussions. The promulgation of the decision of a Council by imperial decree was applied also to Chalcedon. This meant that the faith declared by the Council had to be the one faith of the one Empire. Those dissatisfied with this "faith" or those who did not like the Empire or its capital were thus put automatically in the same position towards the Council of Chalcedon. Now that the Empire no longer exists, how has the situation changed with regard to the "faith" of Chalcedon?

3. The differences of interpretation of history appear especially with regard to the role played by the rivalry of the great ecclesiastical sees in the background of the Council. What was the importance for Chalcedon of the particular interest of such sees as Rome, Constantinople, Alexandria, Antioch, the emerging Patriarchate of Jerusalem or of the bishops of Illyricum with their pecular attitude towards the Tome of Leo? What was the role played by the Roman delegates in the Council?

These questions are implicitly present in our ecumenical discussions. For example, many non-Chalcedonian historians would attach to the Roman delegates in the Council of Chalcedon a role of promoting a certain policy of the Roman see in connection with a similar policy by Constantinople who, according to this view, aimed at becoming the first see of the East at the expense of Alexandria or Antioch. Besides this, there is also the question of the influence Pope Leo's Tome has had on the definition of Chalcedon. Did Chalcedon receive a decisive "Roman" influence on its teaching or was it more "ecumenical" in its dogmatic perspective?

4. To what extent did ethnic and cultural factors play a role in the history of Chalcedon? It is true that in post-Chalcedonian times the cultural frontiers between Byzantines and non-Byzantines were of special significance. But is it right to apply such differences to the time of Chalcedon itself?

The influence of cultural or ethnic factors in the confession of faith is a matter of constant relevance for the ecumenical movement. This is true in a special way for the split between Chalcedonians and Non-Chalcedonians. The overcoming of this split depends very much on the recognition of whether such factors which might have played a role in the past should not be distinguished and placed aside from what constitutes the real issue.

5. What were the theological concerns (motives) behind Chalcedon? Here one may mention various possibilities:

a) The soteriological motive, namely the concern that man is saved only by God (the Logos), and yet that he is saved as a complete human being (perfect man). Both these elements (that salvation can only come from God and that it must refer to the entire man) were alive in the soteriology of the Early Church. Chalcedon's doctrine of two perfect natures, divine and human, in Christ stemmed from this soteriological motive as it was feared that in the theological trends to which the Council reacted this soteriological principle was endangered by an excessive and onesided stress on either the divine or the human factors in man's salvation. This soteriological concern becomes a criterion even for the Church today in its attitude towards the teaching of Chalcedon.

b) The worship motive, namely the question whether the worship of Christ would not in fact mean worshipping a man. This "pious" motive characterized both sides, i.e. both those of "Nestorian" and of "Monophysitic" tendencies, in the controversies which led to Chalcedon. Chalcedon aimed at safeguarding the divinity of the subject to whom worship is rendered (the Logos) but in absolute inseparability from the human nature assumed by him.

c) The concern for establishing the identity of Christ, namely the question who the historical Christ (who walked and suffered in Palestine) in fact was, God or man, and how his historical existence related to his being the Son of God (communicatio idiomatum).

d) An implicit attempt to criticize the neo-platonic image of man in his relation to God, an image which threatened the "otherness" of God and man (hence the insistence on ἀσυγχύτως etc.).

In mentioning these possibilities one should not exclude a combination of some or all of these together, perhaps, with other factors making up for the theological concerns behind Chalcedon. It seems, however, that any understanding of this issue in terms of more philosophical speculation should be excluded.

6. With regard to the content of the Chalcedonian definition itself the following questions arise in connection with the nature as well as the theology of this definition:

(a) Concerning the nature of the definition the question is whether this decision represents simply a setting of "borders" within which one is free to understand whatever he wishes, or is it intended to state something positively. This raises the more general question of what is right or wrong about liberty of interpretation and comprehension in Christian doctrine. (b) Concerning the theology the Chalcedonian definition represents, the question is whether this theology should be seen as expressing an "anti-Monophysitic front" or an "anti-Nestorian" attitude as well. (c) It is also to be seen to what extent this theology depends on particular theologians, like Leo I, Cyril of Alexandria, etc., or represents a synthesis of many trends, including perhaps that of the Antiochene school.

7. This is closely connected with the question of the relation of Chalcedon to the previous ecumenical Councils. Here two kinds of questions arise. One has to do with the position of Chalcedon in Christian tradition compared with that of the previous ecumenical Councils. Does Chalcedon hold the same authority as the ecumenical Councils which preceded it or should we view the latter and especially the first ecumenical Council as the authority *par excellence* to which Chalcedon appears as addition, perhaps "unacceptable", as it may be seen to constitute a threat to the purity of the original faith? The other kind of question refers to the essential or dogmatic relationship between Chalcedon and the ecumenical Council after it; does Chalcedon constitute a point in a certain continued evolution of Christological thinking or should it be seen rather as a response to an entirely new problem?

II. Problems arising from a study of the reception of Chalcedon by the various traditions

A study organized by Faith and Order some years ago on the Councils of the Early Church and their significance for the ecumenical movement showed the importance which reception bears in the understanding of a Council.[4] Reception represents the process by which the local churches accept the decision of a Council and thereby recognize its authority. This process is a multiplex one and may last for centuries. Even after the formal conclusion of such a process and the canonical reception of a Council's doctrinal formula usually through a new Council, the process of reception continues in some way or other as long as the Churches are involved in a self-examination on the basis of the question whether a particular Council has been received and appropriated properly and with justification. In this sense we can say that in the ecumenical movement the Churches find themselves in a process of continuing reception or re-reception of the Councils.

In examining the reception or rejection of Chalcedon in their respective traditions the Churches are faced with questions which bear particular significance for their understanding of reception itself and of the place the Councils have in their consciousness. As the Churches live together in the ecumenical movement in which they experience a re-reception of their traditions the question becomes relevant when they study their attitude towards the Councils: Are the Churches ready to contribute to this emerging of re-reception of Christian tradition today by placing their reception of the Councils in the context of this re-reception? Here the following questions are included:

---

[4] Cf. *Councils and the Ecumenical Movement*, World Council Studies No. 5. WCC, Geneva 1968, esp. pp.15ff.

1. Is it possible to establish a distinction between the content of a Council, especially of its dogmatic decision, and the actual proceedings of the Council? To what extent does the recognition of the doctrine of a Council depend upon the manner of conciliar procedure practised in the Council? Would it be perhaps possible to speak of a reception of the content of a Council without a reception of the Council itself?

2. The fact that reception forms an indispensable part of a Council is accepted by all. But what does it mean that a Council is in the *process of reception?* Is there something irrevocably *given* which has to be gradually understood and appropriated? Or is it an event in the history of the Church which is to be used at a given moment as an *analogy* to the intentions of the Church at a certain point in its history? These questions are closely related with the following:

3. What is the relation of a conciliar definition and its reception to the Apostolic witness? Does a Council (a) develop, (b) interpret, (c) simply point to the Apostolic witness in a certain historical moment? An understanding of the meaning of reception is, perhaps, possible only in the context of the problem of the relation between Scripture and Tradition.

4. To what extent does the process of reception leave unchanged what was once decided by a Council? Here the question is whether reception in fact transforms the original meaning of a conciliar decision. If we look, for example, at the history of the Chalcedonian formula in the West we are perhaps allowed to say that in many cases Western theology went beyond the original intention of Chalcedon, especially when the terms of this formula acquired a certain independence and initiated some new theological idea (cf. the theological ideas which developed on the basis of the proprieties of each nature in Christ, etc.). Thus, it is not only a matter of hermeneutics that we face in the process of reception but also the question of the role history plays in the transmission of a conciliar doctrine from generation to generation.

5. Chalcedon constitutes an example of a Council which was followed both by divisions and by differences of interpretations in the process of its reception. In view of this and of the previous four questions what should the Churches do today? The discussions at the consultation indicated the following trends which might assist the Churches to go forward and, in a positive manner, find a way beyond those differences in the reception of Chalcedon which have hitherto separated or tended to separate some of them. The trends are relevant also to the whole question of Councils within and in relation to the tradition of faith.

a) It is obvious that the way in which we understand the reception of a Council or Councils directly involves our various conceptions of tradition. All Churches are having to re-examine their understanding of tradition in relation to the challenges both of other Churches and of the world. It is to be hoped therefore that this mutual re-examination will contribute to overcoming problems about the reception of a particular Council.

b) In this connection, it seems reasonable to expect that the Churches will be obliged to reconsider the status of any specific process whereby a Church received or rejected a particular Council in the past. For example, both the historical act of receiving Chalcedon and that of rejecting Chalcedon may not be as final for a Church's dogmatic stand and definition as has hitherto been thought. A new understanding of the whole process puts particular incidents in the process into a new light.

c) Similarly, it is necessary to re-examine the relationship of any juridical act of accepting a Council to the restoration of Church unity. It no longer seems sufficient to hold in a simplistic way that in order to restore church unity there must, simply or of necessity, be juridical assent to a list of Councils. Or, alternatively, this point should perhaps be stated in the form of claiming that we are all obliged to take seriously the past and in so doing to reconsider what juridical acceptance of a Council or Councils should mean and what form it should properly take.

d) A particular point to be considered in relation to the more general considerations touched on in (a) - (c) above is the question of how "anathemas" pronounced by Councils are to be received. It would seem necessary both to re-evaluate the total significance of such anathemas and to consider the possibility of distinguishing between "anathemas" referring to particular persons (whose doctrinal stances, incidentally, historical research may lead one to evaluate differently from the judgment of their contemporaries) and "anathemas" referring to particular beliefs.

III. Interpreting Chalcedon today

As the Churches are faced with the present day situation the question of their relation to Chalcedon takes the form: What is it that we are committed to today with regard to the Council of Chalcedon? This question may open new possibilities of convergence for our Churches in their re-reception of Chalcedon today. Raising such a question implies going back to Chalcedon in an attempt to find its relevance for today.

This attempt would include in the first place the question of the meaning which interpretation has in this case. Does interpretation imply here a mere translation of terminology? Or does it require changes in the concepts themselves? And how can one today use concepts that are no longer relevant?

Another question which would be involved in the attempt to find Chalcedon's relevance for today is that of the motives which lie behind the Chalcedonian definition. Should we approach Chalcedon having in mind the question of "how" or of "why" it speaks of Christ in such a way? It has been mentioned earlier in this report that the soteriological motive in all conciliar decisions and in that of Chalcedon in particular should be taken seriously. If this is applied to the reception and interpretation of Chalcedon today it is clear that we should go beyond the "how" of the Chalcedonian definition to the "why" of it, thus basing our re-reception and interpretation of Chalcedon on the intention of the Council.

This approach to Chalcedon leads to the following concrete problems

1. Can we interpret Chalcedon outside the context of God's relation to the world and history? Does Chalcedon allow us to speak of divine nature in an independent and positive way or only in the context of God's personal existence in relation to the world and history? And how would our classical theology be affected should we place the doctrine of Chalcedon in such an existential relationship of God to our historical life?

2. Is the intention of Chalcedon to unveil something about God and the Incarnation or rather to protect the mystery of God? Does Chalcedon by the ambiguity of its formula bind theology or does it open new theological questions?

3. Can Chalcedon be properly understood and received without an understanding of what followed it both in the form of theological debates and of new conciliar decisions in the centuries that follow immediately after Chalcedon (e.g. 5th and 6th

ecumenical Councils)? And what does it mean that a conciliar decision can be received through another Council?

4. What is the importance we should attach to a reception of Chalcedon or of any Council in the form of liturgical life or piety (spirituality)? Is spirituality and liturgical life derived from a Council or is it the conciliar decisions that derive from a certain spirituality? Can we say that Chalcedon has been received by liturgical and spiritual life in East and West in the same way? And could we not find the vision and teaching of Chalcedon in the spiritual and liturgical life of Churches who have not accepted this Council?

IV. The bearing of Chalcedon on the "understanding of man" and the "secular"

A special but central area to which "interpreting Chalcedon" today applies is that of the current discussion on anthropology and secularism. Here the following issues arise:

1. What are the grounds on which the Chalcedonian definition can be brought to bear on our modern discussions on the "humanum"? Here the first question to be asked is whether it is possible to use the method of extracting *data* concerning the humanity of Christ from the discussion about Jesus at Chalcedon, and then relating these data to what in our times is understood as constituting the "human". Does this approach take account of history? Can we discern any "facts" or "data" about Jesus from the reflections of the Church and — in the case of Chalcedon — from the Church of that particular time? Furthermore what sort of anthropology is to be found in Chalcedon? Is it one that Chalcedon finds and utilises or is it one resulting from the Chalcedonian doctrine itself? These questions underline the particular character which any attempt of extracting anthropological *data* from Chalcedon bears in this case. The same questions apply also to data concerning not only Jesus but existence and faith in general, issues involved in our present day assertions about the humanum and the secular.

2. In what way can the Chalcedonian *model* criticize our modern views about man and the "secular"? Although it should be admitted from the beginning that all "models" are limited in their application to other times, nevertheless the basic model offered by Chalcedon (not in its terms which may change, but in its structure) implies some elements which may be relevant to our contemporary anthropological discussions.

a) It points to a fundamental ontological distinction between uncreated and created, yet not in a sense of contradiction or opposition between the two, but of "personal" unity. This leads to an affirmation of created nature and away from any reductionism of reality to either "materialism" or "spiritualism".

b) It involves an idea of *consubstantiality* which offers in the person of Christ a rescuing of anthropology from individualism. Christ's humanity cannot be conceived in isolation from his community life — even from the "impersonal" aspects of his environment (e.g. cultural or economic life) or from the natural elements (e.g. food, sea, etc.).

c) It throws light on the relation between the "personal" and "impersonal" by bringing the two together. The "impersonal" with which modern science and technology are concerned finds its fulfilment on the level of the "personal" while the latter becomes sensitive and responsible towards matter. What concrete possibilities are there in such an understanding of the "personal" and the "impersonal" for defining our attitude towards the affirmation of the "secular" today?

V. Questions which appear to underlie the foregoing and which therefore need consideration for any subsequent agenda

The detailed study of Chalcedon, its antecedents, its subsequent history and its possible implications, which the consultation has encouraged, permitted and carried forward has constantly been raising, explicitly or implicitly, a series of underlying questions which may themselves be seen as questions relevant to one basic theme. That theme is how we are to understand the place of the Councils within the whole process of Tradition and how *that* understanding relates together Tradition, Unity and Truth. Detailed study of a specific Council by men from very varying ecclesiastical traditions tends to show that many, if not all, of the views implied by the various traditions on the relation between church tradition, ecclesiastical unity and the claims made for the truth of doctrine will not stand up in their commonly received form to historical and critical evaluation.

For example, it is difficult to see how allegations of undue imperial influence at Chalcedon (even if they were provable) could legitimately affect judgments about the rightness of rejecting Chalcedon and of being content with the first Council of Nicaea. Historical evidence is at least as clear about imperial dominance at Nicaea as at Chalcedon. Conversely, many devout Christians and many committed theologians cannot easily see how the resultant of imperial pressures, episcopal discussion and theological debate at a distance of 1500 years can be held to be in any way normative for the Church at the present time. Conversely again, there is the question of how the past experience of the Church, particularly that part which the Church in the past has held to be particularly significant can now be understood as relevant to, and at least partially formative of, the Church's present understanding of the Faith.

Thus the study of the Councils or of a particular Council must clearly be pursued in relation to the questions of how the Councils now contribute to the understanding of Faith (the question of Truth) and of how acceptance of Councils is related to common membership of one Church (the question of Unity). In this context the discussions of the consultation may be seen to have reflected three broad questions which need to be related further both to actual available evidence and to further reflection.

Firstly there is the question of the relation between the proceedings of the Council and the significance of the faith which it proclaims. This question should really be extended to cover not only the proceedings leading up to a conciliar formulation but also to subsequent proceedings whereby Churches received or rejected this conciliar formulation. In what way are we to judge that there is "treasure" in conciliar "vessels" no matter how "earthen" they turn out to be and how far is the "treasure" defined as treasure by subsequent recognition, use and interpretation?

The second question which is very closely connected with the first is the question of *motivation*. Can we perceive what the proponents of a particular conciliar solution believed themselves to be protecting and promoting? Did opponents believe they were protecting and promoting different things? And is subsequent reception/rejection of a Council a judgment about the council's aim or the success of the Council's *method?* And how would present judgments about any of these questions affect the present standing and use of Councils and present attitudes and judgments taken up towards them?

It should always be remembered with regard to the Council of Chalcedon in particular that at least *three* groups of Churches and Christians have to be taken into account. There are those Churches and Christians who positively affirm Chalcedon, there are those who positively deny Chalcedon and there are those who are indifferent to Chalcedon (whatever the formal doctrinal position).

Thus the third main question is to see whether agreement could emerge as to what sort of point or stage Chalcedon is in what sort of process. How does the Church receive, formulate and pass on her experience and what is the value of that past experience and the formulation of it for the Church at present as she is called to face the future? Unless ways can be found of studying and answering questions such as these then studies of the reception and interpretation of the Council of Chalcedon are simply matters of ancient history for a decreasing band of specialists rather than matters concerning vital resources for the way in which the Church today confronts her task.

DOCUMENT IV.4

CONCILIARITY AND THE FUTURE
OF THE ECUMENICAL MOVEMENT (1971)

1. The Uppsala Assembly spoke of the World Council as a "transitional opportunity for eventually actualizing a truly universal, ecumenical, conciliar form of common life", and suggested that the member Churches should "work for the time when a genuinely universal council may once more speak for all Christians and lead the way into the future". This suggestion has provoked considerable discussion. The recent world meetings of the Lutheran World Federation, the World Alliance of Reformed Churches, the Old Catholic Congress and the Anglican Bishops at Lambeth have all shown interest in the proposal. The Central Committee at its meeting in Addis Ababa (January 1971) has expressed the hope that the Faith and Order Commission would contribute to the clarification of the idea. The present paper is an attempt to respond to this request.

2. Meeting at Louvain we have considered the twofold suggestion of the Uppsala Assembly in the context of the main theme of our meeting — the Unity of the Church and the Unity of Mankind — and also in the context of the present widespread questioning and debate concerning the nature and goals of the ecumenical movement. No discussion of the future of this movement can take place except in the context of a concern for the whole of mankind. The ecumenical movement is concerned with the purpose of God for all mankind as it is revealed in Jesus Christ, and with the Church as instrument and first-fruit of that purpose. Therefore any discussion of its future must be concerned with the needs of all mankind for true community, and with the forms of church life which are relevant to these needs. It is in this context that we have to consider the suggestion of the Uppsala Assembly.

3. Conciliarity has been, in some form or degree, characteristic of the life of the Christian Church in all ages and at various levels. By conciliarity we mean the coming together of Christians — locally, regionally or globally — for common prayer, counsel and decision, in the belief that the Holy Spirit can use such meetings for his own purpose of reconciling, renewing and reforming the Church by guiding it towards the fulness of truth and love. Conciliarity can find different expressions at different times and places. The ecumenical movement has both challenged and helped us to seek appropriate conciliar forms for our own time. Facing the questions of the contemporary world, and drawn together by a common desire to serve the Lord together in the whole life and mission of the Church, the Churches have been led in our own time to develop new forms of conciliarity — both within each Church, and in councils of Churches at the local, national, regional and world levels. It is important that we should reflect upon this fact, should endeavour to relate it to the conciliar experience of the Church in the past, and should seek more adequate forms of conciliarity for our day. In this connection we draw attention to the studies undertaken by the Faith and Order Commission on "Councils and the Ecumenical Movement" and on the Council of Chalcedon.[1]

---

[1] Cf. WCC Studies No. 5 (1968, Geneva) and *The Ecumenical Review* (Vol. XXII/4, October 1970).

4. The report of the Uppsala Assembly first calls for "eventually actualizing a truly universal ecumenical conciliar form of life" and then asks the Churches to "work towards the time when a genuinely universal council may once more speak for all Christians and lead the way into the future". Though related these two suggestions need to be distinguished. The first points to a permanent feature of the Church's life, while the second refers to an event which may once take place. To accept the first suggestion of the Uppsala Assembly will mean that we seek to deepen the element of conciliarity in the life of the Churches at all levels, local, regional and universal. The New Delhi statement on the nature of the unity we seek spoke of a "fully committed fellowship" both "in each place" and also universally embracing the Church in all ages and places. To accept conciliarity as the direction in which we must move means deepening our mutual commitment at all levels. This does not mean movement in the direction of uniformity. On the contrary, our discussions here at Louvain have emphasized the fact that, if the unity of the Church is to serve the unity of mankind, it must provide room both for a wide variety of forms, and for differences and even conflicts. The conciliarity of the Church requires the involvement of the entire lay membership, including as it should every segment of mankind. There must be opportunity within the life of the Church for each community of mankind to develop and express its own authentic selfhood; for the oppressed and exploited to fight for justice; and for the "marginal" people in society — the handicapped in mind and body — to make their own distinctive contribution. This becomes all the more necessary because modern technology has forced all mankind into a tight inter-dependence which constantly threatens freedom and individuality. The Church's unity must be of such a kind that there is ample space for diversity and for the open mutual confrontation of differing interests and convictions.

5. True conciliarity, moreover, has a temporal dimension; it links the past, the present and the future in a single life. This is part of the meaning of what New Delhi said about the unity of one committed fellowship "in all ages and all places". Through the work of the Spirit in the life of the Church we are enabled to discern his teaching through the words of the Councils of the past. Within the living fellowship of the one Church we are enabled to enter into a conversation with the past, to put questions and to receive illumination on our own problems. We are not called upon simply to reproduce the words of the ancient Councils, which spoke to different situations and in languages other than ours. But it is an essential part of our growth into full conciliarity that we should be continually engaged in a process of "re-reception" of the Councils of the past, through whose witness — received in living dialogue — the same Holy Spirit who spoke to the Fathers in the past can lead us into His future.

6. The councils which have been created as expressions of the ecumenical movement in our time do not possess the fulness of conciliarity as it is to be seen in the great Councils of the early Church. The reason of this deficiency is not in the first place their lack of universality. The central fact in true conciliarity is the active presence and work of the Holy Spirit. A Council is a true Council if the Holy Spirit directs and inspires it, even if it is not universal; and a universally representative body of Christians would not become a true Council if the Spirit did not guide it. But the acceptance of a Council as a true Council in the full sense of the word implies that its decisions are accepted by the Church as fully authoritative, and that it has been marked by or has led to full eucharistic fellowship. However, the full acceptance of a Council

as authoritative has often taken a long period of time. It has not necessarily been the case that the complete binding authority of a Council has been accepted in advance. We must therefore ask such questions as the following: What are the pre-conditions for a true Council? Could there be a "reunion Council" which did not presuppose eucharistic fellowship and full consensus, but met seeking and expecting these as gifts of the Holy Spirit? These — as well as many other questions providing the nature of representation, the role of bishops in a Council, and other matters — require study. It is clear that the World Council of Churches and other similar regional and local councils are not in this full sense Councils of the Church. They are meeting places for Churches which are not yet in full communion and do not yet accept a common authority. They do nevertheless provide a framework within which true conciliarity can develop. In so far as they are guided and inspired by the Holy Spirit they have — if only in an anticipatory form — the character of conciliarity.

7. It follows from what has been said so far that all conciliar bodies — whether local, national and regional councils, or world confessional families, or the World Council itself — should be urged to test their own life and work against this concept of true conciliarity. They should be asked to consider both the question how far a true conciliarity marks their existing life, and also the question whether their life and work are helping to prepare the way for a "genuinely ecumenical Council".

8. We have begun by looking again at the Toronto Statement of 1950 on "The Ecclesiological Significance of the World Council of Churches". This statement marked, as it were, the starting point of our journey. It assured the member Churches of the World Council of Churches that membership did not imply the relativizing of their several ecclesiologies, nor the initial acceptance of any particular doctrine of the nature of the unity which God wills for the Church. It committed the Churches to a serious conversation with a view to "unity based on the full truth", and to solidarity and mutual help. It makes clear that the Council does not claim to be itself the form of unity which God wills; it is not the end but a means — a place within which the Churches can together seek for God's will concerning their unity. This remains true.

9. In the light of the experience of the past 21 years we can now say that the existence of the World Council of Churches has changed the situation in significant ways. For example:

a) While the Council has no binding authority over its member Churches, its only authority being "the weight which it carries with the Churches by its own wisdom" (Temple), nevertheless the decisions of the Council have had a significant effect in the life of member Churches. An outstanding recent example is the effect of the various actions of the Council, from the Second Assembly, on the race question.

b) The World Council, through its own conciliar processes, has promoted the more vigorous development of conciliarity in the life of the member Churches. The effect of its work has been to move the Churches to take counsel together and within their own membership on matters which concern the common witness and service of the Church in the world today.

c) The World Council of Churches has provided a common life in which the area of eucharistic fellowship has been extended among many Churches which previously did not have such fellowship with one another.

d) The World Council of Churches has provided many opportunities for Christians to work and think together in ways which are urgently needed for the total witness of the Church in the modern world, but for which existing structures provided no opportunity.

In other words, certain of the elements of true conciliarity have begun to appear, even if only in a very preliminary way, in the life of the Council. The life of the member Churches, and their relation to one another, have been significantly changed during the past two decades through their membership in the World Council of Churches. The ecumenical movement does move, even if the movement seems slow.

10. We suggest that it will be by strengthening these elements of true conciliarity in the life of the World Council of Churches and its member Churches that we shall move towards that "fully committed fellowship" of which the New Delhi statement speaks. To accept this would mean at least the following:

a) that all the member Churches seek more earnestly to ensure that the ecumenical movement penetrates more and more fully into the life of local congregations, synods and assemblies of the Churches;

b) that member Churches be encouraged to widen the area of organic unity and of eucharistic fellowship among them, wherever their fundamental ecclesiological principles permit;

c) that the World Council of Churches explore still further the ways in which it can provide fellowship, support and guidance for those individuals and groups which are seeking new forms of Christian obedience for which existing ecclesiastical structures provide no opportunity;

d) that the World Council be recognized as a place where the great issues on which Christians are divided may be faced — even at the risk of severe conflict, so that it may in a measure fulfill the ancient function of a Council as a place where Christians can be reconciled together in the truth;

e) that member Churches be encouraged to re-examine and (when appropriate and possible) interpret anew their polemical statements against each other;

f) that the member Churches together endeavour more seriously to achieve unity in faith and to confess together our hope for the world.

11. In the preceding paragraphs we have considered the application of the idea of conciliarity to the World Council of Churches. However, this concept has much wider relevance. The Second Vatican Council was not only a conciliar event of epoch-making importance, but has also led to a ferment of discussion throughout the Roman Catholic Church on conciliarity, and to new experiments in conciliar practice at various levels of the Church's life. It is our earnest prayer that the preparations for the Pan-Orthodox Synod may be so guided and blessed by the Holy Spirit as to bring about a creative renewal of conciliar life for the enrichment of the whole of Christendom. We note also recent developments in conciliarity among the oriental Orthodox Churches and other significant conciliar movements among Churches not in membership of the World Council of Churches. It is our prayer that through the development of fellowship among the WCC member Churches and through co-operation between the World Council of Churches, the Vatican Secretariat for Promoting Christian Unity and other bodies outside the membership of the World Council of Churches, the growth of true conciliarity may be fostered and the way prepared for a genuinely ecumenical Council.

DOCUMENT IV.5
HOW DOES THE CHURCH TEACH
AUTHORITATIVELY TODAY? (1977)

Introduction

The ultimate concern of this study is the faithful witness of the Church today to the Gospel of Jesus Christ as it was proclaimed by the apostles and the apostolic Church. The Church, called into being and kept alive through the centuries by the Spirit, has the responsibility to make known the apostolic truth both to its own members and to the world. How does it fulfil this task today? It finds itself in a new historical situation drastically different from earlier centuries. The changes raise questions about both the content of the message and the ways in which it is presented. The present study is primarily concerned with the second aspect. By what practices and structures today can the Church reach clarity on the meaning of the Gospel and announce it in words and deeds?

Why raise this question in the context of the ecumenical movement? Three major reasons may be mentioned:

1. The churches differ deeply in their understanding and in their practice of authoritative teaching. In the course of history, they have developed different concepts, ways and modes of teaching. Thus, they start from different historical presuppositions as they seek to appropriate and to transmit the apostolic truth today. If they are to advance on the road to the unity of the Church, these different approaches need to be clarified and reconciled. Since particular concepts, ways and modes of teaching have been developed and adopted in controversies and disputes between the churches, agreement cannot easily be reached. The various traditions are strongly attached to their respective approaches; they often consider them to be part of their historical identity.

2. Today all concepts, ways and modes of teaching are being tested. Many churches are experiencing that their inherited practices of teaching are now no longer operative. The problems they face in the contemporary world require not only new answers, but also new ways of answering. There is, for instance, the witness in the political field. Many churches have been led to adopt new forms of teaching in order to provide guidance for their members in their struggle for justice in society. There is also the encounter with a wider range of cultural backgrounds. Many churches, especially in the Third World, discover that the ways of teaching as they developed in European history need to be drastically modified if they are to respond to the needs of the culture in which they live. At the same time, for some churches, certain basic assumptions which had traditionally guided their approach to teaching have been called into question, in some cases to the extent that their ability to speak authoritatively and unitedly has been seriously shaken. Increasing numbers of Christians protest against any form of authoritative teaching "from above". They appeal to "experience" and "praxis" as the only reliable sources for the communication of their faith. For many, the doctrines of their churches are only partially relevant. Sociological analysis calls this phenomenon "partial identification".

Many churches find themselves confronted with similar challenges. The ecumenical movement may provide them with the opportunity of sharing their difficulties and engaging in a common search for new and more adequate approaches to their task. They can assist each other in discerning the changes which are characteristic of the present time and in drawing the consequences for their respective traditions.

3. Finally, the question also arises because the fellowship among the churches is growing. Obviously, they are not yet sufficiently united to speak authoritatively with one voice, but increasingly there are occasions when they are capable of bearing common witness; and even if they continue to teach separately, it is becoming more and more recognized that each church, in its teaching, needs to take into account the teaching of other churches. Though they are not yet one, they have committed themselves to the search for unity and for common witness. In all that they initiate, therefore, in their teaching and witness, they need to act with a sense of mutual accountability. They face the question of how, in their partial fellowship, they are to fulfil responsibly their task of teaching.

In particular, the issue of authoritative teaching requires attention because of the advances achieved in doctrinal conversations. On many issues of doctrine and practice the churches are discovering convergences and common perspectives; they are able to formulate at least partial agreement. How can such agreement be appropriated by the churches? Concrete steps towards unity require decisions by the churches.

The movement towards unity needs to be accelerated through explicit acts of teaching. For this, the churches need to reach mutual understanding on their ways of teaching. This study is to be understood as an appeal to the churches to re-examine their concepts, ways and modes of teaching in the light of the call to bear witness and to advance towards the visible unity for which Jesus prayed.

These three considerations are more fully discussed in the three sections of this paper.

The title of the study has sometimes been misunderstood. A few explanatory remarks may help to clarify the intention of the study.

a) Although the title asks the factual question as to how the churches *do* teach today, it should be clear that the study does not exclusively aim at a description of ways and modes of contemporary teaching by the churches. An adequate analysis of the present situation is of decisive importance for the mutual understanding among the churches, but ultimately the study seeks to answer the questions: How *can* and *should* the Church teach authoritatively today? How can and should the churches act to advance on the road to unity and common authoritative teaching?

b) The study is primarily concerned with the corporate aspect of teaching. How should the *Church* teach in order to guide its members in the truth and to give witness to the Gospel? Obviously, attention is also paid to the witness of individuals and groups as it contributes to and depends on the Church's teaching, but the primary focus remains the representative teaching of the Church.

c) The title may give the impression that the Church must necessarily engage in acts of formal teaching, but the term "teach" does not intend to prejudge the ways in which the Church has to transmit the Gospel today. It is used in a wider meaning and stands for the multiplicity of ways in which the Church as a community communicates authoritatively the apostolic truth to its members and to the world — statements, models of action, forms of worship, and so on.

d) The term "authoritatively" indicates that the attention of the study is primarily directed at authoritative acts of teaching. The Church teaches "authoritatively" when it claims to interpret authentically today the apostolic tradition as witnessed to the Scriptures and the creeds as well as in the whole life of the Church. Ideally, authoritative teaching will be also authentic teaching. It must be recognized, however, that there may be a tension between authority and authenticity. Teaching proclaimed "authoritatively" by the Church can turn out to be untrue (sometimes even after having been enthusiastically received). Authenticity depends on the inspiring and sustaining power of the Spirit. This does not mean that the Church should cease to teach authoritatively. It lives under the promise of the Spirit; strengthened by this promise, it will constantly seek to prepare for authentic teaching. The present study is meant to help in this task.

I. Divergences and convergences among the various traditions

The various confessional traditions differ greatly in their ways and modes of teaching. In order to advance to a common understanding, these divergences need to be seen clearly. How does each church approach its task of teaching authoritatively today? At the consultation in Odessa, the main divergences and convergences among the traditions were discussed under four aspects.

A. Authoritative teaching: past and present

As they seek to interpret authentically today the apostolic tradition, all churches refer to the past. What has been taught authoritatively in the past provides guidance for the task which the Church is called to fulfil today. Scripture, the ancient creeds, the ecumenical councils, the great church Fathers, and the Church's experience have all played a formative role in shaping the teaching which is accepted as authoritative in the various churches, even though each church places different emphases on these factors. Yet, the Church cannot teach authoritatively today by simply repeating the authoritative teaching of the past. The churches all recognize the need to continue to teach when faced with new questions which call for a decisive response. Such teaching can take different forms. Some churches have promulgated new dogmas or confessions of faith, others have sought to provide an authentic explanation of the apostolic tradition by interpreting or re-interpreting the teaching of the past which is recognized as authoritative by the Church. Varying degrees of authority are attributed to the different forms of continuing teaching.

In particular, the churches differ in their attitude to the need of authoritative teaching on certain issues. While some churches feel that they have to speak out on all important issues, others are more hesitant to commit themselves to acts of authoritative teaching: they feel that the Church should leave a wide range of issues to the personal judgment of each member of the Church. If authoritative teaching is offered on too many issues, freedom and creativity can easily be stifled in the Church. If too much is left open, the Church, as a consequence, may lack guidance and cohesion.

B. Continuity in authoritative teaching

All churches affirm the necessity that the ongoing teaching of the Church, in whatever form it takes place, must be in continuity with the apostolic tradition. All teaching must be based on the *memoria* of God's great deeds in history. Radical departure from or discontinuity with the apostolic witness is rejected by all churches.

How is continuity to be understood? Here the traditions differ. Some admit the possibility of developments, changes and even apparent contradictions; others reject in principle any form of discontinuity. Therefore, what appears to some Christians to be a necessary organic development is deemed discontinuity by others.

Inevitably, all traditions recognize that, in the course of the centuries, there have been shifts or modifications. There are at least three different approaches to the relationship between continuity and discontinuity.

a) Some would claim shifts and modifications have been at a lower level of change in terminology, practice and structures. They posit an original purity and completeness of a deposit of teaching which can be preserved through the ages with minor adjustments.

b) Others recognize that there have been real shifts in teaching, but see these as harmonious developments or organic growth.

c) Still others maintain that the discontinuity goes further. In order to make the Gospel actual or contemporary, the teaching of the past may need to be recast. They see continuity rather in the liberating message of the Gospel than in the various teachings in which this message has been actualized. In their opinion, when new situations arise, teaching practice and structures of the Church may need to change. Only the demands of the Gospel can determine what must be retained and what must be altered for the sake of faithfulness.

The issue of continuity and discontinuity has been further complicated by the growing awareness in some traditions of diversity within the apostolic witness itself. Historical critical methods in biblical studies have led to the recognition that the variety of witnesses within the New Testament reaches much further than past generations assumed. While some maintain that this variety by no means calls into question the basic unity of the New Testament and its message, others go so far as to raise the issue of diverse christologies and ecclesiologies within the New Testament. Ongoing authoritative teaching based on the apostolic witness has become more difficult for the churches which acknowledge the variety of witnesses in the New Testament.

C. Who teaches in the Church?

All churches agree that the ongoing teaching of the Church, which is not simply a repetition of the past, is necessary to fulfil the Church's mission to communicate the Gospel to the world. The ongoing teaching is a response to questions raised in the encounter between Church and world. Each act of ongoing teaching must be rooted in the whole people of God. It has its starting point in the consciousness of the Church and must be received by it; but there are persons or groups of persons who have to fulfil specific roles to bring it about.

At various times and in various ways, the following exercise functions in the ongoing teaching of the Church.

a) Church members who have *personal credibility* by their words and actions as "communicators" of the Gospel, like saints, monks, theologians, founders of spiritual movements or even churches, church-reformers. Many of them exercise a prophetic function in the Church.

b) Church members, who have *ministerial authority* to preach and teach in the Church, to administer the sacraments and to oversee the community in order to keep them faithful to the Gospel: pastors, priests, bishops and other church leaders.

c) Representative gatherings within the churches, like councils, synods, bishops' conferences and others, which exercise a *corporate teaching authority* in the Church.

The authority of each of them may either be local or universal. Ministers may have personal credibility and prophetic gifts. Councils and synods may issue prophetic statements as well.

All churches recognize the need for all or several of these roles in one form or another. They differ considerably, however, in understanding their nature and their weight; they also hold different views on the relationship between them and on the way in which the whole people of God need to be involved in the various stages of ongoing teaching. In any case, teaching must be appropriated by the whole people of God.

It is important to distinguish between an anticipatory role in the ongoing teaching of the Church and the formal decisions taken by representative offices or bodies. Saints, prophets, theologians, small communities, and so on sometimes anticipate the teaching which the Church, through its representative instruments, makes its own only at a later date. It is crucial for the teaching of the Church that such voices be heard and heeded; room should be left for creativity and courageous prophecy in the Church.

Some kind of ministerial teaching, some pastoral authority, preserving and promoting the integrity of the *koinonia* in order to further the Church's response to the lordship of Christ and its commitment to mission, is equally indispensable for the Church. They discern the insights of the believing community and give authoritative expression to them, sharing its quest for understanding the Gospel in obedience to Christ and receptive to the needs and concerns of all. Such a function of oversight *(episcope)* is present in most churches, although opinions differ on its forms and structures.

D. Authenticity in teaching

How does the Church acquire certainty that what is being taught is in authentic agreement with the Gospel? Obviously, all churches insist on the need for conformity with the witness of Scripture and tradition. Can further criteria for certainty be given? The answers of the various traditions differ in their emphases.

a) Some, while not excluding other authorities, emphasize the authority which is inherent in a certain office. If the bearer of that office has spoken, the teaching can be trusted as truth. For instance, if the bishops assembled in council with the Bishop of Rome arrive at certain conclusions, their teaching can be taken as authentic interpretation of the Gospel. Sometimes this criterion is viewed as sufficient, while at other times qualifications are insisted upon (for example the teaching must be tested in dialogue with theologians before it can be proclaimed).

b) Other traditions emphasize the role of confessional documents as an important means of safeguarding the authenticity of teaching. Since these documents have been acknowledged by these traditions as being in accordance with the Scriptures, conformity with them can be regarded as a criterion for the authenticity of the teaching. They recognize the need and value of teaching offices, but do not regard them as a criterion of authenticity.

c) Other traditions have difficulties in accepting as criteria either the authority of an office or confessional documents. In their view, there cannot be any criterion for authenticity outside the consciousness of the whole people of God. The Church is the charismatic community; it is taught and guided by the power of the Holy Spirit. Teaching proves its authenticity by being received and appropriated by the people of God, living in conformity with the Gospel, celebrating the eucharist and fulfilling its prophetic and priestly calling in the world.

d) Others still, while not denying the need for an office or the value of confessional statements, insist on the role of every community and every believer in verifying the authenticity of the teaching which is offered. Of course, the teaching has to be examined in the fellowship with the whole people of God, but every community and every believer has finally to judge for themselves whether or not the teaching is conformable to Scriptures as they understand them.

The list of approaches could easily be extended and refined. The various ways of verifying the authenticity of teaching as described above should not be regarded as necessarily excluding each other. On the whole, the individual churches, through historical developments and experience, have been led to place primary emphasis on some particular way of verification. But there is no single criterion for judging the authenticity of teaching. A criterion which proves adequate in one situation may not be adequate in another.

The problem has become more acute today for many churches as a sharper historical awareness begins to call into question the simple reference to a single criterion of verification. Where an official teaching office claims allegiance, the discovery of changes in teaching which have occurred in the course of history may create problems. Confessional statements are often interpreted in contrary ways by groups which adhere to them. As historical examples show, too exclusive a reference to the need for reception by the people of God can diminish the prophetic element in the Church's teaching and lead to immobility. As previously mentioned, some have come to recognize diversity within the Scriptures themselves; judgment on conformity with the Scriptures can lead, therefore, to very different results.

Can the ecumenical movement, by bringing together churches with different ways of verification, lead to a more comprehensive approach? Can churches be strengthened in their witness by the teaching of another church, even if that church has received it as authoritative in a way which differs from their own? Can the churches, by striving to perfect their ongoing teaching within the framework of their tradition but in dialogical relation to each other, move step by step to greater unity and thus reflect more fully the catholicity of the Church?

II. Teaching authoritatively today

As the churches seek to respond to the contemporary world, often the inherited ways and modes of teaching prove to be inadequate; they are led to adopt new approaches. What are the main characteristics of these shifts? What can the churches learn from one another in this respect? Three aspects may be mentioned here:

A. The variety of situations

Both in content and in style, the teaching of a church will be influenced by the situation in which it lives. Today, there is a clearer awareness of the immense variety of situations which the churches have to face. In order to reach a common understanding of the Church's task of authoritative teaching, a careful analysis of this variety is required.

At the consultation in Odessa three statements on particular situations received special attention.

a) A participant from *East Asia* mentioned the importance of looking at the teaching authority of the Church in relation to historical and socio-political changes. That is to say, authority is not something which the Church can take for granted. In the past, the authority of a church in East Asia tended to be a by-product of the privileges enjoyed by western personnel and institutions, be they missionary, political or military. China in the pre-revolution days was a case in point. Under extra-territorial treaties, the Chinese churches established by western mission boards enjoyed privileges and authority far beyond their size and membership. But whatever authority the Church had in that land quickly vanished when these privileges were withdrawn.

In a sense it is true to say that, during the last two or three decades, most churches in East Asia have been forced to look for authority on a radically different ground. As a result, a new understanding of authority in relation to the life and ministry of the Church is emerging. A church is now considered to be authoritative in its teaching and action when it shows faithfulness to the Gospel and demonstrates spiritual strength in adverse social and political situations. The courageous witness of Korean Christians to the sovereignty of God and their defence of human rights is an example here. Thus, authority should be regarded as a dynamic concept closely related to the witness in the life of a nation. The Church gains authority as it becomes engaged in faithful witness regardless of the consequences.

This leads to an important observation that the concept of authority is not to be confined only to a strictly ecclesiastical framework. That is to say, a church gains authority in its teaching and its work when it expresses hopes and concerns cherished not only by Christians, but also by a great number of people outside the Christian community. Numerically, most churches in East Asia are in the minority. But when their witness is truly directed to the deep-seated longings of the people, as in the case of Korean Christians, they acquire authority which exceeds their minority status in society. This, again, shows how hierarchical authority has given way to dynamic authority. Perhaps one can say that such dynamic authority comes from the work of the Holy Spirit at work both inside and outside the Church.

b) A participant from the *German Democratic Republic* (GDR) gave the following report. How can the churches in the GDR teach authoritatively today? The evangelical churches in the GDR see themselves as a fellowship of witness and service in a socialist society. They offer their witness and service not outside or against, but in this socialist society. God's good purpose in and for this society is to be manifested. The Church teaches by the witness to the Gospel of all its members and in particular of its ministers.

What influence does the situation in a socialist society have on the authoritative teaching of the Church? Among others, the following factors play a role in this respect: the socialist society is a secularized society where the Church represents a minority. The Church has lost its former privileges and has been separated from the state. The socialist society is officially based on an ideology which draws its inspiration from Marxism and Leninism. The power structure which exists today guarantees the spreading and application of this official ideology. In such a situation, authoritative teaching must have the character of missionary witness and must involve all church members. Authority will entirely depend on the credibility of the message. True, credibility is ultimately the gift of the Spirit persuading human conscience, but credibility also requires that the witness of the Church can be understood, that it corresponds to human experience, that it provides people with perspective on the meaning of life and the events of history, that it helps them to act responsibly and keeps them united as one community.

Furthermore, authority depends to a large extent on the personal credibility of the witnesses as well as on the style of life of the community. Teaching cannot be imposed, it must be offered as an invitation, and those to whom it is addressed must be in a position to decide freely on accepting or rejecting what is being offered. Authoritative teaching does not exclude variety of opinions. The one Gospel leaves room for various interpretations. At the same time, the recognition of variety points to the fact that the truth of the Gospel cannot be imposed by authoritarian means, but will make its way in the free encounter of different opinions. Finally, in the minority situation of the Church in the GDR, the teaching and the guidance offered by the Church will depend in a special way on the agreement between the leadership and the members of the Church; they need to listen to each other. Synods play an essential role in this process.

c) A participant from *Zaïre* offered the following comment on the situation of the churches in his country. In the past, authoritative teaching occurred not primarily through statements, but rather through styles of worship and communal life. In many communities, the highest degree of authority is being claimed for certain religious attitudes or ethical standards (for example, forbidding smoking, drinking, contracting polygamous marriages, consulting traditional doctors, and so on). Often, charismatic and independent leaders create new laws which bind their community together. In recent times, some churches have begun to speak authoritatively through statements. No doubt the most interesting example is the confession of the faith issued by the Roman Catholic Episcopal Conference in early 1975. It is entitled "One Faith in Jesus Christ", and is an attempt to reformulate authoritatively the fundamental faith and mission of the Church in the midst of a society whose government promotes the ideology of "authenticity" and which is more and more inclined to return to traditional religious beliefs.

In the society of Zaïre, there are different models of teaching. The traditional model is the "bargaining method" within the community, understood and experienced as a corporate personality. The issue at stake is debated by the community, and after long and intricate bargaining palavers, the leader of the community makes the decisive pronouncement. Modern developments in society have caused a crisis for this way of decision making. Today political and religious leaders are no longer convenors and catalysts as their counterparts in traditional society used to be; they have become authoritarian and messianic by personalizing authority and restricting it to governing offices. The churches are called to address themselves authoritatively to the issues confronting today's society in the political, social and economic fields. They need to learn afresh to be a dynamic community; in a renewed way the bargaining method should create a productive, challenging and spiritually committed people whose members all participate in reading the signs of the times.

d) A fourth kind of situation, especially prevalent in traditionally Christian western lands, was also discussed. Here, church membership is often nominal and involves little active participation or living relationship to the community of faith. Conflicts sometimes arise between academic theologians and church leaders, on the one hand, and between "conservatives" and "progressives" on the other, as to how best to bring the Gospel to these partly de-Christianized masses. This contributes to an especially acute crisis of authoritative teaching in these countries.

The description of further situations could be added. The four examples above suffice to illustrate the wide variety which today needs to be taken into account. In the eyes of many, the variety constitutes a threat to the teaching of the Church; the teaching seems to fall apart into teachings which arise from the various contexts. In fact, this is not the case. The variety rather manifests the richness of the tradition as well as its capacity to respond pertinently to different situations. The sharper awareness of variety raises, however, in a new way the question of the relationship between teaching addressed to the whole Church and teaching formulated on behalf of the whole Church in particular situations.

B. Authority in Church and in society

Styles, ways and modes of teaching in the Church are influenced by patterns of authority in society. Teaching processes in the Church must then be seen in relation to the situation in the societal context.

Sometimes structures of authority in the Church are a conscious or unconscious reflection of the structures of authority prevailing in society. For instance, in many churches the emphasis on the role of synods is partly due to the rise of democracy; in many African Independent churches the role of the leader corresponds closely to that of the local chief.

In many cases, the Church will seek to adapt its style of teaching in order to be better heard in society. In societies which place primary emphasis on action and achievement, it may seek to teach through practical commitments and programmes rather than through statements, and the like. In other cases, it may develop its style of teaching in opposition to the values prevailing in society. For instance, in an authoritarian society it may emphasize freedom and participation in the decision-making processes; in a society dominated by structures of injustice it may be led to a critical revolutionary approach and develop a style of teaching which seeks to manifest the identification with the oppressed classes.

Often patterns of teaching in the Church which have legitimately evolved at a certain point of history continue to be used, even if in the meantime the situation in society has changed. For a long time, for instance, the Church maintained concepts of authority which corresponded to the mentality of a feudal society. Sometimes churches, without abandoning their earlier theories about teaching, adapt their teaching processes *de facto* to the requirements of the times. For instance, many churches of congregational type have *de facto* developed new structures at regional, national and universal levels.

Special attention needs to be given to the impact of modern media of mass communication; in some countries they play a considerable part in the life of the Church. But the churches are not yet accustomed to making appropriate use of them in their teaching. Sometimes the vacuum of authority which churches leave is filled by the influence of the mass media. Ways should be found for mass media to serve as means of responsible participation of the whole community.

C. Towards new patterns of credibility

How to teach with authority today? For the faithful and effective exercise of the Church's teaching authority, four aspects require special attention today.

a) *Change:* Today, most churches are much more sharply aware of the changes having occurred in human society and affecting the life of the Church. They realize, therefore, that teaching may need to be adapted to the needs of the present time. While in the past identity with the earlier teaching was considered to be the mark of truth, more and more the churches are coming to the conclusion that faithfulness to the apostolic truth requires a new presentation of the Gospel. Change, which used to be regarded as innovation and betrayal, can, in fact, be faithful witness to the past.

Teaching will always aim at enabling the Church to fulfil its calling to the world, to enter into meaningful dialogue with specific partners, to discern and interpret new perspectives in history, to denounce evil, and so on. Teaching will take place in constant interaction with the world.

b) *Pluralism:* More and more, plurality in teaching is no longer seen by the churches as necessarily illegitimate. Positions which used to be regarded as contradictory are no longer considered as necessarily mutually exclusive. A new appreciation for the richness of aspects in the Bible and the vast variety of situations is emerging.

The growing variety of interpretations may cause the problem of diffusing the visible unity of the Church's teaching and call into question the Church's identity. The acceptance of pluralism does not necessarily militate against unity. Authoritative teaching should seek to maintain the Church in unity, yet not impose uniformity nor deny creative difference. The oneness has its primary root in the eucharistic fellowship and in the common mission and witness of the Church.

Obviously, pluralism must not be misunderstood as "indifferentism" or "relativism". The Church must also know how to say "no". Faithfulness to the apostolic witness implies that there may be unfaithfulness. Obedient listening and the desire to teach aright call for the recognition that sometimes the line between truth and error must be drawn. The churches cannot teach authoritatively unless they recognize that they are not automatically preserved from heresy.

In this context, the question arises to what extent some forms of discipline in matters of faith and morals are necessary in the Church. If there are juridical structures regulating such discipline, they should be strictly subordinated to the calling and mission of the Church and not allowed to deteriorate into juridicism, limiting the freedom of conscience of individual church members and ministers. Disciplinary measures which may be necessary to maintain the clarity of the Church's message must not contradict the ethos of freedom which is characteristic of the New Testament.

c) *Participation:* Today, there are signs in many churches that more people are participating in decision-making processes. Theologians are often asked to advise bishops or synods; leaders of local churches share to a larger extent in the procedures of teaching at the universal level; more frequently the actual experience of parish priests is taken into account by synods; local communities share in shaping catechetical material.

Such participation is theologically based on the fact that the gift of the Spirit is given to the whole Church and that, therefore, the discernment of truth needs to take place through the interaction between all its members. Participation is a way of expressing the *sensus fidei fidelium*.

d) *Reception:* In many churches there is today a stronger emphasis on the need for reception of teaching by the whole Church. Reception is another aspect of participation. To the degree in which teaching has been arrived at through the participation of the entire body of Christ, reception will be facilitated. Structures of participation at all levels of the Church prepare the way for reception.

The term "reception" must not be taken to imply that decisions are arranged "from above" and then simply submitted to the community for passive "reception". Reception is not only official endorsement, but also a profound appropriation *(Aneignung)* through a gradual testing process *(Bewährung)* by which the teaching is digested into the life and liturgy of the community.

In most churches, there are established ways of reception. But the process of reception will not pass exclusively through these regular channels. "Alternative channels" such as youth movements, *ad hoc* gatherings, and so on may influence the process both positively and negatively.

Ultimately, authoritative teaching is always an "event" which happens and cannot be organized or programmed, juridically or structurally. The authority of the Church is based on the authority of God and his design for the world in Jesus Christ; it depends on the gift of the Spirit. The teaching of Jesus was authenticated by his deeds and miracles. So, too, the Church's teaching will be authenticated by the blessings of the Spirit, not by "persuasive words of wisdom, but by the manifestation of Spirit and power".

III. Authoritative teaching in the context of the ecumenical movement

We have examined the ways of teaching in the various traditions. We have pointed to the changed circumstances in which the churches exercise their teaching ministry today. We now turn to the contemporary opportunities and difficulties of authoritative teaching in relation to the ecumenical movement.

In the course of the last decades the churches have come closer to each other. More and more, despite their persisting differences, they are able to witness and act together in the contemporary world. Their common basis is expanding. More and more, churches use the same Bible translations, share in the spiritual life of other churches, adopting their prayers and hymns and so on, develop common terminologies in many fields, especially in social ethics. The need to participate effectively in the ecumenical movement and to share together with other churches in common witness and service has led many churches to introduce new structures facilitating their representative participation.

Though still differing in their understanding of the Church and its unity, the churches have been able to describe at least in outline the goal they are committed to achieve together. The Fifth Assembly of the World Council of Churches in Nairobi offered the following statement on the "unity we seek":

> The one Church is to be envisioned as a conciliar fellowship of local churches which are themselves truly united. In this conciliar fellowship, each local church possesses, in communion with the others, the fullness of catholicity, witnesses to the same apostolic faith,

and, therefore, recognizes the others as belonging to the same Church of Christ and guided by the same Spirit. They are bound together because they have received the same baptism and share in the same eucharist; they recognize each other's members and ministries. They are one in their common commitment to confess the Gospel of Christ by proclamation and service to the world. To this end, each church aims at maintaining sustained and sustaining relationships with her sister churches, expressed in conciliar gatherings whenever required for the fulfilment of their common calling.

The fellowship among the churches today is still preliminary and "preconciliar", but it anticipates and heralds the future goal. The churches are called to advance step by step to full conciliar communion. In particular, through their acts of teaching they should prepare the way to that unity which is capable of common conciliar decisions.

While, on the one hand, the ecumenical movement opens new opportunities of relevant teaching, it also creates difficulties for the teaching within the individual communions. Commitment to the ecumenical movement can lead to dissensus. In response to the call to unity, laity, church leaders, theologians and staffs of ecclesiastical agencies may move in different directions; the tension between conservatives and progressives may find its focus in the commitment to the ecumenical movement.

Often the churches, afraid of possible divergences in their ranks, tend to withdraw from authoritative teaching. They try to preserve peace and unity by avoiding critical issues rather than by taking positions on matters of faith and justice. But there is no escaping. They need to hazard peace and unity and dare to confront error and unrighteousness. Controversy within the Church and conflict with evil in the world may be inevitable if the Church is to be faithful to its Lord.

As the churches engage in the ecumenical movement, they must continue to teach the Gospel. The ecumenical commitment must not lead to a loose attitude to the truth of the Gospel. What in fellowship with other churches has been heard, must in common be proclaimed.

How can the churches, in the ecumenical movement, assist each other to teach more effectively in fidelity to the apostolic heritage of the Church?

A. Common teaching today

a) *Acts of common teaching:* Despite their doctrinal differences, the churches often find themselves capable of teaching together. They may be able to formulate together catechetical material. They may be able to offer guidance on crucial issues facing the society in which they live. In particular, common corporate acts of witness become possible when the churches respond to the need of identification with oppressed people. As they seek to manifest the liberating power of the Gospel in solidarity with suffering humanity, they will find themselves bound together by their witness.

The need for common teaching exists equally in each country. Churches should seek, therefore, to formulate together the authoritative witness required in their situation. Often guidance on new pressing issues arising from the encounter with the contemporary world can more easily be worked out at the international level and provided through the common witness of the churches. In order to respond adequately, some distance from immediate national interests is sometimes needed, and furthermore there are occasions when a wider range of competence is required than is at the disposal of any individual communion. The World Council of Churches and other ecumenical bodies have therefore a special responsibility in formulating common

Christian teaching on such issues in order to encourage, stimulate and guide the churches in their teaching. Studies, statements, recommendations and actions on such issues as peace, race, human rights, the use of nuclear energy, and so on are thus important means to help the churches in their task.

b) *Sharing in the teaching of other churches:* Today, teaching is necessarily taking place in fellowship with other churches. Churches can be strengthened by acts of teaching offered by other churches. Churches whose simplicity of teaching has been shaken can rejoice in the straightforward witness of other churches. Those yet undisturbed in the inherited expression of the Christian faith can learn from others to seek new styles of witness and life. New understanding and commitment may come to the whole Church through the creative encounter between the younger and older churches.

The sharing can take place through explicit acts:

i) In some cases, churches may find themselves stimulated to associate themselves with the teaching of another church on the meaning of faith. The Roman Catholic effort at "receiving" the Lutheran *Confessio Augustana* may be mentioned in this context. A participant from the GDR was able to offer the following example. The Synod of the Roman Catholic dioceses in the GDR issued in 1974 a statement with the title "Faith Today". A committee of the Federation of Evangelical Churches in the GDR decided to examine this document and to ask whether the witness of this Roman Catholic text can be considered by the Evangelical Church as an adequate "Account of Hope" for our time. The committee has worked out a statement which offers a positive evaluation of the document as well as a number of critical remarks. The work was guided by three main questions: (1) Does the document adequately reflect the centre of the biblical witness? (2) Does it repeat doctrines considered by our Fathers as deviations from the Gospel to such an extent that communion was excluded? (3) Does the document make concessions to the spirit of the contemporary world, to the demands of today's society and dominating ideologies which obscure the meaning of the Gospel? The committee said "yes" to the first and "no" to the second and the third questions and, therefore, despite some critical reservations, it was able to see in the document, "Faith Today", the witness of Christian brothers and an expression of the common Christian hope.

This evaluation will be shared with various groups in the Federation of Evangelical Churches and serve as a basis for discussing possibilities and criteria of mutual reception. There are plans to discuss the same issue officially with the Roman Catholic Church.

ii) When Christians denounce injustice in dangerous circumstances, they are acting on behalf of all churches. Their action is a call to other churches. They should declare their support for their witness across confessional boundaries. An example for such support can be found in the recent statement of Baptist ministers in El Salvador associating themselves with a group of Jesuits who had taken a courageous political stand; the statement is particularly important because, going beyond the immediate purpose of support, it seeks to challenge the inherited patterns of Baptist hostility towards the Roman Catholic Church.

iii) Often, teaching in a particular situation is of significance beyond the boundaries of the country and requires a response from other parts of the ecumenical fellowship. In this respect, the World Council of Churches has a special task: it should fulfil a mediating role by bringing the efforts and achievements (as well as sometimes the failures) of the churches in one place to the attention of the churches in other places and offering them the opportunity of a response.

c) *Sharing in the witness of saints and martyrs:* The life and death of extraordinary witnesses have an impact which reaches far beyond confessional boundaries. In a real sense, it could be said that personalities such as Dietrich Bonhoeffer, Martin Luther King, Mother Teresa, Dom Hélder Camara, do not belong to one church, but to all churches. Though not explicitly, they are implicitly recognized by them as their own.

Of course, the formal recognition of saints poses serious problems which cannot easily be solved. But there can be no doubt that saints and martyrs in past and present may witness to Christ in a way which transcends the divisions; they often express the deepest content of the Christian tradition. For Christians, the cross of Christ is the supreme act of identification with suffering humanity. Those who die for Christ testify in a special way to his liberating power. The testimony of a martyr is thus always a call to all churches; each can be enriched by knowing of those from other churches who have died for the cause of the Gospel.

B. Common teaching and "visible unity in one faith and one eucharistic fellowship"

In order to reach unity or conciliar fellowship in the full sense of the terms, it is necessary that the churches are able to recognize each other as confessing the same apostolic faith. The World Council of Churches, especially the Faith and Order movement, has as its aim to lead to this mutual recognition. Obviously, the initiative for advancing towards the goal rests primarily with the churches. While in statements on pressing issues in today's world the World Council of Churches may speak in ways which provoke the churches, with regard to consensus building, it has primarily a facilitating role to fulfil. It can provide impulses by enabling dialogue between the churches, summarizing the findings, interpreting the common experience in the ecumenical movement, raising with the churches appropriate questions which result from ecumenical encounter, and similar activities. The work of the Faith and Order movement needs to be undertaken more and more in close contact with the churches. The decision of the Fifth Assembly to submit the agreed statements on baptism, the eucharist and the ministry to all churches for their considered response indicates a clearer recognition of this interaction between theological work and church response. In the light of the responses received, further theological work will need to be undertaken. Consensus can only be reached in stages.

In order to advance towards unity in one faith and one eucharistic fellowship, conscious actions by the churches are required. Through the ways and means of authoritative teaching which are at their disposal, they need to promote the movement to the goal. For this process, the following suggestions may be offered.

a) The final goal is a consensus which enables the churches to live in communion at all levels of their lives. The one Church will be characterized by rich variety. Bearing witness in different contexts inevitably leads to different expressions of the one faith. Consensus is not to stifle this variety; it should make possible a unity in diversity; it must serve the witness of the local church. In order to restore the communion among the churches, the process of consensus building must proceed, therefore, at all levels at the same time.

b) Multilateral agreements like the agreements on baptism, the eucharist and the ministry have a special role in the process. They provide a framework within which the churches can undertake their initiatives towards unity.

c) Responses to multilateral agreements should be sought both at the level of confessional traditions and at the level of regions, nations and local churches. In their response, confessional traditions should facilitate the growth of communion at all levels.

d) In the light of multilateral agreements, the churches of one region should work towards consensus on faith, taking into account the special confessional constellation and the special historical and cultural conditions of their regions. The elaboration of common responses would provide an opportunity to work out ways of teaching together and of developing the possibility of common acts of teaching in today's world.

e) Churches should associate representatives of other churches at all stages with their decision making. Such presence can take different forms: observers, consultants, participants without vote or even with vote. In some cases, joint sessions of decision-making bodies may be possible.

f) In order to make decisions representative, the community as a whole should be part of the process. Churches will need, therefore, to promote responsible discussion of ecumenical findings within their own ranks. The present practice has many unsatisfactory aspects. Often, ecumenical findings are published without clear address and definite indication about the response expected. They exercise a certain influence, especially in countries where the public means of communication contribute to their dissemination, but they are not taken up by the churches in "concerted action". This very easily leads to a tension between an "ecumenical atmosphere" and the life of the churches as expressed by church authorities.

C. A new self-assessment in the perspective of the ecumenical movement

As the churches engage in the ecumenical movement, they need to re-examine deliberately their ways and modes of teaching. Consensus and communion in conciliar life can be reached only if the ways of teaching become more and more capable of common decision making. At present, the response of the various churches to ecumenical findings both of multilateral and bilateral conversations have very different status. While in some churches a response by the authorities does not commit the church, in other churches it would have so much weight that the authorities prefer to refrain from responding. In order to make consensus real in the churches, the weight of decisions needs to become comparable.

Transformation of modes of teaching will take different forms in different churches. Some examples may serve as illustrations of possible directions.

a) Many churches have developed administrative and bureaucratic structures which in fact exercise considerable power of decision, but have no identifiable roots in the ecclesiological teaching of the church. Since they are regarded as temporary and created for convenience, their actual weight is not spiritually recognized by the church and their growth often not controlled by ecclesiological spiritual considerations. In some cases, the growth of such structures may represent a correction of the inherited way of teaching, in other cases it may represent a distortion of the true exercise of authoritative teaching.

b) Some churches will need to develop ways of teaching which generate more commitment from the whole Church.

c) Most churches will need to find new ways of associating in a more representative way the whole people of God in the process of teaching, for example, men and women, different classes, different age groups.

DOCUMENT IV.6

WORSHIP TODAY (1969)

Introduction

How are Christians to pray and worship? This question is being asked today with growing urgency. In their traditional form at least, prayer and worship have become a problem in many Churches. What form are we to give them so that they should be acts in which the present generation can participate with conviction and not something imposed from the past whose meaning is forgotten? Reforms are being proposed and introduced. All kinds of experiments are being made in the hope of providing opportunities for new forms to emerge. Some begin to doubt the future. They cannot see how the gulf between the world of faith and worship and modern life can ever be bridged. Many, on the other hand, see this disquiet about worship as really a promise of new and important possibilities. Have not the traditional forms of worship been challenged in other periods as well? Did not new answers come from such upheavals? Even though each crisis is *sui generis* and even though we should not play down the present crisis, we may expect to be led by it to new answers.

The present problem of prayer and worship cannot be clarified without first asking what in fact we mean by worship. Otherwise our inquiry runs the risk of being caught up in too narrow an approach to the problem. It is not enough to begin with the symptoms and to propose certain remedies for these. The problem lies deeper: What is worship and what are its basic principles

The Fourth Assembly in Uppsala (1968) made a first attempt in this direction. The draft document for discussion in Section V was entitled: "The Worship of God in a Secular Age". Its discussion, however, could not be expected to achieve conclusive results. Considering the lack of adequate preparation in the Churches, it was in any case a difficult undertaking. The Churches differ in their traditions of worship, and ecumenical discussion of these differences is far from being concluded. They have still to come to know and understand each other thoroughly. The different spiritual backgrounds have only just begun to influence each other. It was not to be expected, therefore, that the Assembly should in bypassing this unfinished task, as it were, reach a common mind on the problems of worship today. But certainly the Assembly did help to introduce new aspects of the theme of worship into ecumenical discussion. One not unimportant contributory factor here was the experience of the clash of old and new forms of worship at the Assembly itself. The now customary practice of ecumenical conferences in the matter of worship was challenged from different angles. A certain impatience was evident; new experiments were tried on the fringe of the Assembly and in isolated cases even in the programme of the Assembly itself.

The discussion at Uppsala made it abundantly clear that the problem of worship does not arise everywhere in the same way. An analysis of the situation may seem to some to be quite accurate whereas by others coming from a different geographical and cultural background it is felt to be inadequate. The different confessional presuppositions also play a role here. Even more important, however, are the various anthropological, cultural and social factors. There is no single analysis of the situation applicable to all places any more than there is one "modern man". The factual variety resists arbitrary simplification. One consequence of this may be that it becomes increasingly impossible for the Church to speak in generalizations about a theme such as "worship". It will have to face up consciously to the coexistence of a variety of assumptions, factors and interpretations.

The Assembly made this particularly clear in its discussion of the suitability of the term "secular". The choice of title had been an attempt to describe the "today" in which Christian worship has to be celebrated. It soon became clear, however, that such a universally applicable description was in fact excluded. The analyses of the situation as well as the conclusions drawn from them with respect to worship diverged widely. Whereas many spoke of a breach with the past, others challenged the view that the secular age was something completely new. Nor was this just a matter of differing opinions but clearly a matter of different experiences of reality.

The Uppsala Assembly assigned to the Commission on Faith and Order the task of pursuing further the inquiry into worship. To carry out this assignment the Commission arranged a consultation in Geneva from 8th to 13th September, 1969. Its purpose was to examine further the questions touched upon by the Assembly, and to define the *status quaestionis* more comprehensively and in greater detail. It was then to consider which questions would in future have to be dealt with first by the Commission on Faith and Order. The present report is an attempt to summarize the results of the consultation.[1] The 40 participants were representative of different traditions, trends and tendencies. The conference was deliberately planned in such a way as to bring differences into the open and to prevent them being smoothed away on either side. Consequently, a rich and sometimes bewildering variety of views emerged in discussion. But difficult as the discussion often proved, there was nevertheless an underlying unanimity of motivation hard to express in words. Despite the extent to which the participants differed, they were one in their deep concern that, both today and in the future, worship should be an authentic act.[2]

I. "Worship" in a "secular" age

The consultation began by asking whether this title was really the right starting point for discussion. It had been chosen for the Assembly to make it clear from the outset that we live in a changed world and that, because of this, worship in its traditional form is called into question. Discussion was not to disappear into general considerations but to face up to this fact. No doubt the title served this purpose, but its attendant difficulties soon came to the fore. There are in the first place terminological difficulties. The term "worship" and still more the term "secular" together with its various derivatives (secularized, secularization, secularism, secularity) lend themselves to so many different interpretations that discussion is constantly exposed to the danger of misunderstandings. The words used in other languages for worship (e.g. *Gottesdienst, culte*) do not have the same meaning. They have such different roots that inevitably they carry very different associations. In the case of the word "secular", the difficulties are even greater. Quite apart from the fact that in some languages the verb "to secularize" primarily implies expropriation of church property, the debate in the Churches in recent years about modern man's sense and experience of life has

---

[1] The papers presented to the consultation are published in *Studia Liturgica*, Vol. 7, 1970, No. 2/3 (Bussim, Nederland) under the title "Worship and Secularization", ed. Wiebe Voss.

[2] For a list of participants see Appendix [not reprinted here].

produced a confusing variety of arguments. Whereas "secularization" and "secularity" usually refer to the process consequent on the loss of the view of a world and history ruled by God, "secularism" signifies the conversion of this process into an ideology. But it is also possible to draw different distinctions and however this may be done, the point of reference in the distinction has always been that of the Church. "Secular", with its derivatives, is essentially a Church concept. Outweighing all these considerations, however, is the fact that the terms used in the title as formulated tend to narrow discussion to one particular aspect, namely the apparent loss of the dimension of transcendence. If discussion should really embrace the full scope of the problem, however, it must be broadened. Some participants in the consultation summed up their misgivings about linking "worship" and "secular" as follows: (a) it is impossible to use the term "secular" in the ecumenical movement in an agreed connotation; (b) the term is ambiguous and therefore open to misunderstanding; (c) it is a relative concept in so far as it is always used as an antithesis to a presumed earlier, non-secular age; (d) it raises additional problems and (e) fails to focus on the real problem.

II. How can we describe "today" in relation to worship?

The consultation was, of course, agreed that we should begin with an analysis of our present situation. Worship does not take place in a vacuum isolated from the circumstances of the day. While it may be true that Christians taking part in worship are not of this world, they do nevertheless belong to this world, no less than other men. However the nature of worship may ultimately be defined in detail, it is essential therefore to agree about the situation in which it takes place.

The consultation was also agreed that there had been an exceptional change of conditions. Admittedly opinions differed as to whether the breach was really as complete as many today were inclined to assume. It was felt that the very rapidity of the change experienced today might possibly have led some to exaggerate the extent of change in comparison with previous breaches in history. But this difference did not affect the need for a careful analysis. At all events every attempt to draw a parallel between the present crisis in worship and previous crises (e.g. the cessation of worship in the Temple after the capture of Jerusalem, or the 16th century upheaval) was treated with scepticism.

Some discovered in the changed position of the Church in and over against the world the key change for the celebration of worship. Whereas the dominant trend had long been to subordinate the reality of the world to church categories and to interpret it accordingly, the world's autonomy and coming of age is now acknowledged. Others thought reference only to this factor insufficient. There had been a radical change of values. The modern consciousness could perhaps be described in terms of the following shifts of emphasis: (a) the stressing of change rather than of the permanent and continuing; and (b) of the particular rather than of the universal; (c) the priority given to plurality rather than to unity; (d) the stress on the relativity of all judgements and statements over against the absolute; (e) the view of conditions of the world not as given but as modifiable and, therefore, (f) of man primarily not as one who is at the mercy of these conditions but rather as one who may be held responsible for actively shaping them. All these shifts of emphasis, it was held, are universal in character. Just as previous values had been shared by all, so today these shifts cut right across all systems and ideologies however different these might be in other respects.

It was generally agreed that the main difficulty was the lack of any reference to the divine in contemporary culture and its consequent inability to provide worship with an environment to support it as a matter of course. Reference to the transcendent Other, a reference which seems absolutely essential to worship, is felt to be something alien. Within this environment worship seems, at least at first sight, outmoded and anti-quated. The cultural forms used in worship stem from a past age.

The question at once arises, however, as to the extent to which this evaluation can claim universal validity. The variety of situations has already been mentioned. Clearly we must reckon with different presuppositions depending on confessional and cultural factors. Even in the technological world of the West these presuppositions are not everywhere the same. The problem does not, for example, present itself in the same way in the United States as it does in the Soviet Union, and still less in Asia and Africa. It is also important not to regard the shifts, which we think we can discern, as being already completed. The altered dimensions do not abolish the past. Most people continue to carry the past within themselves even when they overtly advocate new dimensions and the question regarding what reality must still be attributed to the abandoned dimensions cannot at all be regarded as already settled. In general, it is an open question how far these changes represent a movement which sooner or later will equally embrace all parts of the world. Are peoples for whom there seems to be no breach with cultural forms to be regarded merely as ghettos which will sooner or later be assimilated? Or do they not perhaps bear the seeds of a future which is *sui generis* and therefore does not accord with the situation in the civilizations which are for the moment historically the most powerful? It is clearly not a question here of an alternative. The majority of the participants were inclined to regard the present process as in principle irreversible and all-embracing, while admitting that little could be said concerning the strength of retarding factors and the speed of the process. On the other hand, of course, the importance of constant respect for the openness of history was repeatedly stressed. Absolute judgements may be the fruit not so much of genuine insight as of the messianic pretensions of some specific experience of the present situation.

III. Is it possible in the present situation to worship meaningfully?

How we answer this question will depend largely on how we assess the change which has come about. Many do not put the question in this form at all. They do not believe that there has been any fundamental change. As in the past so in future, worship must be celebrated, they say, essentially in the traditional form it has acquired in history. Forms and formulas may, of course, be changed. No tradition is a static and unchangeable entity. Worship itself, however, is not called in question. Although this attitude may represent accurately the position of large sections of many Churches, the dominant view among the participants in the consultation was that the question as to the essential meaning of worship could not be avoided. The answers given in the course of discussion may be grouped as follows:

1. Although worship in its traditional form is called in question, worship itself is not. In facing up to the modern world, the Church is compelled to re-open the question of the real nature of worship. In doing so it discovers that many apparently essential elements in worship are in fact the results of distortions in the course of historical development. Forms of worship which were possible and even necessary responses to

the Gospel in a particular situation have been absolutized and declared to be the only proper response for all times. It is generally recognized today that the forms of worship are historically conditioned. From this standpoint, the crisis of worship can be regarded as indicator of a process of purification making it possible to reaffirm the true nature of worship. So, for example, by its very nature, worship far from being a "stepping out of the world" can be understood as a recognition and contemplation of the world in its creaturely and historical givenness. Therefore those elements of worship which promote an authentic relation to reality, such as intercession, offertory, experience of active fellowship and so on, are to be emphasized. "Worship is a function of life. There is no way to God which leaves out our fellowmen. Worship is faith, action, suffering."

2. Others regard the tension as being much more serious. The changes taking place put a question mark against prayer and worship as such. If worship is to have any meaning at all, there must be a radical reorientation. Mere adjustment is not enough. "The doors dividing a museum of antiquities from the secular world can either be closed or passed through. But no one can stay for long on the threshold". Thoughts of the kind expressed by Harvey Cox in *The Secular City*, while they may be popular for a time, are ultimately unsatisfactory. We cannot simply modify worship; it must be completely reconstructed on different principles. This is a demand which certainly cannot be met for the present, so long as orientation in the new world is still incomplete. What then is required? The present is a time of seeking and waiting and can only be lived authentically and with integrity if uncertainty is accepted. One way of describing the dilemma was as follows: In the last resort the Christian can only choose between "the ghetto and the desert". He can retreat into an artificially preserved "subculture", within which worship remains meaningful. Or he is compelled to recognize that there are no real bridges to the present world and its culture; he then finds himself in the "desert" with his knowledge, and perhaps even his doubts, of the ultimate relevance of God. The desert is the place of wandering among tormenting ambiguities, in which the Christian searches for new ways of relating to the transcendent, supported only by his hope in something yet to be revealed. There he may perhaps celebrate worship with individuals or with groups, always with the hope of new insights, as yet still unfulfilled.

3. Others begin with the question whether we have not magnified the changes which have taken place as given factors to be reckoned with in a positive sense. That changes have taken place and that worship must take them into account — this is not denied. But, they say, faith can never reckon on being confirmed by its environment; it is always action "when hope seems hopeless". It is therefore not surprising that worship find itself in conflict with the cultural forms of the present time. Tolerant agreement would be even greater cause for alarm. This applies especially to prayer. Prayer has at no time been a matter of course, except when understood simply as a religious exercise which satisfies man's "religious instinct" and not as prayer in Christ. Prayer is the cry of faith to God through Christ against the forces of unbelief. Attempts to reorientate worship radically fail to take seriously enough the reality of God. The full force of the possibility of unbelief and disobedience is not seen. Worship, in one of its intentions, is to be celebrated as a sign of rebellion against the fact that modern society seems to have lost its openness towards God. At this point the Church should not lose its nerve. Above all it must not be afraid of ostracism and suffering.

4. Others, finally, believe that worship is challenged from two sides. A far-reaching change has taken place. A reorientation is needed. Worship must find its appropriate position between two opposing views of the world. On the one side, there is the view that the divine spiritual world is superior to this world, as the upper sphere, its task is to control the lower sphere. On the other side, as a reaction against this view which has prevailed for so long there is the view that the independence and autonomy of the world and of history must be respected. Time and space are seen as primary and not as secondary reality. The Christian faith is not at home with this alternative. Indeed its basis is that in Christ God entered into the world and history. Worship celebrates this event and with it, therefore, the removal or indeed the irrelevance of this apparently insoluble contradiction. It sets its face against both "sacral heteronomy" and "profane autonomy". Its basis is "theandric autonomy".

IV. Where is the starting point for renewal of worship?

The participants in the consultation gave no agreed answer to this question. Some suggested that the biblical witness must provide the starting point for our reflection. Renewal would be achieved by a fresh questioning of the Church's tradition and, within this tradition, of the Old and New Testament. One of the groups adopted this method; it discussed certain aspects of worship, such as authority, fellowship, eucharist, on biblical principles and tried from this basis to illuminate what worship today is or might be. But there were many objections raised against this method. Even though the relevance of Scripture was not questioned and the ultimate importance of the scriptural witness was acknowledged, the objectors expressed fear lest overhasty deductions from Scripture hinder us from facing up to the present reality with sufficient clarity. The existing situation cannot be postulated on the authority of biblical or even church-historical considerations, but should be grasped as it presents itself. To start from the biblical witness and church tradition, in particular, from liturgical tradition, could lead to "dogmatism, loss of touch with the present world" and, above all, to an "antiquarian" and ultimately, fruitless refurbishing of supposedly original forms. Although most participants favoured the renewal of sacramental practice, individual voices urged that even baptism and eucharist need not be regarded *automatically* as settled forms of Christian worship. The first and most important consideration should be the experience of the present generation. Where in our modern world do acts of worship take place? Only when this has been considered can it be profitable to study Holy Scripture afresh.

Of the three groups the one which adopted this method listed moments in human life which approximate to acts of worship insofar as they are expressive of mutual human dedication: common involvement in the struggle for social justice; eating and drinking together; discussion in genuine search of truth; shared silence, and so on. On the basis of these observations, they concluded that genuine worship has the following characteristics: mutual openness and candour, silence, festivity, the spirit of common sharing, freedom for spontaneous expression, restoration of human integrity, commitment, atmosphere of astonishment, physical activity, etc. Obviously these characteristics are not all equally important nor need they find a place in every act of worship. The purpose of the list is rather to show that worship has a basis in the life of modern man and must be fashioned accordingly. The "cultural bridges" can be found if we examine carefully where *de facto* acts of worship take place in modern life.

The ensuing discussion made it clear that the two methods of putting the question are not mutually exclusive. Good reasons can be put forth for both methods. Since faith is related to a definite historical event, we can only understand the nature of specifically Christian worship by considering the biblical witness. To divorce our thinking about worship from the specifically Christian historical roots is bound to result in vague generalizations. The tradition is in fact operative even when we imagine ourselves to be free from it. The selection and listing of contemporary acts to which the description worship can be applied will always be more or less determined by our traditional categories. How for example did the special significance of eating and drinking come to be included, if not in fact because it was suggested by the tradition of the eucharistic meal? The biblical and historical facts therefore remain necessary matter for discussion. But can worship really be connected to what is existentially meaningful for modern man if we do not consistently take actual experience as the point of departure? Is worship not otherwise in danger of becoming a form imposed on men rather than something in which they feel the meaning of their life expressed? This question is by itself enough to indicate the validity of the second method of inquiry. Most participants stressed the need for the broadest possible scope of inquiry.

Even though the two methods of approach can be thought of as complementary, they must not be harmonized. Depending on which side is stressed, a completely different view of worship can be present. Is the Church's worship based on God's revelation in history, supremely in Christ? Or are we to think of worship primarily as a universal human phenomenon? Is it a matter of investigating the way in which men participate in this historical reality and in doing so celebrate worship? Or do we have to start from a religious capacity for adoration inherent in man, which is subsequently to be filled out with the substance of the Gospel? Again and again in the conference this antithesis emerged. While one group maintained that Christ is the constitutive centre of worship and that the problem of worship is simply that of finding the appropriate expression of this fact today, both in form and in content, the other group began by attempting to define worship in general terms. For example, we might define worship as that which gives expression and reality to fellowship and makes visible a relation to that which is of ultimate concern for men. It is characteristic of this view that it adds the following qualification to this definition: "For Christians, that which is of ultimate concern has its centre in Christ". Obviously considerable differences are bound to arise in the attempt to define this universal human capacity for adoration more precisely.

In the course of discussion it was constantly pointed out that worship cannot simply be equated with what takes place in the Churches. Both, among Christians and avowed non-Christians, genuine worship has always taken place in all kinds of situations. Worship must be looked at in this wider sense. The present crisis clearly enhances the importance of this assertion. To many, worship in its traditional form has become something alien. But even if they are no longer churchgoers, this does not mean that they are indifferent to worship as such. Those who stand at the fringe of formal worship may be of special importance for the future.

V. Reforms are needed

However the individual participants in the consultation may have interpreted the present age, they were unanimous about the need for reforms in worship. They differed in the expectations they attached to reform. Whereas some saw it as the sole possibility of solving the crisis, others were unable to pitch their expectations so high. All they could expect from reforms was provisional solutions which certainly ought not to be discarded but whose importance was not to be exaggerated either. No one denied the need for reform, not even those who expressed anxiety that reforms might cover up the deepest questions facing theology and the Church.

The following were the most important suggestions made regarding the renewal of worship:

1. Worship must not be divorced from the world. It must include an expression of responsibility for the world. Worship can only fulfil its function when it consciously takes place in the world. If worship is confined to adoration of God, then in fact the world is not proclaimed as God's creation but tends to become an autonomous sphere closed to God. But worship must make it possible to see God as Lord of history. It is important, therefore, that those elements in worship which express solidarity with the world around us should be given full weight. Worship is service for the world and prayer must, so to speak, be engaged in "with our eyes open". The resistance to mentioning mundane things in worship must be overcome. For example, it was suggested that the offertory and collection should be given a more prominent place in the service. The central importance of the intercessions was emphasized. But above all, the need was emphasized to bring out the connection between explicit acts of worship and worship in daily tasks.

2. Worship must make *koinonia* possible to a far greater degree than hitherto. The participants in worship should not come together in order to pray as individuals; they must "come into contact with each other, and get to know one another. In the name of Jesus they must also be together, bodily and materially, as brothers with a definite goal". Worship must be ordered in such a way as to make fellowship a matter of experience. This is not to say that worship be a "warm togetherness created by bonhomie and easy informality". Fellowship in the sense of *koinonia* makes exacting claims and it is in many ways easier to "worship" if one can remain an individual and not be exposed to these demands of fellowship. But if worship today is to be authentic, fellowship must be made a reality.

Real fellowship can only come about if people stand together in the presence of a third party. *Koinonia* is at once fellowship with God and fellowship with men. Ultimately men do not encounter each other by their own seeking. They stand together before a third party and worship must therefore make this presence evident. A form of worship in which one was only aware of other men would not in fact create fellowship.

3. The question about the third party in worship at once raises the question of authority. The consultation was agreed that authoritarian forms of worship must be abandoned. "Man is accustomed to act for himself." But he cannot do so in worship. He feels that he is being manipulated in a certain way. He takes part in pre-arranged forms he has done nothing to create and to which he cannot contribute anything. What confronts him is an institution; he is subjected to a claim which he views sceptically because he is accustomed to recognize as authoritative only what is capable of convincing him. His thinking is not hierarchical, from above downwards, but from below upwards. This changed attitude lends weight also to the insistence on the need to make fellowship a reality. The presence of the third party should not, therefore, find expression only in static traditional forms, regarded today as authoritarian. It must take

a new form, it must become unmistakeably visible as confronting *all* and acknowledged by *all*. In this connection it was stressed, for example, that responsibility must not rest with an individual vested with authority in the matter but increasingly with the congregation itself. Active participation by all must be the aim. More attention must be given to the element of dialogue, not just in the sermon but in every part of worship. Meeting together must allow the possibility of interchange of ideas.

4. One of the major functions of worship has always been to provide man with a sense of security, to enable him to come to terms with the uncertainties of the world in which he finds himself. In the past man's sense of security has focused upon what he assumed was stable and unchanging. He found a continuity between the past, the present and the future. God himself was unchangeable. Now that man begins to see God as the God of change, as a dynamic presence in the midst of a continually evolving cosmos, he must ask himself seriously whether his security does not lie in change rather than in some imagined unchangeable past which can simply be projected into the future. Man must learn to live with relativity. He must find his security in the midst of change rather than apart from it. This requires a new way of thinking about God and a major reorientation of worship.

5. Worship must become more spontaneous, or, as one group put it, more creative. This means, in the first place, that the participants in worship should be able to feel that they are not just carrying out a set piece, but within certain limits, sharing in its creation. But spontaneity means more than this. Worship must use symbols which are rooted in the experience of modern man and which give immediate expression to what is to be expressed. This is not to say that all symbolic actions no longer rooted in daily life have to be abandoned. Spontaneity means, rather, that fresh links are constantly being forged between worship in its more or less fixed forms and human experience. One of the participants in the conference spoke in this context of the new importance of liturgical "rubrics". Hitherto these "rubrics" were provided to indicate how the main text (the "nigrics", so to speak) was to be performed. But the relation between "nigrics" and "rubrics" must now be changed. What is said must be verified by convincing actions. The new rubrics must be marked by spontaneity, intellectual and ethical integrity, by a drive towards concrete expression and so on. Orthopraxis is not the mere repetition of an action but creativity.

6. Worship is not a self-contained act. It is aimed at the non-believer and is missionary in character. The consultation did not go thoroughly into what this orientation implied for the ordering of worship in detail. It was, however, repeatedly suggested that there should be a clear separation between the celebration of worship by the committed and the service intended explicitly as a missionary activity. The traditional worship service tries to a large extent to fulfil both functions simultaneously. It assumes a congregation of committed Christians but has constantly to be adapted to a wider circle. But the forms are not designed for this and collapse under the strain. In a period when in many places the entire population could be considered as belonging to the Church, this tension was not so apparent but today the Church is increasingly a diaspora almost everywhere and has to learn to live as a little flock without however turning into a ghetto. Worship must, therefore, take a different pattern according to the function it has at any given time. Whereas at one time there is need to give full expression to the claims of the Gospel and common devotion to common tasks, at another time worship must be propaedeutic in character; again and

again the way to the Gospel must be cleared. We can perhaps illustrate the problem here by reference to the eucharist. In theology and in liturgical practice the insight has in recent years increasingly gained ground that insufficient emphasis has been placed on the Lord's Supper as a sign of real brotherly fellowship.

But if a congregation of some established Church concludes from this that the Lord's Supper must be celebrated more often and in the form of a common meal, a false situation arises. The newly recognized purpose of the sacramental sign cannot in fact come to full fruition in this way. Its true context can only be that of genuine commitment. The Church can learn much, *mutatis mutandis*, from the distinction made in the ancient Church between the liturgy of the catechumens and the eucharist. Precisely because it took seriously the obligation arising from baptism and restricted participation in the eucharist to the baptized, the ancient Church was able to be in a special way effectively missionary and open towards the world.

The emphasis on the missionary character of worship raises even larger questions. Does this emphasis not touch on the very nature of worship? Has worship not too often been understood as the adoration of an unchanging God? Does not the very nature of worship change therefore if God is seen as carrying out his own mission in the world? Worship must then be understood as participation in God's activity. It was felt that this aspect needed to be further pursued.

7. Worship services broadcast by radio and television present a special problem. What opportunities do the mass media offer in this respect? Are they capable of communicating the reality of worship or of creating fellowship in worship? Or can they fulfil a different function for worship? How are these services — if they can be called services at all — related to ordinary services of worship? The consultation could only deal cursorily with these problems. But they are of the greatest importance for the ordering of worship, especially if we remember that, in those countries where the Churches are able to use the mass media, more people participate in these services than in any others. The problems raised by the mass media are far from solution. It is at least clear that services on the mass media are services of a special kind. Services which take place in one place and then are transmitted elsewhere change their character. Account has to be taken both of the medium employed and of the situation of the receiver. If the mass media are used for worship, therefore, attention must be paid to their special possibilities. The service must be created with the listener or viewer in mind. The mass media can exercise a far-reaching influence and are, precisely for this reason, indirectly means of establishing fellowship. But they have nothing to do with concrete fellowship and can therefore be said to fulfil only a preparatory function. The connection with concrete Christian fellowship urgently needs clarification.

VI. The crisis of worship cannot be solved by reforms

Although the consultation agreed that reforms were urgently needed, there were constant warnings not to expect too much merely from changed forms of worship. In the first place there were many sharp criticisms of efforts merely to make traditional elements of worship more accessible to modern man. These efforts did not have the desired success. They may make it possible for Christians who were wavering in their allegiance to continue participating in worship. Liturgical reform has often amounted merely to rehabilitating the older and the most ancient forms of worship. Although this has sometimes demonstrated the surprising relevance of certain old forms — we think, for example, of the *agape* — the method of repristination as a rule does not produce forms which are suitable for today. One group distinguished, therefore, between liturgical reform and liturgical creativity. Creativity is really open for what is new. It too has its dangers, of course. Creativity can lead to arbitrariness. It can endanger the really necessary continuity of the Church as well as its unity. It can lose sight of the content of the Gospel and become the slave of aesthetic impressions and other passing fashions. Creative ordering of worship must start from Christ as the really New and continue to be rooted in Him (new in the sense not of *neos*, but of *kainos*). On this assumption worship can only be renewed by creativity.

Many, however, went beyond considerations such as these. They asked whether there really was so radical a difference between traditional worship and modernizing worship. Are not both of these in the same state of unbridgeable tension vis-à-vis the modern world? Indeed, is it not actually easier to celebrate an admittedly traditional service which lays no claim to modernity? To attempt to worship in forms suited to the modern world only serves to sharpen the problem. The participant can no longer use his historical awareness as a basis for taking part in what is happening. He is expressly addressed as a man of today and is thereby exposed to all kinds of difficulties in understanding. It may well be, therefore, that the traditional service, despite its strangeness, can more effectively communicate what is meant, even though of course it cannot continue to be effective indefinitely. Many mentioned here with a certain irony those helpless reforms which are content to pass mechanically from "Latin to the vernacular, from the impressive to the simple, from the pulpit to the table, from Gregorian to jazz, from the sacred to the profane, from the clergy to the laity, from sanctuaries to houses and so on." The result is often that what previously was in its way consistent becomes incoherent.

Whatever the arguments for and against, there was complete agreement that it was no longer possible to conceal the deepest problems raised by the crisis of worship. The Church must address itself to these problems. Some of them were mentioned in the course of the discussions:

1. It is inevitable that reflections upon worship ultimately lead to the question of God. What does it mean today to say "God" in the setting of the Christian tradition? The differences which emerged in the course of the consultation were in part connected with the fact that different answers are given to this question. But it is perhaps still more important that in relation to worship this question is hardly ever raised theologically, but is nevertheless present existentially. Until we seek to clear up this point, our discussion of worship has no sound basis. One aspect of this clarification is investigation into the relationship between the reality pointed to by the term "God" and man's worship. What is the content of worship? Is the experience of God the experience which is or which must be made in worship? Or is the experience of worship nourished from still other sources?

2. Discussion of worship again and again comes up against the question of the relationship between "this" world and the world "to come", between this-worldliness and transcendence. Worship ultimately only makes sense if it is related to a third party of some kind and the worshipper is delivered from self-sufficiency. How are we to understand this relationship today? How are we to speak about the kingdom of God, the world to come, and in connection with these, about death? The question cannot be

solved simply by taking the fullest possible account of "existential this-worldliness" in worship. Otherwise the question will only reappear unanswered in other places.

3. Closely connected with the questions already mentioned, the problem arises as to how we can once again acquire valid symbols. The collapse of symbolic language was frequently mentioned. There is a crisis of symbols, not symbols in the sense of signs but in the sense of natural and encompassing expressions of reality. The proof of this is that most symbols now need explanations. This crisis is not only the consequence of changed cosmological views but of an anthropological mutation. Are there genuine symbols then? What role have psychology and psychoanalysis in this context? And above all, can we expect to find universally valid symbols? The fact that men are increasingly included in one and the same history points to the need. But do such symbols accord with the particular historical origin of the Christian faith? In this respect, how are the particular and the universal related?

VII. Conclusions for the ecumenical movement

The differences which emerged in the consultation were not primarily confessional in character. The dividing lines in the discussion were not identical with the lines dividing the confessional traditions. On the contrary, discussion centered on questions arising from the situation today and presenting themselves to the members of the conference irrespective of confessional loyalties. This does not mean that confessional traditions have ceased to be important. They are particularly important for ordering the newly-arising problems. Undoubtedly support for this or that approach mentioned in this report will have been influenced by confessional presuppositions. But the consultation makes clear above all that the question of worship today is drawing Christians of different traditions together into a questioning and questing fellowship.

Hitherto the ecumenical discussion has been concerned primarily with the ways of worship in the different traditions. It was assumed — consciously or unconsciously — that the act of prayer is the same in all traditions. This assumption made it possible for Christians to join in common prayer despite their differences. This is largely the basis of the Week of Prayer for Unity. The ecumenical discussion was sustained by the hope that this basic agreement would make it possible to overcome differences or so to relate them to each other that they would no longer have to be regarded as divisive. But the consultation showed that the ecumenical discussion has to reach back beyond this assumption. Not to question common prayer; on the contrary, but certainly to face up to the questions which surround prayer and worship today. The different options open here must explicitly become topics in ecumenical discussion. Even if the saying, *lex orandi lex credendi*, may be open to question, it nevertheless surely contains an element of truth, and it is vital that the ecumenical discussion should press on to where decisions pregnant for the future are beginning to emerge.

This new approach to the question is both a fresh opportunity and a fresh task for the ecumenical movement. Christians of different traditions will find themselves on the one hand in closer fellowship, but on the other hand in new conflicts. They are discovering that the problem of unity suddenly presents itself in a new way. One member of the consultation spoke of three groups appearing in the discussion on worship: those who presuppose God, the Gospel, the Church as given certainties and live their faith on this basis; those who set their faces against every security in order to be able to be really open and questioning; and those who consider uncertainty as the genuine expression of faith and are determined to experience this uncertainty to the full. Another member of the consultation declared his allegiance to this third group in these words: "We are they who are one with modern man in his loss of the sense of God in the traditional sense; we are they who are one with modern man in his confusion of doubt; we are they who dare to believe that we are therefore one with the Christ who had not yet passed the gate of death when he said, My God! My God! Why hast thou forsaken me? We are they whose existence is a living death, whose intellectual activity is itself a form of crucifixion..."

The lines could also be drawn differently. In any event, new groupings are appearing and the conflicts which potentially divide them from one another are so great that they can only be held together by the passionate expectation of the New which God wills to do and will indeed do. But it was this passion which was a feature of the whole consultation.

DOCUMENT IV.7

SPIRIT, ORDER AND ORGANIZATION (1971)

Introduction

One of the projects of the Commission on Faith and Order in the period from 1964-1967 was the planning of a study under the title "Spirit, Order and Organization". The work done during these years was considered to be preparatory for the study itself, which was envisaged for another period of about four years. The supervisory committee of the study had decided that the project should not be undertaken unless sufficient funds could be secured. As a matter of fact, no funds could be made available. Rather than altering the programme and scope of the study it was therefore decided to summarize its results, giving the circumstances of its origin and pointing out some of its implications for present discussions and similar ecumenical study efforts.

In the formulation of its theme the study anticipated problems which only today are beginning to receive attention. Their solution would have been easier perhaps if the study on "Spirit, Order and Organization" could have been carried through. To place this report in the right perspective some of these problem areas may be mentioned:

1. We witness today a profound crisis of human institutions. The values which served as ordering principles for human life in society in the past have lost much of their validity. More and more the Churches are drawn into this upheaval and efforts towards Christian unity appear in a new light. Far from being settled the old questions of continuity and change, of unity and diversity or plurality are forced upon us with new urgency.

2. The sudden proliferation of ecumenical activities on the local level, the emergence of numerous action-groups and of underground-church movements turns the former theoretical problem of "order" into a very real one: What are the elements which make the Church the Church? What is the centre of the identity of the Christian community?

3. The emergence and growth of Independent Churches in Africa, of Pentecostal Churches and of Pentecostalism within the established Churches could point to some deficiency of traditional Roman Catholicism and Protestantism. Theology and practice of these Churches has to a large extent neglected the Holy Spirit, except for some standard affirmations about his continuing presence. This negligence which has deep roots in the tradition of the Western Churches becomes apparent today as a consequence of the growing participation of the Orthodox Churches in the ecumenical movement and in confrontation with Pentecostalism. More than ever before it is necessary today that we give serious attention to the question of the relationship between the Holy Spirit and the Church and its mission. The Report of Section I of Uppsala has served to open new lines which have to be followed up.

4. In its methodological approach the study makes it quite clear that theological reflection in this area cannot any longer be pursued in the manner of "doctrinal deduction". But even though it is stated again and again that the traditional deductive method has to be complemented by an inductive and interdisciplinary approach, not much progress has been made as yet towards clarifying the methodological steps which this new approach could follow. The Zagorsk Consultation on "Theological

Issues in Church and Society" (March 1968) has formulated the problem and the needs quite clearly, but we are still far from a satisfactory solution.[1]

The following report will keep these present questions in mind and will return to them in a concluding section. At many places the report will refer to documents which were written in connection with the study.[2]

I. Background and starting point

The study arose out of a specific situation in the work of the Faith and Order Commission.

1. The earliest roots of this study go back to a preparatory document for the Second World Conference on Faith and Order, Edinburgh 1937, with the title: The Non-Theological Factors in the Making and Unmaking of Church Union.[3] The questions of union and division of the Churches were the dominating themes of that early approach. From a later perspective one may question the way in which the problem was defined and especially the justification of the term "non-theological" factors. But this document introduced a question into the work of Faith and Order which today has become of central concern. It took some time until this first impulse came to fruition. After several preliminary discussions a document was prepared for the Third World Conference on Faith and Order, Lund 1952, with the title: Social and Cultural Factors in Church Divisions.[4] It was the Lund Conference which included these concerns in the Constitution of the Commission (see paragraph 4 b). The document mentioned above was widely circulated. It finally led in 1955 to the establishment of a joint commission of theologians, sociologists and historians which was asked to study institutionalism as one of these factors.[5] The commission concluded its work in 1961 by publishing a report on "Institutionalism and Unity"[6] which was then submitted to the Fourth World Conference on Faith and Order in Montreal 1963. In addition a symposium-volume was prepared containing some theoretical papers and case-studies which had developed in connection with the work of the commission.[7]

2. A further significant aspect in the background of the study on "Spirit, Order and Organization" was the fact that the North American Conference on Faith and Order (Oberlin 1957) paid considerable attention to the institutional dimension of the Church.[8] It is in this connection that the polarity between order and organization was first introduced into the discussion. One of the sixteen study-groups which had prepared the conference (the Toronto group) had formulated a report on the theme of "order and organization" which then was incorporated into the conference-report. The conference recommended that theological study in the area of order and organizations should be continued.[9] This recommendation led in 1962 to the formation of a study-commission under the auspices of the National Council of Churches which worked on

---

[1] Cf. *Study Encounter* IV, 2, 1968.

[2] For papers up to Fall 1965 see *Concept* X, Nov. 1965, WCC, Geneva.

[3] Faith and Order Papers, Old Series No. 84.

[4] Cf. Faith and Order Papers, New Series No. 10; see also Lund Report, pp.174-203.

[5] Faith and Order Papers, New Series No. 22, p.11.

[6] Cf. *The Old and the New in the Church*, SCM Press, London 1961, pp.52ff.

[7] Cf. *Institutionalism and Church Unity*, Association Press, New York, 1963.

[8] Cf. the official report *The Nature of the Unity We Seek*, Division II, pp.206 ff., esp. sect. 8, pp.229-236; see also the address by Dean Muelder on "Institutionalism in Relation to Unity and Disunity", *ibid.*, pp.90-102.

[9] Cf. report, p.211.

these questions until 1967. The commission struggled with the conceptual problems posed by the title of the study in much the same way as the WCC study did later. No official report was issued but some of the papers and research documents which emerged from the study were published separately.[10]

3. Mention should be made in this connection of the unity statement of the New Delhi Assembly and its importance for the perspective and approach of this study, especially the passage that the unity "is being made visible as all... are brought by the Holy Spirit into one fully committed fellowship".[11] The New Delhi Assembly is also important in another respect: It was here that the most influential and controversial study on the "Missionary Structure of the Congregation" was inaugurated; this study was connected with a renewed emphasis on mission as a fundamental dimension of the Church. The study on the Missionary Structure and the one on Spirit, Order and Organization covered similar problems, though from different perspectives, and they employed similar methodological approaches.[12]

4. These different roots merged and finally led to the proposal at the Aarhus meeting of the Faith and Order Commission (1964) to start a study under the title "Spirit, Order and Organization".[13] The proposal takes its clue from the unity statement of New Delhi as quoted above and it says that " this understanding of the action of the Holy Spirit in guiding Christians towards unity is important and needs to be fully explored in the light of the biblical and historical doctrine of the Spirit" (p.58). The Spirit, on the one hand, is recognized as "the source of continuity in the life of the Church"; on the other hand "the Spirit as judging and transforming power is to be discerned... in changes...". Some understand the workings of the Spirit as establishing and maintaining the order of the Church, others connect them more with personal, spontaneous experiences. These differences call for investigation. The Commission further recommended that a start be made in this study from an empirical analysis of actual situations in the world and in the Churches, rather than with a deduction from doctrinal principles. Following the New Delhi emphasis on the local Church the Commission proposed to study the status and function of the local Church in terms of "church order". Further the ecclesiastical status of new groups, movements and forms of church life should be investigated and the study finally should also consider the larger structures of the life of the Church as denominations, councils, etc.

5. The proposal is mainly concerned with a new understanding of the doctrine of the Holy Spirit. But, as mentioned above, the renewed emphasis on mission was an implicit second focus for the study. "Mission, renewal, new structures of church life, and the relation between the Holy Spirit and the Church have come to the forefront in recent ecumenical discussions. A growing conviction is evident that engagement in mission in the contemporary world can and should lead to unity in faith and order. Such engagement leads to attempts to restructure ecclesiastical organizations, to

---

[10] See Gibson Winter, *Religious Identity*, Macmillan, New York 1968; Paul M. van Buren, What do we mean by an "Empirical Investigation of the Church?" in: Paul M. van Buren, *Theological Explorations*, London, SCM Press 1968, p.431f. See also the minutes of the Faith and Order committee meetings in June 1965 and January 1967.

[11] New Delhi Report, p.116.

[12] See H.J. Margull, *Mission als Strukturprinzip*, WCC, Geneva, 1965; *The Church for Others*, WCC, Geneva, 1967.

[13] *Cf. Aarhus Minutes*, Faith and Order Papers No. 44, pp.58 ff.

develop new organizational structures, and to renew and revitalize traditional organizations. These attempts involve grappling with the sociological reality of given ecclesiastical structures in order to make them more appropriate for mission in the contemporary world". [14]

II. Reflections about purpose and method

1. The study intended to set an example for a new approach to the whole problem area. Former endeavours in the area of "non-theological factors" were mainly concerned with problems of continuity and change [15] trying to isolate the factors which were preventing or supporting church union. The study on "Spirit, Order and Organization" from the very beginning shared, as has been pointed out, the impulse towards missionary renewal of the Churches. "The basic conviction underlying the proposal for this study is that in allowing ourselves to be led by the Holy Spirit in the contemporary world we shall discover that our forms of church life change. It is the conviction that responsible and obedient engagement in mission may not only lead to change but to deeper unity. It is based on the hope that in obedience in one area we may find fruit growing in others; that mission can and should lead to unity." [16]

The emphasis on mission had implications for the understanding of "order". Both in the North American and in the WCC study-group on Order and Organization it was strongly felt that any conception of an essential order in the Church could no longer be interpreted in "static" or "a-historical" terms, but that order had to be understood as functionally related to the particular historical situation. Contrary to the view that some timeless order provides the criterion for the ever changing expressions of the life of the Church, the hypothesis underlying this approach was that "order" itself is an expression of the Church's response to the calling of God through his Spirit. In order to learn how "order" actually functions in church life it seemed best to investigate how Churches respond to the demand for change in face of situations where the mission is felt to be at stake.

The purpose of the study comes to clearer expression in the fact that "organization" replaced "institution" as the leading concept. [17] In the former study the basic reference of institution had been to continuity, whereas organization is a thoroughly dynamic concept presupposing change as necessary. In addition, the concept of organization avoids the conceptual difficulties which arise when the attempt is made to define institution in empirical terms. The advantage of the change from "institutionalism" to "organization" may be summed up in this way (following Mady A. Thung).

a) Organization allows for the distinction between consciously planned and unconscious processes of institutionalization;

b) Organization, seen as a process of goal-oriented action, introduces the element of "orientation to a common purpose";

c) Organization takes account of the "informal and unorganized processes" that accompany all formal order. It thus avoids the identification between church life and church order;

---

[14] Report of the first consultation, August 1965, *cf. Concept* X, p.9.

[15] Cf. *Institutionalism and Church Unity, op. cit.*, pp.28-30,38 *et al.*

[16] *Concept* X, p. 11.

[17] See the mimeographed paper by Mady A. Thung, "From Institutionalism to Organisation" (1966) for a full evaluation of this transition.

d) Organization leads to a functional understanding of formal order as being subservient to purpose. It brings to awareness the frustrating potential in all formal order.

By connecting the question of organizational renewal of the Church with the other one about the working of the Holy Spirit the study introduced a further new dimension into the reflections. "Ultimately our aim is a broader and deeper understanding of the doctrine of the Holy Spirit and the doctrine of the Church".[18] But in what terms could one speak at all about the working of the Holy Spirit? The Aarhus recommendation had listed some of the antagonisms in the understanding of the Holy Spirit[19] but at the same time had underlined the necessity to start from empirical investigation instead of deduction from doctrinal principles. And if the Holy Spirit indeed signifies in an inclusive way God's present action in the Church and in the world, did not then the very doctrine of the Holy Spirit demand that a study of the working of the Holy Spirit start from the empirical end? During the first consultation in connection with this study someone put it this way: The Holy Spirit is God at his most empirical.[20] This conviction served as a central point of reference for the further deliberations and it led to some important methodological consequences.

2. The demand for empirical study, mentioned already in the Aarhus statement, implied that work should be carried out on an interdisciplinary basis and the discipline of sociology was selected as the specific counterpart of theology in this endeavour. This is an evident choice where the problems of organization and structure of the Church are at stake. The study did not, however, restrict itself to sociological analysis exclusively. Empirical findings resulting from historical investigation were given full attention. It was the stated intention of the study to develop ways of cooperation and dialogue in which the partners could fully express themselves. Until then, it was the impression of the participants, empirical sciences had more or less been dominated by theology in interdisciplinary exchange and it seemed necessary, therefore, to give full attention to their insights.

The study reflects the feeling that this empirical interdisciplinary approach represents a "new way of doing theology". The idea certainly was not new; the study on institutionalism was planned on an interdisciplinary and to some extent empirical basis and also the study on the Missionary Structure of the Congregation had adopted this approach in a very pronounced way. Nevertheless, the conviction of the participants in the "Spirit, Order and Organization" study seems justified — they had embarked on a new way of doing theology. For together with the related study in the USA it was the first ecumenical study in this area which seriously tried to reflect upon its methodological procedure. Meanwhile the approach has become widely accepted, but it may be questioned whether much progress has been made in the clarification of basic methodological presuppositions.

If the study was to proceed with a consciously reflected method it had to take some stand in the long debate concerning the relationship between theology and sociology as sciences. The preceeding discussions under the auspices of Faith and Order had largely been determined by the distinction between theological and non-theological factors. This distinction originally was a reflection of the experience that achievement of union between Churches depended not only on the overcoming of doctrinal differences.

---

[18] *Concept* X, p. 7.
[19] *Aarhus Minutes,* p.58, para. 4.
[20] See *Concept* X, p.7.

More and more one had to realize that social, psychological, political and organizational factors had a strong influence of these processes. But this distinction became increasingly questionable the more the insight was accepted that Churches as a whole are social bodies and that even doctrine is to a certain extent a reflection of specific social and political conditions in which a Church finds itself. One could not any longer proceed on the assumption that while investigating the Church as a social phenomenon some aspects are impenetrable for empirical study and exclusively reserved for the theological analysis and reflection.

In the study it was made clear from the very beginning that the distinction between theological and non-theological factors or areas of investigation had to be abandoned. [21] The difference between sociology and theology was interpreted as a difference of perspective, orientation or interest, rather than as a distinction between different objects of research. Sociologists and theologians do in fact talk about the same empirical phenomenon, the Church as a "body" in society, but they proceed on different presuppositions and ask different questions. This fundamental assumption was not understood as being destructive of the independence of theology. "The entire basis of independent theological examination is rather the realization that all statements of theology are insights derived from the reality of Christ". [22] The mode of cooperation between sociology and theology was interpreted as interaction: Sociology was to formulate on its own terms and as clearly as possible those questions and problems which are put to the Church from the present situation in society. But one was equally aware of the fact that independent and thorough theological reflection was needed in order to secure that the interpretation of empirical data would lead to meaningful theological questions. For not everything that lends itself to sociological analysis by the same fact already has theological significance. But on the basic assumption that God through his Spirit is already at work in the events in Church and world, that the Holy Spirit is God at his most empirical, one could hope that by sociological, empirical study one would eventually arrive at points where the theologian believes that action of the Spirit is encountered. Here, then, a theological interpretation of phenomena and a theological answer to questions arising from the situation would seem appropriate.

It is evident that in this delicate field of interaction between sociology and theology certain precautions are necessary in order to make sure that both partners of the dialogue do in fact continue to speak about the same phenomenon. First of all this is a question of language, of terminology. Secondly, it involves the selection of areas of investigation that are meaningful to both. In the following remarks these two points will be elaborated a little further.

One of the paramount difficulties of any interdisciplinary work is the difference of language between the disciplines. Language defines a certain field of experience. Each language represents a certain interpretation of the world. This is also true for the special languages of scientific disciplines. But there are various overlappings between these special languages since any one of them must, ideally at least, be retranslatable into the common language of the everyday world. The difference in language between sociology and theology is apparent. Where this difference (which only reflects the

---

[21] See papers by H. ten Doornkaat Koolman, *Concept* X, p.52 and by Mady A. Thung, *op. cit.*, pp.4-5.
[22] H. ten Doornkaat Koolman in: *Concept* X, p.52.

difference in perspective) is neglected there follows a misleading usurpation of concepts which necessarily take on a new meaning in the new context. Even though the concept has remained the same the whole system of reference has changed. Interdisciplinary work, therefore, has to face up to the necessity of continuously translating and interpreting the concepts used. The present study, being aware of this demand, tried to develop a number of working definitions of the main concepts like order, organization, institution, institutionalization. The purpose of these working-definitions was to formulate in a preliminary way the common understanding of these concepts; they were to serve as principal keys to translation and thus they should secure that both partners would indeed speak of the same empirical phenomena. This certainly represents an improvement compared to a certain terminological confusion in earlier studies. It was, however, understood that these working definitions were of a preliminary nature and that they would have to be changed in the course of the work to retain their communicative and translating function.

The whole approach reveals some of the theoretical assumptions about the relationship between theology and sociology which stood behind the study. The major theoretical clue came from an essay by Prof. H. Schelsky where he suggested that theology and sociology should mainly try to arrive at "statements of parallel meaning" *(sinnparallele Aussagen)* and that careful analysis was necessary to discover those areas where such statements are possible.[23]

The second demand upon any interdisciplinary work is the selection of meaningful and relevant areas of investigation, i.e. in our case the selection of such phenomena connected with the social reality of the Church which lend themselves to empirical sociological analysis and which at the same time justify the expectation that in the course of empirical analysis questions can be formulated which can be interpreted in theological terms and thus be transformed into meaningful theological questions. Since theological interest in this study centered around the action of the Holy Spirit and a better understanding of the relationship between the Spirit and the Church it was necessary to select such areas for investigation in which on theological grounds the action of the Spirit was to be expected most. Such a selection which narrows down the range of the investigation certainly has far-reaching consequences. It has, however, to be noted that this decision is unavoidable in any scientific work. One has to arrive at a definition of what will be regarded and recorded as relevant data. It is equally clear that this decision is based on certain presuppositions regarding the way in which the Holy Spirit presumably works. Any empirical study is biased to a certain extent but it is important to state explicitly as many of these presuppositions as is possible.

The two areas selected for investigation in this study were "protest" and "unity". To quote from the report of the first consultation: "'Protest' is understood in a very wide sense to cover any group or movement which arises within or in relation to a Church or Churches or a particular element in the life of a Church 'in protest' against features of its life or deficiencies that are believed to exist in that life. This general subject of protest has been chosen as being eventually particularly relevant to the

---

[23] Cf. his article "Religionssoziologie und Theologie" in: ZEE 1959, 3, pp.129-145, esp. pp.131-132; see also his earlier essay "Ist die Dauerreflexion institutionalisierbar? Zum Thema einer modernen Religionssoziologie" in: ZEE 1957, 4, pp. 153-174 and the reactions to it: see also Mady A. Thung, *op. cit.,* p.5.

question of the work of the Holy Spirit as protest groups in church life presumably believe that in making their protests they are being obedient to the Holy Spirit... The choice of the topic of 'unity' is sufficiently explained by the concerns and presuppositions of the ecumenical movement... We propose to make a start in this topic by concentrating on the organizational aspects of re-union, that is by studying examples of the coming-together or attempted coming together of churchly bodies."[24]

3. The participants agreed that after an initial period of clarifying concepts and terms and of defining the problem sociology should take the lead. In order to arrive at a true dialogue between theology and sociology it was necessary first of all to provide and analyse the relevant material. It was planned to work on the basis of case-studies which should include contemporary as well as historical examples. Possible case-studies were listed for the two major areas: protest and re-union. In order to make these case-studies comparable and to be able eventually to code the important data for thorough analysis the group developed a research-design or "theoretical framework for investigation". This scheme was intended to provide the individual investigators, both sociologists and historians, with some guide-lines and to pinpoint the major questions to be asked. The case-studies were to be developed along these lines. Furthermore, thought had been given to the appropriate distribution of case-studies in order to ensure that the most important or the not yet sufficiently investigated areas were covered by them.

After a preliminary analysis of the case-studies was available the study was to proceed to its second phase. Theology and its empirical counterparts should now be brought into genuine interaction, i.e. into a process of mutual questioning and answering. It was the expectation that certain questions would arise from the case-studies which would inspire theology to enter upon some complementary biblical, theological and doctrinal studies in a new and original way. Questions like the following were anticipated:[25]

a) How can the action of the Spirit be recognized and by which criteria?
b) What is the nature of "order" and to which empirical phenomena does this concept correspond?
c) How is the tension between order and organization to be interpreted and how can it be solved?
d) What is the proper relationship between the "given" presence of the Spirit in Church and world and the eschatological hope?

III. The development of the study

It is not the purpose of this section to give a detailed chronicle of the development of the study, but rather to use this study as a paradigm to show how interdisciplinary work between sociologists and theologians could be pursued, what the major problems and difficulties are that can arise on the way and where the procedure of this study could have been improved.

1. The study developed in three stages or phases which correspond closely to the three years during which the work was done. Starting from the Aarhus recommendation the *first phase* was mainly devoted to the task of agreeing upon a preliminary

---

[24] See *Concept* X, p.13.
[25] Cf. *Concept* X, pp.15-16.

definition of the purpose of the study and of the method to be followed. A first consultation in 1965 mainly served this function.[26] After three theologians from different church traditions had presented a doctrinal statement about the relationship between Spirit, Order and Organization the difficulties which had led to the recommendation of this study became vividly alive. It was apparent that these differences could not be bridged on the basis of doctrinal discussion alone. Being committed to start from the empirical end the consultation took as its primary task to come to some terminological agreement in order to define the problem in such terms that empirical investigation was possible. For this purpose the consultation developed four working definitions the function of which has already been referred to in the preceding section. They are quoted here from the consultation report.[27]

a) By the term "organization" we understand a historically given, empirically explorable social system or social group which is characterized:

i) by a certain set of goals and values

ii) by a certain set of means destined to realize the goals and values

iii) by a more or less consciously planned arrangement of i) and ii) which is called structure.

b) The theological term "order" as used in the Faith and Order discussions is not a normal or natural term in sociology. However, an attempt has been made to relate the observed theological use of this term in such discussions to normal sociological terms. It is suggested that "order" may be considered as the equivalent of those elements in the set of means which are acknowledged by the members of the organization (or by groups of members) as indispensable parts of the set of goals and values.

c) By the term "institution" we understand a pattern of collective behaviour. (This broad and simple working definition is adopted in deliberate opposition to the unreflective current use of the term in the sense of an organization, an institute, or a social structure and also against the presupposition that the term must automatically have a pejorative sense.)

d) By the term "institutionalization" we understand all those processes by which patterns of collective behaviour are established. These may range from spontaneous action at the one end to highly formalized action such as bureaucratization at the other. Any of these processes may lead to rigidity at any stage but need not necessarily do so.

2. The *second phase* again was marked by a consultation (in 1966) but not even one third of its participants had been present at the first meeting. It is not astonishing, therefore, that much of the discussion was given to a critical evaluation of the work done so far. The initial impulse came from the paper by Mady A. Thung which has already been mentioned above and a report by Walter Hollenweger about further progress in the study on the Missionary Structure of the Congregation. It became clear in the following debate that the working definitions had not yet sufficiently solved the problem of the difference in language between sociology and theology and among theologians and sociologists themselves. The difficulties centered mainly around the interpretation of the concept of "order". Some theological participants thought that the

---

[26] For the papers and a report of this consultation see *Concept* X.

[27] See *Concept* X, pp.12-13.

working definition which was adopted previously was too narrow but no satisfactory agreement could be reached.

This terminological problem is reflected in subsequent difficulties about the definition of the problem. What precisely is the problem? Is it the discrepancy between claim and reality of the Church, or is it rather the tension between the calling or the task of the Church and its present state? Can the concept and the notion of "order" simply be replaced by "calling" or "task"? How are these in turn to be defined and what are the criteria for the discernment of the task of the Church in a specific situation? Can the demand for radical renewal of the Church simply ignore the traditional *notae ecclesiae* and what is their relationship to the concept of "order"? These were some of the questions which arose in the course of this discussion.

There was agreement that a static and timeless interpretation of "order" had to be overcome but the consultation did not produce any positive consensus. The major achievement of the consultation was a significant refinement of the research-design, i.e. towards a better inter-relation between protest-movements and processes of change in organized bodies. Some examples of pertinent theological questions were given but it is quite clear that the sociologists in the group, lacking sufficient support or criticism from the side of the theologians eventually found themselves defining the problem in their own terms. To remain fair to both partners it should, however, be added that the reluctance of the theological participants to enter the debate at this stage was intentional. They had not only been assigned the function of "listeners" but they deliberately assumed this role in order to learn more about the ways of reasoning among their sociological partners. In addition, nobody expected this to be the last meeting of the study group and if it was to be the time of the sociologists at this consultation so the time for theological reflection would come.

3. After the second consultation had defined the problem as described above the necessary next step in the *third phase* was to design a *strategy* for the clarification of this problem. Several lines and ways of investigation were proposed: case-studies, a review and consequent coding of relevant literature, comparative studies, and finally a thorough comparative analysis of all the material and data collected. These reflections about strategy resulted in a new proposal for the study as it was adopted by the Commission on Faith and Order at its meeting in Bristol, August 1967. If one compares this last statement on the study with the first proposal of the Aarhus Commission meeting, a certain change of emphasis is apparent. The suggested study about the doctrine of the Holy Spirit and the relationship between the Spirit and the Church has turned into a study which "would serve to provide a contribution to the understanding of the sociology of organizations". Only in the third instance its possible theological value is described as providing "one way of gaining insight into the relationship between the Holy Spirit and the Church". The study was now divided into two parts, the main purpose of the second part being to find out how the empirical findings in the first part could best "be reflected upon theologically". Theological reflection thus had been postponed to a later stage.

An interdisciplinary study has to define its problem in terms that are meaningful not only theologically but which open up possible lines for empirical research. But the question arises at this point whether the study as proposed in this final statement was indeed an interdisciplinary study any longer. It was one among the sociological participants who questioned the approach on just these grounds. This self-criticism could even take the form of the query whether the group had not defined away to some extent what at this stage really was the principal problem, i.e. getting the problem defined. However this may be, there was a strong feeling that some theological work should go on parallel to empirical analysis in order to keep the study an interdisciplinary one. As one possibility in this direction it was suggested that the findings on ecclesiology and pneumatology in previous Faith and Order studies be reviewed and summarized so that they could be used for the present study.

A similar self-limitation of the study can be discerned in the treatment of the concept of "order". Lacking a commonly agreed statement what the theological meaning of the term was, one decided in favour of a "pragmatic" definition of meaning. The study thus limited its purpose to the investigation of the empirically observable consequences that follow from the theological use of the concept. Since the notion of order in all of its different interpretations was connected with the preservation of identity and continuity of the Church in situations of change one expected to learn something about the actual functioning of this notion by investigating the reactions of organized church bodies which are challenged by protest-group. Many protest-groups at least claim that in their protest they are obedient to the Holy Spirit. Thus one could hope to learn something about the relationship between the Holy Spirit and the Church.

IV. Results and critical evaluation

The immediate results of the study have already been discussed. They are limited and perhaps would not even warrant such a detailed report. But in science even such experiments which have failed to produce the expected results or which have produced no results at all are regarded as potentially significant. This study, to be sure, did not even enter the experimental phase because the necessary funds were lacking. But one could, nevertheless, make a "thought-experiment" and try thereby to assess the expected value of the study. Three main areas could be considered in this context; they correspond closely to the reasons for an undiminished significance of the study suggested in the introduction:

— The function of empirical research for theological reflection, especially in the field of ecclesiology.
— The usefulness of an analysis of the Church as a social unit in terms of organizational sociology and the consequences which follow from this perspective for the problem of order.
— The relationship between ecclesiology and pneumatology.

1. In its *methodological reflection* the study certainly has contributed valuable insights for similar ecumenical study projects. Its import is seen mainly in three elements:

a) The study has made evident that it is necessary for any interdisciplinary investigation to arrive at some common working definition of the principal concepts to be employed. The failure of this attempt with regard to the concept of "order" in the present study can only serve to underline this point.
b) After this study it should be impossible in ecumenical discussions to fan back into the language of "non-theological" factors. The study has at least succeeded in stating a convincing case for an interdisciplinary investigation of the Church as a social phenomenon attributing the distinction between the disciplines to a differ-

ence in perspective and interest. No part of actual church life, not even the doctrine of the Church, is closed to analysis from either perspective.

c) The study, by taking up the suggestion to work for "statements of parallel meaning", has described a possible line of co-operation and inter-action between sociology and theology. After this study it should be difficult to repeat the simple scheme of thought which assigns to sociology the task of asking the questions whereas it is the privilege of theology to provide the answers.

After this has been said, a number of critical questions could be asked and the study group itself was aware of most of them:

A certain widespread enthusiasm for empirical studies among theologians is a phenomenon that is worth some empirical study itself. Even where agreement is reached that the traditional "deductive" method in theology has to be complemented by a more "inductive" and empirical approach it is not yet clear how empirical methods can be used most fruitfully for theological reflection. Theology, it seems, would be meaningless, if it had no points of reference among empirically observable phenomena or simply no basis in experience. But what does the sentence: "The Holy Spirit is God at his most empirical" really imply for the relationship between empirical observation and theological judgement? Further, empirical data do not speak for themselves. Any empirical research is based on certain theoretical presuppositions. It operates with some theory which functions to provide critical control of the research process and which gives the principal clue for the interpretation of data. What, then, is the status of a theological interpretation of data in relation to their interpretation in the sociological context? It does not yet constitute interdisciplinary research when theologians incorporate the findings of empirical studies into their own reflections without taking account of the theoretical framework in which these findings are located.

The study group tried to arrive at "statements of parallel meaning". However, the group was unable to agree upon some statement about what in fact they were looking for when they attempted to study the action of the Holy Spirit empirically. Theological doctrine or the different doctrinal traditions of the Holy Spirit provide no clue for empirical research, unless they are interpreted and transformed into empirically meaningful hypotheses. As long as theology only operates with the vague affirmation that the Holy Spirit is God at his most empirical without further specifying his relationship to empirically observable phenomena sociology will be of no help at all. Sociological research will trace the action of the Holy Spirit just as little as it will help to solve problems of church order. The most it can do is to observe what difference it makes whether certain events are claimed as being actions of the Holy Spirit or not. Interdisciplinary work between theologians and sociologists will not be fruitful unless theologians try to interpret traditional and present doctrine in the direction of its empirical reference. Thus one would have to ask: What are the theological reasons to look for action of the Spirit in the area of protest and change rather than in the area of continuity and order? Should one look for the action of the Spirit in individual experience rather than in collective phenomena, and what are the theological reasons for either option?

2. The study has given some clues regarding the usefulness of *the concept of organization* for an analysis of the Church. To some extent it has proved the advantages of this conceptualization over against the former one which thought in terms of "institution". Meanwhile organizational sociology has been further developed

and a number of studies on political, economic and bureaucratic organizations have been published. Perhaps a further differentiation between different models of organization would be required today if research along the lines suggested in this study should be pursued. But in spite of several interesting applications of concepts from organizational sociology for the analysis of the Church,[28] the ecclesiological implications of this way of conceptualization have still to be spelled out.

In the title of the study "order" and "organization" are put alongside each other. They seem to form a new "dualism" similar to the more familiar ones between *koinonia* and institution, event and institution, invisible and visible Church. What is the significance of this new distinction in comparison with the older ones and what is the theological reason for these distinctions? With respect to the polarity between order and organization one would have to ask whether it is understood in terms of "primary order" and "secondary organization"[29] and whether this interpretation is acceptable in the light of the sociological understanding of the concept of organization. Can Churches be exhaustively analysed in terms of organization or is there something left which transcends organization? Is it only the fact that order traditionally has been interpreted unhistorically and statically which makes this category sociologically opaque? Further, what would be the theological consequence if order were interpreted functionally rather than as normative?

These are some of the questions which might have been asked if the study had been continued. Things standing as they do, it can, however, be doubted whether case-studies of protest groups and of the reactions of organized Churches to them would have arrived at any theologically meaningful results unless theological reflection at the point indicated above had been carried much further.

3. The study in its preliminary state is least satisfactory with regard to the central question which originally gave the initial impulse: i.e. *the relationship between the Holy Spirit and the Church*. Perhaps the principal reason for this failure is the fact that the doctrine of the Holy Spirit and even more the sensitivity to his active presence in the Church and the world were and still are underdeveloped in the western tradition of Christianity. The unity statement of New Delhi with its reference to the Holy Spirit anticipated a consensus which still had to be worked out. Meanwhile the report about "The Holy Spirit and the Catholicity of the Church" of Section I of the Uppsala Assembly has opened new dimensions of understanding the working of the Holy Spirit. Not only catholicity, "the quality by which the Church expresses the fullness, the integrity and the totality of her life in Christ"[30] is seen as the Spirit's gift. He is equally asserted to be the origin of a constitutive diversity in the life of the Church. For, by such diversity, which serves the calling of the Church, "the Spirit leads us forward on the way to a fully catholic mission and ministry".[31]

The question should, however, be asked — and it has been asked by some participants — whether the study did not in fact proceed on the basis of a silent and implicit assumption about the Holy Spirit and his action. In associating the Holy Spirit mainly with protest and change it has again come close to the dualism of event and

---

[28] See e.g. J. Klein, "Structural Aspects of Church Organisation", in: *International Yearbook in the Sociology of Religion*, Vol. 4, 1968, pp.101ff.

[29] Cf. *The Nature of the Unity We Seek*, p.210.

[30] Cf. *Uppsala Report*, p.13.

[31] *Ibid.*, p.13.

institution and has to some extent foreclosed the possibility of interpreting order in terms of the action of the Spirit. This procedure, which evidently is very close to the radical protestant approach to the problem, could be interpreted as betraying a certain theological bias that has not been sufficiently examined.

Moreover, any serious attempt to relate in this study the doctrine of the Holy Spirit with the doctrine of the Church would evidently have to interpret the action of the Spirit in terms of "organization". No serious attempts were undertaken in this direction which is all the more regrettable since the whole set-up of the study called for a revision of the antagonism between Protest/ Spirit and Order/Spirit. Perhaps this could have been accomplished if the doctrine of the Spirit would have been explicitly related to organization.

These critical reflections, however, show that the whole approach still is extremely important and valid and it can only be hoped that the Faith and Order Commission will not lose sight again of the questions which have been formulated in this study.

DOCUMENT IV.8

THE ECUMENICAL MOVEMENT AND CHURCH LAW (1974)

I. Why Church Law is Becoming an Ecumenical Problem

The ecumenical movement is striving for "the visible unity of the Church in the one eucharistic fellowship". Inevitably, sooner or later, this effort will raise issues of church law. The churches differ in their order and their constitution. But so far not much attention has been paid to this aspect of the search for unity.

On the whole, the ecumenical discussion on the unity of the Church has concentrated on issues of doctrine and worship as the most obvious causes for the division of the Church. With the advance of the ecumenical movement, the debate will need to include more and more constitutional and legal issues. Wherever churches consider concrete stops on the way towards the unity of the Church, they face, inevitably the question as to how their different orders can be brought closer to one another. Therefore, if the churches are to go beyond the present state of their divisions, the ecumenical movement needs to provide them with some help in dealing with the legal issues arising from their mutual encounter.

At this stage we cannot visualize the structure of legal organization of the one Church, which is the ultimate goal of the ecumenical movement. But in working towards that goal, we are faced by intermediate problems of a legal nature in the life of the various churches. When trying to solve these problems, the separate churches should be aware of their commitment to the ecumenical cause and try to work out solutions which will further or at least not hinder the process of convergence towards unity which has already started.

In order to achieve this, the ecumenical movement and especially its Commission on Faith and Order needs to make a conscious effort to help member churches in this particular field by engaging in a serious study of the legal aspects of inter-church cooperation and eventual church union. For even if the ultimate goal may still seem very distant, there are at present several features in the progress of the ecumenical movement which make it urgent to take up these kinds of questions within the framework of the Faith and Order Commission. Several factors point in that direction:

a) The growing ecumenical fellowship among the churches has made practically inoperative certain statements or rules in the various churches, e.g. condemnations, rules against contact with heretics, etc. This raises the question of the continuing validity of these statements and rules.
b) Ecumenical fellowship has led to new structures and regulations not foreseen in the traditional legal system of the different churches, e.g. representative systems which did not exist before, new financial arrangements, etc. Some churches have put explicit references in their constitution to the ecumenical movement or their membership in the World Council of Churches, National Councils or other ecumenical bodies.
c) Agreements reached in ecumenical dialogue call for juridical implementation. They may imply changes in the constitutions of the churches, e.g. references to confessions of faith, etc., or changes in the discipline of the churches, e.g. rules concerning ordination, intercelebration, intercommunion, etc.

d) When dialogue leads to closer collaboration, often new ecumenical structures come into being. What is their juridical significance? Can the competence of decision which a church has be transferred to such "para-constitutional" bodies?

e) Implementation of ecumenical agreements and common action of the churches at the international level require freedom of decision and action on the part of the individual churches. How far have the churches — especially churches in close relationship with a state — the freedom to decide as a church and to dispose of its resources in order to give priority to solidarity with the rest of the churches?

Against the background of such considerations, it is recommended that the Faith and Order Commission undertake a study of issues of church law with the aim of identifying and clarifying differences and to provide a forum where concerted action can be worked out.

II. The Underlying Issues

To raise the question of the ecumenical significance of church law is to call attention to a whole range of underlying issues which must be kept in mind. Whatever its theological position, confessional allegiance, or institutional past, every Christian community has some concrete social and legal form. It has both an inner structure of its own and occupies a "social space" acknowledged by the larger society. In some way, every Christian community relates both its internal legal structure and its external legal form to its understanding of the Gospel. The way these elements are related differs from one situation to the next. So does the way in which churches conceive of these relationships.

These considerations point to what one might quite simply call the concrete presence of God's people in history. No Christian body, whether institutionally or anti-institutionally oriented, can avoid it. To own property, to receive and pay out money, to gather as a voluntary society, to have both an internal and an external legal form. It is in fact the vehicle for worship, witness and service. It is the structure in and through which a church responds, or fails to respond, to the ecumenical challenge. Thus the practical and theological importance of "church law in the ecumenical perspective" can hardly be overstated.

Many differences in the structures and legal systems of the churches have their roots in different confessional traditions. In order to reach a full understanding of the differences, the different confessional approaches need to be analysed and adequately described. In fact, it can be argued that the confessional heritage persists most powerfully in the different ways in which the churches are constituted and perpetuate the inherited order. The differences concern not only the actual order which the churches have, but also the general orientation by which their legislation is inspired. A very careful analysis is required in this respect. No exhaustive list of the different approaches can be given here, but the importance and the weight of the confessional differences need to be underlined. There are differences even as to the role attached to law as such in the life of the Church. While the Roman Catholic Church tends to understand the Church as an institution which can be described in juridical terms, Lutheran and many Free Churches are inclined to visualize the Church as "spiritual institution" and to deal with the juridical questions at a non-theological level. While some churches have a tendency to present their legal tradition in a systematic way, others feel that the nature of the church law is betrayed by a systematic approach. They hold the view that church law must constantly arise out of the sacramental fellowship. They reject the idea of a constitution of the Church.

Obviously the question of the law of the Church and its setting in the law of the civil community is inseparable from a full panoply of cultural and sociological considerations. To focus attention on legal structures is a way of making the inquiry tangible and pointed. Law and precedent can be studied in church canons, constitutions and by-laws as well as in the record of their practical application. The same is true of civil customs and codes. Their relation to society and culture is itself an open question. Even more so the question of the underlying essence of law. But laws and their application inside and outside the church do have a practical bearing on how a church understands itself and how it behaves.

Of special importance is the *interaction* between the church's own legal structures and its civil setting. We must ask how the legal situations of the churches affect their relations to each other and, more concretely, how each particular style of interaction affects the possibilities for cooperation in the wider ecumenical community. Many examples can be given. What does financial support from the state imply? Does it simply assure the salary of clergy or also preclude the use of funds for purposes outside the nation concerned? To what extent does the Church's status as one voluntary society among others enhance freedom and limit influence? What does it mean for the ecumenical commitment of a church if it does not possess the full right of assembly and association? What role do Church institutions play (schools, hospitals, etc.)? To what extent should churches be free to receive or reject financial help from abroad?

A basic dilemma arises when Church leaders and public authorities have different views of what church structures are for. In the eyes of the state, the Church may have legal standing because it is good for public morale. Under some circumstances, the Church may be happy to play this role, even if its own perspective on the role is different. At other times, a church may find itself in opposition to an officially-backed state religion. Or the Church may play a socially affirmative role in one respect and a prophetically critical role in another. A nation's past traditions, embodied in the Church's legal position, may be invoked against public policies being followed in the present. Each legal pattern, each structure of internal church organization, offers a range of possibilities while excluding others. Each makes possible certain kinds of ecumenical participation while inhibiting others.

Societies the world over are changing rapidly. So are the roles open to churches within them. While on the one hand, new opportunities may arise, on the other hand, functions so far fulfilled may disappear. There is, for instance, a distinct possibility, especially in the Western world, that the position of voluntary associations will gradually be weakened as public administration and mass communication become more centralized and as social services become nationalized. Electronic information storage and retrieval limits personal privacy and places the affairs of voluntary associations under surveillance. Increasing religious pluralism undermines any claim the Church may have for special treatment. Institutions of every kind, governmental as well as churchly, inspire less confidence.

In such a fluid situation, we urgently need to study the range of possibilities open to the Church in different circumstances and different parts of the world. A comparative study, or typology, of existing and emerging forms of the Church in legal perspective would help us. The relation of such structures to theological self-understanding, their practical strengths and weaknesses, their kinds of responsiveness to ecumenical responsibility, could all be considered. Four fundamental questions might well underlie such a comparative survey.

1. How do the different churches conceive the *relation* between the notion of the people of God theologically considered and that people of God juridically embodied? Is this a question of the relation of church law to civil law, a question of the foundations of law as such, a matter of grace and law related or grace and law opposed? Or must the issue be formulated in some other way?

2. How do the different churches understand the content, style and functioning of their internal legal systems? How is the law applied? What role does ecumenical commitment play in these codes, written and unwritten, now? What issues are at stake as the different churches reconsider and reformulate their canons, constitutions, by-laws and guidelines?

3. Have the churches any common convictions about the sorts of relation to the civil community which best make for faithfulness to the Gospel and ecumenical responsibility to each other? Is there a trend towards "disestablishment" or is the tendency now the opposite? Is there any agreement about what "establishment" and "disestablishment" mean? Do the churches advocate the notion of the "secular state"? Do they agree what this means?

4. What do the churches see as the critical issues affecting their integrity and identity in modern societies? Do they feel that circumstances tend to force a certain identity upon them? Do they feel free to redefine and reexpress their identity as insight and circumstances demand? Are they able, in concrete terms, to affirm an ecumenical identity? How?

III. The Implications of the Ecumenical Movement for the Legal Systems of the Churches

The ecumenical movement has led to the recognition of partial communion already existing among the churches. The churches do not exist any more in isolation from the others. They recognize that the Holy Spirit has been at work in other churches. Much of their legislation does not reflect this recognition however. Each church needs, therefore, to examine itself to what extent the progress of the ecumenical movement calls for changes and revisions in its legal systems.

a) Though the ultimate goal of the ecumenical movement may still be in a distant future, each church should make clear its commitment to it. This may mean that it needs to give clear public expression to its intention to work towards this goal. This implies the willingness to adopt results reached in ecumenical discussions.

b) The ecumenical movement has led to first and partial results. Some churches have united. Some churches have found bilateral agreements which have juridical implications. Such achievements should be examined and taken into account by all churches. All achievements in the ecumenical movement have consequences for all churches.

c) Many structures of ecumenical collaboration have been created in the course of the last decades. Does church law take sufficient account of them?

d) While the ultimate goal cannot be described in full detail, there are steps imposing themselves at this stage of the ecumenical movement. Each church must ask itself whether the partial insight already gained has found expression in its constitution and legal rules.

i) Rules governing the relations with Christians of other churches (mixed marriages, common worship, etc.).

ii) Role of the whole people of God in the decision-making processes of the Church.

iii) Freedom of action which is required if the churches are to participate effectively in the universal fellowship of all churches (church-state relations, synodical structures, etc.).

iv) Each church faces the question of representation. Who speaks for the church in dialogue and ecumenical assemblies? Who is entitled to take decisions?

IV. The Next Step

It is not enough simply to state the problem. Steps must be taken to focus the attention of the churches upon it. This will not be easy. There may be in the churches, as in other institutions, a tendency to accept uncritically the prevailing juridical forms, and to resist change. Certainly the question is rarely asked whether the internal laws of a particular church, or the public or civil laws of the state in which it operates, contribute to, or hinder the progress of the ecumenical movement at the national or international level.

How can we encourage the churches to open these questions? We believe that the essential first step must be to devise a method by which individual churches can make a judgement, each upon its own situation. To pave the way for comparative studies, it is necessary for each to ask whether its legal framework is sufficiently flexible to allow the people of God to discharge their responsibilities fully in worship, witness and service not only denominationally but also ecumenically. Is a church free to act in cooperation and partnership — and, if it so desires, to go forward to organic unity — with other churches? A church must be encouraged to seek the answers to these questions by looking closely at the rules which govern its internal life — how far do these match up to the challenge of its ecumenical commitments? For example, if a church is to be represented in ecumenical bodies, does its existing constitution or juridical rules allow it to give sufficient authority to those who represent it in such bodies? In many cases there will be need to examine closely the particular relation which a church has to the state. In some cases a close relationship may be found to be of advantage to the particular church and in some measure also to the whole ecumenical cause. But in other cases a church may find itself possessed of constitutional, economic or other privileges, conferred or protected by the state, which in themselves either weaken its ability to reach out in mission and service to the wider community, or which are incompatible with the development of ecumenical cooperation. There may be in the particular juridical forms which the church has adopted — or in some parts of them — features which create obstacles to ecumenical cooperation and to the achievement of organic unity.

In opening these questions for study, the aim is not to establish everywhere a uniform juridical pattern. There are wide divergences now and we must expect wide divergences so far ahead as we can see. But no situation is static, and we believe that an increased awareness of the juridical issues may help in changing the circumstances towards a gradual convergence to exercise a prophetic ministry and to be able to respond fully to the claims of its ecumenical commitment both in the particular society and internationally. Putting the same point in another way, any church which makes changes either in its internal rules or in its public legal framework should always in future take ecumenical considerations fully into account.

Who is to suggest the method by which the churches can apply themselves to this task? We recommend that the Faith and Order Commission should establish a small committee to undertake the task. This should include theologians, legal, administrative and sociological experts with experience of different types of situations. Their first task would be to produce a working paper, which would include a series of questions to be put to the churches. We envisage that the working paper would then be circulated to member churches.

We think, however, that initially only certain selected member churches should be asked to respond. This would, in effect, constitute a pilot study. The answers from this pilot group would then be considered by the supervisory committee, giving an opportunity to check the effectiveness of the method, and allowing for modification of the questions before the churches generally were asked to participate.

It is suggested that the pilot group should include a range of situational types. Thus, taking first churches which are members of the World Council of Churches, we think that the initial list should include examples as follows:

1. A West European established national church, with the Free Churches of that country.
2. An East European Protestant church.
3. Some examples of Orthodox churches, including an East European case.
4. A range of Third World examples, illustrating:
   i) situations where Christianity is predominant,
   ii) situations where Christianity co-exists with other living faiths,
   iii) situations where the Christian Church is numerically small.
5. Some North American examples, carefully differentiated.
6. Some examples of non-structured, independent Christian movements.

We think it important that the Roman Catholic Church should fully participate in the project. We hope that some studies might be based upon Roman Catholic experience in particular countries. It will also be important to receive comments from those concerned in canon law revision and in the preparation of the Lex Fundamentalis. We see this latter comment as invaluable in making any overall judgement on Roman Catholic experience.

In sending the working paper to the churches, the Faith and Order Commission would be asking them to engage in self-criticism or, as we should prefer to say, in self-study. We expect that each church would remit the task to a group comparable with the committee appointed by the Commission. We expect that at both levels — national and international — the work will often require calls to be made upon people who are not normally drawn into consideration of the ecumenical issues, and certainly not into international ecumenical issues. We see this as an important by-product of the study which we propose.

DOCUMENT IV.9

GOD IN NATURE AND HISTORY (1967)

1. Introduction

Without any deliberate choice on his part, modern man has entered into a new experience and understanding of nature and history. For many centuries there was a general tendency to consider non-human nature as an entirely earthbound static reality, this planet being conceived as the stage for the drama of human life. In European culture, history was thought of as covering a short period of but a few thousand years, and also as a basically static reality, within which Fall, Incarnation and Consummation were seen as three incidents, of which the second and the third aimed at the restoration of a supposedly perfect beginning.

This world-view underwent a gradual disintegration in the period succeeding the Renaissance. The process speeded up about 1850. Now, since 1950, the quick destruction of its last remnants has become manifest, as it has given way to a radically new and dynamic concept of nature and history.

For modern man nature is thus no longer a static, geocentric, limited entity, but a process in an indeterminate space and an almost endless time. The earth is a tiny satellite of a little star in one of the many galaxies discovered by terrestrial telescopes. The process of development of this earth began about four billion years ago. That process went on through all kinds of events, in a chequered career, as matter, then life, and then conscious life came to be, through ever higher and more complex unities, characterized by a gradually increasing possibility of freedom — until about 2 or 1 million years ago the phenomenon of man emerged.

According to the now dominant theory of evolution, man is the product of age-long natural development, moved forward by the forces of heredity and selection. Since the days of Darwin, there has been a latent temptation to use this theory as the basis of a materialistic and monistic ideology. Science itself, in virtue of its nature and limits, refuses to make this extrapolation, yet on account of its important role in modern society, cannot help creating for countless people an atmosphere which makes them feel like elements in a powerful and irresistible evolutionary process. For some this feeling results in optimism, because they believe themselves driven towards a future of greater freedom and welfare. Others, on the contrary, fear that this freedom, as expressed in the power of nuclear fission, of keeping alive the congenitally weak, etc. will in the long run destroy the human race.

The Christian Church shares in the bewilderment created by this new experience and understanding. For centuries the Bible has been thought of as witnessing to a small geocentric and static world, governed by a wise and almighty God, whose main interest is to help man, the crown of his creation, to his eternal destiny. Now, however, man looks insignificant indeed against the background of the vast dimensions of time and space. The question must arise whether the God of the Bible has any relation to the modern scientific world-view, or has anything to say to the feelings of either optimism or pessimism which it creates in the hearts of contemporary men.

Christendom, embarrassed by these facts and questions, has often given evasive answers to this new challenge. These answers have either denied the clear facts of science (fundamentalism) or the essentials of the Christian faith (modernism), or else have tried to separate the realms of faith and of science, by limiting God's work to the inner life and to existential decision, and by denying his relations to the visible realities of nature and history (pietism, theological existentialism). We may nevertheless acknowledge with gratitude that the Christian Church in its rich tradition has preserved many precious insights which can help us in this situation.

We feel the obligation to look for such answers, and to seek a new and better mutual relationship between the Christian message and the modern view of life and of the world. In trying to accept that obligation, this paper will start from the biblical side, aiming at a fresh understanding of what the Old and the New Testaments teach about God's active presence in nature and history.

This subject is so closely connected with all the major themes of Christian faith that we shall be in constant danger of losing sight of the specific issue, unless we limit ourselves to it as strictly as possible. Our readers will in consequence miss the consideration of many problems intimately related with the subjects of our different chapters. We must keep in mind, however, that we are writing, not a treatise on Christian dogmatics as a whole, but on one specific question. We must therefore invite our readers themselves to integrate the insights given here into the whole of their Christian faith. This limitation has also its implications for the way in which, in the following chapters, we shall be reading the Bible. We are aware of the fact that in this study we approach the Bible with a specific pre-understanding which former generations did not have to the same extent. We are not ashamed of it. We believe that the biblical message comes alive in a special way when we direct our existential questions to it. The abiding truth of the Bible is manifested in its power to give relevant and decisive answers to the life-questions which every age poses to it. It does so under the condition that we are ready, if necessary, to correct and widen our questions in light of the biblical answers. Whether we are on a fruitful way with our pre-understanding must be proved by the extent to which the biblical message becomes alive and visible along the way on which we approach it. We must never forget that this is not more than one way among many others, all of which are complementary to one another. On the one hand, we cannot absolutize our approach. On the other hand, we believe that our approach is meaningful, because it is the same God who speaks in the Bible and who under the pressure of our time urges us to ask the questions expressed here. Finally, we must admit that we are aware of the limitations of our work in yet another way. This study has no pretention of being our contribution to the dialogue of the Church with modern scientific man. We are not yet prepared for that dialogue. What we have to do first is to have a conversation within the Church itself. We have to help one another to discover the relations between the biblical message and modern world-view. The modest intention of this study is to contribute to that primary and urgent task. We express the hope that it will help many to overcome in their hearts and minds the gap between their Christian faith and their expectations and embarrassments as modern men.

II. The God of History as the God of Nature

The heart of Israel's faith, as set forth in the Old Testament, was that God has made Himself known in some special decisive events of history. This was a radically new idea and experience in the world of religions. For the primitive and ancient religions of the Middle East, God or the gods are mainly revealed in nature. Nature is the external aspect of divine reality. God is as nature is — blessing and harming, ambiguous, capricious. And history is primarily a part of nature, partaking in the same divine natural reality, obeying the same laws as the seasons, the stars and the weather.

Through Moses, Israel encountered this God of history. She met Him at that great turning-point in her story when she was rescued from her life in Egypt, the "house of bondage". This new God was nameless. He called Himself "I am I". This meant a refusal to give a name by which He could be conjured. It meant at the same time a strong promise: you will experience My presence as you need it; "I shall be with you in the way in which I shall be with you". This God goes before his people through the desert, leading the way to the future, to the promised land. This does not mean that his way is always evident to the faithful. Mostly his guidance and purposes are hidden. "Thy footprints were unseen" (Ps. 77:19). Time and again, however, when his people in disobedience and distress need it, He speaks in judgment and in grace through the events of history. Then Israel sees anew, repentant and encouraged, her way ahead through history. And she knows that this same God in a hidden way is the Lord of all history, both of Israel's and also of that of all the nations.

History for Israel was no longer a part of nature. Unlike nature, it is directed towards a goal. This goal is higher and wider than Israel itself. It embraces all the nations. The history of Israel is the preparation for a universal history, for in Israel "all the families of the earth will be blessed" (Gen. 12:3).

In worshipping a God of history, Israel inevitably developed an attitude to history different from that of religions of the nations around; but her attitude to nature was also different. In earlier stages, the encounter with God again and again took place in phenomena of nature (burning bush, Mount Sinai), but always so that the revelation in these phenomena pointed to God's purpose in history. In a later stage, nature loses this role. More and more history becomes the vehicle of revelation. Therefore the old nature-feasts which Israel inherited from her neighbours, the feast of unleavened bread, the feast of the first-fruits and the feast of booths, were in the course of Israel's history turned into memorial feasts of God's historical deeds (cf. Ex. 23:14-17 with Deut. 16:1-17). Nature is not so much the realm where God is revealed to man, as the realm in which man, created in God's image, has to realize God's purpose for his creation (Gen. 1:26-30). This does not imply that Israel had a negative attitude towards nature. On the contrary, she believed and confessed that the God of history is also the last secret of nature. God is one, and his creation is one. History and nature therefore are governed by the same will. When history is believed to be the realm of the covenant God, and the way towards his kingdom, then nature also must serve Him and his goal. The whole earth responds to his glory (Is. 6), and the fertility of the promised land is the expression of his covenant-love. So the creation of nature is conceived of as the opening act of history. In the ancient religions, history is naturalized; in Israel nature is historicized. In her scriptures, particularly in the Psalms, nature plays a great role, but almost without exception in connection with God's acts in history and his covenant with Israel, to which nature also bears witness and responds (cf. Psalms 19, 29, 65, 67, 74, 75, 89, 96, 104, 136, 147 and 148). After God's character in his historical deeds is discovered, this character can also be discerned and these deeds seen prefigured in the processes of nature, and nature can be invested with the same grace as history discloses. The order of nature can now be interpreted as a prefiguration, on the one hand, and a confirmation, on the other, of God's steadfast truth and loyalty towards his people (cf. Is. 42:5f., Jer. 31:35-37).

Thus for Israel, history came first in the order of knowledge. Israel experienced God's deliverance at the Red Sea and trusted Him as her covenant God long before her prophets and teachers formulated a clear understanding of God as creator of heaven and earth. One of the first of such formulations appears in the second creation story (Gen. 2:4b-25), where nature in general, and the Garden of Eden in particular, are the stage-setting of human history, with its challenges and failures. Through her further historical experiences, not least through the tragedy of the exile, Israel learned more deeply that if her God were to be trusted at all, he must be a God who completely controls the world. The second Isaiah in particular confesses this belief with impressive eloquence. For him, God's work in creation is the presupposition and reflection of his redeeming work in history (Is. 40:21ff., 42:5ff., 44:24ff., 45:12f., 51:9f.). In the same period, the writer of Gen. 1 delineated creation as the week-long opening phase of the history of mankind and of Israel. History and creation were thus joined together in Israel's faith in God and her commitment to serve Him alone.

It is also clear that history cannot be an end in itself, but must have an end beyond itself. God's creative and redemptive work will not be complete until all the powers of darkness are definitely brought beneath the rule of the God who wants the whole earth to be full of the glory of his covenant. So creation is the beginning of a chain in which nature, history and consummation are inseparable links. This continuum can be seen in its true character and unity, however, only from the middle of God's revelatory deeds in history, whence both a backward and a forward look are possible.

A good illustration of this faith is Psalm 75. It starts with the praise of God's "wondrous deeds" in history. Then the poet hears God say that He maintains and continues in history the work which He began in creation: "It is I who keep steady the pillars of the earth", even "when the earth totters and all its inhabitants". This conviction fills the poet with boldness. He now turns to God's enemies and reminds them of God's sovereignty over history. "It is God who executes judgment, putting down one and lifting up another". The poet looks forward to the moment when "all the wicked of the earth" shall be defeated. Then the promise of creation, of the God who makes steady the pillars of his earth, will be completely fulfilled.

So Israel believed in the ultimate significance of her historical encounter with God; she believed that in this encounter the final reality was disclosed, and that this reality is the key to the understanding of all things, in nature and history, from creation to consummation.

III. Christ, the Agent of Redemption and Creation

The New Testament witnesses to the fact that in the life, death and resurrection of Jesus Christ, God has finally reconciled the world to Himself. The event of Jesus Christ is thus a new disclosure event, in which all the meaning of past disclosure events is gathered up, the human situation is exposed in all its potentiality for good and evil, and the final achievement of God's purpose for the world affirmed beyond all that evil and mortality can do to frustrate it. This Christ-event surpasses previous disclosure events (such as the Exodus) for the following reasons:

a) The Christ-event is both the confirmation and the turning-point of the covenant-relation. Jesus Christ is both the fulfilment of God's action in wrath and grace, and the true covenant-partner, who acts vicariously on behalf of his people, in his life, teaching and sacrifice.

b) In his resurrection and in the outpouring of his Spirit, the great eschatological future is anticipated. Consequent upon these events, the Church comes into being, and the message of the radical justification of the godless and of the renewal of life is proclaimed.

c) The finality of this event is shown in the wiping out of the boundaries between the Chosen People and the nations, and in the spreading of the Gospel and the growth of the Church over all the earth, as the foretaste of the Kingdom in accordance with the eschatological expectancy of the prophets.

This involves a complex relationship between the Christ-event and the preceding revelations, a relationship which can be set out only under several heads — parallelism, cohesion and confirmation, as well as renewal, deepening and surpassing, and at times even contradiction. It is important to see how the framework of the unity of creation, nature, history and consummation is maintained, and how at the same time this whole concept is deepened and elaborated through the experience of God's incomparable action in history in Jesus Christ. The same order will here be taken as in chapter 2, that of history, creation and consummation. The specific application of all this to the problems of nature will follow in a later chapter.

The deepest driving powers of *history* are revealed in the double event of cross and resurrection. The witnesses see history as the battlefield of God with the powers of guilt and destruction. They see his rescuing initiative, as well as human resistance and rebellion. They see how God seemingly yields to this rebellion, but in reality uses it and gears it to his redemptive purpose. They see how God overcomes the resistance and makes grace and life triumph over sin and death. From this centre and perspective the witnesses look back to the history of Israel, which they see as a continuous struggle between the covenant-God and his resistant people (Matt. 21:33-39, Acts 7:1-53, Rom. 7:7ff.), and to the history of the nations, which they regard as being governed by the patience of God (Acts 14:16, 17:30, Rom. 3:25f.) but subjected to the consequences of Adam's sin (Rom. 5) and to "the elemental spirits of the universe" (Gal. 4:3). At the same time, the witnesses look forward and see future history, under the influence of the Gospel, as a continuous and increasingly wide and intense display of the mystery of the cross and resurrection, of the struggle between the powers of the Spirit and powers of darkness, and of the final victory of Christ's kingdom (II Thess. 2, the Book of Revelation). New Testament scholars have pointed to the analogy and connection between the Passion-story and the eschatological passages (Mark 13, at the opening of the Passion-story) and to the parallels between christological and eschatological events (persecution, darkening of the sun, appearance of the Son of Man, resurrection).

To take seriously the final events in Christ, must also mean that he is confessed as the ultimate secret of *creation*. The key to the understanding of history must at the same time be the key to the understanding of creation, since both are essentially one. This confession of Christ as the agent of creation is found in a particularly articulated form in three traditions, in John 1, Col. 1 and Heb. 1. All these passages make use of expressions borrowed from the popular Hellenistic philosophy of their time (probably in its turn influenced by Jewish Wisdom-speculations) about an intermediary hypostasis between the Most High God and the created world. Without interruption, however, they pass from the work in creation to the work in history (cf. Col. 1:17f. and Heb. 1:3). In John it is almost impossible to say where the one ends and the other begins. In all these passages both actions are ascribed to the same Person, called the Word (John), the Son (Hebrews), the Son of His Love (Colossians). Moreover in all these passages the main emphasis is on the historical work of the revelation of God's glory (John), of atonement and restoration (Colossians), and of purification for sins (Hebrews). Apparently this historical work is considered as the consequence and completion of his creative work. Compared with similar passages in Hellenistic philosophy, these authors are not interested in a separate Logos-substance in creation and nature. They point to history as the only realm where the secret of creation is revealed and fulfilled. On the other hand, we must also say that what is revealed in history is no unrelated incident, but the realization of a condition which had been God's purpose from the very beginning. The crucified and risen Jesus of Nazareth is the key to the understanding of the meaning of the whole created world. One should notice the way in which Colossians plays with the word "first" (15c, 17a, 18b; a play unfortunately obscured in various translations). This close connection of what God meant in creation and what he accomplished in Christ was expressed by these writers, using contemporary patterns of thought, in the confession that the world was created in and through Jesus Christ. God's creation of the first Adam was effected with the last Adam in view, and the latter had to complete creation and to rescue the world from its incompleteness and estrangement. Just as in the Old Testament creation is described in terms of the Exodus (God's deliverance from chaos, darkness and flood), so in the New Testament it is described as the first revelation of Christ, the new man, the true image of God.

Here arises an old argument in Christian theology, concerning the motives of the Incarnation. Most classical theologians believed that the only motive was God's purpose to rescue a sinful and lost mankind. They saw the Incarnation as the great emergency-measure by which God decided to bring the world back to its original perfection. A minority, however, maintained that Christ is more than that, that he is also the crown of creation, the new man for which creation has been waiting from the beginning (Antiochene School, Duns Scotus, several forms of liberal theology, Barth). The consequence drawn is that Christ would have come anyway, apart from the fall and sin. The question was usually treated in this form. This is an unhappy way of posing the question, because it presupposes something unreal. Nevertheless, when a choice has to be made, the decision has to be in favour of the second doctrine, because the first cannot give a satisfactory explanation of the three passages in the New Testament which deal with Jesus Christ as mediator of creation.

All this leads also to a renewed concept of the *consummation*. For Israel the future is the crown of history, as the victory of Yahweh over all the rebellious powers and the elevation of Israel as the centre of the nations. In the New Testament we find basically the same approach to eschatology: the future is seen as the complete and radical display of God's victorious work in history. To those who had witnessed the resurrected Jesus, the outpouring of the Spirit and the beginning of the world-wide mission, the consummation could be nothing other than the glorious revelation of this Jesus, a world-wide resurrection, the judgment of all men according to their attitude towards his first appearance, and the ordering and renewal of the world according to his new humanity. That is what the New Testament confesses, nothing less, nothing more. "We are God's children now; it does not yet appear what we shall be, but we know that when he appears, we shall be like him, for we shall see him as he is" (I John 3:2).

Both the doctrine of Jesus as the agent of creation and what is traditionally called the doctrine of his "second" coming (though he was never absent; he also came in the Spirit!) point to the finality of his historical appearance as disclosing the ultimate meaning of the whole indivisible process of creation, nature and history.

The consequence of all that has been said is that *consummation is a far higher work than creation*, far more than only the restoration of an original situation. If it were that — as traditional conservative theology presents it — history would in the end be conceived of as not more than a circular movement (paradise lost and paradise regained), not essentially different from the concept in naturalistic cultures. Christ is, however, the new man who leads the process of history to its ultimate goal. Genesis 2 does not picture a perfect state but a point of departure. Rev. 20 and 21 do not present a repetition of the Garden of Eden, but a city, symbol of culture. In this context particular attention should be paid to the passage I Cor. 15:44b-49; here Christ is compared, not with the fallen Adam (as is often supposed), but with the first created Adam, who is "from the earth, a man of dust"; the latter is nothing but "a living being", far surpassed by the last Adam, since he comes "from heaven" and is "a life-giving spirit". The old adamic humanity was the starting-point of history; a new pneumatic humanity, built around the new man, the resurrected Christ, is the goal of history. At the same time, with regard to John 1, Col. 1 and Heb. 1, it must be said that the last Adam is the original one, meant and implied in the creation of the first. All this gives us the image of one great movement from lower to higher, going through estrangement and crises, but also through atonement and salvation, and so directed towards its ultimate goal, a glorified humanity, in full communion with God, of which goal the risen Christ is the guarantee and the first-fruits.

IV. "Nature", "Creation", "World", "The Universe", "History"

Before these biblical insights can be elaborated and applied, terminology must first be clarified. The word *nature* has already been used several times, connoting the totality of non-human reality. This use of the word has no equivalent in Scriptures — for two reasons: 1) It makes a separation between man and this reality, which surrounds and bears him, and of which he himself also partakes; yet such a separation is unknown in biblical thinking. 2) This word in its Latin and also in its Greek meanings *(natura, phusis)* suggests something centred in itself, with an immanent origin and growth; dependence on the Creator God cannot be expressed by it.

The New Testament, instead of nature, uses the word *creation (ktisis)* and even more the verb *create*, which includes the notions that are missing from "nature", as can clearly be seen in Rom. 8:18-25, where creation includes both man and non-human nature (the popular interpretation that Paul thinks mainly of the sufferings of animals and the disasters of nature presupposes a modern romantic concept, which is absent in Paul; man is primarily meant, and non-human nature is included in his fate). According to those passages, creation is entirely in the hand of the Creator God; it goes through a history of groaning and longing, until in the end it partakes of the glorious liberty of the children of God. In the Old Testament even the word "creation" is absent. There such expressions are found as "heaven and earth", "the earth", "all that lives", "all things". A predilection is shown for this last word in the Epistle to the Ephesians, where *ta panta* is often translated as *the universe*. This translation could mislead us into thinking mainly of outer space, planets and galaxies. The main emphasis lies on our well-known earthly and human realities. The *earth (eretz)* in the Old Testament often means the nations, as over against Israel. The same may be the case in Ephesians, where so much emphasis is laid on the unity between Israel and the Gentiles. "The universe" does not at any rate point to cosmic speculations, but to an earthly human historic process (see Eph. 1:9-14). We must, however, also say that the use of the word *ta panta* in a world of cosmological speculations implies that this historic process has its consequences also for the non-human world.

The word *world (kosmos)* has a similar meaning. It is used especially by Paul and John, sometimes in a neutral way, but even then in the sense of "human world". For the most part it expresses man's rebellion against God and God's saving love for this rebellious world.

This terminology supports what has been already stated: the unity of non-human and human reality, the emphasis on man's place in God's creation, the unity of creation and redemption and the historical connotation of all the words used. The world is a creation, never without relation to the Creator God. Man is the junction, where all the lines between God and his earthly creation come together. The world view is geocentric, not because the existence of other beings is denied (think of the angels!), but because revelation is addressed to man, and man bears no responsibility except for his own world.

The word *nature* will continue to be used in this paper, because it would seem impossible to abolish it from ordinary speech. Modern man is accustomed to making a stricter distinction between human and non-human reality than does the Bible. In itself this is not objectionable. Such a distinction can help to illuminate the Christian message concerning this realm of reality. Nevertheless, it must not be forgotten that this reality does not subsist in itself, but exists because of God's continuous preservation, and that it is regarded as being the stage-setting for the history of God's dealings with mankind.

The word *history* has different meanings. It can be the name for all that happened in the past; or for the records and the study of the past; or for the total field of human responsibility, for man's acting as a subject, as well as for the results of these actions. In this study, the word indicates mainly the totality of human events in past, present and future, as governed by God and directed towards his goal.

V. The Biblical and the Modern World-View

Deepened understanding of the world of biblical speech, and an ever more sophisticated understanding of the nature and self-limitation of scientific speech, make it possible in our time for faith and natural science to begin a quite fresh conversation about our understanding of the world. This is so for the following reasons:

a) Creation is the first history, and nature is part of this prehistory. The word "generations" *(toledoth)* is used in Genesis not only for the succession of human generations, but also for the history of creation: "These are the generations of the heavens and the earth when they were created" (Gen. 2: 4). Both Israel and modern science have a radically historicized conception of creation and nature.

b) Creation and nature are prehistory, directed towards man. Man is rooted in this prehistory. At the same time this history comes in man to a new decisive phase.

c) According to this, creation as the opening act of history is not complete. When we read that "God saw that it was (very) good" (Gen. 1), we should understand the word "good" in the sense not of being perfect, but of being fit and suitable for its function, for the goal it has to serve — in this case, for the history of God and man, for which it has to serve as a stagesetting.

d) God reveals Himself through his words and deeds in history. Looking back from this work of God, man can recognize also in his stagesetting work some traces of his being (e.g. his majesty, his power, his inscrutability).

e) The process of God's creative work has not yet come to an end. New developments are still to be expected. Living in a great historical process means looking constantly forward, believing in an open future.

Now the question arises: supposing all this is true, why then did it remain hidden for so long? Why did the Church so strongly resist the historicizing of nature in modern evolutionary theories? Why was the Church, which by her preaching led the ancient world out of a naturalistic life-concept into God's history, so reluctant to draw the consequences of her own convictions? Why did she cling for so many centuries to a static, unhistorical concept of life?

The reason is that for centuries the Church in Western Europe not *only* preached the Christian message, but also saw it as her duty to preserve and develop the Graeco-Roman scientific heritage, embodied in works such as those of Ptolemy of Alexandria. This was a heritage of static conceptions about nature and history. The Christian message was thus framed in a static world-concept, which was handed down with the same ecclesiastical authority. Since the Enlightenment, this concept has been attacked. Both attackers and defenders have seen the attack as an assault upon Christianity. This misunderstanding could easily arise and be maintained, because the attack often used mechanistic and deterministic categories unsuitable for the Christian faith, whereas Christians tried to refute it on the basis of a literal acceptance of the creation narrative in Genesis. So in the nineteenth century, one was urged to make an unnecessary choice between a static Christian conception of creation and history and the modern idea of evolution. This situation lasted until the middle of this century, when the conviction gained ground on both sides that the alternative was a false one.

This does not mean that the Christian faith can identify itself with the modern world-view. Science is a specialized range of techniques, applied to the study of defined ranges of phenomena and problems by persons specially trained for this work. Some believe that science suggests a more general world outlook applicable to the whole of human life; but such suggested "scientific" world outlooks are lacking in the vigour and precision of science itself. Moreover, science frequently finds itself unable to make assertions on a higher level, such as assertions of purpose, goal or meaning, about the phenomena which it describes. Scientists who sometimes try to make such assertions appear to assume the role of philosophers and theologians, and have to accept criticism by the procedures of philosophy and theology. Christians believe that some such higher level assertions have to be made, and that these higher level assertions must take account of the encounter with God in history, centred in Jesus Christ.

Thus Christian faith is not identical with modern science or any world-view claiming to depend upon it. But it is deeply indebted to modern science, because the scientific approach and its results have compelled Christians to re-examine their convictions and to free their faith from elements which, though long supposed to be integral to the Christian message, are now seen not to be so. Christians should therefore be grateful for the way in which God has used science to clarify and deepen the insights of faith. The growth of science has elements in common with, or parallel to, the assertions of faith in its growth of consciousness against the background of the ancient world-views. The next chapters will elaborate these biblical insights along different lines.

VI. Nature and Man

The full marvel of human existence in the midst of nature is perhaps best indicated by the fact that two almost contradictory statements are equally true. Now as never before, man has it in his power through technology to assume responsibility for nature, and to release himself from the supposedly inherent limitations nature has imposed on him. Yet it is equally true that today, as never before, we recognize the abiding continuity of man, even in his most spiritual activities, with the energy particles and the behavioural mechanisms that constitute material and animal nature. Christians, reflecting on God's presence in nature and history, must take into account the astonishing fact that our condition is equally well described in both ways. Therefore the following elements may be mentioned:

1. *Man is part of nature*. This is not only the thesis of a materialistic world-view, but of the Bible as well (cf. Gen. 2:7, I Cor. 15:47). One should particularly notice the structure of Genesis 1, where creation is recounted as a single history, proceeding from lower to higher realities and crowned by the appearance of man. This, of course, is not identical with the evolutionary causalistic conception. Here is no immanent process, but a God who acts. Nevertheless there is more analogy here than between Gen. 1 and the older static view about the world. In Gen. 1 man is rooted in nature. According to Genesis 2 his first companions are the animals. This line of thought in the Bible reminds one of the thinking of men like Marx, Darwin and Freud, who strongly reacted against the way in which philosophical idealism had detached man from nature. Until recently, Christian anthropology has leaned upon idealism and spiritualism in a way which finds no support in biblical thinking. And now man is in danger of surrendering himself to a kind of existentialism which, not unlike idealism, or even more than that, detaches him from nature and one-sidedly stresses his standing over against nature. It should not be forgotten that even the most specifically human characteristics, like mobility, freedom and consciousness, have a foreshadowing and analogy in non-human nature.

2. *Man is nurtured by nature*. According to Genesis, man is given plants and trees, and later on even animals, for his food. Without nature man cannot exist; and not only so, but nature nurtures man in many other aspects of his life. It offers him aesthetic delight, meditation, companionship (esp. the animals), consolation, and inspiration (poets and painters). In times of inner crisis, nature helps man to come to himself. Man today lives in a culture in which he is in danger of underestimating this highly important role of nature in human life. Nature has become so much his servant that he

forgets that she is also his sister. His desire for holiday-camps does not really help him, nor his modern vacation techniques in general. These aim more at transporting his daily conveniences to other, and often crowded, spots, rather than at making possible a deep and quiet encounter with nature. Here the Church should not only lift her finger warningly, but also help our short-sighted generations to a new experience of the beneficient riches of our sister nature.

To this end, Christians should support all those responsible for nature conservation in various countries in their long-standing struggle against the pollution of air and water, in their demand for an afforestation which counteracts the denudation and erosion of vast regions, and in their plea for a policy of habitation which takes into consideration the much endangered biological balance of many areas. What these groups claim for biological reasons, the Church has to support for basic theological reasons.

3. *Man is threatened and challenged by nature*. Nature is ambiguous. She is man's mother and his enemy. She brings forth thorns and thistles. Hers are the hurricanes, the floods, the droughts, the earthquakes, the famines, the abortions. When man does not resist nature, she can swallow and suffocate him.

4. *Man is made by nature*. By compelling man to offer resistance, nature makes man into what he should be — more than a part of nature: a controller of nature; the only being who refuses "to take life as it is"; an inventor, a fighter, a builder. This leads us on to recognize that

5. *Man guides and transforms nature*. This is an unparalleled event in the age-long history of evolution: the product becomes the leader. Since the appearance of man, nature has become more and more domesticated. Her own unconscious ends are now submitted to man's conscious planning. This is the great turn that can be observed in the history of evolution. We now live more and more in an unnatural nature, reshaped by man, a world of concrete and plastic, of parks and medicines.

6. *Man is the master of nature*. When Gen. 1:27 says that God created man in his own image, the whole passage 1:26-28 makes it clear that what is mainly thought of is man's dominion over nature. As God is the Lord over his whole creation, so He elects man as his representative to exercise this lordship in God's name over the lower creation. This was an unprecedented insight in the ancient world. As long as man believed nature to be the external manifestation of divine powers, he was more or less doomed to passivity. Every deeper change in the course of nature was an act of Promethean recklessness. That is why the primitive and ancient cultures in general limited themselves to cattle-raising and agriculture; and even these were surrounded by magical practices in order to propitiate the envious gods. According to Genesis 1 and Psalm 8, God stands no longer on the side of nature over against man, but on the side of man over against nature. Man is encouraged and even instructed by God to dominate the world.

7. *Nature's meaning surpasses man's understanding*. God has also his own relation with nature. The pedestrian way in which the Enlightenment tried to prove that all phenomena in nature are there for man and for man only, has served to prove just the opposite. The very fact that so many phenomena are meaningless and incomprehensible to man, is extremely meaningful, in so far as it teaches him the limits of his knowledge and task. That is the way in which nature appears in the mighty chapters 38-41 of Job. The abundancy and inexhaustibility, the absurdities and irrationalities of

nature (i.e. what man calls so, from his limited viewpoint) reflect, in their own way, the majesty and inscrutability of the Creator.

Finally, this conception of man's relation to nature excludes two others:

a) The conception which sees man as essentially an "outsider" in the world, through the fact that he is the bearer of "existence". In that case man's existential attitude is the only thing which counts; nature and history are meaningless. This radical separation between existence and the world in which it is grounded is, in our conviction, incompatible both with biblical faith and with modern science. Man's existence is embedded in nature. Lower and higher form a unity. Body and soul belong together. An artificial isolation of existence impoverishes man's faith and makes his life in the world ghostly.

b) The conception which sees man almost exclusively as a product of nature, to the extent of biologizing man and naturalizing history. Out of the process of evolution a unique phenomenon emerges, which brings a decisive turn, and not only continues evolution, but also takes the load. Moreover man makes life risky by his freedom, which he can use in different ways. This is an entirely new element, and forbids the view that man is only a continuation of nature.

VII. Nature, Man, Sin and Tragedy

The use of the word "sin", and even more the use of the word "fall", suggests an interruption, a disruption, and discontinuity in the great nature-history process to which many are unable to give a place in their thinking. This attitude may be due to a mythological conception of sin and fall, but is in itself unnecessary. To begin with, evolution in nature is a road full of risks, detours, frustrations and deadlocks. It has nothing to do with a mechanistic, smooth and straightforward causality. The reality which is the outcome of this process is, statistically speaking, of the highest improbability. At no stage was there the slightest guarantee that the way of natural development would go steadily upwards. It did not need so to do, nor did it do so. Now that it is possible to look back, however, this road can be seen to be a way towards ever more complicated, higher, and more mobile entities. The highest level is reached with man as a being endowed with freedom. Here nature stops acting merely spontaneously and unconsciously. In the phenomenon of man, nature starts to act consciously and responsibly. In that very fact the terrible possibility of sin is given. This is, however, the reverse side of the possibility of acting freely and responsibly. This open possibility is one of the greatest steps forward in the evolutionary process. This does not imply a naturalization of sin. Sin is not natural. Man's nature as distinct from lower nature means that man is no longer bound to act merely naturally. He can transcend his nature in either the right or the wrong direction. When he does the latter, he acts "unnaturally", he becomes guilty. There is no excuse for guilt. The possibility of becoming guilty is however man's high privilege, the counterpart of his being created in the image of God. Genesis 2 and 3 belong together. Their togetherness does not mean a temporal succession. At the same time, these chapters are distinct from one another, indicating that sin is not a logical consequence of creation, but something unnatural. At the same time, we have to face the fact that this misuse of freedom is far more than an accident; it is an enigmatic distortion of our created nature.

There is yet a second and even more serious reason to see a cleavage between the biblical and the modern world-view on this point. That is the way in which sin, according to the Bible, affects human and non-human nature, by introducing evil and suffering, thorns and thistles, and human death. Passages like Genesis 3 and Romans 5 give the impression of a "fallen creation". In modern scientific thinking, however, there is no place for the conception that an alteration and deterioration took place in man's physical nature, and in the biological world around him, as a consequence of his culpability. According to our experience, death is inherent in all life. Strife and suffering belong to nature. Floods and earthquakes are part of the same reality to which majestic mountains and fertile valleys belong. In Scripture, an identifiable connection between sin and suffering is sometimes definitely denied (Job, Luke 13:1-5, John 9:3), but more often it is strongly posited. In the latter case, the biblical writers — basing themselves on the world-view, and using the common mythological language, of their time — tried to express something which is as near to modern man as it was to them: the unity of man and nature and of soul and body, and the decisive role which man plays in the process of nature. Man, who is in fact sinful man, on the one hand is rooted in nature and, on the other hand, transforms nature. He lives in three relations: as child of God, as his neighbour's partner, and as master of nature. If one relation is distorted, it also affects the others. When man, as the master of nature, fails to put his mastery to the service of God and of his neighbour, he denies the true purpose of his dominion, and thereby harms nature. Again, when man does not feel himself sheltered in the Fatherhood of God over his life, nature becomes to him a threat and an enemy. What Genesis 3 expressed in terms of substance (nature under a curse) is better expressed today in terms of relation. This applies to human death also. Death in itself is natural. But there is no such thing as "death-in-itself", only the death of this or that kind of being. Man is not nature. It is his nature to transcend his nature. So his death is not natural, but personal, existential. It differs widely from animal death. It is the end of a life of responsibility and guilt. Man by the very fact of his transcendence of nature, rebels against death. To him it is more than a fate. As soon as man is confronted with the revelation of God, this general anthropological observation is deepened and understood as part of a new pattern. Death then becomes the sign and seal of the imperfect and preliminary state in which the sons of the "first Adam" still dwell. Fresh attention must be paid in this connexion to Romans 8:18-25. The longing and groaning creation is in the first place mankind outside the Church, without the knowledge of salvation. Man is longing, but he does not know for what. His groaning is the sign that God has destined him for a far higher form of existence than the bondage to decay (v.21) in which he now lives, namely for liberty (v.21) and the redemption of his body (v.23, i.e. his total existence). Therefore his groaning is a "groaning in travail" (v.22); out of this preliminary existence a new world will be born, of which mankind in its rebellion against bondage and decay is dimly aware, and which the Christian community of the resurrected Jesus has to explain. In the light of Christ human death is seen as a preliminary stage belonging to the "first things" which will "pass away" (Rev. 21:4). The same holds good for sin. That is why Paul takes them together in a "causal" relation in Romans 5. We are, however, unable to follow him in affirming this connexion. This "creation" in Romans 8 also includes non-human nature, which, since man appeared, depends on him for its situation and for its future. Paul, who points to the future of man with the words "liberty" and "resurrection", makes no attempt to describe what this future will mean for non-human nature.

These considerations bring to our mind what is often called the "tragic" element in God's creation. Much evil and suffering, death included, cannot be explained either as a consequence of man's sin or as an expression of God's providence. The process of God's work in nature and history has also its deep dark sides. Man can partly remove them, but can never overcome them. They belong to the "futility" and the "dust" which are inherent in this first creation (Rom. 8:20, I Cor. 15:47). To us they seem to be inconsistent with the love of God as revealed in Jesus Christ. They remind us of the fact that the Kingdom has not yet come, and that accordingly our knowledge is also only "in part". We are not able to find meaning in the evil of the world. We are not called upon to explain the tears, but to hope for a future in which God will wipe them away.

VIII. Nature in God's History with Man

God's work in history deals directly with man and indirectly with nature; its aim is the salvation of man. The work upon history and the work upon nature, however, cannot be completely separated. The degree to which God, in his history with man, uses events on a natural level appears to vary between one stage and another of the process, as the biblical narrative depicts it. In early stages of Israel's life, and from time to time in the prophetic tradition, any natural phenomenon can be seen as dependent on God and is used as an instrument of his revealing, judging and rescuing will: winds, thunderstorm, famine, rain, etc. The deliverance of Israel from Egypt is depicted in categories of natural catastrophe. But much of the development of Israel's history with God takes place not through events of this kind, but through political and military history, and especially Israel's relation with the surrounding nations. In this era, in which God's guidance of his people is expressed primarily in social and political terms, the reference to natural events is less.

In the story of Jesus, however, the role of nature in God's judging and saving work is more emphasized, as we see in the darkening of the sun at the time of the crucifixion, and in the way in which, in the eschatological parts of the New Testament, nature is involved in the great changes of the consummation. These and similar statements expressed anew the conviction that God's history with man, as well as man's life itself, is embedded in the processes of nature, and that there is a continuous interrelation between both. God's salvation has wider dimensions than the existential one.

More important in the New Testament, however, is another line — the dominion of nature by the new man Jesus Christ. Usually we see Jesus' perfect manhood in his relation to God and to his fellow-men; but the authors of the Gospels were equally aware of a third dimension: Jesus' mastery over the forces of nature, as evidence of the messianic times. It is difficult, if not impossible, for us to distinguish in these pronouncements and stories between memories of real facts and expressions of the belief of the Early Church. No doubt this last element plays an important role; but it must have been based on and inspired by real facts which many had witnessed. We cannot draw a line between the two elements. For our subject this is less important, however. The main thing is that Jesus is seen and confessed as the New Man who has nature with its threatening powers under his control. "He was with the wild beasts" (Mark 1:13); he walks on the waters, signs of the chaos; he heals the sick and casts out the demons. All this is ascribed not to his Godhead, but to his true humanity; such a new relation to nature, therefore, cannot be completely alien to his followers either (Matt. 14:31, Mark 9:28 f.). At the same time this relation is the anticipation of the coming fulfilment of man's relation to nature, in which the roles of servant and of companion will be in full harmony (cf. Is. 11:6-9).

Here a word must be said about miracles. Does God's saving relation disrupt the natural order by miraculous incidents? Or is this order a closed chain of causes and results? It was in this way that the contrast between orthodoxy and modernism was formulated in the nineteenth century. This contrast is now obsolete. Deeper study of the Bible, as well as modern science, has removed the problem in this form. Both consider the natural order as not a closed but an open reality. The Bible sometimes reports miracles which reflect either a primitive understanding of nature or a desire for the miraculous. In its central message, however, it is not interested in anomalous happenings as such, but only in "signs and wonders" (Heb. *otot umofetim*, Gk. *semeia kai terata),* events in which we see something of God's restoring and elevating work, pointing to the new creation. Where the eye of faith discerns how God uses the natural order as his instrument, signs and wonders are declared. Such words do not belong to an objective realm (the "sign" character of certain events can never be proved by scientific means), nor are they mere projections of subjective feelings; they express the discovery by faith of a higher reality which makes the lower realities instruments of, and windows for, its purposes.

The crucial miracle, on which the Christian's hope for the world and himself depends, is Christ's resurrection. This is indeed the "defining" miracle, on which the meaning of miracle as such has to be based. It is the powerful affirmation that in the life of Jesus of Nazareth the grace of the living God was present indeed; it is at the same time the dawn of God's new order, the first-fruits of the consummation. This new order includes our total existence, both body and soul. When we try to subsume this unique event under the laws of our ordinary life, we deny the meaning of the resurrection. What is possible and real with God is indicated by this sign disclosing the future order towards which we are under way. We now know that what we call "life", "history" and "nature" is part of a preliminary order surrounded and limited by the order of God's salvation and re-creation. The scientist may not deem himself qualified to affirm or to deny such extraordinary events. When as a Christian he believes their reality, he will welcome the new perspective they give to the field of his research. He will beware of conceiving physical reality as a closed and ultimate reality, and he may find certain analogies and models which help him in a fruitful way, to confront his faith with his scientific pattern of thinking, though such never can furnish an explanation of the miracle.

IX. Christian Faith and Technology

During the last decade the conviction has often been voiced that modern technology is a fruit of the Gospel, a result of man's calling to dominate the earth in the name and as the image of God. There is a great deal of truth in this assertion, but a careful distinction has to be made. God's restoring and renewing work evokes in man abilities and attitudes which were previously underdeveloped, but it never creates them out of nothing. Man has always to some extent tried to control nature and to make tools which could help him in this struggle. Hampered, however, by his belief that nature was the external manifestation of the Godhead, and that a deep change of its course and function might evoke the wrath of the gods, his technical skill and outreach necessarily remained very limited. Graeco-Roman culture, however, already brought a certain turn in man's attitude towards nature. The greatest stumbling-block for a radical display of man's dominating force was removed when, as a result of Christian preaching in the Western world, nature was understood as the creation of a transcendent God, and was thus desacralized and de-demonized.

The relation between Christian faith and technology is nevertheless not a direct one, because centuries passed after the victory of Christianity before the technical age set in. The reason for this long delay was partly that under the deep influence of past traditions, European man stood in the same awe of nature as a divine revelation as did his pagan ancestors. Moreover, theological motives can never explain the whole of history any more than economic or social ones can. The great display of technical sciences after the eighteenth century had as its prerequisite specific scientific and economic conditions which were not previously ripe. It is nevertheless true that Christian faith prepared the soil and set man free for an ever more radical dominion over, and use of, nature. Christendom should not have hesitated, therefore, to welcome the immense progress in controlling and using nature which gave relief to innumerable men in their struggle for life, and disclosed innumerable riches for a deeper humanization of mankind. The ambiguous way in which many Christians regarded new inventions and new achievements, both criticizing and using them at the same time, has been a cause for shame. These achievements are signs of the kind of life which God has intended for his children at the consummation.

However, we still live this side of the consummation, in a sinful world. Technics are not sinful in themselves; on the contrary, they are a means towards fulfilling God's commandment. The means are in the hand of sinful man, and are therefore never free from the possibility of misuse for selfish ends. Here the Christian Church has to exercise a critical function. Not in an unfair way, as is often done when technical progress is labelled as Babylonian tower-building, yet at the same time is gladly used; nor by drawing a line where science and technics ought to stop (e.g. where research into and use of nuclear energy or of outer space begins), since it is against the nature of science and of technology to be given artificial limits. The Church has to exercise her critical function by putting three questions to this technical generation:

1. *What kind of dominion is being exercised?* Here the seven points in chapter VI should be recalled. Nature is both man's servant and his sister, and these two aspects have to be kept in balance. In this age, the desire for handling, changing, using and transforming nature is so one-sidedly developed, that man is in danger of forgetting what nature has to contribute in her sister-function. Man no longer gives names to the animals; they have mainly become objects. His housing areas devour the natural resources of open space. His industries defile the air and the streams. So he exercises a dominion which more and more makes the display of nature's sister-aspect impossible. Man will pay the price for this fault. This one-sidedness of his dominion will hollow out and undermine his humanity.

2. *What are the aims of man's technical dominion?* We all know that war and the preparation for war are the great promoters of technics. Whether technics are a blessing or not, depends entirely on man. His mastery of nature should be in harmony with the fact that he is a child of God and a partner with his neighbour. Up to the present this harmony has been lacking. A joint effort of all industrialized nations could

dispel hunger and poverty from the earth in not more than a few decades; yet man prefers to put his technical skill into the service of his narrow national aims, his anxiety, his pride and his competition. For outer space projects, there is far more money available than for anti-hunger campaigns. Nuclear fission has so far been applied more for constructing means to destroy mankind than for promoting welfare.

The question of aims has become far more crucial still in recent years, since not only nature but also man himself can now be manipulated and changed in many ways, not only through drugs but also through interference in the genetic code. Here questions of great import arise, all of which circle around the problem of what it means that man is a person and what the relation is between the core of man's personality and the objectifiable elements of his nature. We are no more than dimly aware as yet of these questions, which can be answered only through the co-operative effort of scientists and students of the behavioural sciences, of ethics and of theology.

3. *What is the result of man's actual technical dominion?* What are the results upon man as a human person? On the one hand, modern man is freed from bondage to nature to an extent of which his ancestors would never have dreamed. On the other hand, however, technics and industry have transformed man in such a way that he is now more than ever functionalized, and adapted to the laws of his own tools — and therefore, also, more in a hurry, more nervous, more a "mass man". He suffers from the relative hypertrophy of his mastery-relation to nature, the concomitant of which is too often the atrophy of his relationships with God and with his fellow-men. Modern man is deformed. He becomes a function and a product of his own achievements. First he was enslaved to nature, now he is enslaved to his mastery of nature. As a consequence of this situation, we even see the possible destruction of the human race, either by a nuclear war or by degeneration.

Nevertheless, we do not advocate a stop to technical development. Man has to do not less, but more. He has to subjugate his technical possibilities to the other relations of his life, instead of allowing technics to supersede these other relations. Otherwise he will lose as much as he gains, and in the long run he will lose far more than he gains. Already in many highly-developed countries complaints are heard of the menace of boredom, because man is satiated and has lost the notion that he is called to be more than a consumer. In less developed countries the joy of freedom, made possible by science and technology, is still rightly dominant. Everywhere, however, man has to be reminded of the fact that what seem to be the ambiguities of technics are in reality the ambiguities of man himself, and that in view of the immense power which he now possesses, it is high time for him to seek a fresh understanding of his nature and destiny.

X. God in Universal History

It has already been seen how Israel's concept of history, born out of her encounter with God in history, contrasted with the way in which history was conceived of before and around Israel. The self-revelation of the God of covenant and promise was directed towards one small particular nation, but it was never meant for that nation exclusively. On the contrary, in her meeting with the God of history Israel is treated as representative of the whole of mankind, and considered as suffering and acting on behalf of all mankind. In this very particular (and often seemingly particularistic) revelation, the unity of mankind is presupposed and aimed at. This is clear from the universal background which the writer of Gen. 2-11 gave to his account of Israel's history, from the universal outlook in the prophets (Isaiah, Deutero-Isaiah, Deutero-Zachariah, Jonah, etc.), and especially from the whole trend of the New Testament. Mankind is understood as a whole, with a common nature (created from one head), with common problems (sin, suffering, death), with a common future (the Kingdom of God for every nation, people and tongue, the uniting of all things in Christ), and with a common calling (to faith, love and hope). So God's history must sooner or later give birth to the conception of universal history, in the sense that all groups, tribes, nations, imperia, races, and classes are involved in one and the same history. This conviction was not without a certain preparation in former political events (Alexander the Great, Pax Romana) and philosophical thinking (Stoicism), but all this had no power to break through the feeling of separation, as it existed between Greeks and barbarians. So long as in the West Christianity was identified with a special "Christian culture", limited to Europe, no more could the germs of universality in the Christian message bear fruit either. The universalizing and unifying of history started in the ages of mission and colonialism, and is now in this generation penetrating human minds everywhere as never before. This last fact is not so much due to the impact of the Gospel as to the technological revolution, which in itself has a universal tendency. These different sources of universal history cannot, however, be separated, because, as has been seen, the advance of technological science and practice cannot be understood apart from the influence of the Gospel.

The present movement towards the unification of mankind and its history lays a heavy pressure on all the Christian Churches to seek, with greater earnestness and haste than ever before, the world-wide unity of the Christian Church. The prayer of our Lord "that they may all be one" (John 17:21) has always disquieted and inspired many Christians. However, now as never before, the Churches are challenged because the world needs the united witness and service of the Church. Only the one Church can be the adequate counterpart of the one world. We see it as the guidance of the Spirit that in our century, and exactly in face of the dividing forces of two world wars, the Churches everywhere have begun to seek a world-wide unity. The interdependence between this fact and the present search for world unity can help us to a deeper understanding of the meaning and the call of the Spirit, and stimulate us not to be disobedient to this call, lest the coming one world be deprived of the guidance of the partner who once sowed the seed of her unity.

The growing awareness of being involved in one universal history appeals to the Church, particularly because this fact has also an ethical thrust. It inspires men to react against all kinds of social, racial and economical discrimination and to strive with all their strength for world peace and world co-operation. In all this can be seen realizations of God's purposes for this world, signs of the coming Kingdom.

We dare not use a stronger word than "signs", however, because the present universalizing of history partakes of that ambiguity which is characteristic of this world in its preliminary and sinful phase. Christ evokes the powers of the Spirit — and at the same time those of the Anti-Christ. He brings new shadows as well as new light. Universal History, experienced apart from Christ, can become a threat as well as a blessing. What is the goal towards which Universal History is developing? For very many of our fellow-men there is no goal beyond the creation of a well-balanced, smoothly-organized, technically perfect universal welfare-state. Now already we see the indications that this will result in a society of boredom. A society which has no purposes beyond its own welfare must die. The alternative is that it devotes all its superfluous powers to new irrational and even anti-humane adventures. The unification of societies is not in itself a good thing. The value of universal history depends on the good it serves and the goal towards which it is directed. Here may be recalled Genesis 11, where the Tower of Babel is the expression of a strong universal will, but a will directed against God's purpose.

For this and other reasons, many are inclined to see little or no connexion between God's history in Israel and in Christ, on the one hand, and man's "profane" history, universal history included, on the other hand. But such a connexion does exist, and must be affirmed. History is one and indivisible. We partake today in that same history in which Abraham was called, Israel was judged and delivered, Jesus died and rose from the dead, and the Holy Spirit was poured out. What modern man sees around him are risks and detours, guilt and frustration. Things are ambiguous or inscrutable. The same is true, however, for God's history as it is told in the Bible, which, though it is a history of rebellion and failures, is nevertheless God's history. The difference is that God's work in Israel and in Christ is interpreted by the Word, that here we have to do with disclosure-situations in the highest sense of the phrase, that here and particularly in the appearance of Jesus Christ, God lays aside his anonymity. All this can be said only by faith. A double disclosure is needed: one in the events and one in men's hearts through the Spirit. The revelation which is given in this double disclosure is not exclusive, however, but inclusive. God's mind and purpose are here disclosed in their relevance for all times and nations. So we are summoned to understand all history, and especially our own history, with its good and evil, in the light of this History. The same God is present, there in a more disclosed way and here in a more hidden way; but it is one presence and therefore one history. He goes on with his judging and saving work on a world-wide scale. That is what we confess. And this confession, far from making us passive spectators, inspires us to share in the tensions and risks of human history. As God's fellow-workmen, we are called to make way for the healing forces of his love on a world-wide scale, through our mission and our service, knowing that in the Lord our labour is not in vain.

XI. God and Man in History

The God who historicizes human existence frees man from entangling bondage to the powers of nature, and calls him to come of age and to become the master of the powers whose slave he previously was. In this statement, which summarizes much of what has been said in the previous chapters, two confessions are inseparably connected: God's sovereignty over man and his history, and man's freedom in history. These two confessions, so often put over against one another, are in the Christian faith two sides of the same reality. And this not as a result of penetrating philosophical thinking, but of the reality which is discerned in the disclosure-situations. God frees man for responsibility. The terrifying mystery is that man is inclined to mobilize his freedom not to pursue his divine calling, but to act counter to God's will. Even so, God accepts him and grants him full room for his self-chosen role. The whole of Israel's history and particularly the life, death and resurrection of Jesus reflect the unity of man's autonomy and God's sovereignty. Man's freedom in history is unlimited: he can even expel God's presence. Nevertheless, God is not defeated, but victorious. He takes man's rebellious freedom into his service, bending man's aims and actions towards his purpose (cf. Gen. 50:20, Is. 10:5-21, Acts 4:27f.). God's work through Christ and the Spirit everywhere in the world liberates man to autonomy; and man everywhere is tempted to use his new freedom against God. The history of Jesus' life, death and resurrection is displayed and repeated on an ever wider scale. For the world-wide scale on which it will be repeated in the final stages of history, the New Testament uses the images of Anti-Christ and the Millennium.

History is the work of the sovereign God. He is never a helpless spectator of man's autonomy. Nor does He use men as passive instruments. The divine character of his omnipotent grace is seen in the fact that it admits and even presupposes the highest measure of human liberty. God's freedom does not jeopardize nor even limit man's. The confession of God's Providence (a far too static and poor a word for his ways through history!) can never be an excuse for irresponsibility nor a shelter for passivity. It functions in the life of God's children, in the midst of so many baffling events, as a source of confidence, consolation and challenge.

These insights are particularly relevant since, through the knowledge of nuclear fission, the power fell to mankind to destroy itself and its world. From now on, we have to live with this terrifying possibility. This situation makes an appeal to our responsibility as never before. For Christians who know about the depth of sin in man, this implies a constant struggle to bring and to keep the powers of destruction under a strict control. We are challenged to pray and to work afresh for the renewal of the world through the powers of the Spirit. At the same time, we will do so in a deep confidence, knowing that our concern is far more God's own concern, and that his sovereign love for his sinful creatures will prove itself stronger than all our resistance.

XII. History and Nature in Consummation

In wide circles of Christendom the relation of history and consummation is mainly seen in a context of pessimism: this world will come to a drastic end, and on its ruins (if any are left) an entirely new world will be created. This presentation is in contradiction to even the most apocalyptical passages of the New Testament (cf. Matt. 24, Mark 13, Luke 21, I Cor. 15, II Thess. 2, Rev. 18-22), where the new world is found in the identical setting of the old, and where often even between this age and the age to come no sharp line can be drawn. This is quite different from the dualistic tendencies in the Jewish apocalyptic literature of that time. This applies even to the most "dualistic" passage in the N.T., II Pet. 3:5-10, where the fire is not so much destroying as purifying and where, according to the better manuscripts, the last words have to be read: "and the earth and the works that are upon it will be found" (instead of: "will be burned up").

The relation between history and consummation is one of both continuity and discontinuity. The new world will be this earth renewed. The eschaton will be the complete and glorified unfolding of what God has already begun in history in his Son and in his Spirit. This work is in contrast with much in this world, which has to be removed. The world will be recreated according to the new humanity of the risen Christ. As he could become the new man only through suffering and death, so this whole creation has to undergo an analogous process: in this way "He will change our lowly existences to be like his glorious existence" (Phil. 3:21). That is what the dark features in New Testament eschatology want to express. The cross is the way to the resurrection; for this lower and sinful humanity there is no other way. But in all this are disclosed, not signs of frustration, but the travail of the coming glorious liberty of the sons of God (Rom. 8), which is the goal of human history.

Discontinuity serves continuity. It may be believed that our works in the Church of Christ (I Cor. 3:14) and our cultural achievements (Rev. 21:24,26) will be used as building-stones for the Kingdom of God. All deeds and achievements which help the world to more freedom, humaneness and love, according to God's purposes, have such a function of continuity. But who knows which of his works will stand the great Test? (I Cor. 3:13).

Since there is some kind of continuity between history and consummation, the suggestion of a contrast between history and consummation is to be rejected. Of course the human mind is here at the limits of what can be thought or said. Nevertheless it should be boldly stated that the alternative, consummation as a timeless motionless eternity, is alien to the Christian faith. The historicizing of life has been experienced as God's own liberating work. The end of such a work never can mean its abolition, only its glorification, its preservation in a wider context of life. The expression in the New Testament that mankind in the consummation will reign with Christ (Rom. 5:17, II Tim. 2:12, Rev. 3:21, 5:10, cf. also Luke 19:17) seems to express this conviction. Consummation will mean a new and far more thorough-going display of man's freedom and dominion.

Nature in consummation has to be spoken of in an analogous way, because of the close unity between man and nature, and the continuity between this world and the consummation. The Revelation of John uses an illuminating imagery: the sea is no more, the waters are transparent like crystal, the trees yield their fruits each month. These images express the thought that nature will completely lose its uncertain, chaotic and threatening character to man, and will be entirely subservient to him. To modern man there is nothing strange in this message, except that what the Bible expresses in terms of substance, he prefers to express in terms of relation. Renewed nature is the product of a renewal of man in his relations to God and to his neighbour. Such renewal will affect our relation to nature in the widest sense, nature beyond our planet included. Man will participate more fully in the divine joy in creation, and be more fully aware of the meaning of this larger order. The renewal of nature in its relation to man will also and even primarily affect man's most intimate connection with nature — his body. The confession of the resurrection of the body means that man's corporality is not something accidental but essential, and that he lives with the promise that his complete rebirth will also imply that his bodily existence, now so often a burden and a hindrance, will become a perfect instrument of his personality in his communion with God and with man.

In the progress of technical and medical sciences may be seen the foreshadowing of this renewal of nature in the consummation. At the same time their limits, risks, darker sides and misuses are reminders of the fact that these sciences are still instruments in the hands of man as yet unrenewed. This ambivalent situation foreshadows the fact that the Kingdom will come only through the deep crisis of divine judgment.

XIII. Our Situation in History: Interpretation and Commitment

Can we interpret history? On this point we find two opposite opinions in Christian theology. The first is a clear "yes". Its defenders point to Matt. 16:3, where Jesus rebukes his adversaries with the words: "You know how to interpret the appearance of the sky, but you cannot interpret the signs of the times". They speak of the prophets as the great interpreters of their time, of the way in which Paul in Romans 11 and II Thess. 2 interprets the present and the near future, of the Book of Revelation and other apocalyptic passages, etc.

Over against this opinion the following objections can be made: man can never see more than very limited fragments of God's great history. He does not live in God's disclosed history, but in the midst of events in which He is present in a hidden way. We believe his presence; we cannot indicate it. Consider what is said in the Bible about those who wanted to explain contemporary events! (Cf. Job 42:7, Luke 13:1-5, which follows right after the Lucan version of "the signs of the times".) No survey, no blueprint of history, has been given. We are men, not God. We live on this side of the consummation. Prior to that, history remains still incomplete. And before the great divorce, good and evil are still inseparably mixed. In the Lucan version of "the signs of the times", Jesus asks: "Why do you not know how to interpret the present time?", i.e. the fullness of time, the meaning of his appearance. There is one great Sign of the time and of all times: Jesus Christ and none besides Him. Moreover, the history of all interpretations of "the signs of the times" is a strong warning. Hardly any of these interpretations has survived the interpreters. Think of the so-called "German Christians", who interpreted the Third Reich as a new outpouring of the Holy Spirit. All this should warn against interpreting special events and contemporary developments as signs of the work of Christ or of the work of the powers of evil. Christians are called not to interpretation, but to repentance and commitment.

It would thus seem that the "no" has far stronger arguments than the "yes". Yet this is not the case. The "no" separates between interpretation and commitment, which is impossible. Commitment always implies a decision in favour of something and against something else. Repentance is always repentance concerning concrete deeds, which now are rejected as being against God's will. Conscious human life is always interpreting. As responsible human beings we can never avoid it. Nor can we avoid it as Christians; for the same God who was revealed to us in Israel and in Christ, is He whose hidden presence we believe in the events of our time. We believe that the last secret of our world is the double secret of cross and resurrection. Christians are called to a life which in service, suffering and resistance will share in this ultimate reality of cross and resurrection. So they are obliged to take the risk of interpreting their historical situations to the extent that this is necessary for their commitment.

A parallel can here be drawn with what we do in our personal lives. The Christian believes that in everything God works for good with those who love Him (Rom. 8:28). This faith is again and again a reason to try to discern God's guidance in daily life, in order to see what the next step should be. Our interpretation may, in the light of later events, be confirmed or be negated. In either case faith in God's guidance remains unshaken. The Christian's faith is independent of interpretations. At the same time, in its encounter with the ambiguities and decisions of life, it makes interpretations.

God calls us to make our decisions, in the light of his coming Kingdom, against hunger, suffering, poverty, discrimination and oppression, and for welfare, freedom, equality and brotherhood. The Christian has to know for himself where he sees the forces of the Spirit at work, in order that he may join them, and where he sees the forces of darkness at work, in order that he may resist them. It is often far from easy to make such interpretations. In this age good and evil are never present in pure forms. Always, or almost always, man has to do with a "more or less". This is a source of much difference among Christians in interpreting their historical situations. Interpretation is primarily a personal decision, but is never meant to remain a mere private opinion. It calls for confirmation, amendment or rejection by the common body of Christ. Christians need a fresh understanding of what, in the New Testament, is called "the gift of prophecy"; some members of the Church receive more than others the ability to discern and to formulate the will of God in the problems of the present day.

There is no clear and absolute authority in interpreting history. The Church has no guarantee against great mistakes in this realm. We think e.g. of the quite different views which we now hold of the French Revolution, compared with that of contemporary Christians. This cannot make us passive, however, particularly not in our time when our commitment is required on a world-wide scale.

Here the World Council of Churches has a major task. We may hope that this body will sometimes speak the right prophetic words on behalf of the Churches. On the whole, however, its main task will be in preparing its member Churches for such a witness, through bringing together their different interpretations, providing fuller information, widening their horizons, and challenging them to distinguish between pure and wrong motives in their initial interpretations. So the Churches in this community can wrestle to find a common interpretation of the contemporary situation, as the basis for their common endeavour.

All our interpretations have to be built on the foundation which is laid, Jesus Christ (I Cor. 3:10-15). He, as the rejected and victorious Lord, is the key to the understanding of our universal history. On this foundation, however, we can build in very different ways, with gold, silver and precious stones, or with wood, bay and stubble. No authority can decide who is building well, who is building badly. "The Day will disclose it, and the fire will test what sort of work each one has done". This is not said to make us passive; on the contrary, it is an appeal to us to test ourselves, "with all the saints", "that we may prove what is the will of God".

God is present in human history. He is present in a hidden way. Even the forces which resist Him serve his purposes. At the same time He is not present as an anonymous God. He has a name. "Truly, thou art a God who hidest thyself, God of Israel, the Saviour" (Is. 45:15). This Saviour-name is the key to our understanding of nature and history. And in God's saving history man is called to partake.

DOCUMENT IV.10

THE CHURCH AND THE JEWISH PEOPLE (1967)

I. Introduction

There is a growing awareness in many churches today that an encounter with the Jews is essential. On various occasions in the past the World Council of Churches has condemned any form of anti-semitism. It is, however, necessary to think through the theological implications and the complex questions bound up with the Church's relation to the Jewish people in a more explicit and systematic way. This was, for instance, urged in the report of Section I on "The Church in the purpose of God" at the Fourth World Conference on Faith and Order in Montreal in 1963. We hope that what follows here may be a contribution to such a study. We cannot pretend to offer more than that. We are aware of the shortcomings of this statement, and particularly that differences of opinion among us, which we have not yet been able to resolve, impose limits on what we can say. However, what we offer is, notwithstanding its limitations, new in the history of the World Council. We hope that this statement will stimulate a continuing discussion and will pave the way for a deeper common understanding and eventually a common declaration.

Both in biblical and contemporary language the words "Israel" and "Jews" can have various meanings. To avoid misunderstanding, in this document we have used the term "Israel" only when referring to the people in Old and New Testament times; no present-day political reference is intended or implied. When we speak about the people in post-biblical times we prefer to use the terms "Jews" or "Jewish people", the latter being a collective term designating the Jews all over the world. We find it hard to define in precise terms what it is that makes a Jew a Jew, though we recognize that both ethnic elements and religious traditions play a role.

In drawing up this document we set out to answer two distinct questions which were put to us: 1) in what way does the continuing existence of the Jews have theological significance for the Church, and 2) in what way should Christians give witness of their faith to Jews. The structure of this paper is to a great extent conditioned by this starting-point. It should also be kept in mind that we speak as Christian theologians; we are conscious of the fact that theological statements often have political, sociological or economic implications, even if that is not intended. That consideration, however, cannot be a reason for silence; we merely ask that this paper may be judged on its theological merits.

In our discussions we constantly kept the biblical writings in mind and tried to understand our questions in the light of the Scriptures. We realized that the evidence of the Bible, both Old and New Testaments, is varied and complex, and that we are all in constant danger of arbitrarily excluding parts of it. In re-thinking the place of the Jews in the history of salvation, we should recognize that the question of Israel is very important in parts of the gospels and the Pauline letters, but it seems to be less in evidence in other parts of the New Testament literature, though it is perhaps rarely entirely absent. The problems of interpreting the biblical evidence in regard to this question are just as difficult as they are in regard to other significant theological issues. Being aware of the danger of building one's thinking upon particular proof-texts, we have refrained from pointing to specific verses. We have tried, however, to be faithful to the overall meaning of the Bible and trust that the scriptural basis of what we say will be evident.

II. Historical Considerations

The first community of Christians were Jews who had accepted Jesus as the Christ. They continued to belong to the Jewish communities and the relationship between them and their fellow-Jews was close, notwithstanding the tension that existed between them — a tension caused by the fact that the Christian Jews believed that the fulness of time had come in Christ and in the outpouring of the Spirit and that they therefore came to know themselves to be found in one fellowship with Gentiles who also believed in God through Jesus Christ. The two groups of Jews broke apart as the consequence of various facts: for example, the attitude of Christians towards the Law, the persecution of the Stephen group by Jews, the withdrawal from Jerusalem of the Christians during the great uprising 66-73 A.D., the increasing hostility between Jews and Christians which found expression in their respective liturgies, and in other ways. In the same period Christians of Gentile origin came greatly to outnumber the Jewish Christians. From this time on the history of Jews and Christians is one of ever increasing mutual estrangement. After Christianity became the accepted religion of the Roman state, the Jews were discriminated against and often even persecuted by the "Christian" state, more often than not with ecclesiastical support. As a consequence, the so-called "dialogues" between Christian and Jewish theologians which were organized from time to time were never held on a footing of equality; the Jewish partners were not taken seriously.

In the past the existence of Jews outside the Church and their refusal to accept the Christian faith prompted little serious theological questioning in official church circles. Christians generally thought about these questions in very stereotyped ways: the Jews as the Israel of the Old Testament had formerly been God's elect people, but this election had been transferred to the Church after Christ; the continuing existence of the Jews was primarily thought of in terms of divine rejection and retribution, because they were regarded as those who had killed Christ and whose hearts were so hardened that they continued to reject him.

Despite all this the separation between the Church and the Jewish people has never been absolute. In the liturgy of the Church many Jewish elements have been preserved. And when in the middle of the second century Marcion tried to cut all ties by rejecting the Old Testament as God's revelation and by clearing the New Testament as far as possible of all its Old Testament concepts and references, the Church, by holding fast to the Old Testament, testified to the continuity between the old and the new covenants. She thereby in fact testified also to the common root and origin of the Church and the Jewish people, although this was not clearly realized; and only few Christians have been aware that this common root meant some kind of special relationship.

At the scholarly and theological level also there has always been contact between the two groups. In the Middle Ages especially, Christian theology and exegesis were strongly influenced by Jews, who for instance transmitted Aristotelian philosophy to them; the influence of Jewish mysticism upon Christian mystics, moreover, has been much stronger than is generally known. In the 16th century among Christians of the Western world a new awareness of their relationship with Jews arose, partly under the influence of humanism with its emphasis on the original biblical languages, partly because of the Reformation. Protestant attitudes were, however, by no means always positive. In Pietism a strong love and hope for the Jewish people awoke, which in the 18th and 19th century found expression in the many attempts to come into missionary contact with Jews. But even so, there was little change in the thinking by Christians generally about the Jews. The time of the Enlightenment, with its common move towards toleration, brought improvement in the position of the Jews, at least in Western Europe. This happened in a cultural atmosphere in which there was a tendency to deny the particularity of the Jewish people. Outright anti-semitism, with its excesses and pogroms, seemed a thing of the past, although in most countries religious and social discrimination remained, the more insidious because it was often not fully conscious.

It is only since the beginning of this century, and even more especially since the last war, that churches, and not merely various individual Christians, have begun to rethink more systematically the nature of their relationship to the Jews. The main theological reason for this is probably the greater emphasis on biblical theology and the increased interest which the Old Testament in particular has received. It is self-evident that this emphasis was to a great extent caused by the preceding outbreak of anti-semitism in Germany and its rationalization on so-called Christian, ideological grounds. In the realm of biblical scholarship there is today increasing co-operation among Christians and Jews; many Christian theologians are aware of what they have learned from men like Rosenzweig, Buber and other Jewish scholars. The question of what is meant by election and the irrevocability of God's love is being asked again in a new way. The biblically important concept of "covenant" has become more central, and the relationship between the "old" and the "new" covenant is being restudied. In addition, Paul's wrestling with the baffling question of the disobedience of the greater part of his fellow-Jews has come up for consideration.

Besides these theological grounds, two historical events in the last thirty years have caused churches to direct their thinking more than before to their relationship to the Jewish people. In Europe persecution has taken place, greater and more brutal than could have been thought possible in our time, in which some six million Jews were annihilated in the most terrible way, not because of their personal actions or beliefs, but because of the mere fact that they had Jewish grandparents. The churches came to ask themselves whether this was simply the consequence of natural human wicked-ness, or whether it had also another, theological, dimension.

The second event was the creation of the State of Israel. This is of tremendous importance for the great majority of Jews; it has meant for them a new feeling of self-assurance and security. But this same event has also brought suffering and injustice to Arab people. We find it impossible to give a unanimous evaluation of its formation and of all the events connected with it, and therefore in this study do not make further mention of it. We realize, however, especially in view of the changed situation in the Middle East as a result of the war of June 1967, that also the question of the present State of Israel, and of its theological significance, if any, has to be taken up.

III. Theological Considerations

We believe that God formed the people of Israel. There are certainly many factors of common history, ethnic background and religion, which can explain its coming into existence, but according to Old Testament faith as a whole, it was God's own will and decision which made this one distinct people with its special place in history. God is the God of the whole earth and of all nations, but he chose this particular people to be the bearer of a particular promise and to act as his covenant-partner and special instrument. He made himself known specifically to Israel, and showed this people what his will is for men on earth. Bound to him in love and obedience, it was called to live as God wants his people to live. In this way it was to become, as it were, a living revelation to others, in order that they also might come to know, trust, love and obey God. In dealing with Israel, God had in view the other nations; this was the road by which he came to them. In other words, in his love for Israel his love for mankind was manifested; in its election Israel, without losing its own particularity, represented the others.

In the Old Testament Israel is shown to be an imperfect instrument; again and again it was untrue to its calling so that it often obscured rather than manifested God's will on earth. But even in its disobedience it was a witness to God — a witness to his judgment, which however terrible was seen as a form of his grace, for in punishment God was seeking to purify his people and to bring them back to himself; a witness also to his faithfulness and love, which did not let his people go, even when they turned away from him.

We believe that in Jesus Christ God's revelation in the Old Testament finds its fulfilment. Through him we see into the very heart of God, in him we see what it really means to say that God is the God of the covenant and loves man to the very end. As he became the man who was the perfect instrument of God's purpose, he took upon himself the vocation of his people. He, as its representative fulfils Israel's task of obedience. In his resurrection it has become manifest that God's love is stronger than human sin. In him God has forgiven and wiped out sin and in him he created his true covenant-partner.

A part of Israel recognized in Jesus as the Christ the full revelation of God. They believed that in him God himself was present, and that in his death and resurrection God acted decisively for the salvation of the world. Numerically they were perhaps only a very small minority, yet in these "few" God's purpose for the whole of Israel is manifested and confirmed. And together with Israel the Gentiles too were now called to the love and service of God. It cannot be otherwise; for if in Jesus Christ the fulness of time has really come, then the nations also must participate in God's salvation, and the separation of Israel is abolished. This is what the Church is: Israel having come to recognize God in Christ, together with the Gentiles who are engrafted into Israel, so that now Jew and Gentile become one in Christ. It is only in this way that the Church is the continuation of the Israel of the Old Testament, God's chosen people, called upon to testify to his mighty acts for men, and to be his fellow-workers in this world.

Christ himself is the ground and substance of this continuity. This is underlined by the preservation of the Old Testament in the Church as an integral part of her worship and tradition. The existence of Christians of Jewish descent provides a visible manifestation of that same continuity, though many Christians are hardly aware of this. The presence of such members in a Church which in the course of time has become composed predominantly of Gentiles, witnesses to the trustworthiness of God's promises, and should serve to remind the Church of her origin in Israel. We are not advocating separate congregations for them. History has shown the twofold danger which lies in this: the danger of discriminating despite all intention to the contrary, and the danger that such separate congregations tend to evolve sectarian traits. But more important than these considerations is that in Christ the dividing wall has been broken down and Jew and Gentile are to form one new man; thus any separation in the Church has been made impossible.

However, without detracting in any way from what has just been said, we should remember that there is room for all kinds of people and cultures in the Church. This implies that Jews who become Christians are not simply required to abandon their Jewish traditions and ways of thinking; in certain circumstances it may therefore be right to form special groups which are composed mainly of Jewish Christians.

The fact that by far the greater part of Israel did not recognize God in Jesus Christ posed a burning question for Paul, not primarily because of the crucifixion, but because even after Christ's resurrection they still rejected him. The existence of Jews today who do not accept him puts the same question to us, because in this respect the situation today is basically the same as it was in Paul's time.

We are convinced that the Jewish people still have a significance of their own for the Church. It is not merely that by God's grace they have preserved in their faith truths and insights into his revelation which we have tended to forget; some of these are indicated in chapter V. But also it seems to us that by their very existence in spite of all attempts to destroy them, they make it manifest that God has not abandoned them. In this way they are a living and visible sign of God's faithfulness to men, an indication that he also upholds those who do not find it possible to recognize him in his Son. While we see their continuing existence as pointing to God's love and mercy, we explicitly reject any thought of considering their sufferings during the ages as a proof of any special guilt. Why, in God's purpose, they have suffered in that way, we as outsiders do not know. What we do know, however, is the guilt of Christians who have all too often stood on the side of the persecutors instead of the persecuted.

Conscious of this guilt we find it impossible to speak in a generalizing way of Christian obedience over against Jewish disobedience. It is true that we believe that Jesus Christ is the truth and the way for every man, and that for everyone faith in him is salvation. But we also know that it is only by grace that we have come to accept him and that even in our acceptance we are still in many ways disobedient. We have therefore no reason to pride ourselves over against others. For Christians as well as Jews can live only by the forgiveness of sin, and by God's mercy.

We believe that in the future also God in his faithfulness will not abandon the Jewish people, but that his promise and calling will ultimately prevail so as to bring them to their salvation. This is to us an assurance that we are allowed to hope for the salvation of all who do not yet recognize Christ. So long as the Jews do not worship with the Church the one God and Father of Jesus Christ, they are to us a perpetual reminder that God's purpose and promise are not yet realized in their fulness, that we have still much to hope for the world, looking for the time when the Kingdom of God will become plainly and gloriously manifest.

All this we can say together. However, this considerable agreement, for which we are grateful indeed, should not conceal the fact that when the question is raised of the theological identity of Israel with the Jewish people of today we find ourselves divided. This division is due not only to the differences in the interpretation of the biblical evidence, but also in the weight which is given to various passages. We might characterize our differences, rather schematically, as follows:

Some are convinced that, despite the elements of continuity that admittedly exist between present day Jews and Israel, to speak of the continued election of the Jewish people alongside the Church is inadmissible. It is the Church alone, they say, that is theologically speaking, the continuation of Israel as the people of God, to which now all nations belong. Election and vocation are solely in Christ, and are to be grasped in faith. To speak otherwise is to deny that the one people of God, the Church, is the body of Christ which cannot be broken. In Christ it is made manifest that God's love and his promises apply to all men. The Christian hope for the Jews is the same as it is for all men: that they may come to the knowledge of the truth, Jesus Christ our Lord. This does not imply any denial of the distinctive and significant witness to Christ which the Jews still bear. For their continued separate existence is the direct result of the dual role which Israel as God's elect people has played: through them salvation has come to the world, and they represented at the crucial time of human history man's rejection of God's salvation offered in Christ.

Others of us are of the opinion that it is not enough merely to assert some kind of continuity between the present-day Jews — whether religious or not — and ancient Israel, but that they actually are still Israel, i.e. that they still are God's elect people. These would stress that after Christ the one people of God is broken asunder, one part being the Church which accepts Christ, the other part Israel outside the Church, which rejects him, but which even in this rejection remains in a special sense beloved by God. They see this election manifested specifically in the fact that the existence of the Jewish people in this world still reveals the truth that God's promises are irrevocable, that he will uphold the covenant of love which he has made with Israel. Further they see this continuing election in the fact that God has linked the final hope of the world to the salvation of the Jews, in the day when he will heal the broken body of his one people, Israel and the Church.

These two views, described above, should however not be understood as posing a clear-cut alternative. Many hold positions somewhere in between, and without glossing over the real disagreements which exist, in some cases these positions can be so close, that they seem to rest more on different emphases than to constitute real contradictions. But even where our positions seem practically irreconcilable, we cannot be content to let the matter rest as it is. For the conversation among us has only just begun and we realize that in this question the entire self-understanding of the Church is at stake.

IV. The Church and Her Witness

In the foregoing it is set forth that the Church stands in a unique relationship to the Jews. Every one who accepts Christ and becomes a member of his Church shares thereby in this special relation, being brought face to face with the Jewish people. That is to say that the problem we are dealing with in this paper is not one which confronts only the so-called Western churches, but concerns every Christian of whatever race, cultural or religious background he may be. So too the Old Testament is not only of importance for those whose culture is to a greater or lesser degree rooted in it, but becomes also the spiritual heritage of those Christians whose own ethnic culture is not touched by it.

The existence of this unique relationship raises the question as to whether it conditions the way in which Christians have to bear witness of Jesus to Jews.

We all agree that the Church is the special instrument of God, which is called to testify in her word and her life to his love revealed in its fulness in his Son. She has to proclaim that in Christ's cross and resurrection it has become manifest that God's love and mercy embrace all men. Moreover, being rooted in his reconciliation, she is called to cross all frontiers of race, culture and nationality, and all other barriers which separate man from man. Therefore we are convinced that no one can be excluded from her message of forgiveness and reconciliation; to do otherwise would be disobedience to the Lord of the Church and a denial of her very nature, a negation of her fundamental openness and catholicity.

In the World Council of Churches much thinking has been done about the question of how the Church can give her witness in such a way that she respects the beliefs and convictions of those who do not share her faith in Christ, and perhaps, with God's help, bring them in full freedom to accept it. It is agreed that in an encounter with non-Christian people real openness is demanded, a willingness to listen to what the other has to say, and a readiness to be questioned by him and learn from his insights. This means that at all times Christians have to guard against an arrogant or paternalistic attitude. Moreover, the way in which they approach different men in different circumstances cannot be a single one; they should do their utmost to gain a real understanding of the life and thinking of the non-Christian, for only thereby can they speak to his situation in their witness.

That this is the generally accepted attitude for Christians to men of other faiths can be seen from the statement on "Christian Witness, Proselytism and Religious Liberty" accepted at the Third Assembly of the World Council of Churches in New Delhi, 1961, and from the declaration of the Commission on World Mission and Evangelism at Mexico City, 1963. It will therefore be evident that we consider the alternatives of mission or dialogue, which formerly was perhaps justified, untenable today. We are convinced that an encounter with non-Christians on the lines indicated above can be a real enrichment for the Church in which she not only gives but also receives.

The very fact that the particular situation in which the Christian witness is given must always be taken into account, applies of course also to the Jews. Moreover, where they are concerned this consideration receives a special dimension, for with no other people does the Church have such close ties. Christians and Jews are rooted in the same divine history of salvation, as has already been shown; both claim to be heirs of the same Old Testament. Christian and Jewish faiths share also a common hope that the world and its history are being led by God to the full realization and manifestation of his Kingdom.

However, in an encounter between Christians and Jews not only the common ties are to be considered but also their agelong alienation and the terrible guilt of discrimination which Christians share with the world, and which in our own time has culminated in the gas-chamber and the destruction of a large part of European Jewry. Though certainly not all Christians are equally guilty and though anti-semitism has played no particular role in the Oriental and in the so-called younger churches, we all have to realize that Christian words have now become disqualified and suspect in the ears of most Jews. Therefore often the best, and sometimes perhaps even the only way in which Christians today can testify to the Jewish people about their faith in Christ may be not so much in explicit words but rather by service.

We all are thus basically of one mind about the actual form which in practice the Christian encounter with the Jewish people has to take. We differ, however, among ourselves when we try to analyse and to formulate this common attitude in theological terms. The differences which exist in this respect are closely connected with the ones we noted before. There it was remarked that the very self-understanding of the Church was at stake (par. 22). Here even more, our differences are bound up with differences in ecclesiology, or rather with the different ecclesiological points on which we lay stress. If the main emphasis is put on the concept of the Church as the body of Christ, the Jewish people are seen as being outside. The Christian attitude to them is considered to be in principle the same as to men of other faiths and the mission of the Church is to bring them, either individually or corporately, to the acceptance of Christ, so that they become members of his body. Those who hold this view would generally want to stress that besides service to the Jews it is also legitimate and even necessary to witness in a more explicit way as well, be it through individuals, or special societies, or churches.

If, on the other hand, the Church is primarily seen as the people of God, it is possible to regard the Church and the Jewish people together as forming the one people of God, separated from one another for the time being, yet with the promise that they will ultimately become one. Those who follow this line of thinking would say that the Church should consider her attitude towards the Jews theologically and in principle as being different from the attitude she has to all other men who do not believe in Christ. It should be thought of more in terms of ecumenical engagement in order to heal the breach than of missionary witness in which she hopes for conversion.

Again it should be pointed out that these views are not static positions; there are gradual transitions between the two and often it is more a question of a more-or-less than of an either-or. That is in the nature of the matter. For the Church must be thought of both as the body of Christ and as the people of God, and these two concepts express the one reality from different angles.

But even though we have not yet reached a common theological evaluation of the Christian encounter with Jews, we all emphatically reject any form of "proselytizing", in the derogatory sense which the word has come to carry in our time, where it is used for the corruption of witness in cajolery, undue pressure or intimidation, or other improper methods (see the New Delhi declaration on "Christian Witness, Proselytism and Religious Liberty").

V. Ecumenical Relevance

We are convinced that the Church's re-thinking of her theology with regard to the question of Israel and her conversation with the Jewish people can be of real importance to the ecumenical movement. In this way questions are posed which touch the foundation and the heart of Christian faith. Though these questions are also being asked for other reasons, it is our experience that here they are being put in a particularly penetrating form. Because there is no doctrine of Christian theology which is not touched and influenced in some way by this confrontation with the Jewish people, it is impossible for us here to develop fully its implications. We can only indicate some salient points.

1. The documents of the Old Testament belong to the heritage which the churches have received from and have in common with the Jews. In a theological encounter of the two groups the question of the right understanding of these writings will necessarily come to the fore, the Jews placing them in the context of the Talmud and Midrash, the churches in that of the New Testament. Thereby Christians are called upon to analyse the criteria they use in their interpretation of the Bible. Clarity in this respect will help the churches in their search together for the biblical truth.

2. The Old Testament is also part of the common heritage that lies beyond the separation of the churches themselves. Differences in its evaluation and interpretation may result in different understandings of the New Testament. When in their meeting with Jewish theologians the churches are driven to reconsider whether they have understood the Old Testament aright, and perhaps coming to new insights into it, it may well help them also to understand the Gospel in a deeper and fuller way and so overcome one-sided and different conceptions which keep them apart.

3. Jewish faith regards itself as being based on God's revelation written down in the Bible as it is interpreted and actualized in the ongoing tradition of the Jewish believing community. Therefore, in their theological dialogue with Jews the churches will be confronted with the question of tradition and Scripture. When this problem, which has been a cause of dissension between Christians for a long time, is considered in this new setting, the churches may gain insights which can contribute to a greater understanding and agreement among themselves.

4. The emphasis made by Jews in their dialogue with Christians on justice and righteousness in this world reminds the churches of the divine promise of a new earth and warns them not to express their eschatological hope onesidedly in other-worldly terms.

Equally, reflection in the light of the Bible on the Jewish concept of man as God's covenant-partner working for the sanctification of the world and for the bringing in of the Kingdom should prompt the churches to reconsider their old controversy over the co-operation of man in salvation.

5. The existence of Jews, both those who have become Christians and those who have not, compels the churches to clarify their own belief about election. They must ask themselves whether election is not a constitutive element in God's action with men, whether it does not have an unshakable objectivity which precedes the response of those who are elected, but which on the other hand requires ever anew acceptance by faith, realized in human acts of obedience. A study of these questions may bring closer together those who stress the prevenient grace of God and those who put the main accent on the human decision of faith.

VI. Some Implications

Finally we want to point to some implications of this study. Needless to say, they can be indicated only briefly; we hope that in the future some of these points will be taken up and further elaborated and acted upon. In this connection we recall the following words of the Third Assembly in New Delhi, which renewed the plea against anti-semitism of the First Assembly in 1948, adding that "the Assembly urges its member churches to do all in their power to resist every form of anti-semitism. In Christian teaching the historic events which led to the Crucifixion should not be so presented as to fasten upon the Jewish people of today responsibilities which belong to our corporate humanity and not to one race or community. Jews were the first to accept Jesus and Jews are not the only ones who do not yet recognize him".

The last sentences of the statement just quoted refer to the question of the responsibility of the Jews today for the crucifixion. This question has both a historical and a theological dimension. 1) Modern scholarship has generally come to the conclusion that it is historically wrong to hold the Jewish people of Jesus' time responsible as a whole for his death. Only a small minority of those who were in Jerusalem were actively hostile to him, and even these were only indirectly instrumental in bringing about his death: the actual sentence was imposed by the Roman authorities. Moreover, it is impossible to hold the Jews of today responsible for what a few of their forefathers may have participated in nearly twenty centuries ago. 2) Theologically speaking we believe that this small minority, acting together with the Roman authorities, expressed the sin and blindness common to all mankind. Those passages in the New Testament which charge the Jews with the crucifixion of Jesus must be read within the wider biblical understanding of Israel as representative of all men. In their rejection of Christ our own rejection of him is mirrored.

We recommended that, especially in religious instruction and preaching, great care be taken not to picture the Jews in such a way as to foster inadvertently a kind of "Christian" anti-semitism. In addition to the way in which the crucifixion is often taught, we have in mind, among other things, the historically mistaken image often given of the Pharisees, the misconception of the Law of the Old Testament and its so-called legalism, and the stress repeatedly placed upon the disobedience of the Jews according to the Old and New Testaments, without it being made sufficiently clear that those who denounced this disobedience were also Jews, one with their people notwithstanding their denunciation.

Similarly, some Christian prayers contain expressions which, whatever their meaning formerly was, can easily promote misunderstanding today. We feel that it would help if the churches would re-examine both traditional liturgies and also lessons, hymns and other texts used in worship from the point of view set out in this document.

The fact that the Jewish people is of continued significance for the Church should also have its effect on the way history is presented. Because of this special relationship all through the ages, church history cannot rightly be taught without taking into account its impact on the history of the Jews, and vice versa. We are of the opinion that theological teaching and text books are in general inadequate in this respect and need to be reconsidered and supplemented.

There is a general tendency among Christians to equate the faith of the Old Testament with Jewish religion today. This is an oversimplification which does not do justice to Jewish understanding of the Old Testament and to subsequent developments. Here the oral law must be specially mentioned, for it has played such a central role in shaping Jewish life and thought, and still continues to be of paramount importance for large groups.

We should also be aware that many, while affirming that they belong to the Jewish people, do not call themselves believing Jews. For a real encounter with the Jews we consider it imperative to have knowledge and genuine understanding of their thinking and their problems both in the secular and in the religious realm. We should always remain aware that we are dealing with actual, living people in all their variety, and not with an abstract concept of our own.

* * *

We have often been aware in our discussions that no problem should be examined in isolation. Nor should this one be, since there may be a danger that, instead of reducing anti-semitism, we may even increase it by concentrating on this issue.

Through our study together it has been brought home to us that much thinking still has to be done, and how impossible it is to ignore or avoid the theological questions in this area. We feel assured that an ongoing encounter with Jews can mean a real enrichment of our faith. Christians should therefore be alert to every such possibility, both in the field of social co-operation and especially on the deeper level of theological discussion. We realize that at the moment many Jews are not willing to be involved with Christians in a common dialogue; in that case Christians must respect this expressed or silent wish and not force themselves upon them. But when such conversation is possible, it should be held in a spirit of mutual respect and openness, searching together and questioning one another, trusting that we together with the Jews will grow into a deeper understanding of the revelation of the God of Abraham, Isaac and Jacob. What form this further understanding may take, we must be willing to leave in his hands, confident that he will lead both Jews and Christians into the fulness of his truth.

V
Ongoing Faith and Order Tasks

In addition to the main Faith and Order themes and the more specific, limited projects surveyed in chapters III and IV, there are a number of ongoing tasks. They are not limited to a particular working period and are important complementary parts of the full picture of Faith and Order activities.

The oldest among these ongoing tasks is the support for the **Week of Prayer for Christian Unity**. Since its beginnings the modern ecumenical movement has been conscious of the importance of common prayer as an essential source and condition of all ecumenical endeavour. The Faith and Order movement has supported all efforts to establish regular periods of prayer for Christian unity, and involvement in the Week of Prayer for Christian Unity has taken a more tangible and regular form since 1966. Every year the Pontifical Council (formerly the Secretariat) for Promoting Christian Unity and Faith and Order organize a joint consultation to prepare the material for the Week of Prayer on the basis of proposals from a local ecumenical group. In connection with these consultations, surveys of the observance of the Week of Prayer have been undertaken and the participants have continuously reflected on its significance and suggested ways of broadening its observance and impact.

A second ongoing task is related to **united and uniting churches and church union negotiations**. The growing number of church union negotiations has become an important expression of ecumenical endeavours, especially since 1948. In order to share information about these developments, Faith and Order in 1954 began publishing *Surveys on Church Union Negotiations* every two years in *The Ecumenical Review* and as Faith and Order Papers (nos 11: 1937-1952; 11a: 1952-1954; 11c: 1954-1957; 28: 1957-1959; 35: 1959-1961; 43: 1961-1963; 47: 1963-1965; 52: 1965-1967; 56: 1967-1969; 64: 1969-1971; 68: 1971-1973; 78: 1973-1975; 87: 1975-1977; 101: 1977-1979; 115: 1979-1981; 122: 1981-1983; 133: 1983-1985/86; 146: 1986-1988; 154: 1988-1991). Since united/uniting churches have no worldwide organization of their own, Faith and Order has been asked to organize consultations for these churches to enable them to share their experiences and to reflect together on their special contributions to the ecumenical discussion and movement. Such consultations were held in 1967 in Bossey, Switzerland (papers and reports in *Mid-Stream*, vol. VI, no. 3), in 1970 in Limuru, Kenya (papers and reports in *Mid-Stream*, vol. IX, nos 2-3), in 1975 in Toronto, Canada (report in *Growing together into Unity*, ed. Choan-Seng Song, Madras, Christian Literature Society, 1978, pp.13-17), in 1981 in Colombo, Sri Lanka (*Growing towards Consensus and Commitment: Report of the Fourth International Consultation of United and Uniting Churches*, no. 110, 1981) and in 1987 in Potsdam, German Democratic Republic (*Living Together towards Visible Unity: The Fifth International Consultation of United and Uniting Churches*, no. 142, 1988). The next consultation is planned for 1994. In addition, two volumes of essays on the relation of united churches to Christian World Communions and to the ecumenical movement have been published (*Unity in Each Place... in All Places... United Churches and Christian World Communions*, ed. Michael Kinnamon, no. 118, 1983; *Called to be One in Christ: United Churches and the Ecumenical Movement*, eds Thomas F. Best and Michael Kinnamon, no. 127, 1985). An occasional newsletter has provided a forum for sharing information and ideas within the united and uniting churches community (no. 1, June 1977; no. 2, November 1977; no. 3, October 1979; no. 4, February 1981; no. 5, August 1981; no. 6, February 1982; no. 7, September 1982; no. 8, April 1986).

The late 1960s saw the emergence of **international bilateral dialogues**. This new ecumenical initiative was one of the consequences of the entrance of the Roman Catholic Church into the ecumenical movement during the time of the Second Vatican Council. The rapidly growing number of these dialogues between the Roman Catholic Church and Christian World Communions and soon also between these communions raised the question of their relationship to the multilateral dialogues, especially in Faith and Order. Already in an early stage of this new development, representatives of the two ecumenical methods and endeavours met in the context of the meetings of the secretaries of Christian World Communions, in order to seek ways of relating bilateral and multilateral dialogues to each other. "Complementarity" became the guiding perspective and also, to a large degree, the result of these efforts. A first step in this direction was taken when in 1972 Faith and Order published a first survey on bilateral conversations (Nils Ehrenström and Günther Gassmann, *Confessions in Dialogue: A Survey of Bilateral Conversations among World Confessional Families 1962-1971*, no. 63, 1972; 3rd rev. ed. 1975, no. 74). Since 1978 Faith and Order has organized five meetings of a forum on bilateral conversations under the auspices of the Christian World Communions (*The Three Reports of the Forum of Bilateral Conversations*, no. 107, 1981; *Fourth Forum on Bilateral Conversations 1985: Report*, no. 125, 1985; *Fifth Forum on Bilateral Conversations: Report* together with *International Bilateral Dialogues 1965-1991: Commission, Meetings, Themes and Reports*, compiled by Günther Gassmann, no. 156, 1991). The sixth meeting of the forum will take place in 1994 and will consider the experiences and concepts of *reception* in bilateral and multilateral dialogues. In preparation for the official theological dialogue between the Orthodox church and the Oriental Orthodox churches which began in 1985, Faith and Order sponsored four non-official consultations between these churches from 1964 to 1971 (reports and a selection of papers in *Does Chalcedon Divide or Unite? Towards Convergence in Orthodox Christology*, eds Paulos Gregorius, William H. Lazareth and Nikos Nissiotis, Geneva, WCC, 1981).

Co-operation of Faith and Order with the **Joint Working Group** (JWG) between the Roman Catholic Church and the WCC is not an ongoing task in the more formal sense, but has been a reality since the establishment of the JWG in 1965. This co-operation is based on the official representation of the Roman Catholic Church on the Faith and Order Commission, and on the reflections in the JWG on the visible unity of the church. In a more specific way Faith and Order has been the partner in several studies conducted under the auspices of the JWG, which have led to reports on *Catholicity and Apostolicity* (papers and report in *One in Christ*, vol. VI, no. 3, 1970; report in *The Ecumenical Review*, vol. XXIII, no. 1, 1971), *Towards a*

Confession of the Common Faith (cf. Document III.17), and *The Notion of "Hierarchy of Truths": An Ecumenical Interpretation* together with *The Church: Local and Universal* (no. 150, 1990). During the new working period of the JWG since 1991 Faith and Order has again been asked to co-operate in one or two joint projects.